GOD

AND

THE END OF SATAN

DIEU

ET

LA FIN DE SATAN

Victor Hugo Assis, by Walery, detail, 1876,
Musée Victor Hugo-Maison Vacquerie

God

AND

The End of Satan

*

Dieu

ET

La Fin de Satan

Victor Hugo

SELECTIONS: IN A BILINGUAL EDITION

Edited, Translated, and with an Introduction by R.G. Skinner

VICTOR HUGO (1802–85) was a great French poet, novelist, playwright, and statesman. Living in exile on the islands of Jersey and Guernsey for eighteen years, the author of *Les Misérables* and *The Hunchback of Notre Dame* wrote some of his most influential work during that time. Highly esteemed for his poetry, *Dieu* and *La Fin de Satan* were works in progress at the time of his death and published posthumously.

RICHARD G. SKINNER is an independent scholar and poet.

Swan Isle Press, Chicago 60611
 Published 2014.
Printed in the United States of America
Second Printing (February, 2024)
28 27 26 25 2 3 4 5
ISBN-13: 978-0-9833220-4-7 (paperback)
ISBN-13: 978-0-9833220-5-4 (e-book)

The French text of this translation is based on the original manuscripts that were bequeathed by Victor Hugo to Bibliothèque nationale de France and part of the BnF's extensive archival collection. Originally published as *Œuvres inédites de Victor Hugo: La Fin de Satan.* Paris: J. Hetzel et A.Quantin, 1886. and *Œuvres inédites de Victor Hugo: Dieu.* Paris: J. Hetzel et A.Quantin, 1891.

Swan Isle Press gratefully acknowledges that this book has been made possible, in part, with generous grants and support from:

THE FRENCH MINISTRY OF FOREIGN AFFAIRS AND THE CULTURAL SERVICES OF THE FRENCH EMBASSY IN THE UNITED STATES

for providing a Hemingway Grant to help advance the publication of this edition by Victor Hugo.

"Cet ouvrage, publié dans le cadre d'un programme d'aide à la publication, bénéficie du soutien du Ministère des Affaires étrangères et du Service Culturel de l'Ambassade de France aux États-Unis."

"This work, published as part of a program of aid for publication, received support from the French Ministry of Foreign Affairs and the Cultural Services of the French Embassy in the United States."

FRANCIS J. HIGGINS

EUROPE BAY GIVING TRUST

Library of Congress Cataloging-in-Publication Data

Hugo, Victor, 1802-1885.
[Poems. Selections. English & French]
God and the End of Satan = Dieu and La Fin de Satan : selections, in a bilingual edition / Victor Hugo ; edited, translated, and with an introduction by Richard G. Skinner ; foreword by E.H. Blackmore and A.M. Blackmore. — First edition.
pages cm
Includes bibliographical references.
ISBN-978-0-9833220-4-7 (pbk.)
I. Hugo, Victor, 1802-1885—Translations into English. I. Hugo, Victor, 1802-1885. Dieu. II. Hugo, Victor, 1802-1885. Fin de Satan. II. Title.
PQ2283.P24 2013
843'.7—dc23

2013042597

♾ This paper meets the requirements of ANSI/NISO Z39.48–1992 (Permanence of Paper).

www.swanislepress.com

CONTENTS

PART TWO FROM *La Fin de Satan* | The End of Satan

LIST OF ILLUSTRATIONS

Victor Hugo, *Marine Terrace with Initials,* 1855 May 21, private collection

FOREWORD

VICTOR HUGO WROTE many books, but none more adventurous—or more challenging—than *Dieu* and *La Fin de Satan.* He drafted them at the very height of his powers, between his two spells of work on *Les Misérables.* When they were first published after his death, as the master's final masterpieces, they amazed and deeply influenced a whole era of French poets (including Mallarmé, Valéry, and Claudel). Today, *Dieu* is often considered Hugo's single finest achievement. There is nothing quite like it in our language. Its first English readers compared it to the strange late poems of Blake; and that is probably still the closest analogy.

Hugo never quite finished either of these books. Yet, in both cases, their incompleteness has often been regarded as a strength rather than a weakness. The main body of *La Fin de Satan (The End of Satan)* was to be a three-part narrative tracing the rise and fall of evil in prehistory (a Central Asian legend about Nimrod), ancient history (the crucifixion of Christ), and modern history (the French Revolution). Hugo completed the first two-thirds of the narrative—but there he stopped, apart from a few sketches. Yet many French readers have felt that he was wise to do so, and that the existing sections' consistent linguistic brilliance and mastery of storytelling would have been tarnished by an attempt to go further.

Dieu (God) is both closer to, and further from, completeness. It consists of two main parts. In the first part—"Le Seuil du gouffre" ("The Threshold of the Abyss")—the narrator's quest for God is blocked by the Human Spirit, a creature speaking with many voices, all but one of which deride any attempt to venture beyond the mainstream and the conventional. (The solitary exception—Voice XI, placed last in Hugo's papers—encourages him to press ahead regardless.) In the second part—"L'Océan d'en haut" ("The Ocean of the Heights")—the narrator soars upward and encounters eight successive winged creatures proclaiming eight successive notions about God. Each of these views, while it is being uttered, seems to express at least some truths; but each is quickly supplanted by its successor.

Until the very last line of its second half, *Dieu* seems to be a work of a familiar nineteenth century kind: a work like Hegel's *Lectures on the Philosophy of Religion,* in which various incorrect views of the subject are exposed before the writer reveals the correct view. Sure enough, the eighth and last speaker—"La Lumière" ("The Light")—seems to present Hugo's own ideas about God. But when the Light has stopped speaking, yet another winged creature is glimpsed beyond it—and two rows of dots show that the series is to continue endlessly. The notions expressed by the Light were just as finite and limited as all their predecessors; and the reality remains forever at an infinite distance ahead, no matter how far the narrator travels toward it. The poem's deepest convictions are that its deepest convictions are not only short of the truth, but *infinitely* short of the truth.

In Hugo's manuscripts, the second half of *Dieu* is absolutely complete, and the first half seems virtually complete; only a few lines here and there remain to be filled in. (In fact, most of his revisions to that half were cuts rather than additions. He had written far more for it than he needed.) So, whereas we have only the first two-thirds of *La Fin de Satan,* apparently we have all but a few lines of *Dieu.*

However, the existing text of *La Fin de Satan* can be read as a coherent narrative, whereas it is far from clear how the existing sections of *Dieu* should fit together. The crucial link between its two great masses of material remains tantalizingly elusive. According to overlapping drafts in Hugo's papers, the narrator cries out in protest against the Human Spirit, insists on knowing more, is granted his request—in the form of death—but then finds himself still at an infinite distance from his goal. This looks like a single episode—but is it? And if it is, where should it be placed? As an alternate ending to the Human Spirit episode (replacing the Voices)? Between the work's two main halves (so that the second half—"L'Océan d'en haut"—becomes a posthumous quest)? Or at the end of the entire work? No answer yet given to these questions has met with general acceptance. One thing is certain: for a book that celebrates with boundless zest and in multitudinous ways the intangible and inaccessible, nothing could be more appropriate than a central incompletely resolved mystery.

Richard Skinner's carefully edited texts and clear, easily readable translations allow the overall structure of both books to be followed in a single volume, for the first time in our language. This volume rightly claims to offer only "Selections," but the selections are large and representative of the whole; and nearly all the omitted sections can be found elsewhere in English in other volumes. Indeed, English-language readers now have access to everything that Hugo finally earmarked for publication in *Dieu* and nearly everything that he earmarked for publication in *La Fin de Satan*—as well as a considerable amount of material that he drafted for these projects but published in other forms or not at all. The most serious gap in English translations of Hugo has now been filled.

—E.H. Blackmore & A.M. Blackmore

INTRODUCTION

MANY PEOPLE CONSIDER Victor Hugo (1802–1885) the greatest writer of his century. In America he is known as a novelist, author of *Les Misérables* and *The Hunchback of Notre Dame (Notre-Dame de Paris)*. In nineteenth-century France he was also known for seven other novels as well as twelve plays. These plays included the popular *Hernani* and *Le Roi s'amuse* (The King's Fool), both turned into operas by Verdi ("Rigoletto" was based on the latter), as well as *Cromwell*, unproduced, but whose preface was a famous manifesto of the Romantic movement, encouraged in its writing by Nodier, Nerval, and others. Nonetheless, despite his great success in these areas, Hugo was first and foremost a poet. That is what he called himself and that is his reputation in France. By the age of sixteen an admirer had secured for him a royal pension, and when he reached twenty, Louis XVIII, himself, awarded him an annual stipend for his first volume of poetry. When only 25, he was called the "prince of poets" by Delacroix, Musset and the young romantics in the Cénacle group who recognized him as their leader.[1] As late as 1895, Mallarmé wrote in the chapter "Crise de vers" in his book *Divigations*, that Hugo was "poetry incarnate."[2] However, his reputation as a writer began to suffer for a number of years following his death in 1885. He was hardly taught in school, and in some circles was considered a *mauvais maître* (bad teacher). In 1923, in the Surrealist review *Littérature*, he was belatedly celebrated as one of the "French pioneers of the poetry of irrational insights,"[3] and in a later essay, as one of the "greatest poets of the nineteenth century,"[4] in the company of Nerval, Baudelaire, Lautréamont, Rimbaud, and

Mallarmé. By 1927 there was a Victor Hugo Chair at the Sorbonne, and in that year writer and poet Joseph Delteil said of him, "All the other French poets, Ronsard, Racine, Rimbaud, play the part of angels. He, alone, is god." (Tous les autres poëtes français, Ronsard, Racine, Rimbaud, font figure d'anges. Lui seul est dieu).[5] Nearly sixty years after his death, in March of 1943, French poet and essayist Léon-Paul Fargue saluted Hugo as "a poet of the future" (un poëte d'avenir).[6] Today, Hugo is a major part of the curriculum in college departments of French and Romance Languages.

Although the years 1828 through 1843, the year his eldest daughter Léopoldine died, had been very fruitful ones for Hugo's writing, after 1843 he was creating less, while becoming more involved in politics. He was made a Peer of France in 1845, and elected to the Constitutional, and then Legislative Assemblies in 1848 and 1849; in those forums he spoke out strongly against slavery, capital punishment, war, child abuse, and the ill-treatment of women. When a *coup d'état* occurred in 1851 resulting in the repressive Second Empire of Napoleon III and the dissolving of the National Assemblies, Hugo resisted, and then, December 11th, fled to Brussels. During his eight months there, he wrote *Napoléon-le-petit* (Napoleon-the-little), a harsh pamphlet denouncing Napoleon III, and began *L'Histoire d'un Crime* (The History of a Crime), a novel about the *coup d'état* which was eventually published in 1877. Officially expelled from France by a decree of January 9th, 1852, with a price on his head, and with the Belgian government becoming wary of his politics and in fear of the potential embarrassment upon publication of *Napoléon-le-petit*, he made a final move into self-exile, initially to the island of Jersey in the English Channel, 1852–55. When his politics became too controversial there, he moved to the neighboring island of Guernsey where he stayed until August of 1870, the year the Prussian army ended the reign of Napoleon III.

At midnight on August 4th, 1852, Hugo and his eldest son Charles left Southampton, England, for Jersey, aboard the steamer *Dispatch.* They experienced a stormy voyage, but unlike the other passengers, avoided seasickness by spending the night on deck. At dawn they passed the beautiful port of Guernsey, where the houses were arranged like an amphitheatre, admired the nearby islet of Sark, and arrived at Jersey by midday. There they joined Hugo's wife Adèle, daughter Adèle, and Auguste Vacquerie, poet, family friend and one of Hugo's future literary executors, who had preceded them by a few days.[7] Eleven days later, on August 15th, Hugo wrote to André van Hasselt, a Dutch poet living in Belgium:

> I am enveloped in poetry, dear poet, amid rocks, meadows, roses, clouds, and the sea, and naturally my thoughts turn to you.
>
> What fine lines you would write if you were here! They spring as it were of themselves from this splendid scenery. When the view is not grand, it is lovely.
>
> Tomorrow I take up my abode in a little den near the sea, which the newspapers of the island describe as a "superb house on the Azette shore."[8]

Hugo's daughter, Adèle, kept a journal during these Jersey years, to which Hugo, himself, sometimes contributed. An early journal entry reads, "[M]y father is pleased to have finally realized his dream: to be on an island and have the sea at his feet."[9] He called his house "Marine Terrace," after the street on which it stood.

Initially at loose ends, Hugo describes a pivotal conversation with his son, François-Victor, which occurred later that fall:

> One morning at the end of November (1852), two of the inhabitants of this place, the father and the younger son, were seated in the dining-room. They kept silence, like shipwrecked people who reflect. Without it rained, the wind blew, the house was as if benumbed by this angry noise outside. Both the two were plunged in thought, absorbed perhaps by this coincidence of a beginning of winter and a beginning of exile. Suddenly the son raised his voice, and asked the father, "What do you think of this exile?" "I think that it will be long." "How do you mean to occupy it?" The father answered, "I shall look at the ocean." There was a silence. The father broke it; "And you?" "I," said the son, "will translate Shakespeare."[10]

François-Victor shared his father's political views, and had been jailed for seditious writings. Delayed afterwards in Paris, joining his family in Jersey at a later date, he did eventually produce an excellent prose translation of the works of Shakespeare. Hugo, himself, far from the distractions of Paris, where, prior to his exile, it had been twelve years since he had published a book of poetry, eight since he had written a play, and seventeen since he had produced a prose work,[11] began to write with a renewed sense of urgency.[12]

Napoléon-le-petit was published and went on sale soon after Hugo's arrival in Jersey. He then began *Les Châtiments* (The Chastisements), a collection of scathing poems also critical of the Emperor, which was secretly published in 1853. In

1856, after the expulsion from Jersey to Guernsey, he finished and published *Les Contemplations*, a collection of personal and metaphysical poems, some written in the early 1830's (Hugo later altered many of the dates) but changing in tenor in 1843 following the drowning death of his eldest daughter, Léopoldine, and her husband Charles Vacquerie, brother of Auguste. In 1859 he published the first part of *La Légende des siècles* (The Legend of the Centuries), epic poetry telling the story of mankind's struggle through the ages upwards towards the light, towards the ideal, and during the next eleven years, continued writing for the theatre while publishing four visionary social novels, including *Les Misérables*, as well as three other books of poetry and essays. In *Les Contemplations,* Hugo's poetic epigraph to the work, written in 1839, contained the verses:

> Poet, you do well! Poet with the downcast brow,
> You dream beside the sea,
> And you draw from that ocean many things which lie
> Beneath her unfathomed waves![13]

It was during this time of exile that he began to write two of his last poems, the visionary epics that are considered by many to be his greatest literary work, *Dieu* (God), and *La Fin de Satan* (The End of Satan). *La Fin de Satan* was begun on Jersey during 1854, and stopped just short of completion during 1859–60 on Guernsey. *Dieu* was started on Jersey perhaps as early as 1854, and then taken up again on Guernsey during the years 1856–57, and again during 1869–1870, his last years in exile. It was brought to near completion in the mid-seventies, and then left untouched. Due to their incomplete state, as well as critical and commercial considerations, these two poems were left unpublished during Hugo's lifetime.

A year into his stay on Jersey, a seminal event occurred. Hugo began participating in a kind of séance, table-turning, in which messages from the dead were tapped out, in most circumstances, by a three-legged pedestal table. Still mourning the death of his daughter, Hugo was convinced, during one of the first séances, that Léopoldine had spoken to them. For the next two years he, his family, and friends communicated with as many as 110 entities from the past including Shakespeare, Socrates, Isaiah, Moses, Cain, Mozart, Jesus, and Galileo. These dialogues influenced his writing of *Dieu* and *La Fin de Satan*. Earlier in his life, Hugo had spent over ten years studying occult matters; the secrets of the *Zohar* in particular—one of the foundations of Kabbalistic study—had been disclosed to him by Alexandre Weill, French writer and polemicist.[14] These séances reinforced that interest, and helped lessen his personal grief. Kabbalistic symbolism informs *La Légende des siècles*, and is found in great abundance in *Les Contemplations* and *Dieu*.[15] The influence of Éliphas Lévi, the famous occult Illuminist formerly known as the Abbé Constant, and whom Hugo finally met and befriended in 1873, is apparent, as well. Auguste Viatte relates how Hugo borrowed the idea of the angel Liberty for the last part of *La Fin de Satan* from Lévi's book *le Testament de la liberté*, published in 1845:

> A comparison between *La Fin de Satan* and *Testament de la liberté* seems even more instructive.
>
> Like Victor Hugo, the Abbé Constant shows us first of all the fall "of the angel who, when born, refused to be a slave" and who pulled down with him, into the night, "a shower of suns and stars, attracted by his glory"; but Lucifer, his Intelligence proscribed, gives birth to two sisters, Poetry and Liberty, and "the spirit of love assumes their features in order to subdue and save the rebellious angel!"[16]

An entry in Adèle's journal dated May 1st and 2nd, 1855, describes Hugo's late-night reading to family and friends of his early version of *Dieu*, the verses describing the history of religions that eventually became the last and main section of the poem, referred to by him in 1869 as "L'océan d'en haut" (The Ocean of the Heights). At midnight, after two hours of reading, his audience insisted he continue:

> My father speaks about revelations made by the Tables; then he arrives finally at his own religion, which is summarized in this great word: Love. This poem ends with a series of dots, that is, it only comes to an end on the brink of the Infinite.
>
> It was half past two when my father ended this poem of 1946 lines, this account of the religions which tried to find God without ever succeeding.
>
> [Family friend] Kesler, the atheist, begins nevertheless to believe in God, to whom this gigantic poem is the ladder of fire. He goes away saying: it is as beautiful as the *Book of Revelation*; and we all withdraw, moved and lost in wonder....My father remains alone, clambering up to his room to search the sky for the moonlight, the friend who has sat near him in this poor room of exile. He gazes at the moon.[17]

In a letter of January 4th, 1855 to Delphine de Girardin, an influential French author, and the friend who had introduced the Hugos to the turning tables over a year earlier, Hugo wrote:

> The tables do in fact tell us some surprising things. How I should like to talk with you, and kiss your hands, your feet, or your wings! Did Paul Meurice tell you that a whole quasi-cosmogonical system, hatched by me and half committed to paper for twenty years, had been confirmed by the tables with splendid amplifications? We live in a mysterious landscape which opens out prospects, and we think of you, to whom we owe this glimpse into another world.
>
> The tables enjoin on us silence and secrecy. You will therefore find nothing from them in the *Contemplations*, with the exception of two details, of great importance, it is true, for which I have *asked permission* (I underline these words), and which I will indicate by a note.[18]

The sometimes brooding, sometimes exhilarating seascape as viewed first from his Jersey cottage, where he wrote most of *La Fin de Satan* and the main body of *Dieu,* and then from the high vantage point of his studio atop Hauteville-House on the Guernsey shore, where he lived and wrote the prologue to *Dieu*, as well as most of *Les Misérables*, was also a contributing factor, as was the effect of the eighteen year exile in this isolated part of the world (his wife and children were eventually to leave for the allures of Brussels and elsewhere, his daughter Adèle later institutionalized following a prolonged and fruitless pursuit of a British soldier met on Jersey. Hugo made extended visits to family during the last years of exile, or traveled, usually in the company of his mistress, Juliette Drouet, a constant presence over many years). In a letter of January 14th, 1855, to Émile Deschanel, a poet also forced into exile and living in Brussels, Hugo wrote from Jersey: "[All is] rosy for you, somber for me. . . . *I* have wedded the sea, the hurricane, a vast sandy shore, sadness, and the starry canopy of heaven."[19] Over a year later, on April 10th, 1856, Hugo, now moved to Guernsey, was to write in a different vein to Franz Stevens, a young Belgian poet:

> Try to realize the state of my mind in the splendid solitude in which I live, perched as it were on the summit of a rock, with all the grandeur of the waves and the sky before me. I dwell in this immense dream of the ocean. I am gradually becoming a somnambulist of the sea; and in face of all these stupendous phenomena and all this

> vast living thought in which I lose myself, I end by being only a sort of witness of God.
>
> It is from this never-ending contemplation that I arise to write you.[20]

His daily writing routine at Hauteville-House, that great domicile on Guernsey that Hugo was able to purchase due to the extreme popularity of *Les Contemplations,* never varied. He awoke before dawn, bathed quickly in cold water, and after having coffee, wrote for most of the morning standing at his foldout desk, facing east towards France. This house was also a refuge for other writers and exiles. Hugo set aside a guest room near his studio for fellow countrymen in need of a haven. He called this guest room "the raft of the Medusa."[21] Loyal family friend and writer, Hennett de Kesler, who had been present at that initial midnight reading of *Dieu*, was staying there when he died, in 1870.

Many fellow political exiles corresponded with Hugo, as did many fellow writers. On April 30th, 1857, he wrote Baudelaire to praise *Les Fleurs du Mal*, which had just been published and condemned as immoral: "I received your noble letter and your beautiful book. The art is as the azure, it is infinite terrain: you have just proved it. Your *Fleurs du Mal* shine and dazzle as stars. I shout bravo with all my might to your powerful spirit."[22] Alexis Lykiard, translator of the enigmatic Isidore Ducasse's long prose-poem *Les Chants de Maldoror*, written under the pen name le Comte de Lautréamont, quotes a letter Ducasse wrote to Hugo at Hauteville-House in 1868: "For ten years I cherished the desire to come and see you...I who in this century am nothing yet, while you, you are its Everything."[23] Hugo's return letter has been lost.

In their final form, these two poems were originally meant to form a trilogy with *La Légende des siècles.* When the first version of the latter was published in 1859, he spoke of this future trilogy in the preface:

> It is an attempt towards the ideal. Nothing more.
>
> ...[W]hen several other parts of this book are published, one will see the bond which, in the design of the author, links *La Légende des siècles* to two other poems, almost finished at this hour, and which are, one the denouement, the other the crowning-piece: *La Fin de Satan*, and *Dieu.*
>
> The author...outlined in solitude a kind of poem of a certain scope wherein reverberates the single problem, Being, under its three-fold aspect; Humanity, Evil, the Infinite; the progressive, the relative, the absolute; in what one could call three songs: *La Légende des siècles*, *La Fin de Satan*, *Dieu.*[24]

In a letter written from Guernsey on June 7th, 1856 to Barthélemy (Prosper) Enfantin, social-reformer and co-founder of Saint-Simonism, Hugo had spoken, earlier, of these two poems:

> The ideal is the real. Like you, I live with my eyes fixed on a vision. To do my best so far as my strength will allow to help mankind, that hapless crowd of brothers we have there who are walking in darkness, and I endeavor, bound to the chain myself, to aid my fellow-travelers, by my example as a man in the present, and by my writings as a poet in the future....
>
> In those two books, *Dieu* and *La Fin de Satan*, you may be sure that I shall not pass over woman; I shall go even further, just as I shall go beyond the things of this world. These two works are almost finished; nevertheless, I want to leave an interval between them and the *Contemplations*. I should like, if God gives me some measure of strength, to carry the crowd to certain altitudes; yet I'm well aware that there is little air there which it can breathe. I therefore wish it to rest awhile before I make it attempt a fresh ascent.[25]

Dieu narrates the plight of a human protagonist who is searching for God. He imagines a flight into the heavens, where he meets a multi-faceted creature called the Human Spirit, who reveals to him the many aspects, good and bad, of human nature. In Hugo's final conception, this is followed by thirteen separate, distinct 'Voices' emerging from the Human Spirit, reminiscent of the entities from the séances, all but one warning him of the many obstacles lying ahead in his search. The final part, read to family and friends that late evening in early May of 1855, consists of symbolic, winged creatures—bat, owl, raven, vulture, eagle, griffin, Angel, and Spirit of Light—tracing the stages of humanity's conception of the Divinity, from primitive earth gods, through Manichaeism's perpetual conflict of good and evil, ancient Greece's polytheistic myths, Christianity's doctrine of the fall and redemption, etc., which become increasingly enlightened, but which Hugo ultimately rejects one by one as well as the systems of religion that espouse them[26], or, as he wrote sometime around July 15th, 1856, "...each religion an improvement on the preceding one, and rebutting it, the spiritualization increasingly freed until its arrival and disappearance as pure spirit."[27] One reaches at last the Spirit of Light representing Hugo's ideal sphere, where all are pardoned, and where compassion is the essence of a God who "...has only one countenance: Light! and only one name: Love!"[28] However, even in death will that light never be revealed in full.

Dieu having been announced in the 1859 preface to *La Légende des siècles,* in 1869 Hugo wrote part of a new preface with the apparent intention of publishing some of it soon:

> It will be one of the splendors of this great nineteenth century to have posed in a kind of immense free and open debate, with every latitude allowed, negative or positive, inside and outside of religion, the supreme question: *God.*
>
> We are the ones who entreat and who embrace this formidable question mark, unceasingly seen on the horizon, obscure by day, luminous by night.
>
> From there this poem, of which we publish the first part today, *Le Seuil du gouffre*—The second part will appear later and will be entitled *L'Océan d'en haut.* The first part tackles the question. The second resolves it.[29]

When *Dieu* was published in 1891, it was at last the realization of this vow, expressed in verse around 1856:

> Embrace the Vastness, seize Eternity,
> Restrain, wrench out, take hold this fleeing shadow,
> Divulge the secret of the abyss, reveal the enigma of
> God, in spite of the mystery and despite the Infinite.[30]

Written in the prophetic, visionary tradition, these late poetic works have been compared to the late work of William Blake by such poets and critics as Anthony Hartley:

> Of all the Romantics, Hugo is without doubt the greatest, but his greatness has been hidden by the insufficient attention paid to the last part of his work....[He is] a poet more akin to Blake, filling his works with monstrous cosmologies, where the terror of the abyss draws the poet's mind cascading from void to void in unending vertigo.... Wherever Hugo took his cosmology from (the Kabbala or Swedenborg? It does not much matter), he made it peculiarly his own, and embodied it in a series of poems which, for epic sweep and primitive strength, have hardly their equal.[31]

The French Catholic poet, Paul Claudel, compared Hugo to Blake as well when he wrote of Hugo, in 1925, "No one can contest the sincerity of the great poet, nor the fact that he was really and truly a seer, in the manner of the Englishman Blake."[32] But noting that in this work Hugo spoke less of God than of the absence of God, Claudel wrote:

> And I also think that Victor Hugo was not the only grieving soul from this moor full of ruins and excavations which is the literature of the 19th century. Other great moonstruck beings are staggering about in this graveyard dug by the spirits of the dead: Blake, Goethe of the *Second Faust*, Michelet, Carlyle, Ibsen, Wagner who was the first to be illuminated by a redemptive light, and finally Nietzsche who was devoured whole by this monster by which the others were only pursued.[33]

In 1894, three years following its publication, A. C. Swinburne, England's premier poet of the time, successor to Tennyson and Browning, published his thoughts on *Dieu*. Swinburne, a correspondent of Hugo, almost single-handedly introduced contemporary French literature (especially Hugo, Baudelaire, and Gautier) to England. He also saw the prophetic function of the poet and he, himself, wrote in the tradition of Blake, Shelley, Baudelaire, and Hugo. His reaction to Hugo's *Dieu* is as informative today as it was then:

> But it is rather of Blake than of Tennyson that an English reader will be usually reminded by the passionate and apocalyptic utterance of horror and of hope, of anguish and of faith, which rings and thrills through every line of this incomplete yet perfect poem....[To] Blake as to Hugo these sufferings and these wrongs were the ciphers or the figures of a problem insoluble except by faith, and unendurable to contemplate unless by the eyes of faith. Not Blake himself is more extravagant, excessive, outrageous to the instincts or the inductions of common sense and practical reason...than the greatest and most inspired writer of our own day....
>
> The adoring reverence of Hugo for the sacred name which is used here to express the ideal of divine or glorified humanity stands out singularly in contrast with the apparent aversion excited by its association with creeds and churches....[W]e hear again an unconscious echo of the spirit and indeed the very voice of William Blake....
>
> Of this great new song which comes to us from the grave of Victor Hugo... [t]hose who would know what it contains and what it conveys—its dramatic force,

its philosophic insight, its evangelic passion—must be content and thankful to study it reverently and thoroughly for themselves.[34]

Swinburne was as great an admirer of *La Fin de Satan,* published prior to *Dieu,* in 1886, a year after Hugo's death, as he was of *Dieu.* In a long, detailed review, he referred to "ET NOX FACTA EST" (And then there was night), the opening section describing Satan's ten thousand year fall from heaven:

> More than thirty years have elapsed between the announcement and the appearance of the great religious poem which has done for the nineteenth century what was done for the thirteenth by the *Divina Commedia* and for the seventeenth by *Paradise Lost*....Only the poet's matchless mastery of language, his incomparable command of radiant symbol and rolling music, could make a western student not all unwilling to accept this more than Cyclopean or Titanic architecture of fancy without a sense of incredulous distaste for incongruous or inconceivable conceptions. But all demur, all question, all doubt is swallowed up in wonder and delight at the glory and the beauty of the indefatigable song. The flight of the fallen archangel towards the dying sun through chaos is given with that all but unique effect which Dante alone could hitherto achieve by alternation or combination of the very homeliest with the very sublimest images or comparisons.[35]

In one of his manuscripts, in a brief outline of *La Fin de Satan*, below the title "ET NOX FACTA EST" and above the words "Antres noirs du passé" (Dark caverns of the past) that begin the last stanza, Hugo had penned in, then cancelled, the phrase "Words of the dreamer writing this book."[36]

From a November 3rd, 1854 entry in Adèle Hugo's journal, in which she speaks of an after-dinner reading by her father in the parlor, we get an insider's view from someone who was there at the inception of this poem:

> My father read a piece of verse from his poem *Satan Pardonné.* It was called "Nimrod." The poem is meant to denounce the three scourges of the Old World: War, Capital Punishment, and Prison. War came from the spike that Cain, the first criminal, drove into the skull of his brother Abel. The spike served as the sword for Nimrod, who embodied war. Capital Punishment would be represented by the Cross of Christ....The Prison is incarnate in the Bastille. The Revolution destroyed the Prison through the capture of the Bastille.[37]

We learn from this entry that *Satan Pardonné* (Satan Forgiven) was, at one time, Hugo's provisional title for what ultimately became *La Fin de Satan*. In the final version, the poem was divided into eight parts: "Le Glaive," "Le Gibet," "La Prison," a four-part "Hors de la terre," and "La première page." The stanzas entitled "Satan Pardonné," written in 1860, became the unfinished ending to the poem. One of the inspirations for this poem was an event that had occurred earlier, pre-exile, in 1851. Hugo's son Charles, like his brother, was also sentenced to months in jail and fined, he for advocating the abolition of the death penalty. As Adèle tells it, an indignant Victor Hugo, for twenty years an opponent of the death penalty, spoke passionately in Charles' defense at the trial, bringing to the attention of the jury the irony of having a large painting of Christ on the Cross hanging behind the presiding judge, dominating proceedings that upheld the use of capital punishment:

> [T]his law from before which the human conscience recoils with an anxiety every day becoming deeper, is that which sanctions the infliction of the penalty of death.
>
> Well, gentlemen, it is this law which has provoked the trial which we have now in hand. It is this law that is our adversary. I am sorry for the advocate-general, but I perceive this law just behind him! (Strong sensations in the audience).[38]

One of Hugo's subsequent reactions was noted by his daughter: "The death of the Man-God is, in my father's opinion, an admirable subject for a poem."[39] Adèle makes the further observation:

> Contrary to all the classic Satans who do not love God and who, consequently, far from suffering from his absence, must be very happy to be rid of him, the romantic Satan of my father's poem loves God, and his suffering is a result of being separated from him.[40]

Hugo was, in fact, continuing a French Romantic tradition of transforming Catholicism by creating myths more in tune with nineteenth century ideas of progress and evolution,[41] as well as redefining the feminine as the embodiment of redeeming compassion through the intervention of a female angel, a tradition begun with de Vigny's *Éloa, ou La Sœur des anges* and found as well in the work of others such as George Sand, Edgar Quinet, Alexandre Soumet, and, as we've seen, Alphonse Constant.[42] In exile, in that setting, and from the fruits of his brooding introspection, Hugo gave this view its most fully developed expression not only in *Dieu*, but in *La Fin de Satan,* that the most advanced form of spirituality, beyond organized religion, is that represented by forgiveness and love.

Although not Catholic dogma, per se, Hugo's resolution consisting of mercy and *bonte* (goodness, kindness, benevolence) is akin to Christian conception, just as "Le Griffon," describing Christianity's doctrine of the fall and redemption, is not strictly an indictment of Christian thought. It is also representative of Leibniz's and Huxley's idea of the Perennial Philosophy, as well, and thus of universal concordance. In the end, it might be said that the theme of *La Fin de Satan* is an accord rendered between evil and good. As stated above, when Satan falls from heaven, one of his feathers is left behind—and from that feather God creates the angel Liberty. The arrival of that angel, the daughter of Satan and God equally, anticipates an eventual pardon and rehabilitation of Satan; and despite the poem's fragmentary ending, this rehabilitation does appear to be realized following the poem's alternating episodes showing Satan's work on earth and those showing Christ's work and death. In Hugo's view, humankind eventually inherits this liberty through the French Revolution, and must live with the implied dichotomy and the struggle inherent in it.

In 1921, Madame Duclaux, English poet and essayist living in France, and long a connoisseur of French letters, wrote:

> On the morrow of the death of Victor Hugo a light cloud passed across his solar glory. Men were tired of calling Aristides the Just. He had left the stage free for lesser men, the pupils of Baudelaire and of Sainte-Beuve: Parnassians and Symbolists on the one hand, on the other Intimists, like the delicious Verlaine and the insipid François Coppée. And these too had their day.
>
> Meanwhile the works of Victor Hugo still came pouring from the Press—the brilliant *Choses vues*, the exquisite *Théâtre en liberté*, the admirable rhythms of *Dieu* and *La Fin de Satan*. . . . Only one voice in France could utter all we felt, *had* uttered it, had voiced all the courage, intensity, fury, patience, and burning pity of our souls:
>
> *La grande âme d'airain qui là-haut se lamente!*[43]
>
> And France, more than ever entranced, enchanted, listened in gratitude and glory to the voice of her unique, supreme lyric poet—Victor Hugo.[44]

In *Situation de Baudelaire,* French poet and philosopher Paul Valéry, whom some consider the greatest poet of the first half of the twentieth century, wrote of Hugo's late poems in 1924:

> In *Corde d'Airain*, in *Dieu*, in *Fin de Satan*, in the piece on the death of Gautier, the septuagenarian artist—who saw his followers dying all around him, who could see his influence on a whole new generation of poets, even profiting from the invaluable lessons that the disciple can give the Master if the Master lives long enough—the very illustrious old man reaches the very heights of poetic power and of the versifier's noble art.[45]

In 1927, writer and critic Erneste Seillière said of Hugo: "His apogee, as artist, is at the beginning of the exile…." (Son apogée, comme artiste, est au début de l'exil….).[46]

As to the relevance of this late work of Hugo today, it, along with the poetry of Mallarmé, Rimbaud and Lautréamont, is seen as a precursor to the freedom of expression of 20th Century poetry. Some would even say that all of the poetry of those poets, as well as Baudelaire and Verlaine, can be found in Hugo's verse.[47] Florian Rodari, poet, art historian, and author of, amongst others, the 2007 book *Victor Hugo, précurseur a posteriori*, and the catalogue for *Victor Hugo, dessins visionnaires*, Fondation de l'Hermitage, Lausanne 2009, wrote in the catalogue to the 1998 exhibition *Shadows of a Hand: The Drawings of Victor Hugo* at The Drawing Center in New York City that, in addition to Mallarmé's "Un coup de dés," Rimbaud's sonnet "Voyelles," and Lautréamont's *Maldoror*, verses from *La Fin de Satan* and *Dieu*

> …ushered in a new way of seeing and reading in which the poetic norms of the day were redefined by the range of the questioning and the anguish of a response that never seems quite capable of being uttered; Hugo's prosody forces the reader who wishes to enjoy to the full the disturbing nature of this splendid yet worrying vision to participate almost physically in the torment that carries his lines along.[48]

Victor Hugo died in 1885. He left in manuscript two book-length poems, each nearly 6000 lines in length, with more than an equal amount in fragments.

When J.C. Ireson published his comprehensive *Victor Hugo: a companion to his poetry* in 1997, he concluded his introduction with these apposite words:

> On his likely standing with posterity he has remained silent, though it is not difficult to guess at his assumptions. He envisioned an art integrating a conspectus of human life with intuitions about the cosmic mystery within which it evolves. He had seemed at one stage (1854–9) to have established a vast poetic plan tracing the evolution of an individual life (his own), the uncertain movement of progress visible through history, and a divine principle working through the confusion and violence of historical events towards a distant redemption. Its completion demanded the spiritual epic of which he left two unfinished parts, ultimately preferring to order his work according to the issues and pressures of time, and leaving its coherence and scope to be judged in the perspectives of a future age.[49]

JERSEY AND GUERNSEY

This is as much a tale about two islands—with their coasts and bays, vast horizons, profound skies, their ancient ruins and prehistoric dolmens, their charming countryside, and the solitude they provided—as it is about two poems written in exile. Philip Stevens' book *Victor Hugo in Jersey* captures some of what it was that bound Hugo to this part of the world, and so inspired his poetry:

> The Hugos felt, especially in the Jersey countryside, that they had never left France. Hugo often alluded to the fact that the island was once joined to Normandy, and for him it was a morsel of France stolen or gathered up by England. "In its rocks [it] is like Brittany, in its fields...like Normandy," say both Adèle and Vacquerie, and Hugo was probably the source of these similes for we find him saying: "Normandy in the South, Brittany in the North, for us [Jersey] is France." Both Jersey and Guernsey have "pleasant interiors and harsh, brooding coasts, but Jersey is neater than Guernsey, prettier but less beautiful. In Jersey the forest has become a garden, in Guernsey the cliffs stand colossal. More grace here, more majesty there." Jersey, where all is scent, sunshine and pleasantness, is an "idyll in the midst of the sea."[50]

During Hugo's free afternoons when he would go off to write, Rozel Bay, on the northeast coast of Jersey, with its ancient dolmens, was one of the places he would revisit for that purpose. "Ce que dit la bouche d'ombre" (What the

Mouth of Shadows Says), the concluding poem of *Les Contemplations*, greatly influenced by the séances and written in the same visionary style as *Dieu* and *La Fin de Satan*, was written there, as was "Un spectre m'attendait" (A specter awaited me), also from *Les Contemplations*, and "Nous nous promenions parmi les décombres a Rozel Tower" (We walked amidst the ruins of Rozel Tower), from *Les Châtiments*. In *Les Mages* (The Magi) Hugo tells of "The dark cromlech, scattered in the grass...on the silent hill."[51]

St. Brelade's Bay, on the southwest coast, "surrounded by jagged hills and rocks," was also a favorite place for excursions, as was Queen's Valley, "the valley where I go every day...."[52] On Guernsey, the turreted Victoria Tower, with a spectacular view of the island, was a place Hugo visited often. It was there, April 11–15, 1860, that he wrote "Chanson des oiseaux" (Song of the Birds), translated in this edition.

Stevens quotes Hugo's reaction to the charms of Jersey, as conveyed to Jules Laurens, an artist who was visiting him in March of 1855:

> When you have seen the bay of St. Aubin (the second of the island), the admirable granite cliffs of the north, Grève de Lecq with its tunnel traversable at low tide, the cape of Mont Orgueil; when you are sufficiently amazed by the southern appearance of certain plants, holm-oaks, fig-trees, due to the effect, even at this latitude, of the warm currents of the Gulf Stream, but with an underlying freshness always in the air, well, why don't we go to Guernsey, the archipelago of Alderney, Sark, Herm, Jethou, in the full roughness of the Ocean? Terrible and sublime equinoctial effects are found there in particular.[53]

He did make an excursion to Sark, which he had admired on the original trip from Southampton to Jersey, and had found it a "fairy castle, full of wonders."[54] Hugo could not have known that a mere eight months after this conversation, he would embark on a boat trip to Guernsey, not to visit, but to make a new home in exile for another fifteen years, the island to which he dedicated this poem:

> These rocks of the ocean encapsule everything, terror and grace,
> Heavens, seas, escarpment behind which all pass,
> Somber sound which sometimes seems a blessèd hymn,
> Patience to bear the weight of the infinite;
> And, in these proud deserts which a frightening order rules,
> One feels one's wing grow, and the Soul becomes an Eagle.[55]

Victor Hugo, *Vieux Guernesey* (Old Guernsey), date unknown, Bibliothèque nationale de France

A NOTE ON HUGO'S ART

We are beginning, in this generation, to rediscover from exhibits like *Shadows of a Hand*, that Hugo was an artist of immeasurable talent as well. He was considered a master by those of his friends and contemporaries who knew his work, which was compared to that of Goya or Dürer. Much later, van Gogh called Hugo's drawings "astonishing things"[56] in a January 3rd, 1890 letter from Saint-Rémy to his brother Theo, and elsewhere as grand, immense, and infinite; but Hugo's own estimate of his art was less laudatory, in part because he did not want it to compete with his writing. On April 29th, 1860 he wrote to Baudelaire of the "... things I call my pen drawings... [that] amuse me between verses."(...des choses que j'appelle mes dessins à la plume....Cela m'amuse entre deux strophes).[57] In a letter from Hauteville-House dated October 5th, 1862 to André Castel, who wished to publish an album of his drawings entitled *Dessins de Victor Hugo*, he called them "...these insignificant pen strokes dashed more or less clumsily down on paper by a man with other things to do...."[58] Another time he called them "a bit wild" (un peu sauvages).[59]

Victor Hugo, *Clocher dans la dune* (Steeple in the Dunes), detail, 1870-71, Musée Maison de Victor Hugo

In truth Hugo was a superb draftsman, and did many extraordinary drawings from his imagination as well as in his travels. At the same time, he loved to experiment, and relied on unorthodox techniques to free his imagination. Just as his poetry anticipated that of the twentieth century, so some of his graphic techniques anticipated those of the surrealists and abstract expressionists. In that April 29th letter to Baudelaire he also described his method: "I end up combining pencil, charcoal, sepia, coal, soot, and all kinds of bizarre mixtures."[60] Philippe Burty, one of the more progressive French art critics and writers of that time, who coined the term "japonisme," and was an early champion of the Impressionists, wrote of Hugo's technique:

> Victor Hugo has done hundreds of drawings, and has used every conceivable process, all shades of colour, all kinds of paper—common ink, the coffee left at the bottom of

> his cup at dessert, a charred lucifer-match, the feather of a goose-quill, a handkerchief applied to half-dry portions of the paper.[61]

He was as prolific in his artwork as in his writing during those years spent on the Channel Islands—"[Hugo] pursued, from sketch to sketch, the grand impossible project of *Dieu* and *La Fin de Satan*."[62] "His exile inspired compositions which are tinged, some with the bitterness that runs through the *Châtiments*, others with the melancholy that pervades the *Contemplations.*"[63]—but as Burty wrote in 1875, five years after Hugo's repatriation: "Since his return to France he has only done one—a series rather, of arabesques....The yearly deprivation of such a precious gift makes me often tell him that I wish him as many more years of exile as there are empty places in my portfolio."[64]

Twelve years after Hugo's death, the artist Pierre-Georges Jeanniot visited Hauteville-House on Guernsey and wrote:

> There is only one other man who possessed to so great a degree this faculty for creating the fantastic and visionary; this was Gustave Doré; but the fantastic of Doré is commonplace and without dignity, whereas that of Hugo is superb and original. And why? Without doubt because Hugo was transmuting his own particular dreams, while Doré realized those of all the world. There is no scientific skill in the vulgar sense in Hugo's drawings, but a spontaneous creativeness, contemptuous of all rule and of everything ever seen before....These observations seem to me to explain why Victor Hugo, in his manifestation as a graphic artist, remains an inimitable master, and of a power equal to that which he displayed in a literary direction.[65]

André Breton named his daughter Aube (Dawn) in tribute to one of his drawings.[66] Would that Hugo had done as William Blake, and illustrated his own poetry.

LOUIS MORÉRI

Hugo was often accused, in some quarters, of making up names when he needed a rhyme; the word *Jérimadeth,* from "Booz endormi," is a well-known example. However, scholars have shown these accusations to be primarily false.[67] Instead, just as Mallarmé and Valéry used the long-forgotten meanings of common words culled from a dictionary for poetic effect, so Hugo sought out and used obscure proper nouns not only for their literal meaning, but for their allusive quality. Aside from the Old Testament, his favorite source was *Le Grand Dictionnaire historique*, subtitled: *ou le mélange curieux de l'histoire sacrée et profane* (or the curious anthology of sacred and secular history); published originally in a single folio volume by French priest and encyclopaedist Louis Moréri, and eventually changed in emphasis and expanded by later editors to ten folio volumes in 1759, it was first published in Lyon in 1674 by Jean Girin et Barthélemy Rivière. In it were found rare, odd terms, as well as names of places or characters little known or unknown. French critic and man of letters Émile Faguet wrote in the July 16th, 1911 issue of *Le Temps*:

> Moréri is the mine where Victor Hugo descends every day and several times per day. Moréri gives him the history, which he is given the responsability to make picturesque, especially the odd proper names, strange, and worrying, which awaken one's attention and draw it to them, as a bright color attracts the eyes.[68]

Thanks to research done by René Journet and Guy Robert in their edition, *Dieu (Le Seuil du gouffre)*,[69] we know that in "L'Esprit humain" and the thirteen 'Voices' of the prologue, alone, there are over forty references from Moréri's dictionary.

A NOTE ON THE TRANSLATION

The text of these selections is that of Victor Hugo's original manuscript, and thus adheres closely to the work of René Journet and Guy Robert in their editions, *Dieu (L'océan d'en haut)*, 1960, *Dieu (Le Seuil du gouffre)*, 1961, and *Contribution aux études sur Victor Hugo: vol. 2. Le texte de "La fin de Satan" dans le manuscrit*, 1979, which editions, along with their 1969 three volume *Dieu (fragments)*, I will refer to as the JR. This work consisted of careful transcriptions of the MSS that established the text for later scholarly editions such as *Œuvres complètes,* Édition chronologique, vols. IX and X, 1968–69, edited by Jean Massin (hereafter the CF), and *Œuvres Complètes:* Poésie IV, 1986, edited by Jacques Seebacher and Guy Rosa (hereafter the RL). As well as some stanzaic changes, my *Dieu* text differs from that of those editors in my choice of variants. When Hugo left one or more alternative words or phrases, I made subjective choices, whereas the above chose Hugo's initial word or phrase, and other important editions usually chose his second. Unlike the JR and RL, but in accord with the CF and other important earlier and later editions, I adhere more closely to the manuscript of *La Fin de Satan* by placing chapters XIII–XVI of Satan's monologue after "L'Ange Liberté" and "La Prison," and entitle them "Satan Pardonné," as indicated by Hugo on the verso of folio 232r of the MS. The former two place them before "L'Ange Liberté." (Although "La Prison" was not entirely finished, of all these editions, only the CF chose not to include it in the main text.)

As did the JR and the RL, I chose to use, for the ending of *La Fin de Satan*, the fragment entitled "Dénouement," found on folio 279r, beginning with the lines "Voix à travers l'infini / Non, je ne te hais pas." The other editions, including the first three early editions, chose the text of the dénoûment, as well, but replaced the first two lines with those written upside down atop folio 198r, "DIEU PARLE DANS L'INFINI / Non, je ne te hais point!..." For some reason, the first two editions of this poem, *Œuvres inédites de Victor Hugo*: *La Fin de* Satan, 1886, (which, along with the 1891 Hetzel-Quantin *Dieu*, will hereafter be referred to as the HQ), and the Imprimerie nationale edition *Œuvres complètes de Victor Hugo, Poésie XI, La Fin de Satan. Dieu.*, 1911 (hereafter the IN), left out the last line of the denouement, whereas the next Bibliothèque de la Pléiade edition, *La Légende des siècles. La Fin de Satan. Dieu.*, 1950 (hereafter the BP), included it. I added, as an epilogue, the poems "Le Point du Jour," "Les Grands Morts," and a two-verse fragment, all verses that Hugo indicated he wished placed at the end of the poem, and all published in the notes or the appendices of the earlier editions of this work.[70] Unlike the first four important editions of *Dieu*, I did not include the poem "Le Jour" as epilogue. After much study of the MS and the critical literature, I felt, as later editors, that the poem was an invention of the literary executors, and chose to return the verses, of which it was mostly comprised, to their original place in the MS.

The first excerpts are from the prologue to *Dieu* entitled "Le Seuil du gouffre" (The Threshold of the Abyss) by Hugo in 1869. They include the section entitled "L'Esprit humain" (The Human Spirit), as well as eight of Hugo's original thirteen 'Voix' (Voices). Following the prologue, I include excerpts from the second part of *Dieu* entitled "L'ocean d'en Haut" (The Ocean of the Heights).[71] The three excerpts are "I. La Chauve-souris" (The Bat), "VI. Le Griffon" (The Griffin), and "VIII. La Clarté" (The Light). The second part of this book includes excerpts from all eight parts of *La Fin de Satan* beginning with "ET NOX FACTA EST," the wonderfully high-wrought telling of Satan's

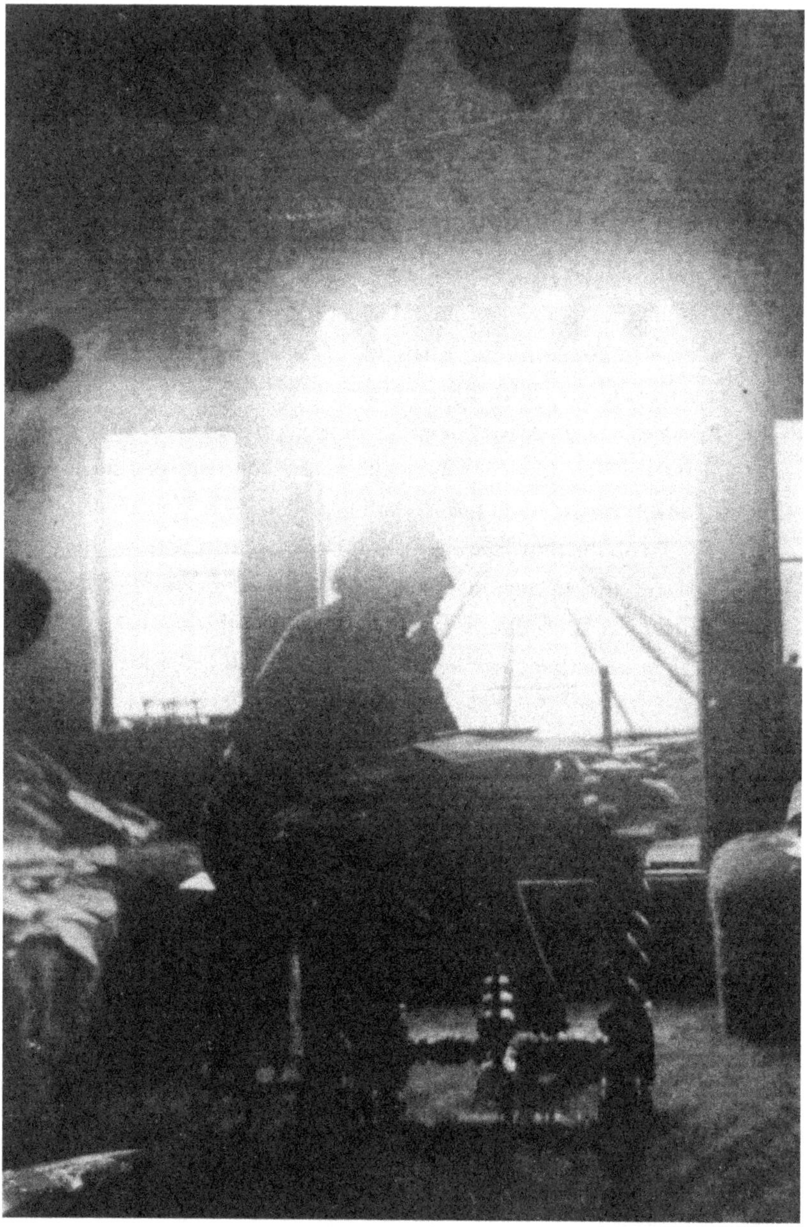

Anonymous, *Victor Hugo dans son cabinet de travail, avant la création du look-out,* (Victor Hugo in his study, before the creation of the "Look-Out "), 1859-61, Musée Victor Hugo-Maison Vacquerie

fall from heaven referred to above. In an attempt to condense the combined twelve thousand lines of these two poems into one volume of almost one-half that length, I have had to select parts that I believe best represent the whole.

To illustrate the scope of Hugo's writings, the difficulty of constructing a cohesive edition of this poetry given the ocean of verses written for these projects, to hint at the byways these poems might have taken, and the wealth of poetry still left to discover amidst the unpublished verses, I include a selection of other fragments, published in the IN, that could just as well have been included by those given the task of preparing this work for publication.

I chose not to translate Hugo's verse as rhymed couplets, a precedent set by previous translators, allowing his inherent imagery to hopefully carry the day. Given that Hugo's poems are narrative, and even thought of by some as reading like novels, my translations are essentially prose translations bordering on prose poems, organized as verse or free verse, and closely approximating Hugo's syntax and grammar. As prose translations, they follow the tradition of such editors of Nineteenth and Twentieth Century French and German poetry anthologies as Anthony Hartley, Elaine Marks, and Patrick Bridgwater, of Oliver Bernard in *Arthur Rimbaud–Collected Poems*, and even of François-Victor Hugo in his translation of Shakespeare.

A PUBLICATION HISTORY OF *DIEU*

Pierre-Jules Hetzel was a Paris publisher and fellow exile who met Hugo in Brussels in 1851, following the *coup d'état*. He became his literary agent, traveled to London to help arrange for translations, and facilitated the publication of his work in Brussels and Paris. At great personal risk, he worked tirelessly to make Hugo's anti-imperialist writings available to the public. In 1852 he arranged for the denunciatory *Napoléon-le-petit* to be published secretly by Baptiste Tarride. In order to protect Tarride from any retaliation by the French or Belgian government, the London publisher, William Jeffs, had agreed to have it published under his name, with some persuasion by Hugo. In 1853, Hetzel arranged for the secret release of *Les Châtiments*, initially entitled *Les Vengeresses*, published by Antoine Mertens and printed by Henri Samuel,[72] also in Brussels. That year, through the Librairie Marescq and the Librairie Blanchard in Paris, he published the two volume *Œuvres Illustrées de Victor Hugo,* with Victor Lecou began an English edition of the complete works of Hugo, and with Tarride, the *Œuvres oratoires.* He remained in exile until a general amnesty allowed his return to Paris in 1859, frequently corresponding with Hugo and periodically visiting him on the islands (Hugo refused to return to France until Napoleon III was deposed, and so stayed on Guernsey for another eleven years, much of the last five years spent traveling or writing in Brussels, near his family, as noted above).

It was following the publication, in Paris and Brussels, of the popular *Les Contemplations* in late April of 1856, arranged by Hetzel and a team organized by Hugo, that Hetzel wrote to Hugo offering a fifteen year contract for the purchase of all his written work. Hugo's favorable response in a May 20th letter from Hauteville-House on Guernsey highlighted his works in progress, *Dieu*, *La Fin de Satan*, and the *Petites Épopées* (Minor Epics), as being part of the bargain.[73] Yet, within the next three weeks Hugo decided to delay publication of the former two poems, after all, as he explained in the June 7th letter to Prosper Enfantin, quoted above. Despite this hesitation, Hugo scholars René Journet and Guy Robert found a fragment of Adèle Hugo's journal which they date most likely from July 2nd, 1856, indicating, once again, a change of heart:

> My father speaks this morning to us about his project of publishing the poem *Dieu* at once; [he] fully responds to what Mme. Sand calls for, a sequel and continuation of the *Contemplations*; one must strike while the iron's hot.[74]

Apparently, in spite of following Auguste Vacquerie's advice to remove, from Book VI of *Les Contemplations* (where it was meant to follow the verses "Solitudines Terræ"), and print separately, the poem "Solitudines cœli" (The Lonelinesses of the Heaven *or* Deserted Spheres of the Summit[75]), later renamed *Dieu*, and aside from the approval of George Sand, some of his friends and family did not want what they considered its continued somber mood perpetuated, a mood exemplified by its concluding verses, "Ce que dit la bouche d'ombre," equally influenced by the turning-table séances of 1852–53. Hugo could not help but be affected by the attitude of his entourage, and even that very same day, July 2nd, Adèle noted that her father later "…[suggested] creating a contrast of style, by publishing some prose,"[76] a view shared by his son François-Victor that day, as well.

Working in tandem with Hetzel was Paul Meurice, a writer and younger friend of Hugo, who had introduced the two in Brussels at the beginning of exile, and who was handling Hugo's affairs in Paris. In the autumn of that year he wrote Vacquerie for news of activity on Guernsey. Vacquerie wrote back on October 7th:

> What are we doing? *He* is finishing *Dieu* and *La Fin de Satan*; at present he reads us nothing; but he wakes up at five o'clock in the morning to write. The immense success of the *Contemplations* has put him in great form; you probably know that Hetzel just bought 5 thousand more copies of it from him. That translates into balconies and fountains in the new house.[77]

Over six months later, in a March 17th, 1857 letter, Hetzel, to whom Hugo was now bound by contract, further postponed the possibility of publishing *Dieu* and *La Fin de Satan*. He suggested that the success of *Les Contemplations* had aroused some envy, and that more pure poetry would invite a critical response:

> Your volumes of *Dieu* and *Satan* for example would find lain in ambush all the enemies that *Contemplations* had put to rout.
>
> Remembering what you told me in Guernsey, I imagine that you have in portfolio something to dismay all those who await you with articles already written for your announced works *Dieu* and *Satan*, I wish to speak of the *Petites Épopées*. If you are ready with these two volumes or one of the two, for which *le Revenant* is a marvellous advertisement, I am sure of a second triumph.[78]

September 11th of that year Hugo and Hetzel signed a contract to publish *Petites Épopées*. As Hugo continued to write, influenced by his current mystical and philosophical inspiration, he began to see the potential for this new work being the human part of a poetic system comprised of *Dieu* and *La Fin de Satan*, a development of which Hetzel was wary. In the summer of 1858, a serious illness tempered Hugo's zeal, poems more to Hetzel's liking were written, and one year later, after Hugo had changed the title to La Légende des siècles (The Legend of the Centuries), subtitled *Petites Épopées*, the work was published. Hugo still maintained his plan to add *Dieu* and *La Fin de Satan* in a future edition, in order to comprise a trilogy, and, as we recall from above, announced the immanent appearance of one or both of these poems in the preface to that first 1859 edition, and again in an 1869 draft of a preface for the next edition. Yet despite these announcements, despite speaking of *Dieu* in a May 21st, 1869 letter to the publisher Lacroix,[79] and once again advertising them both, this time on the back cover of volume I of the 1869 inaugural edition of *L'Homme qui rit*, they were never published. At Guernsey Hugo had moved on to other poems, plays and novels, such as the continued writing of *Les Misérables*, and upon returning from exile in 1870, had set aside his writing to again engage in urgent political matters. In 1967 René Journet and Guy Robert wrote a paper giving an account of Hugo's last times spent with this work:

> ...[B]efore leaving for France in August of 1870, Hugo stores the poem *Dieu* in two trunks which he deposits in a Guernsey bank [the Old Bank—Trans.] on the 13th. He will only reopen these trunks in April of 1875, during a brief stay in Guernsey. During that interval, he had not thought about publishing *Dieu*, and subsequently he will hardly think of it again. One notices here and there a slight trace of interest shown in this work: in 1876, for example, the poem *À l'Homme* carries the heading: "For the poem *Dieu*"; but this reference was crossed out, and the poem added, in 1877, to the Second Series of *La Légende.*[80]

This paper, published by L'Association internationale des études françaises, was accompanied by a transcription of a subsequent discussion by Hugo scholars, presided over by the Association head, Maurice Piron, who pointed out that the publisher Lacroix had wanted novels, Hetzel had said outright that *Dieu* was not a good commercial venture, and the public, after much poetry, would certainly have preferred a novel. Recognizing this, but still wishing to continue in this apocalyptic vein, Hugo had resorted to publishing a lesser poem, *Le Revenant* (The Ghost), "...a cheap, vulgar kind of Apocalypse" (...de l'Apocalypse à bon marché, vulgarisée).[81] As time went by, Hugo, more withdrawn and bereaved due to the loss of most of his family, admitted that he had too many projects, and too little time.[82] Piron then concluded:

> Later, he will pursue the work on one of the parts of his poem *Dieu*, but numerous projects will intervene, and it is true to say that his creative power will be less and less worthy of the great poem *Dieu.*[83]

*

Hugo did wish that all his work be eventually published, including the smallest fragments, and had intended to leave his manuscripts, for that purpose, to his sons. On Sept. 23rd, 1875, both sons having died, he wrote a new Literary Testament, in which he named Paul Meurice, Auguste Vacquerie, and Ernest Lefèvre, Vacquerie's nephew, his literary executors, charging them with the task of publishing everything in his unpublished manuscripts. He subsequently contracted with Hetzel to publish his complete works, including the unpublished work, with notes and variants. From 1880 to 1889 forty-eight volumes[84] of the previously published work were released under the supervision, at Hugo's request, of Meurice, who was effectively assuming his literary executor's duties as absolute textual authority. When Hugo died unexpectedly in 1885, Meurice, perhaps joined by Auguste Vacquerie, began work on the posthumous work. Vacquerie's nephew, Ernest Lefèvre, who died in 1889, seems never to have been involved in the project.[85] From 1886 to 1892, nine of these volumes appeared, including *La Fin de Satan,* in 1886, and *Dieu,* in 1891, and this entire fifty-seven volume edition published by Hetzel-Quantin (HQ) became known as the "ne varietur" (definitive) edition.

Auguste Vacquerie died in 1895. By the turn of the century, Meurice began another edition of Hugo's complete works, this time from the presses of what had been the official Royal printing house and later became that of the French government, the Imprimerie nationale (IN). This publishing project was to continue from 1904 through 1952, first under the auspices of the publisher Ollendorff and from 1933 on, Ollendorff-Albin Michel. Although later supplanted as a scholarly work by future editions, it still gives the best account of the reception of many Hugo works. On December 11, 1905, after publishing *Notre-Dame de Paris*, *Les Contemplations*, and an edition of plays, Paul Meurice died, just short of his 88th birthday, while working at his desk. Meurice's younger friend and protégé, writer Gustave Simon, became Hugo's literary executor and keeper of the manuscripts. He would continue publishing this edition through 1914 and then take it up again in 1924, until his death in 1928.[86] Mme. Cécile Daubray, who had worked with Meurice and Simon for many years, would undertake the completion of this work from 1933 through 1952, applying the same dedication as her two predecessors, and according to scholars, publish volumes that are still considered philologically sound today, due to her "...more scrupulous return to the letter of the manuscripts." (...un retour plus scrupuleux à la lettre des manuscrits...)[87]

Six months after Meurice's death, Simon wrote a long tribute to him in *La Revue de Paris*, portraying his mentor's feelings regarding this work:

> And he felt joy reading and rereading these manuscripts that he would draw from a Breton cupboard beside his bed. They were dear treasures unknown to the public and it was a pleasure thinking of the endless surprises that he was preparing for the readers....[88]
>
> —I especially want to produce the more difficult volumes and those of which I have the most personal memories, but I will not finish the job. Just think, forty or forty-one volumes! *Le Rhin* will appear; after that there will be *La Fin de Satan* and *Dieu*...I have found some unpublished fragments of *Dieu*, of such great beauty.[89]

In 1911, following publication of several volumes beginning with the 1906 *Le Rhin*, Simon published *POÉSIE XI, La Fin de Satan. Dieu.,* for the first time uniting both poems in a single volume. This IN edition was to be a true *édition critique* of this work, and we begin to get the first inkling of the state in which the MS was left. Simon spoke of finding a dossier containing:

> "...nearly a thousand fragments of all sizes, some rare full pages, others on the back of an envelope, a newspaper wrapper, a summons, a circular, or a handbill; when letters addressed to his wife or children came into his hands, he used the blank spaces; some verses are placed in an area a mere centimeter high. This ocean of verse bore the title: Dieu. Rather than publishing this dossier as *Reliquat* [Remainders, remnants, left-over verses, originally either Meurice's or Hugo's term—Trans.]... we have extracted passages suitable to the text published in 1891, and inserted them throughout the volume...."[90]

We gain insight into the earlier approach of Meurice and perhaps Vacquerie when Simon explains that in 1891 it was thought

> ...preferable, in the interest of the work, to present it as much as possible as a finished work; rhymes had to be matched, whole passages deleted. Wouldn't lines of dots in the middle of an interesting passage distract and confuse the readers of the original edition?
>
> In this edition, which has a quite definitive, documentary character, and which is addressed to students and researchers, we believe we have restored in full all of Victor Hugo's verses.

> ...[T]oday it is considerably longer and, in a way, complete; it was not bound yet when it came into our hands, we added entire pages bearing the word: DIEU, or the title of one of the sections....[91]

Because Victor Hugo's MSS remained exclusively with Simon's successor, Mme. Daubray, no independent scholarship on *Dieu* and *La Fin de Satan* had been possible until the late 1940's when others were finally allowed access to them.[92] As a result, the next critical edition of the two poems was not published until 1950, when the Bibliothèque de la Pléiade (BP) edition was released, edited by Jacques Truchet, the first editor to be openly acknowledged as being responsible for a publication of this work. The volume was entitled *La Légende des siècles. La Fin de Satan. Dieu.*, and was the first publication of the trilogy as Hugo conceived it.

Each important edition of this work appeared to improve upon its predecessor in terms of accuracy of scholarship. More verses were added from the MS, finer distinctions were made dealing with fragments or variants, and attempts were made to define some of Hugo's obscure terms, discussed above, each editor rationalizing what he considered these advances in scholarship. Starting in 1960, due to this new access to the MS, Hugo scholars René Journet and Guy Robert began publishing their aforementioned editions, *Dieu (L'océan d'en haut)*, 1960, *Dieu (Le Seuil du gouffre)*, 1961, and *Dieu (fragments)*, 1969, considered veritable variorum editions of this work.[93] There would be a supplementary volume, *Boîte aux lettres*, published in 1965, as there would later be twenty-seven pages of *Dieu* rough drafts published in their 1979 *Contribution aux études sur Victor Hugo: vol. 1*, as well as 367 pages of *Dieu* fragments presented by Journet and Hugo scholar Evelyn Blewer in the 1990 book *Chantiers*. As before, I refer to these editions as the JR.

Dieu next appeared in the earlier discussed 1968–69 Club français du livre edition, *Œuvres complètes*: Édition chronologique, volumes IX and X, edited by Jean Massin (the CF), followed, in 1972, by a version published in *Poésie*, tome 3 (Éditions du Seuil), edited by Bernard Leuilliot (the ES), and in 1986, a Robert Laffont edition, *Œuvres Complètes:* Poésie IV, edited by Jacques Seebacher and Guy Rosa (the RL). The ES was greatly influenced by the scholarship of the JR, as evidenced by its notes and commentary, and by the Journet and Robert paper, "Pourquoi Victor Hugo n'a-t-il pas publié son poème 'Dieu'?." The editor, Leuilliot, also contributed extensively to the CF and the RL. As noted above, a close scrutiny reveals that the CF and the RL, considered, to this day, the most scholarly and accurate editions of Hugo's work, appear to have duplicated the JR's painstakingly transcribed text of *Dieu*, to the letter (and the RL that of the JR's *La Fin de Satan*, as well), thus paying the highest form of tribute to the JR, and reiterating the praise that the editors of these two editions had lavished on Journet and Robert elsewhere in prefaces and scholarly journals.

Guided by the portfolio and piece numbers stamped on each MS folio or fragment by Hugo's notary,[94] Journet and Robert were able to establish the state of the MS at the time of his death, thus revealing how the HQ and IN had rearranged the order of folios prior to the IN's pagination[95] and binding of it. They discovered the thirteen 'Voices' in Hugo's original conception, and pointed out the seemingly contrived nature of the poem "Le Jour," placed as epilogue to *Dieu* by the three previous editions and reluctantly but with strong reservations by the JR, itself. They returned the forty-two verse section, verses 375–416 of our text, beginning with "O méditations! oh! comme l'esprit souffre," not included in the main text of the three earlier editions, to where Hugo indicated he wished them placed, in a left-hand marginal note on folio 22r. Moved by the IN and placed as folios 230r and 231r, their piece numbers 127 and 128 reveal that they were originally placed by Hugo between folio 21r (piece 126) and folio 22r (piece 129).

As brought to our attention by the Hugo scholars and translators E.H. and A.M. Blackmore, Journet and Robert discovered through inspection of the piece numbers that Hugo had written two versions of "L'Esprit humain," one introducing the 'Voices,' and another ending in an early death of the protagonist, precluding an encounter with the 'Voices.' The HQ had torn in two the first bifolio of the version introducing the 'Voices,' set aside the first folio, the introductory verses of that version, and added the rest to the second version, thereby utilizing the verses of both versions, and enabling them to successfully incorporate the 'Voice' section. Where this fusion of the two versions caused inconsistancies (due to Hugo's indecision as to what direction to take the text), as well as an overlapping of text, the HQ or both the HQ and the IN used variant verses to remedy those inconsistancies, the creation of "Le Jour" perhaps being one example, and, prompted by another of Hugo's marginal notes, the verses "After the Voices" perhaps being another. One assumes this was all done in the spirit of trying to create a "finished work."

Of the fifteen hundred and seven fragments identified as belonging to *Dieu*, only the approximately twelve hundred and fifty in the MS at the Bibliothèque nationale de France were included in the three volumes of the JR's 1969 *Dieu (fragments)*, and were divided into three sections: those from portfolio 106, all connected to *Dieu*, those not found in portfolio 106, but clearly belonging there by virtue of their contents, and those that in some way seemed a product of the same inspiration that produced *Dieu*.[96]

In the 1990 *Chantiers*, Journet reveals in more detail the general state of Hugo's MS, giving us a final look at the mass of papers that Hugo had saved for posterity, and the difficulties facing those taking on the task of publishing them. After the IN had created their version of *Dieu*, with the accompanying fragments, they then faced, according to Journet:

> ...an imposing residue that they organized as methodically as possible: hence the thirty-five manuscript volumes entitled *Océan* or *Tas de pierres*: smaller and smaller fragments classified by genre or by subject. The final volumes of the series...are truly a catch-all: scraps barely legible, notes of all kinds, sometimes practical, or intimate....The material was overflowing....Subsequent publications have pecked through what was left, without exhausting it....[97]
>
> ...By examining the contents of certain portfolios in Guy Robert's concordance notebooks, or in the Extract of the Inventory made by Jacques Seebacher [see note 94—Trans.], we have the impression of a kind of shambles, the notary, or one of his clerks, extracted, sometimes at random, an armful of papers....[f]ragments of verse....[f]ragments of prose for the greater part without visible link.... [m]anuscripts of all kinds without visible link....[98]

After spending much time with the MS and the published editions of *Dieu*, one could argue that the poem *Dieu*, as we know it, is a fiction, a product of Hugo's literary executors, and a fiction maintained by future editors, albeit a fiction not only encouraged by Hugo, but mandated by him. One could maintain that, given the ocean of unused fragments, there are as many potential *Dieu*'s as there are potential editors, or conclude, as did Jean Gaudon, that a certain poem written by Victor Hugo entitled *Dieu* may not, in fact, exist at all.[99] However, until someone accepts the task of putting himself in Hugo's shoes, and studying all the related texts for possible incorporation into the current text, we can be but grateful to the literary executors and eminent scholars who have devoted much of their professional lives to heroically transforming these incomplete works into the masterworks they are today.[100]

ACKNOWLEDGMENTS

WHEN I STARTED THIS project in 1998, I could find neither poem translated into English, and so decided to begin the task myself. While in the process some years later, I discovered that in the period 2000–02, new translations of Hugo's poetry had been published by E.H. and A.M. Blackmore, Brooks Haxton, and Steven Monte, celebrating the bicentenary of Hugo's birth in 1802. These translations included excerpts from *Dieu* and *La Fin de Satan*. I hope that my contribution can begin to approach the high standard they have set.

Acknowledgment is due to Lakhdar Choudar, at Wayne State University, who read my first thousand verses and attempted to save me from blunders. His patient generosity and critical comment were invaluable. I would also like to thank Richard Hill for reading my initial manuscript and for his positive response and encouragement in general, as well as Matthew Loving, the French Librarian at the University of Florida, for his initial and on-going encouragement in this project. Without his research assistance, tips, and suggestions, this would not have been possible. I'd like to thank Proust scholar, Harold Augenbraum, for looking at my early efforts and encouraging me to translate the entire works; and at U.F., John Van Hook, the English Librarian, who helped me discover the Journet/Robert variorum edition of these works and pointed out the history of the Imprimerie nationale, Blake Landor, the Classics Librarian, who was especially helpful and encouraging, and without whose intervention this edition would not be possible, Christine Ross, the Scholarly Communications Librarian, who helped me with international copyright law, and Dr. Audrey Viguier, now at the University of Texas, Brownsville, for their invaluable help. As well, I would like to thank University of Florida French Professor Emeritus, George Diller, for looking at my manuscript, and suggesting what eventually became "A Publication History of *Dieu*," and Dr. Bernadette César-Lee, French Linguistics, for her very kind assistance and consideration.

I wish to express a special thanks to Phil Martin for his general encouragement and advice over the years, Richard Hoffman for his early, enthusiastic advocacy, Bess Buckley for her greatly appreciated support and advice, and to Keli Conroy, Sylvia Ashwell, and Jeff Dreisin, the ILL staff of the Alachua County library system, and James Stevens, Lisa Bailey, Robin Haskins and the rest of the staff at the University of Florida's Library West and Smathers Rare Book Library, who were so helpful accessing books for my research. Once again, this work would not have been possible without access to the vast resources of the library systems of the University of Florida and Alachua County, Florida.

I would also like to thank Marva Barnett, professor and Hugo scholar at the University of Virginia, for her kind suggestions, and art historian Florian Rodari, in Paris, for his help in the search for Hugo art images, and a deep and heart-felt thank-you especially goes out to Hugo scholars and translators E.H. and A.M. Blackmore, whose numerous suggestions, help, advice, support and encouragement went well beyond all possible expectations, and whose generosity seemed without limit. Our shared enthusiasm for these two particular poems was a great source of strength and joy.

I would like to express a feeling of deep appreciation to David Rade, editor and publisher of Swan Isle Press, for his warm understanding and encouragement throughout this process. We are the beneficiaries of his love of and receptiveness to world literature, which gift he bestows on us through his editions of translation. The invaluable editing assistance, as well, of Margaret Mahan, is much appreciated.

Finally, I thank my parents for their support and encouragement over the years, and especially my wife, Cat O'Reilly, for her support, suggestions and patience, without which this work also would not be possible.

—*R.G. Skinner*

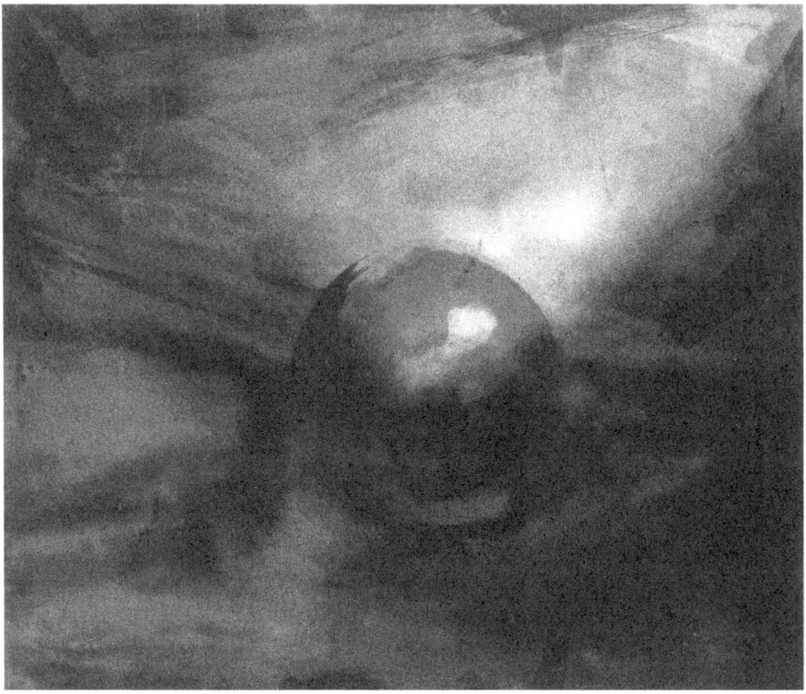

Victor Hugo, *Planète* (Planet), ca. 1854, Collection Krugier-Poniatowski

from **GOD**

---

from **DIEU**

Que ce poème au vol de feu
Effleure le siècle où nous sommes,
Qu'il passe vite et brille peu,
Et qu'a travers l'oubli des hommes,
Sombre, il s'en retourne vers Dieu.

Le Seuil du gouffre

L'ESPRIT HUMAIN

...
Et je voyais au loin sur ma tête un point noir.

Comme on voit une mouche au plafond se mouvoir,
Ce point allait, venait; et l'ombre était sublime.

Et l'homme, quand il pense, étant ailé, l'abîme
M'attirant dans sa nuit toujours de plus en plus,
Comme une algue qu'entraîne un ténébreux reflux,
Vers ce point noir, planant dans la profondeur blême,
Je me sentais déjà m'envoler de moi-même

May this poem with the flight of fire
Touch, lightly, the century wherein we reside,
May it pass quickly, shine briefly,
And, through the neglect of Man,
Return, saturnine, to God.

The Threshold of the Abyss

THE HUMAN SPIRIT

...
And I could see, far above me, a black speck.

As a fly one sees moving about overhead,
This speck came and went, and the darkness was sublime.

And because Man becomes wingèd when he muses, the abyss
Drew me more and more into its night,
Like seaweed drawn by a dark ebb tide.
Soaring into the pale heights,
I felt myself already flying off towards this black speck

Quand je fus arrêté par quelqu'un qui me dit:
—Demeure.—

En même temps une main s'étendit.

J'étais déjà très haut dans la nuée obscure.

Et je vis apparaître une étrange figure;
Un être tout semé de bouches, d'ailes, d'yeux,
Vivant, presque lugubre et presque radieux.
Vaste, il volait; plusieurs des ailes étaient chauves.
En s'agitant, les cils de ses prunelles fauves
Jetaient plus de rumeur qu'une troupe d'oiseaux
Et ses plumes faisaient un bruit de grandes eaux.
Cauchemar de la chair ou vision d'apôtre,
Selon qu'il se montrait d'une face ou de l'autre,
Il semblait une bête ou semblait un esprit.
Il paraissait, dans l'air où mon vol le surprit,
Faire de la lumière et faire des ténèbres.

Calme, il me regardait dans les brouillards funèbres.

Et je sentais en lui quelque chose d'humain.

—Qu'es-tu donc, toi qui viens me barrer le chemin,
Être obscur, frissonnant au souffle de ces brumes?
Lui dis-je.

Il répondit:—Je suis une des plumes
De la nuit, sombre oiseau d'ombres et de rayons,
Noir paon épanoui des constellations.

Je suis ce qui court, vole, erre, s'enfle, s'apaise;
Je suis en même temps ce qui retombe, pèse,
Saisit l'aile qui va, retient l'essor qui fuit,
Et descend; car le fond de mon être est la nuit.

When I was stopped by someone who exclaimed:
—Stay.—

At the same time a hand reached out to me.

I was even now high up in the obscure cloud.

And I saw a strange figure appear,
A Being entirely sown with mouths, wings, eyes,
Alive, nearly sorrowful, nearly radiant.
He was vast, in flight, and several of his wings were threadbare.
The fluttering lashes of his fulvous eyes
Were more clamorous than a flock of birds,
And his feathers made the sound of mighty waters.
A nightmare of the flesh or the vision of an apostle,
Depending on whether he showed one face or another,
He seemed beast or he seemed spirit.
In the air where my flight surprised him,
He appeared to create both light and darkness.

He calmly watched me in the sinister fogs.

And I sensed in him something human.

—Who are you, you who come to bar my way,
Strange Being, shivering in the stir of these mists?
I said to him.

He answered:—I am one of the feathers
Of night, somber bird of darkness and light,
Black peacock strewn with constellations.

I am that which runs, takes wing, wanders, grows turgid, and abates,
Just as I am that which again falls back, has weight,
Seizes the moving wing, restrains soaring flight,
And descends; for the heart of my being is night.

—Ton nom?—dis-je.

Il reprit:

—Pour toi qui, loin des causes,
Vas flottant, et ne peux voir qu'un côté des choses,
Je suis l'Esprit Humain.

Mon nom est Légion.
Je suis l'essaim des bruits et la contagion
Des mots vivants allant et venant d'âme en âme.
Je suis Souffle. Je suis cendre, fumée et flamme.
Tantôt l'instinct brutal, tantôt l'élan divin.
Je suis ce grand passant, vaste, invincible et vain,
Qu'on nomme vent; et j'ai l'étoile et l'étincelle
Dans ma parole, étant l'haleine universelle;
L'haleine et non la bouche; un zéphyr me grandit
Et m'abat; et quand j'ai respiré, j'ai tout dit.
Je suis géant et nain, faux, vrai, sourd et sonore,
Populace dans l'ombre et peuple dans l'aurore;
Je dis moi, je dis nous; j'affirme, nous nions.
Je suis le flux des voix et des opinions,
Le fantôme de l'an, du mois, de la semaine,
Fait du groupe fuyant de la nuée humaine.
Homme, toujours en moi la contradiction
Tourne sa roue obscure et j'en suis l'Ixion.
Démos, c'est moi. C'est moi ce qui marche, attend, roule,
Pleure et rit, nie et croit; je suis le démon Foule.

Je suis, comme la trombe, ouragan et pilier.

En même temps je vis dans l'âtre familier.
Oui, j'arrache au tison la soudaine étincelle
Qui heurte un germe obscur que le crâne recèle,
Et qui, des fronts courbés perçant les épaisseurs,

—What is your name?—I said.

He responded:

—For you who are drifting
Far from the causes, and can see only one aspect of things,
I am the Human Spirit.

My name is Legion.
I am the swarm of sounds and the contagion
Of living words moving from soul to soul.
I am Breath. I am ash, smoke and flame.
Sometimes brutish instinct, sometimes the divine élan,
I am this great passer-by, vast, invincible, and vain,
Named Wind; and my speech enfolds star and spark,
Since I am the universal breath,
Not the mouth. A zephyr makes me grow tall
And then casts me down; and when I have breathed, I have
Said all. I am giant and dwarf, falsehood, truth, silence and sound,
Rabble in the darkness, and People in the dawn;
I say me, I say us; I affirm, we deny.
I am the flood of voices and opinions,
The yearly, monthly, weekly phantom
Come from the fleeting human host.
Man, in me contradiction always
Turns its obscure wheel, and I am its Ixion.
I am Demos. It is I who walks, waits, wavers,
Cries and laughs, denies and believes; I am the dæmon Throng.

Like the waterspout, I am both storm and pillar.

In the same breath, I live in the familial hearth.
Yes, I extract from the firebrand the unexpected spark
That collides with an obscure seed concealed in the cranium,
And which explodes in the minds of thinkers,

Fait faire explosion à l'esprit des penseurs.
Je vis près d'eux, veilleur intime; je combine
Le vieux houblon de Flandre et la vigne sabine,
La franche joie attique et le rire gaulois;
L'antique insouciance avec ses douces lois,
Paix, liberté, gaîté, bon sens, est mon breuvage;
J'en grise Érasme et Sterne, et même mon sauvage,
Diderot; et j'en fais couler quelques filets
De l'amphore d'Horace au broc de Rabelais.

Il poursuivit:

—Je crie à quiconque commence:
—Assez! Finis!—Je suis le Médiocre immense.
Toutes les fois qu'on parle et qu'on dit:—mitoyen,
Mode, médiateur, méridien, moyen,—
Par chacun de ces mots on m'évoque, on m'adjure,
Et tantôt c'est louange, et tantôt c'est injure.

Je suis l'esprit Milieu; l'être neutre qui va
Bas sans trouver Iblis, haut sans voir Jéhovah;
Dans le nombre, je suis Multitude; dans l'être,
Borne. Je m'oppose, homme, à l'excès de connaître,
De chercher, de trouver, d'errer, d'aller au bout;
Je suis Tous, l'ennemi mystérieux de Tout.
Je suis la loi d'arrêt, d'enceinte, de ceinture
Et d'horizon, qui sort de toute la nature;
L'éther irrespirable et bleu sur la hauteur,
Dans le gouffre implacable et sourd, la pesanteur.
C'est moi qui dis:—Voici ta sphère. Attends. Arrête.
Tout être a sa frontière, homme ou pierre, ange ou bête,
Et doit, sans dilater sa forme d'aujourd'hui,
Subir le nœud des lois qui se croisent en lui.
Je me nomme Limite et je me nomme Centre.
Je garde tous les seuils de tous les mondes. Rentre.—
Tout est par moi saisi, pris, circonscrit, dompté.

Penetrating the depths of their curved brows.
I live close to them, intimate watcher; I combine
The old hops of Flanders and the Sabine vine,
Honest Attic joy and Gallic laughter;
The ancient unconcern with its lenient laws,
Peace, freedom, gaiety, common sense, this is my drink;
I intoxicate Erasmus and Sterne with it, and even my savage,
Diderot; and I make a thin trickle of it flow
From the amphora of Horace to the pitcher of Rabelais.—

He continued:

—I shout to whomsoever begins:
—Enough! Be done!—I am the immense Undistinguished One.
Every time that someone speaks and says:—middle,
Mode, mediator, meridian, mean,—
By each word I am evoked, I am entreated,
And at times it is praise, at times, insult.

I am the Median spirit; the neutral Being that goes
Below without finding Iblis, on high without seeing Jehovah;
In number, I am Multitude; in being,
Limit. I am opposed, Man, to the excesses of knowing,
Of seeking, of finding, of wandering, of going to the bitter end;
I am Everyone, the mysterious enemy of Everything.
I am the law of cessation, of enclosure, of cincture
And of horizon, which emerges from the whole of nature;
I am the unbreathable, blue æther on the heights,
And gravity in the unrelenting, dark pit.
It is I who says:—Here is your sphere. Wait. Stop.
Every Being has his boundary, be he man or stone, angel or beast,
And must, without enlarging his present form,
Submit to the bondage of laws that intersect in him.
I am called Limit and I am called Center.
I guard all the thresholds of all the worlds. Return.—
Everything by me is seized, taken, circumscribed, subdued.

Je me défie, ayant peur de l'extrémité,
De la folie un peu, beaucoup de la sagesse.
Je tiens l'enthousiasme et l'appétit en laisse;
Pour qu'il aille au réel sans s'écarter du bien,
J'attelle au genre humain ce lion et ce chien;
Et, comme je suis souffle et poids, nul ne m'évite,
Car tout, comme esprit, flotte, et, comme corps, gravite.
Et l'explication, je te l'ai dit, vivant,
C'est que je suis l'esprit matériel, le vent;
Et je suis la matière impalpable, la force.
Je contrains toute sève à rester sous l'écorce;
Et tout miroir, étant piège, à mon souffle est terni.
Contre l'enivrement du splendide infini
Je garde les penseurs, ces pauvres mouches frêles.
Je tiens les pieds de ceux dont l'azur prend les ailes.
Je suis parfum, poison, bien, mal, silence, bruit.
Je suis en haut midi, je suis en bas minuit;
Je vais, je viens; je suis l'alternative sombre;
Je suis l'heure qui fait sortir, en frappant l'ombre,
Douze apôtres le jour, la nuit douze césars.
Du beau donnant sa forme au grand, je fais les arts.
Dans les milieux humains, dans les brumes charnelles,
J'erre et je vois; je suis le troupeau des prunelles.
Je suis l'universel, je suis le partiel.
Je nais de la vapeur ainsi que l'eau du ciel,
Et j'éclos du rocher comme le saxifrage.
Je sors du sentier vert, du foyer, du naufrage,
Du pavé du chemin, de la borne du champ,
Des haillons du noyé sur la grève séchant,
Du flambeau qui s'éteint, de la fleur qui se fane:
Je me suis appelé Pyrrhon, Aristophane,
Démocrite, Aristote, Ésope, Lucien,
Diogène, Timon, Plaute, Pline l'ancien,
Cervantès, Bacon, Swift, Locke, Rousseau, Voltaire.
Je suis la résultante énorme de la terre:
La raison.

I am wary, being afraid of the extreme,
Of madness a little, and of wisdom much.
I hold enthusiasm and appetite in check;
So that it leads to the real without deviating from the good,
I harness to humankind this lion and this canine;
And, as I am breath and weight, no one evades me,
For everything, being spirit, levitates, and everything, being body,
Gravitates, and the explanation, as I have said, living Being,
Is that I am the material spirit, wind;
And I am the intangible matter, energy.
I constrain all sap to remain under the bark;
And my breath tarnishes all mirrors, they being pitfalls.
Against the intoxication of the splendrous infinite
I protect the thinkers, those poor frail flies.
I seize by the feet those whose wings have been drawn to the azure.
I am perfume, poison, good, evil, silence, sound.
I am midday in the heights, I am midnight in the depths;
I go, I come; I am the somber alternative;
I am the hour that makes emerge, overtaking the gloom,
Twelve Apostles by day, twelve Caesars by night.
Bestowing beauteous form on the grand, I give birth to the arts.
Into the human milieu, into the carnal mists,
I wander and I see; I am the profusion of eyes.
I am the universal, I am the particular.
I am born from vapor as well as from the water of the sky,
And I blossom from the rock like the saxifrage.
I emerge from the green footpath, the hearth, the shipwreck,
The paving stone of the road, the boundary stone of the field,
The rags of the drowned man drying on the shore,
The dying torch, and the fading flower.
I am called Pyrrho, Aristophanes,
Democritus, Aristotle, Æsop, Lucian,
Diogenes, Timon, Plautus, Pliny the Elder,
Cervantes, Bacon, Swift, Locke, Rousseau, and Voltaire.
I am the enormous consequence of the earth:
Reason.

J'étais là, pensif, troublé, muet;
Pendant que j'écoutais, l'être continuait:

—Homme, à nous le mystère est ouvert. Nous en sommes.
Pour l'abîme, je suis un spectre; pour vous, hommes,
Je suis la Voix qui dit: allez, mais sachez où.
J'erre près du néant le long du garde-fou.
J'avertis.

Il reprit:
—Écoute, esprit qui trembles,
Et qui ne peux pas même entrevoir les ensembles:
Hommes, vous m'ignorez, mais je vous connais tous;
Et je suis encor vous, même en dehors de vous.

Entre les brutes, foule, et les anges, élite,
Il est, sur chaque terre et chaque satellite,
Un être à part; pensée et chair; matière esprit;
Page mixte du livre où la nature écrit,
Dernier feuillet du Monstre et premier du Génie;
Créature où la fange et l'or font l'harmonie,
Dans la bête à moitié, dans l'idée à demi,
Flamme accouplée avec le corps son ennemi,
Double rayon tordu d'ombre et d'aube ravie,
Mystère; ayant un pied, dans l'échelle de vie,
Sur une fin, un pied sur un commencement;
Cet être comparant, sentant, voyant, aimant,
C'est l'homme. Que la mort conserve, accroisse ou fauche
Cet à peu près sublime et ce chef-d'œuvre ébauche,
Qu'il ait ce qu'il appelle une âme, en ce moment
Je ne t'en parle pas, je te dis seulement
Que partout l'homme existe, étant un milieu d'êtres.
Il vit près des soleils, foyers, astres, ancêtres.
Sur des terres, qui sont plus ou moins loin du feu,
Il vit, domptant son globe; il est grand, il est peu;

I remained there, pensive, disturbed, and mute;
While I listened, the Being continued:

—Man, for us the mystery is revealed. We are of it.
For the abyss, I am a ghost; for you, Man,
I am the Voice that says: Go, but know whereunto.
I wander beside nothingness along the parapet.
Be forewarned.

He continued:
—Listen, spirit that trembles,
And who cannot even sense the whole:
Man, you are unaware of me, but I know you all;
And I am still you, even apart from you.

Between the animals, a bestial multitude, and the angels, an elite,
On each world and each satellite, you are
A Being apart; thought and flesh; material Spirit;
A mixed page of the book of nature,
The last page of the Monster, and the first page of the Genius;
A creature in whom mud and gold become harmonious,
Half in the beast, half in the idea,
A flame coupled with the body, its enemy,
An entwined double beam of darkness and enraptured dawn,
A mystery; having one foot on an end of the ladder of life,
And one foot on a beginning;
This Being—comparing, feeling, seeing, and loving—
Is Man. That death preserves, augments or reaps
This nearly sublime, this rough-hewn masterpiece,
That it has what it calls Soul, of that
I do not speak as yet, I say to you only
That man exists everywhere, being a medium of Beings.
He lives close to the suns, sources, stars, and ancestors.
On lands which are more or less far from fire,
He subsists, taming his planet; he is large, he is small;

Par la forme divers, mais un par sa nature;
Il a l'hydre animal et plante pour ceinture;
Il est sur le sommet de son visible à lui;
Et, larve où deux lueurs se croisent, point d'appui
De tout un phénomène, identique à lui-même,
Marque partout le même étage du problème;
Entre l'aile et le ventre il est l'être debout;
Il est partout le roi planétaire; partout
Il possède et régit l'astre intermédiaire
Entre l'ombre et le grand soleil incendiaire.
Car tout globe qui tourne autour d'une clarté
Est planète de loin, de près humanité.
Or,—puisque jusqu'à moi ton œil plonge et pénètre,—
C'est moi qui suis l'esprit collectif de cet être,
Partout, sous toute forme, et dans l'immensité.
Tu n'es qu'homme, ô passant; je suis humanité.
L'être effrayant, planant dans l'ombre inaccessible,
Ajouta:

—Nul ne doit sortir de son possible;
Nul ne doit transgresser son réel. Cependant
Je veux, puisque tu viens dans cette ombre, imprudent,
Faire une exception pour toi que je rencontre.
Quelque soit ton dessein, je ne ferai rien contre;
Homme, je consens même à contenter tes vœux
Étant de l'infini, je peux ce que je veux;
Ma main peut ouvrir tout puisqu'elle peut tout clore;
Qui puise de la nuit peut puiser de l'aurore,
Et ce que tu voudras, je te l'accorderai.
Que demandes-tu? parle.—

Et dans l'effroi sacré
Je me taisais; roseau ployant, vil brin de chaume.

—Tu n'es pas jusqu'ici venu, dit le fantôme,
Pour ne pas demander quelque chose. Voyons,

Varied in form, but in his nature one;
He wears the hydra, both animal and plant, for a belt;
He is at the apex of what he can see;
And, larva where two faint rays of light intersect, fulcrum
Of the whole phenomenon, identical to himself,
He reveals everywhere the same stage of the enigma;
Between those on the wing and those on their bellies, he is
The upright Being. He is the planetary king everywhere;
Everywhere he possesses and governs the intermediate star
Between the darkness and the great burning sun.
For any sphere that revolves about a luminosity
Is a planet from afar, and humanity up close.
Yet—since you have plunged headlong and discovered me—
I am the collective spirit of this Being,
Everywhere, in every form, throughout the vastness.
You are only a man, O passing one; I am Humanity.
The frightful being, hovering in the inaccessible gloom,
Added:

—No one should move beyond his own given possibilities;
No one should transgress his reality. However,
Since you come into this darkness, imprudent one,
I will make an exception for you whom I have just met.
Whatever was your intention, I shall not oppose it;
Man, I even agree to satisfy your wishes.
Being infinite, I may do as I wish;
My hand can open all since it can close all;
That which draws forth the night can make flow forth the dawn,
And what you wish I shall grant you.
What do you request? Speak.—

And in sacred fear
I kept silent—I, bending reed, contemptible strand of thatch.

—You did not come this far, said the phantom,
Seeking nothing. Come! Speak!

Parle. Veux-tu des feux, des nimbes, des rayons?
Que veux-tu de ce gouffre où, lorsque je me penche,
La colombe nuée accourt, farouche et blanche?
Veux-tu savoir le fond du serpent, ou du ver?
Veux-tu que je t'emporte avec moi dans l'éther?
Je t'obéirai. Parle. Ou faut-il qu'on te montre
Comment l'aurore arrive, et vient à la rencontre
Du parfum de la fleur et du chant des oiseaux?
Veux-tu que nous prenions la tempête aux naseaux,
Et que nous nous roulions tous deux dans la tourmente,
Quand la meute du vent court sur l'onde écumante
Et quand l'archer tonnerre et le chasseur éclair
Percent de traits la peau d'écailles de la mer?
Veux-tu qu'à pleines mains, tous deux, dans l'invisible,
O passant, nous puisions l'illusion terrible?
Veux-tu que nous penchions nos yeux sur les secrets,
Et que nous regardions la nature de près
Pendant qu'elle produit dans l'immense pénombre?
Parle. Es-tu curieux de l'accouchement sombre?
Veux-tu voir dans le germe, et voir comment éclôt
Le songe ou le rocher, le sommeil ou le flot,
Et prendre sur le fait la création, mère
De la réalité comme de la chimère?
Veux-tu d'une naissance entendre la rumeur,
Regarder un éden poindre, avoir la primeur
D'une sphère, d'un globe en fleur, d'une lumière?
Ou voir surgir l'idée, éblouissante, fière,
Cherchant l'époux Génie au fond du ciel lointain?
Dis, veux-tu dans la nuit, veux-tu dans le destin
Voir quelque lever d'astre ou quelque lever d'âme?
Tu peux choisir. Demande, interroge, réclame,
Parle. J'attends. Faut-il ressaisir, je le puis,
Une étoile aux cheveux dans la fuite des nuits,
Et te la rapporter splendide et frémissante?
Que veux-tu? Veux-tu voir dix soleils, vingt, soixante,
Se lever à la fois dans soixante univers?

Do you desire fires, halos, or rays of light?
What do you want from this pit where the flock of doves,
Timorous and pure, hastens to me when I brood?
Do you want to know the essence of the snake, or the worm?
Shall I carry you off into the æther?
I will do your bidding. Speak. Or must I show you
How the dawn appears, and comes to where the
Bird's song melds with the flower's perfume?
Do you want us to breathe in the odor of the storm,
And for us both to whirl in the gale,
Where the winds run on the foaming wave
And when the Archer's thunderclap and the Hunter's
Lightning bolt pierce the scaled skin of the sea?
Do you wish, O passer-by, for us both, with firm resolve,
To plumb the terrible illusion in the realm of the invisible?
Do you wish for us to rest our eyes on the unseen,
And to watch nature up close
While she gives birth in the immense half-light?
Speak. Are you curious about mysterious childbirth?
Do you wish to look into the source, and to see how are born
Dream or rock, sleep or flood,
And to catch in the act Creation, mother
Of reality as well as of vain fancy?
Do you wish to hear the sound of birth,
To see an Eden burst forth, to look upon a young sphere,
A terrestrial globe in flower, a new light?
Or to see Idea emerge, dazzling, proud, and seeking
Her husband, Genius, at the bottom of the remote sky?
Tell me, do you wish to see in the night, in the future,
Some rising of stars or some rising of Spirit?
You can choose. Question me, interrogate, demand,
Speak. I am waiting. Shall I recapture, this I can do,
A comet from out the fleeing nights,
And return it to you all resplendent and quivering?
What do you desire? Do you wish to see ten suns, twenty, sixty,
Rising at once in sixty universes?

Veux-tu voir, sur le seuil des cieux tout grands ouverts,
Le matin dételant les sept chevaux de l'Ourse?
Ou veux-tu que, dans l'ombre où le jour a sa source,
Homme, pour te donner le temps d'examiner,
Les mondes, qu'un prodige éternel fait tourner,
S'arrêtent un moment et reprennent haleine?
Parle.

L'esprit baissa ses ailes de phalène,
Et se tut. L'air tremblait sous mes pieds hasardeux.
Et l'âpre obscurité qui nous voyait tous deux
Et s'étoilait au loin de vagues auréoles,
Put entendre ce sombre échange de paroles
Entre l'esprit étrange et moi, l'homme ébloui:
—Non, rien de tout cela.—Que demandes-tu?—LUI.

Tout sembla devant moi se fermer; et l'espèce
De clarté qui tremblait dans la nuée épaisse
Sombra dans l'air plus noir qu'un ciel cimmérien.
J'entendis un éclat de rire, et ne vis rien.

Hélas! n'étant qu'un homme, une chair misérable,
Dans cette obscurité fauve, âpre, inexorable,
Dans ces brumes sans fond, sans bords, sous ce linceul,
Je songeai qu'il était horrible d'être seul.
Puis mon esprit revint à son but:—voir, connaître,
Savoir;—pendant que l'ombre affreuse, louche, traître,
Roulant dans ses échos ce noir rire moqueur,
Grandissait dans l'espace ainsi que dans mon cœur.

Et je criai, ployant mes ailes déjà lasses:
—Dites-moi seulement son nom, tristes espaces,
Pour que je le répète à jamais dans la nuit!—

Et je n'entendis rien que la bise qui fuit.

Do you wish to see, on the threshold of the vast open skies,
Morning unharnessing the seven horses of Ursa?
Or, Man, in order to be given time to observe them,
Do you desire that the worlds, which an eternal Wonder
Makes turn, stop for a moment and rest
In the darkness where the day has its source?
Speak.

The spirit lowered his moth-like wings,
And was silent. The air trembled under my foolhardy feet.
And the cold, harsh gloom which observed us both
And became studded with dim, distant aureoles,
Could hear this somber exchange of words
Between the strange spirit and me, the man entranced:
—No, none of those—What do you want, then?—HIM.

All seemed to close before me; and the kind
Of luminosity that glimmered in the thick cloud
Sank in air blacker than a Cimmerian sky.
I heard a burst of laughter, and saw nothing.

Alas! Being only a man, miserable flesh,
In this wild, bitter darkness, inexorable,
In these endless, bottomless fogs, under this shroud,
I felt the unbearable solitude.
Then my mind returned to its objective: to see, to understand,
To know, while the darkness—frightful, deceitful, treacherous,
Cascading this black, mocking laughter in its echoes—
Grew in space, as in my heart.

And I shouted, drooping my already weary wings:
—Tell me only his name, sad spaces,
That I may repeat it forever in the night!—

And I heard only the north wind fleeing.

Alors il me sembla qu'en un sombre mirage,
Comme des tourbillons que chasse un vent d'orage,
Je voyais devant moi pêle-mêle passer
Et croître et frissonner et fuir et s'effacer
Ces cryptes du vertige et ces villes du rêve,
Rome sur ses frontons changeant en croix son glaive,
Thèbes, Jérusalem, Mecque, Médine, Hébron;
Des figures tenant à la main un clairon,
Et des arbres hagards, des cavernes, des baumes
Où priaient, barbe au vent, de ténébreux Jérômes,
Et, parmi des Babels, des tours, des temples grecs,
D'horribles fronts d'écueils aux cheveux de varechs;
Et tout cela, Ninive, Éphèse, Delphe, Abdère,
Tombeau de saint Grégoire où veille un lampadaire,
Marches de Bénarès, pagodes de Ceylan,
Monts d'où l'aigle de mer le soir prend son élan,
Minarets, parthénons, wigwams, temple d'Aglaure
Où l'on voit l'aube, fleur vertigineuse, éclore,
Et grotte de Calvin, et chambre de Luther,
Passages d'anges bleus dans le liquide éther,
Trépieds où flamboyaient des âmes, yeux de braise
De la chienne Scylla sur la mer calabraise,
Dodone, Horeb, rochers effarés, bois troublants,
Couvent d'Eschmiadzin aux quatre clochers blancs,
Noir cromlech de Bretagne, affreux cruach d'Irlande,
Pœstum où les rosiers suspendent leur guirlande,
Temples des fils de Cham, temples des fils de Seth,
Tout lentement flottait et s'évanouissait
Dans une sorte d'âpre et vague perspective;
Et ce n'était, devant ma prunelle attentive,
Que de la vision qui ne fait pas de bruit,
Et de la forme obscure éparse dans la nuit.

Et, pâle et frissonnant, je fis cet appel sombre,
Sans oser élever la voix, de peur de l'ombre:

Then it seemed to me that in a dark mirage,
As whirlwinds chased by a stormy wind,
I could see pass, pell-mell, before me,
And grow and tremble and flee and disappear,
These crypts of vertigo and these cities of dream:
Rome on her pediments transforming her sword into a cross,
Thebes, Jerusalem, Mecca, Medina, Hebron;
Figures holding in their hands bugles,
And storm-tossed trees, caves, healing places
Where somber Jeromes prayed, their beards to the wind,
And, among the Babels, towers, Greek temples,
Hideous brows of reefs with their hair of kelp;
And there were, as well, Nineveh, Ephesus, Delphi, Abdera,
The tomb of Saint Gregory where a candelabrum keeps vigil,
The stone steps of Benares, the pagodas of Ceylon,
Mountains from where the eagle of the sea takes off in evening
Flight, minarets, parthenons, wigwams, the temple of Aglauros
Where one sees bloom the dawn, that vertiginous flower,
And the grotto of Calvin, and the room of Luther,
Passings of blue angels in the liquid æther,
Braziers where souls blazed, fiery eyes
Of the bitch Scylla on the Calabrian Sea,
Dodona, Horeb, bewildered crags, disturbing woods,
Echmiadzin Cathedral with its four white bell-towers,
Black cromlech of Brittany, dreadful cruach of Ireland,
Pœstum where the rose-bushes suspend their garlands,
Temples of the sons of Ham, temples of the sons of Seth,
All slowly floating and vanishing
Into a kind of harsh and indeterminate vista;
And before my attentive eyes, it became
Only a soundless vision,
An obscure form scattered in the night.

And, pale and shivering, I made this somber plea,
Without daring to raise my voice for fear of the darkness:

Êtres! lieux! choses! nuit! nuit froide qui te tais!
Cèdres de Salomon, chênes de Teutatès;
O plongeurs de nuée, ô rapporteurs de tables;
Devins, mages, voyants, hommes épouvantables;
Thébaïdes, forêts, solitudes; Ombos
Où les docteurs, vivant dans des creux de tombeaux,
S'emplissent d'inconnu comme d'eau les éponges;
O croisements obscurs des gouffres et des songes,
Sommeil, blanc soupirail des apparitions;
Germes, avatars, nuit des incarnations
Où l'archange s'envole, où le monstre se vautre;
Mort, noir pont naturel entre une étoile et l'autre,
Communication entre l'homme et le ciel;
Colosse de Minerve aptère, aux pieds duquel
Le vent respectueux fait tomber ceux qui passent;
Flots revenant toujours que les rocs toujours chassent;
Chauve Apollonius, vieux rêveur sidéral;
O scribes, qui, du bout du bâton augural
Tracez de l'alphabet les ténébreux jambages;
Époptes grecs, fakirs, voghis, bonzes, eubages;
O tours d'où se jetaient les circumcellions;
Sanctuaires, trépieds, autels, fosse aux lions;
Vous qui voyez suer les fronts pâles des sages,
Cimetières, repos, asiles, noirs passages
Où viennent s'essuyer les penseurs, ces vaincus;
Monstrueux caveau peint du roi Psamméticus;
François d'Assise, Scot, Bruno, sainte Rhipsime;
O marcheurs attirés aux clartés de la cime;
Sept sages qui parlez dans l'ombre à Cyrselus;
Du rêve et du désert redoutables reclus
Qui chuchotez avec les bouches invisibles;
Fronts courbés sous les cieux d'ou descendent les bibles;
Spectres; effarements de lampe et de flambeau;
Toi qui vois Chanaan, montagne de Nébo;
Moines du mont Athos, chantant de sombres proses;
Libellules d'Asie errant dans les jamroses;

Beings! Places! Things! Night! Cold Night that conceals you!
Cedars of Solomon, oaks of Teutates;
O plungers from clouds, O divulgers of tables;
Soothsayers, magi, seers, terrifying men;
Thebaids, forests, solitudes; Ombos
Where the astrologers, alive in the hollows of tombs,
Are filled with the infinite like sponges with water;
O sleep, obscure mingling of abysses and dreams,
White conduit of apparitions;
Origins, transformations, night of the incarnations
Where the archangel takes flight, where the monster wallows;
Death, natural, black bridge between one star and another,
Communication between Man and the heavens;
Colossus of Minerva Apteros at whose feet
The reverential wind makes stumble and fall those who pass by;
Billows always returning what the rocks always turn away;
Bald Apollonius, old sidereal dreamer;
O scribes, who with the ends of augural sticks
Trace the mysterious down-strokes of the alphabet;
Greek Epopts, fakirs, voghis, bonzes, eubages;
O towers from which the Circumcellions throw themselves;
Sanctuaries, tripods, altars, lions' dens;
You who see the pale, glistening brows of sages,
Cemeteries, retreats, asylums, black passages
Where thinkers, those defeated ones, come to suffer;
The monstrous painted vault of king Psamtik;
Francis of Assisi, Scotus, Bruno, Saint Rhipsime;
O walkers attracted to the luminosities of the summit;
Seven wise men who speak in the dark with Cyrselus;
Redoubtable recluses of desert and dream,
Who whisper with invisible mouths;
Curved brows under skies from which the bibles descend;
Apparitions; terrors of lamp and torch;
You who see Canaan, mountain of Nebo;
Monks of Mount Athos singing somber hymns;
Dragonflies of Asia hovering amidst the rose apples;

Isthme de Suez fermant l'Inde comme un verrou;
O voûtes d'Ellora, croupes du mont Mérou
D'où s'échappe le Gange aux grandes eaux sacrées;
Ombre, qui n'as pas l'air de savoir que tu crées;
O vous qui criez: deuil! vous qui criez: espoir!
Spherus qui, toujours seul dans l'antre toujours noir,
Cherches Dieu par les mille ouvertures funèbres,
Blanches, tristes, que font à l'âme les ténèbres;
Prêtres qu'en votre nuit suit le doute importun;
Vous, psalmistes, David, Éthan, grave Idithun;
Jean, interlocuteur de l'oiseau chéroubime;
Et vous, poëtes; Dante, homme effrayant d'abîme,
Grand front tragique ombré de feuilles de laurier,
Qui t'en reviens, laissant l'obscurité crier,
Rapportant sous tes cils la lueur des avernes;
Dompteurs qui sans pâlir allez dans les cavernes
Forcer le hurlement jusque dans son chenil;
Pilotes nubiens qui remontez le Nil;
O prodigieux cerf aux rameaux noirs qui brames
Dans la forêt des djinns, des pandits et des brames;
Hommes enterrés vifs, songeant dans vos cercueils;
O pâtres accoudés; ô bruyères; écueils
Où rêve au crépuscule une forme sinistre;
Pythie assise au front du hideux cap Canistre;
Angles de la syringe où les songeurs entrés
Distinguent vaguement des satrapes mitrés;
Vous que la lune enivre et trouble, sélénites;
Vous, bénitiers sanglants des seules eaux bénites,
Yeux en pleurs des martyrs; vous, savants indécis;
Merlin, sous l'escarboucle inexprimable assis;
Job, qui contemples; toi, Jérôme, qui médites;
Est-ce qu'on ne peut pas voir un peu de jour, dites?

Et, sombre, j'attendis; puis je continuai:

Isthmus of Suez closing India like a bolt;
O vaults of Ellora, croups of Mount Merou
Whence the great sacred waters of the Ganges escape;
Darkness, which does not seem to know that you create;
O you who shout: Mourning! You who shout: Hope!
Spherus who, always alone in the eternally black cave,
Seeks God through the thousand funereal fissures,
Both wan and sad, that make darkness in the soul;
Priests who, in your night, pursue the persistent doubt;
You, psalmists, David, Ethan, grave Idithun,
John, interlocutor of the bird-like cherubim;
And you, poets; Dante, you of the great, tragic brow
Shaded by laurel leaves, frightful man of the abyss,
From which you return, letting the darkness shout, bringing back
Under your eyelashes the glimmerings from the infernal lakes;
Wild animal tamers who, without blanching, go into caverns
To force the howling beast back into its kennel;
Nubian pilots who sail up the Nile;
O extraordinary stag with the black antlers who troats
In the forest of the djinns, the pundits and Brahmans;
Men buried alive, musing in your coffins;
O idle shepherds resting on your elbows; O heathers;
Reefs where a sinister form dreams in the twilight;
Pythoness seated on the brow of hideous Cape Canistro;
Cornerstones of the royal, Egyptian tomb where entering
Visionaries vaguely distinguish mitered satraps;
Selenites, you whom the moon intoxicates and disorders;
You, blood-stained basins of the only true holy water,
Tears from the eyes of martyrs; you, irresolute savants;
Merlin, seated under the ineffable carbuncle;
Job, who contemplates; you, Jerome, who meditates;
Can one never see daylight? Tell me.

And, somber, I waited; then I continued:

—Quoi! l'homme tomberait, hagard, exténué,
Comme le moucheron qui bat la vitre blême!
Quoi! tout aboutirait à du néant suprême!
Tout l'effort des chercheurs frémissants se perdrait!
L'homme habiterait l'ombre et serait au secret!
Marcher serait errer! l'aile serait punie!
L'aurore, ô cieux profonds, serait une ironie!

Alors, tout haut, levant la voix, levant les bras,
Éperdu, je criai:—Cela ne se peut pas!
Grand inconnu! méchant ou bon! grand invisible!
Je te le dis en face, Être! c'est impossible!

On éclata de rire une seconde fois.

Et ce rire était plus un rictus qu'une voix;
Il remua longtemps l'ombre visionnaire,
Et, s'évanouissant, roula comme un tonnerre
Dans ce prodigieux silence où le néant
Semblait vivre, insondable, immobile et béant.

O méditations! oh! comme l'esprit souffre
Sous les porches hagards et difformes du gouffre!
Comme le souffle noir de l'horreur vous poursuit,
Sinistre, en vous jetant du trouble et de la nuit!
Comme on sent que le rêve est un être qui vole
Et passe...—On m'adressait dans l'ombre la parole;
Et de funèbres voix que sur mon front j'avais
Comme les endormis en ont à leurs chevets,
Chuchotaient au-dessus de moi des choses sombres.
Je sentais la terreur muette des décombres
Et je me demandais:—Qui donc murmure ainsi?
C'était, dans le ciel morne et de brume épaissi,
Comme un nuage obscur de bouches sur ma tête;
Des faces me parlaient dans un vent de tempête;
Puis ces voix s'éteignaient comme le vague son

—What! Man would fall, haggard, exhausted,
As the midge that beats the pale pane!
What! Everything would lead to some ultimate nothingness!
The entire effort of the trembling seekers would be lost!
Man would live in darkness and be left with silence!
To walk would be to wander! The wing would be punished!
The dawn, O deep skies, would be an irony!

Then from on high, raising my voice, raising my arms,
Desperate, I shouted:—That must not be!
Great Unknown, be you malicious or good! Great Invisible One!
I tell you to your face, Being! I say: Impossible!

For a second time, laughter burst forth.

And this laughter was more a grimace than a sound;
It long stirred up the visionary shadow,
And, disappearing, rolled like thunder
In this extraordinary silence where nothingness
Seemed to live, fathomless, immovable, and gaping.

O meditations! Oh! How the spirit suffers
Within the ghastly and deformed portals of the abyss!
How the black breath of horror pursues you,
A sinister thing, casting on you confusion and darkness!
How one senses that the dream is a Being
Winging its way and then passing on...
—Someone spoke to me in the darkness; and funereal
Voices, like those that sleepers have at their bedheads,
Whispered somber things above my brow.
I felt the mute terror of ruins
And I wondered:—Who is murmuring to me thus?
In the bleak sky thick with fog, it was
Like an obscure cloud of mouths above my head,
Faces speaking to me in a windy tempest;
Then these voices died away like the vague sounds

Qui n'est plus la parole et devient le frisson.
Noirs discours! l'ironie y grinçait dans le râle;
Des plaintes, sanglotant dans l'ombre sépulcrale
Comme entre les roseaux gémit le gavial,
S'achevaient en sarcasme amer et trivial;
Je croyais par moments qu'en ces vagues royaumes
J'assistais au concile effrayant des fantômes
Que nous nommons raison, logique, utilité,
Certitude, calcul, sagesse, vérité;
Il me semblait, parmi le grand murmure austère
De l'horreur, de la nuit, du tombeau, du mystère,
Entendre Aristophane; et voir, après les pleurs,
Toutes sortes d'éclairs cyniques et railleurs,
Moqueurs, étincelants, percer l'ombre ennemie,
Et Diderot passer à travers Jérémie;
J'écoutais frémissant et par moments vaincu.
Était-ce des esprits d'hommes ayant vécu?
Était-ce les conseils qui flottent dans les nues
Pour quiconque s'égare aux routes inconnues?
Mon front sous l'infini ployait lugubrement.
L'espace affreux, éther, ténèbres, firmament,
Espèce de taillis sans branches étoilées,
Où les brouillards fuyaient en confuses mêlées,
Semblait d'une forêt le redoutable dais.
Qu'était-ce que ces voix? je ne sais. J'entendais.
Et ma raison tremblait en moi, diminuée,
Dans des tressaillements d'orage et de nuée.

Cependant par degrés l'ombre devint visible;
Et l'être qui m'avait parlé précédemment
Reparut, mais grandi jusqu'à l'effarement;
Il remplissait du haut en bas le sombre dôme
Comme si l'infini dilatait ce fantôme;
De sorte que l'espace effrayant n'offrait plus
Que des visages, flux vivant, vivant reflux,
Un sourd fourmillement d'hydres, d'hommes, de bêtes,

That are no longer words but become shudders.
Ominous discourse! The irony creaked there in a death-rattle;
And as the gavial groans amidst the reeds, so lamentations,
Sobbing in the sepulchral shadows,
Ended in bitter and commonplace taunts.
I believed, at times, that in these indistinct realms
I was witnessing a frightening council of the phantoms
That we name reason, logic, utility,
Certitude, calculation, wisdom, truth;
It seemed to me, amidst the great austere murmurs
Of horror, of night, of the tomb, of mystery,
That I heard Aristophanes; and saw, after the tears,
All kinds of cynical, scoffing, and mocking lightning
Flashes brilliantly piercing the hostile darkness,
Diderot passing through Jeremiah;
I listened, quivering, at times overcome.
Were these spirits of men who once lived?
Was this counsel floating in the clouds
For whomsoever is straying onto unfamiliar roads?
My brow yielded mournfully under the weight of the infinite.
This dreadful space, æther, darkness, firmament,
A kind of thicket without starlit branches,
Where the fogs fled in confused tumult,
Seemed the frightening canopy of a forest.
What were these voices? I know not. I listened.
And my reason trembled within me, diminished,
In shudders of storm and cloud.

However, by degrees the darkness became visible;
And the Being who had spoken to me ere now
Reappeared, but grown to frightening proportions;
He filled this somber dome from top to bottom
As if dilated by the Infinite, so that this
Alarming space was filled
With nothing but the ebb and flow
Of faces, a muted swarm of Hydras, of men and of beasts,

Et que le fond du ciel me semblait plein de têtes.
Ces têtes par moments semblaient se quereller.
Je voyais tous ces yeux dans l'ombre étinceler.
Le monstre grandissait en silence, sans cesse.
Et je ne savais plus ce que c'était. Était-ce
Une montagne, une hydre, un gouffre, une cité,
Un nuage, un amas d'ombre, l'immensité?
Je sentais tous ces yeux sur moi fixés ensemble.
Tout à coup, frissonnant comme un arbre qui tremble,
Le fantôme géant se répandit en voix
Qui sous ses flancs confus murmuraient à la fois.
Et, comme d'un brasier tombent des étincelles,
Comme on voit des oiseaux épars, pigeons, sarcelles,
D'un grand essaim passant s'écarter quelquefois,
Comme un vert tourbillon de feuilles sort d'un bois,
Comme, dans les hauteurs par les vents remuées,
En avant d'un orage il vole des nuées,
Toutes ces voix, mêlant le cri, l'appel, le chant,
De l'immense être informe et noir se détachant,
Me montrant vaguement des masques et des bouches,
Vinrent sur moi bruire avec des bruits farouches,
Parfois en même temps et souvent tour à tour,
Comme des monts, à l'heure où se lève le jour,
L'un après l'autre, au fond de l'horizon s'éclairent;
Et des formes, sortant du monstre, me parlèrent:

And the sky at the horizon seemed to fill with
Heads that at times seemed to quarrel.
I was seeing all these eyes gleaming in the darkness.
The monster grew and grew without cease.
And I no longer knew what it was.
Was this a mountain, a Hydra, a chasm, a city,
A cloud, a congeries of gloom, boundlessness itself?
I was sensing all these eyes fixed on me.
Suddenly, shaking as a tree that trembles,
The giant phantom spilled forth from his indistinct flanks
Voices, which murmured all at once.
And, as sparks fall from burning coals,
As birds, pigeons, teals are sometimes seen
Flying out from a great passing flock,
Or green swirls of leaves appear out of a wood,
Or as, before a storm, clouds fly up
Into the heights that are stirred by the winds,
So all these voices, mixing song with cries and howls,
Detaching themselves from this immense black and formless
Being, came toward me making savage noises,
Dimly showing me faces and mouths,
Sometimes all at once, often separately,
Just as, when day begins to break, mountains light up
One after the other at the bottom of the horizon.
And as they emerged from the monster, these forms spoke to me:

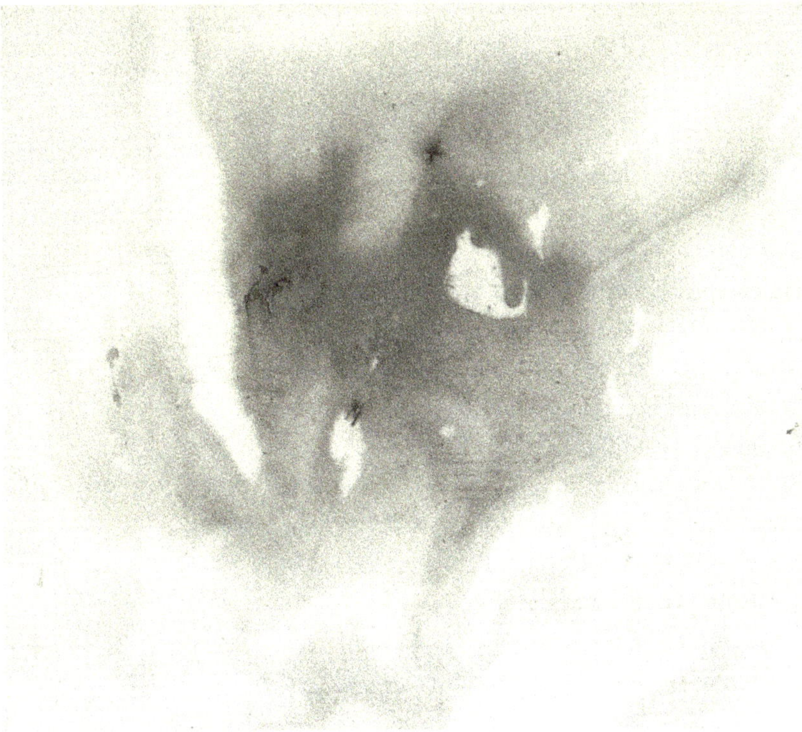

Victor Hugo, *Croquis* (Sketch), detail, ca. 1875,
Bibliothèque nationale de France

LES VOIX

.:.:.:.:.:.:.:.:.:.

II
UNE AUTRE VOIX

Ne nous demande pas, ô songeur, qui nous sommes.
S'ils nous entrevoyaient, nous ferions peur aux hommes.
Soit en bien, soit en mal, nous avons conseillé
Quiconque a médité, cherché, pensé, veillé,
Tous les grands insensés, tous les sages célèbres.
Nous volons d'arbre en arbre aux forêts de ténèbres;
Tout ce que l'homme appelle Énigme, Doute, Mort,
Brume, Silence, Effroi, Hasard, Mystère, Sort,
Est pour nous, sous l'horreur des voûtes éternelles,
Comme un taillis obscur par où passent nos ailes;
Nous sommes les flottants de l'immense azur noir;
Si quelque mage osait essayer de nous voir,
De saisir un de nous, de compter notre nombre,
Nous nous dissiperions comme des oiseaux d'ombre.

C'est nous que vous nommez démons; homme, tu sens
Sous des souffles confus tes cheveux frémissants,
C'est nous. Nous versons l'ombre aux jours que tu consommes;
Nous jetons des lueurs dans ton sommeil. Nous sommes
Pris dans l'obscurité comme vous dans la chair.
Nous sommes les passants sinistres de l'éclair,
Les méduses du rêve aux robes dénouées,
Les visages d'abîme épars dans les nuées.
Tout ce que vous voyez, nous ne le voyons pas.
Nous ne distinguons point votre terre, vos pas,
Vos faces, d'un soleil invisible inondées,
Mais dans votre cerveau nous voyons vos idées;

THE VOICES

.:.:.:.:.:.:.:.:.:.:.

II
ANOTHER VOICE

Do not query, O dreamer, who we are.
If they sensed us, we would frighten the people.
For better or worse, we have counseled those who have
Meditated, searched, thought, or merely kept vigil,
All the great madmen, all the celebrated wise men.
We fly from tree to tree in the forests of darkness;
All that Man calls Enigma, Doubt, Death,
Uncertainty, Silence, Dismay, Chance, Mystery, Fate,
Are for us, beneath the horror of the eternal vaults,
Like a dark thicket through which we wing;
We are those who soar in the immense black azure,
And if some mage dared to seek us out,
To seize one of us, to count our number,
We would vanish like birds of darkness.

It is we whom you call demons; Man, you feel
Your hair stirred as if by some strange winds—
It is we. We pour darkness into your spent days.
We cast light into your sleep. We are
Captive in darkness as are you in flesh.
We are the sinister passers-by of lightning,
Medusas of the dream in flowing robes,
Faces of the abyss scattered amidst thick clouds.
Nothing that you see, do we see.
We do not discern your earth at all, your movement,
Your faces, bathed by an invisible sun,
But in your mind we see your ideas;

Votre pensée est nue à nos regards moqueurs;
Nous voyons le dedans vertigineux des cœurs.
L'haleine de la nuit nous chasse et nous oublie,
Et fait flotter le fil mystérieux qui lie
Vos sciences, vos plans, vos travaux, vos desseins,
Vos efforts, vos projets, vos vœux, à nos essaims.
Nous mêlons notre nuit avec votre ignorance;
Vous appelez cela savoir. La transparence
De l'Être parfois laisse apercevoir nos fronts.
Parfois jusqu'à vos cœurs, la nuit, nous pénétrons,
En rêve, et vous sentez comme une vague étreinte.
Sans cesse des courants d'espérance ou de crainte,
Des flux et des reflux de sentiments divers
Vont, dans les profondeurs de l'espace, à travers
Le vide, l'aquilon, le tombeau, le décombre,
De vous le peuple aveugle à nous le peuple sombre.
L'Inconnu nous tient tous dans ses fatals filets.
Nous sommes vos échos, vous êtes nos reflets;
Car tout est l'unité. Forme joyeuse ou triste,
Tout se confond dans Tout, et rien à part n'existe,
O vivant! Et sais-tu ce que dit l'abîme? UN.
Sans que vous le sachiez, nous pensons en commun;
Nous tremblons au-dessus de vous, livide armée;
Et de votre feu noir nous sommes la fumée.
Nos formes de la nuit sont le lugubre jeu;
Nous allons, nous flottons.—Et toi, tu cherches Dieu?
Hélas!

III

UNE AUTRE VOIX

Qui que tu sois, redoute, au gouffre où tu te plonges,
Le vague coudoiement des vains passants des songes.
Fuyez d'ici, vivants, dont l'esprit, fléchissant
Sous l'incompréhensible et sous l'éblouissant,
Peut à peine porter le poids d'un évangile.

Your thought is exposed to our derisive glance, and
We see the dizzying interior of hearts.
The night wind chases us away and forgets us,
But makes flutter the mysterious thread that binds
Your skills, your plans, your works, your intentions,
Your efforts, your projects, your wishes, to our gathering.
We combine our night with your ignorance,
Which you then call knowledge. The translucence
Of Being sometimes also allows our brows insight.
At night we sometimes penetrate your hearts,
In dream, and you sense a light embrace.
Currents of hope or fear, the ebb and
Flow of diverse feelings, move
Ceaselessly in the depths of space, across the void,
Across the north wind, across the grave, across the ruins,
From you, the blind ones, to us, the dark ones.
The Unknown holds us all in his fateful nets.
We are your echoes, and you our reflections,
For all things merge. Joyful or sad, all becomes
Blurred, nothing remains separate, O living being!
And do you know what the abyss says? ONE.
Without your knowing it, we think in common;
A pale host, we tremble above you,
And of your dark fire we are the smoke.
Our forms express the mournful amusement of the night;
We move, we drift.—And you, you seek God?
Alas!

III

ANOTHER VOICE

Whoever you may be, you must dread nebulous encounters with futile,
Fleeting spirits of dreams, in this abyss where you are plunging.
Flee from here, living beings, whose souls, yielding
Under the incomprehensible and under the dazzling,
Can scarcely bear the weight of a gospel.

Ce n'est pas sans danger que des hommes d'argile,
Tremblants quand ils sont las, glacés quand ils sont nus,
Dialoguent dans l'ombre avec des inconnus.

A force de songer, ô pâle solitaire,
Tu sentiras de l'air sous toi; tu perdras terre...—
Oh! les souffles! craignez les souffles de la nuit!
Où vous emportent-ils? Ceux qu'un rêve conduit
Deviennent rêve eux-même, et, sans être coupables,
Tombent dans l'essaim noir des faces impalpables.

C'est alors qu'éperdu, terrible, tu tendras
Les mains comme les morts sous leurs lugubres draps.

Mais à quoi bon? Tout fuit. Un vent qui vous pénètre
Vous roule dans l'espace à jamais...—O deuil! être
Des espèces d'esprits misérables chassés!
Oh! n'entendre jamais ce mot céleste: assez!
Un souffle vous apporte, un souffle vous remmène.
On a, sur ce qu'on garde encor de forme humaine,
D'obscurs attouchements et des passages froids;
Toute l'ombre n'est plus qu'une suite d'effrois;
On sent les longs frissons des roseaux de l'abîme.
Jamais le jour. Jamais un rayon qui ranime.
Errer! errer! errer! errer! faire des nœuds
D'ombre, dans l'invisible et le vertigineux!
Monter, tomber, monter, retomber! sort terrible!
Être à jamais l'informe égaré dans l'horrible,
Le contraire du jour, de l'hymne et de l'encens!
Des témoins de l'énigme, à jamais frémissants
Devant le ténébreux, devant l'inabordable,
Et face à face avec un voile formidable!
Être, en dehors de l'être, en dehors du trépas,
Quelque chose d'obscur qui souffre et ne vit pas!
Être de la clameur dans l'infini semée,
Un vague tourbillon pleurant, une fumée

It is not without danger that men of clay,
Trembling when they are weary, chilled when they are unclad,
Discourse in the dark with the unknown.

By dint of dreaming, O pale recluse,
You will feel the air beneath you, losing your sense of the Earth...—
Oh! The winds! Fear the night winds!
Where do they lead you? Those guided by a dream
Themselves become dreams, and, blameless,
Sink into the black swarm of intangible faces.

It is then that frantic, terror-stricken, you will extend
Your hands like the dead under their dreary winding-cloths.

But to what end? Everything is fleeting. A piercing wind
Carries you through space forever...—O mourning!
To be some kind of hunted, miserable spirit!
Oh! Never to hear this celestial word: Enough!
A wind brings you close, a wind carries you off.
On what you still retain of your human form, you sense
Strange touches and chill grazings;
The entire darkness is no more than a series of terrors;
You feel the prolonged trembling of the reeds of the abyss.
Never day. Never a ray of light to enliven you.
To wander! To stray! To roam! To wend your way!
To make eddies of darkness in the invisible and the ever-swirling!
To rise, fall, rise, fall again! Terrible fate!
To be forever formless, lost in the dreadful,
The reverse of day, opposite the hymn, the incense!
Witnesses of the enigma, forever quivering
Before the darkness, before the unapproachable,
And face to face with a formidable veil!
To be, beyond existence, beyond death,
Some unknown thing which suffers, yet does not live!
To be some outcry scattered in the infinite,
A ghostly, weeping whirlwind, a billowing

De larves, de regards, de masques, de rumeurs,
De voix ne pouvant pas même dire: je meurs,
Passant toujours, toujours, toujours, comme un flot sombre,
Sous les arches sans fin du hideux pont de l'ombre!

IV

UNE AUTRE VOIX

Malheur au curieux lugubre, qui s'acharne
A la vertigineuse et sinistre lucarne!
Malheur aux imprudents penchés sur l'absolu!
Pour avoir trop sondé, pour avoir trop voulu,
Pour s'être trop plongés dans l'abstraction triste
Où rien de saisissable et d'humain ne persiste,
C'est fini; les voilà sur les fatals sommets,
Égarés en dehors de l'homme désormais,
Sortis du bien, du mal, de l'orgueil, de l'envie,
De l'amour, de la haine, et plus grands que la vie!
Leur esprit, emporté loin de vous, ô vivants,
Prend, dans la vision des gouffres décevants,
Dans on ne sait quoi d'âpre et d'horrible et d'immense,
Cette divinité que vous nommez démence.
Ils ne sont plus jamais éveillés ni dormants.
Terrestre et claire encor dans ses commencements,
Leur pensée, obscurcie en s'élevant, achève
D'ouvrir ses vagues yeux dans le monde du rêve.

Oh! monde redoutable! oh! ce que nous voyons!—
Des échelles d'esprits dans de pâles rayons;
Les flamboiements, les feux, les cratères, les soufres,
Les éclairs, gouvernés par les anges des gouffres;
Des sons de voix qu'on a dans la joie entendus;
D'affreux escarpements dans des mondes perdus;
Des astres, dans des mains portés comme des lampes;
Et là-bas, dans la nue aux tortueuses rampes,
Errent ceux qui vivaient et ne sont plus; ils vont,

Of larvae, glances, masks, a muffled din
Of voices that cannot even exclaim: I am dying,
Passing, forevermore, like a melancholy tide,
Under the endless arches of the hideous bridge of darkness!

IV

ANOTHER VOICE

Woe unto the curious gloomy one, who perseveres
In the vertiginous and sinister light!
Woe unto the foolhardy persons, bent on the absolute!
For having fathomed too much, for having wished too much,
For having plunged too far into the sad abstraction
Where nothing graspable or human remains,
It has ended; there they are on the fateful summits,
Lost to humankind, forever,
Removed from what is good and evil, from pride, envy,
From love, hatred—and larger than life!
Their spirit, carried far from you, O living ones,
Chooses, in sight of the deceptive chasms,
Out of something indescribably bitter, horrible and immense,
This divinity you name Madness.
They are no longer awake or asleep.
Terrestrial and still lucid in its beginnings,
Their thought, darkened as it grows, ends
By opening its dim eyes in the realm of dreams.

Oh! Fearsome world! Oh! What a sight!
An ascent of spirits bathed in pallid light;
Flames, fires, craters, brimstone,
Flashes of lightning, governed by the angels of the abysses;
The sounds of voices once heard as joyful;
Hideous escarpments in lost worlds;
Stars carried like lamps;
And over there, in the cloud with its tortuous slopes,
Wander those who once lived but are no more; they roam,

Tous ces crânes à l'œil monstrueux et profond,
Tous ces squelettes blancs venus des ossuaires;
Ils vont, tous ces linceuls, tous ces hideux suaires,
Tous ces draps frissonnants, foule effrayante à voir,
Et, chassant devant lui, dans l'affreux chemin noir,
Leur conscience nue et leur âme sans voiles,
L'ange fouette les morts avec son fouet d'étoiles.
Et l'on voit des lueurs, on entend des appels;
Les constellations, flamboyants archipels,
Brillent au zénith sombre, et le chaos conspue
Le ciel avec son eau sinistre et corrompue.

Des fantômes sans nom passent. Qui donc sont-ils?
Sont-ce des esprits morts? Sont-ce des corps subtils?
Ils tombent on ne sait de quelle obscure cime,
Tantôt plus noirs, tantôt moins sombres que l'abîme;
Leur chute flotte au gré de l'air qui les poursuit;
Ils seraient les flocons, s'il neigeait de la nuit.
Qu'est-ce que ce nuage inexprimable d'êtres,
Phalènes se heurtant à de vagues fenêtres?
Les uns n'ont qu'un regard et sont comme les yeux
De l'infini glacé, sourd et silencieux;
D'autres vont droits et blancs dans la profondeur blême;
D'autres, plus effrayants que les ténèbres même,
Luttent contre la nuit dans les horreurs du vent,
Poussant des cris, mordant l'ombre, n'apercevant
Que la lividité des mornes étendues,
Ne distinguant qu'un flot de formes éperdues,
Et que ce qu'on peut voir de nuée et de cieux
Dans des renversements de torses furieux.

Et ces larves s'en vont. Est-on sûr qu'elles soient?

Et les contemplateurs sont là. Tristes, ils voient.
Quoi? l'inconnu, muré dans sa muette loi.
Et qui dira jamais ce qu'expriment d'effroi

All those skulls with deep and monstrous eyes,
All those white skeletons from the ossuaries;
They run, all those shrouds, those hideous winding-sheets,
All that quivering cloth, so terrible to see,
And, driving them before him, on this frightful dark path,
Their consciences bared and their souls veilless,
Goes the angel, whipping the dead with his lash of stars.
Lights are seen, plaints are heard;
The constellations, those blazing archipelagoes,
Shine in the dark zenith, while chaos decries
The sky with its sinister and corrupt waters.

Nameless phantoms pass by. Who are they?
Are they dead spirits? Are they subtle bodies?
They fall from some unknown, obscure summit,
Sometimes darker, sometimes less somber than the abyss;
They fall at the whim of the air that carries them;
They would be flakes, if night were snowing.
What is this unspeakable cloud of beings,
These moths colliding against leaden window panes?
Some have but one gaze, secret and silent,
As are the eyes of the glacial infinite.
Others go virtuous and pure into the colorless deep;
Still others, more terrible than darkness itself,
Battle night in the horrors of the wind,
Shouting, gnawing at the darkness, perceiving
But a flood of scattered and frantic
Forms, furious torsos in upheaval, ashen
And gloomy, yet discerning only what could be seen
From the thick clouds, from the heavens.

And these ghosts depart. Are we certain that they exist?

And the contemplators are there. They sadly look on.
What do they see? The unknown, immured in its silent law.
And who can ever say what dismay is expressed

Ces profils ténébreux, ces figures fatales,
Ces yeux hagards noyés dans des aurores pâles?
Ils pensent, échoués dans l'immobilité;
La terreur sans espoir fait leur tranquillité;
Leur épaule fléchit comme s'ils portaient toute
La charpente du monde avec toute la voûte;
Et, comme en un caveau, goutte à goutte, la nuit
Filtre sous leur front blême où leur œil fixe luit.
Ils ont pour vision éternelle la Chose
Sans nom, sans jour, sans bruit, sans bord, sans fin, sans cause,
Jamais ne s'arrêtant, jamais ne s'achevant,
Terrible, avec des vols de spectres dans le vent.

Que viens-tu demander à ce monde nocturne?
Un Dieu! Pourquoi viens-tu plonger ta main dans l'urne?
Job en tire Satan et Mahomet Iblis.
Les gouffres ont-ils Dieu dans leurs profonds oublis?
Ce Dieu sert-il de centre à leurs circonférences?
Le voit-on à travers leurs sombres transparences?
Ou bien est-ce ce Tout, cette âpre immensité,
Ce ciel, que vous prenez pour une volonté?
Sont-ce ces profondeurs, ces vents, ces fondrières,
Ces forêts de nuée aux livides clairières,
Ces éléments, ces nuits, ces mornes régions,
Que vous appelez Dieu dans vos religions?
Avez-vous pour mirage, ô fils du cimetière,
De voir la chose Dieu sous la chose Matière?
Est-ce Dieu qui paraît, quand s'enfuit l'alcyon;
Quand l'hydre de l'écume entre en convulsion;
Quand partout on entend dans la sombre nature
Comme un bruit d'ouragan brisant une mâture,
Quand le ciel lamentable éclate en tristes voix;
Quand le nuage accourt; quand les bêtes des bois
Tremblent; quand les lions, hagards, baissent la tête
Sous des écrasements d'éclairs et de tempête?
Est-ce lui que la mer appelle en sa clameur?

By these dark forms, these fateful figures,
These haggard eyes drowned in pale dawns?
They think, while stranded in their immobility;
Their hopeless terror makes them still;
Their shoulder sags as if they bore the
Entire weight of the world and its vault;
And, as in a grotto, night seeps, drop by drop,
Under their pallid brow where their fixed eye gleams.
They have, for eternal vision, the Thing, nameless,
Sunless, soundless, boundless, endless, without cause,
Never stopping, never finishing,
Terrible, with flocks of specters in the wind.

What are you going to ask of this nocturnal world?
A God! Why do you come to plunge your hand into the Urn?
Job drew forth Satan from it, and Muhammed drew forth Iblis.
Do the abysses have God in their forgotten depths?
Does this God serve as the nave of their circumferences?
Is he seen through their dark translucencies?
Or is it Everything, this bitter vastness,
This sky, which you take for a Will?
Are these deeps, these winds, these morasses,
These forests of thick cloud with their pale glades,
These elements, these nights, these sad regions,
What you call God in your religions?
Is it a mirage, O son of the cemetery,
Seeing the thing, God, beneath the thing, Matter?
Is it God who appears when the halcyon flees;
When the hydra froths in convulsive rage;
When, all around dark nature, sounds are heard
Like a hurricane breaking the masts of ships;
When the pitiful sky bursts into sounds of plaintive voices;
When the cloud comes scudding and when the beasts of the
Forest tremble; when the wild lions lower their heads
Under the crashing of lightning and storm?
Is it he whom the sea calls in her roaring?

Homme, est-il quelque part un effrayant semeur
Qui jette dans l'azur des chiffres et des nombres,
De la graine d'abîme éclose en larves sombres,
Des vivants comme nous qui te semblent des morts,
Des esprits comme toi qui nous semblent des corps,
Et qui voit, dans le champ des espaces sonores,
Ondoyer des épis d'étoiles et d'aurores?
Qui peut répondre oui? qui peut répondre non?
Un geôlier rôde-t-il autour du cabanon?
Qu'importe! Vis. Tais-toi. Va-t'en. Aime ton père,
Ta mère et tes enfants. Qui cherche désespère.

.:.:.:.:.:.:.:.:.:.:.

IX

UNE AUTRE VOIX

Te figures-tu donc être, par aventure,
Autre chose qu'un point dans l'aveugle nature?
Toi, l'homme, cendre et chair, te persuades-tu
Que d'une fonction l'ombre t'a revêtu?
Quel droit te crois-tu donc à chercher, à poursuivre,
A saisir ce qui peut exister, durer, vivre,
A surprendre, à connaître, à savoir, toi qui n'es
Qu'une larve, et qui meurs aussitôt que tu nais?
J'admire ton néant inouï s'il suppose
Qu'il est par l'infini compté pour quelque chose!
Quelle idée, ô songeur du songe humanité,
As-tu de ton cerveau pour croire, en vérité,
Qu'il peut prendre ou laisser une empreinte à l'abîme?
Ta pensée est abjecte, étroite, folle, infime;
L'homme est de la fumée obscure qui descend.
T'imagines-tu donc laisser trace, ô passant?
Rêves-tu l'absolu comme ton fleuve Seine
Coulant entre les quais de ta ville malsaine,
Recueillant les égouts de toutes tes maisons,

Man, is there somewhere a terrible sower
Who casts, into the azure of figures and numbers,
Some seed of the abyss which then hatches into dark larvae,
Living creatures like we who seem to you dead,
Spirits like you who seem to us mere bodies,
And who sees undulating, in the fields of sonorous
Space, waves of stars and dawns?
Who can answer yes? Who can answer no?
Does a jailer prowl the dark cell?
It does not matter! Live. Be silent. Go away. Love your father,
Your mother and your children. He who searches, despairs.

.:.:.:.:.:.:.:.:.:.:.

IX

ANOTHER VOICE

So, do you thus imagine yourself, perchance, being
Something other than a speck in this sightless world?
You, Man, ash and flesh, are you convinced
That the darkness has endowed you with some purpose?
By what right do you thus suppose yourself allowed to seek,
To pursue, to seize that which can exist, endure, and live,
To surprise in the act, to understand, to know, you who are
But an embryo, and who die as soon as you are born?
I marvel at your unparalleled nothingness if it supposes
That it is counted for something by the Infinite!
What sort of mind do you think you have, O dreamer
Of the dream Humanity, to indeed believe that
It can benefit from or effect the abyss?
Your thought is despicable, narrow, mad, infinitesimal;
Man is just some nebulous vapor descending.
Do you, thus, imagine leaving some trace, O passerby?
Do you dream of the Absolute as you do your river Seine,
Flowing between the quays of your sickly city,
Collecting the sewage from all your houses,

Doctrines, volontés, illusions, raisons,
Ayant dans son courant, si quelqu'un te réclame,
Quelque pont de Saint-Cloud où l'on repêche l'âme?
Crois-tu que cette eau vaste et sourde, Immensité,
Ne t'enveloppe pas d'oubli, de cécité,
De silence, et sanglote à ta chute, et soit triste?
Crois-tu que ta chimère en ce gouffre persiste,
Qu'elle y garde sa forme, espoir, rêve, action;
Et qu'on retrouve, après ta disparition,
Quelque chose de toi, ton cadavre ou ton ombre,
Aux noirs filets flottants de l'éternité sombre?

X

UNE AUTRE VOIX

As-tu vu les penseurs s'en aller dans les cieux?
Les as-tu vus partir, hautains, séditieux,
Jetant dans l'inconnu leur voix terrifiante,
Espérant abuser de la nuit confiante,
Méditant des larcins prodigieux, rêvant
D'aller toujours plus loin et toujours plus avant,
Se proposant d'atteindre à la source première,
Au centre, au but; de prendre ou l'ombre ou la lumière
Ou l'être, et de saisir le météore au vol,
Emportés comme Élie, ailés comme saint Paul,
Et de trouver le fond, dût-on faire le vide,
Dût-on escalader le mystère livide,
L'obscurité, les cieux brumeux, les cieux vermeils,
Avec effraction d'azurs et de soleils?
Les as-tu vus, fuyants, blanche robe du prêtre,
Bras levés du devin, décroître et disparaître
Dans la profondeur sourde où tout s'évanouit?
Parle? et les as-tu vus devenir de la nuit?
Es-tu resté tremblant, cherchant leur trace vague?
Puis, regardant l'éther, les ténèbres, le vague,
Passant les jours, les nuits, seul debout sur une tour,

Doctrines, intentions, illusions, reasons;
Stretching across its current, if someone lays claim to you,
Some bridge of Saint-Cloud from which they can fish out the soul?
Do you believe that this vast and voiceless water,
This immensity, will weep and mourn at your fall,
Without enveloping you in forgetfulness, blindness, silence?
Do you believe that your chimera will persist in this abyss,
That it will maintain its form, its hope, its dream, its exploits;
And that, after your disappearance, we shall find
Something of you, your corpse or your spirit,
Floating in the blacks nets of dark Eternity?

X

ANOTHER VOICE

Did you see the thinkers going off to the heavens?
Did you see them leaving, haughty, rebellious,
Casting into the unknown their terrifying voice,
Hoping to deceive the trusting night,
Contemplating enormous thefts, dreaming
Of going always further and further ahead
In order to reach the first source, the core,
The goal: to steal either Darkness, Light,
Or Existence, and to seize the meteor in flight,
Borne off like Elijah, wingèd like Saint Paul,
And, even if they must create the void, or scale the
Wan mystery, to find, in the end,
Darkness, the heavens in the mist, the vermilion skies,
While stealing, as well, the azures and suns? Did you see them,
Fleeing, with the white robe of the priest, and the raised
Arms of the soothsayer, fading away and disappearing
Into the voiceless deep where everything vanishes?
Speak! And did you see them becoming Night?
Were you left trembling, seeking their uncertain whereabouts?
Then, looking into the æther, the darkness, and empty space,
Spending days and nights, alone, up on a tower,

O songeur, as-tu vu ces hommes au retour?
Les as-tu vus de l'ombre énorme redescendre?
Et toi, l'obscur veilleur vêtu du sac de cendre,
Te dressant au-devant de leur vol éperdu,
Leur as-tu dit:—Eh bien?—Et qu'ont-ils répondu,
Ces noirs navigateurs sans navire et sans voiles?
Et qu'ont-ils rapporté, ces oiseleurs d'étoiles?

Ils n'ont rien rapporté que des fronts sans couleur
Où rien n'avait grandi, si ce n'est la pâleur.

Tous sont hagards après cette aventure étrange;
Songeur! tous ont, empreints au front, des ongles d'ange,
Tous ont dans le regard comme un songe qui fuit,
Tous ont l'air monstrueux en sortant de la nuit!
On en voit quelques-uns dont l'âme saigne et souffre,
Portant de toutes parts les morsures du gouffre.

XI
UNE AUTRE VOIX

. . .

Les monts sont vieux; cent fois et cent fois séculaires,
Muets, drapés de nuit sous leurs manteaux polaires,
Leur âge monstrueux épouvante l'esprit;
Sur leur front ténébreux tout l'abîme est écrit;
L'âpre neige des jours a neigé sur leur tête,
Le temps est un morceau de leur masse; leur faîte,
De loin morne profil qui s'efface de près,
Livre au vent une barbe épaisse de forêts;
Ils ont vu tous les deuils, toutes les défaillances,
Toutes les morts passer autour de leurs silences;
Ils ont vu s'écrouler des astres dans le puits
De l'horreur infinie et sourde; ils ont depuis
Bien des millions d'ans la lassitude d'être;
Eh bien, sur leurs noirs flancs décrépits, le vent traître,

Did you see, O dreamer, these men return?
Did you see them coming back down from the enormous darkness?
And you, the humble watcher dressed in a sackcloth
Cloaked in ash, standing before their desperate flight,
Did you ask them: Well?—and what did they answer,
These gloomy navigators with neither ship nor sails?
And what did they bring back, these fowlers of stars?

They brought back only their colorless brows
Where nothing had grown, save, perhaps, the pallor.

All are haggard after this strange adventure;
Dreamer! All have, imprinted on their brows, the scratches
Of angels, all seem to have in their gaze a fleeting dream,
All have the air of the monster, emerging from the night!
One sees in them those whose souls are bleeding and suffering,
And who bear, on every side, bites from the abyss.

XI

ANOTHER VOICE

...
The mountains are ancient; a vast number of centuries old,
Mute, and draped by night under their polar coats,
Their monstrous age frightens the spirit.
On their dark brows the entire abyss is written, and
The bitter snow of days has snowed upon their heads.
Time is now embodied within them; their summit, at a distance
A sad profile which fades away when seen up close,
Offers to the wind a thick beard of forests;
They have seen all bereavements, all failures,
All deaths moving about their silences;
They have seen stars collapsing into the pits
Of infinite and echoless horror; they have felt for
Many millions of years the weariness of existence;
Now, on their black, decrepit sides, the treacherous wind,

L'orage furieux, l'éclair fauve, ce ver
Qui serpente dans l'ombre immense de l'hiver,
L'ouragan qui, farouche, aux grands sommets essuie
Sa chevelure d'air, de tempête et de pluie,
L'aquilon qui revient quand on croit qu'il s'enfuit,
La grêle, et l'avalanche, et la trombe, et le bruit,
Toutes les visions des affreuses nuées,
La tourmente et ses chocs, la bise et ses huées,
S'acharnent; et ne font, sous leurs dais de brouillards,
Pas même remuer ces effrayants vieillards.

Sois comme eux: si tu vas dans l'espace terrible,
Ne chancelle pas, homme; et garde un calme horrible.

XII

UNE AUTRE VOIX

Remonte aux premiers jours de ton globe; voilà
Une muraille; elle est prodigieuse; elle a
Dix mille pieds de haut, et de largeur dix lieues.
Falaise, alluvion, dans les profondeurs bleues
Ce haut boulevard monte, altier, froid, surprenant,
Et d'une mer à l'autre il barre un continent.
Vaste géométrie, on dirait que l'équerre,
Assise par assise, a fait ce mont calcaire,
Et que, forgeant l'espace, on ne sait quels marteaux
L'un sur l'autre ont cloué ses plans horizontaux.
L'escarpement à pic monte en bandes étroites,
Ses couches s'allongeant fermes, égales, droites,
Rides profondes, plis de ce front de la nuit.
Contre ce mur se heurte et flotte et roule et fuit
Ce que chaque saison pêle-mêle charrie.
Ce massif colossal de la maçonnerie
Terrible, que construit et détruit l'élément,
Semble un coffre de pierre immense renfermant
Les archives d'une âpre et sombre catastrophe,

The furious thunderstorm, the savage lightning—that worm
That wends its way in the dark immensity of winter—
The ferocious hurricane which lashes the great
Summits with its hair of wind, storm and rain,
The north wind which returns when it is thought to have fled,
The hail, and the avalanche, and the whirlwind, rending the
Skies, all the visions of the hideous thick clouds,
The storm and its shocks, the wintry blast and its howls,
Set upon, and yet do not even make move these
Terrible old men, under their canopies of fogs.

Be like them: if you enter dreadful space,
Be not moved, Man, and keep a terrible calm.

XII

ANOTHER VOICE

Return to the first days of your world.
Behold! A wall; it is prodigious; it is
Ten thousand feet in height, ten leagues in width.
This high bulwark, cliff, alluvial, rises in these
Cerulean deeps, lofty, cold, astonishing,
And from one sea to the other divides a continent.
A vast geometry, it seems as if the cross-staff,
Stratum by stratum, has created this limestone mountain,
And, forging space, who knows what hammers
Have nailed, one to the other, its horizontal planes.
The escarpment climbs precipitously in narrow bands,
Its layers stretching out firm, equal, straight—
Deep wrinkles, folds on this brow of night.
Against this wall collides and floats and tumbles and flees
The manifold handiwork of the seasons.
This colossal massif of terrible masonry
That the elemental forces build and destroy,
Seems like an immense vault of stone containing
The archives of a bitter and somber disaster,

Et tout un monde mort ployé comme une étoffe,
Avec ses fleurs, ses champs, ses rocs boisés ou nus,
Et ses fourmillements de monstres inconnus.

Dans des millions d'ans, ses pierres ruinées,
Ses moellons croulants seront les Pyrénées.

En attendant, vois: large, auguste, encombrant l'air,
Il est encor tout neuf, comme bâti d'hier;
Rien n'ébrèche sa ligne entière et régulière;
Et son sommet correct semble une seule pierre
Plate comme le toit d'un palais d'orient;
Le matin et le soir, en se contrariant,
Font de cette muraille épouvantable et sombre
Tantôt un banc d'aurore et tantôt un bloc d'ombre.

Et fais attention à présent:—l'air s'émeut;
Voici que sur le haut du mur géant, il pleut.
La pluie erre et s'en va, par le vent emportée;
Mais une goutte d'eau sur le faîte est restée.
Le lendemain, la brume, humide et blanc rideau,
Revient; il pleut encore; une autre goutte d'eau
S'ajoute à la première; et, sous cette rosée,
Une vasque s'ébauche, et la pierre est creusée.
Désormais sur ce point l'eau va s'obstiner. Vois,
Il pleut; et l'on entend comme une triste voix;
Peut-être est-ce un démon sous la roche, qui grince
De sentir l'eau plus forte et la pierre plus mince.
Il pleut, il pleut, il pleut; janvier livide et mort
Passe avec l'ombre, il pleut; la goutte tombe, mord,
Et creuse; avril arrive et rapporte la nue,
Il pleut; la goutte d'eau, féroce, continue;
Et la première assise est percée; et déjà
La deuxième, qu'en vain le granit protégea,
Est atteinte; et la goutte, implacable, acharnée,
Qui dépense le siècle aussi bien que l'année,

And an entire dead world folded like a fabric,
With its flowers, its fields, its wooded or bare rocks,
And its teeming of strange monsters.

In millions of years, its ruined stones,
Its crumbling rubble, will be the Pyrenees.

In the meantime, see: wide, august, encumbering the air,
It is still quite new, as if built yesterday;
Nothing damages its pristine and uniform line;
And its pure summit seems a single stone,
Flat as the roof of an Oriental palace;
Morning and Evening, by turns,
Make of this dreadful and dark wall sometimes
A ledge of dawn and sometimes a headland of darkness.

And take heed now:—the air is in motion;
Behold, on top of the giant wall, it is raining.
The rain meanders and then departs, swept away
By the wind; but on the summit, a droplet remains.
The next day, the fog, a moist, white curtain,
Returns; it is raining again. Another drop of water
Is added to the first, and under this dew
A basin is outlined, and the stone hollowed out.
At this point, the water will hereafter grow persistent.
Look, it is raining; and it sounds like a melancholy voice;
Perhaps there is a demon under the rock, who groans
When he feels the water stronger and the stone shallower.
It is raining, raining, raining. Pale, dead January passes with
The darkness, and it rains still; the raindrops fall, biting
And hollowing; April arrives and brings back the clouds,
And it continues to rain. The fierce droplets persist,
The first layer is pierced, and now
The second, which the granite protects in vain.
And the raindrop, merciless, relentless, which labors
Throughout the century no less than throughout the year,

Revient, et plonge, et troue et mine, dur foret,
Et le dedans du mont, formidable, apparaît,
Zone à zone, et voilà que, là-haut, l'aube éclaire,
La goutte étant sphérique, un bassin circulaire.
Un étang que le ciel dore, azure, rougit,
Sur le plateau désert s'étale et s'élargit.
La goutte d'eau revient, revient, revient encore,
Et tombe opiniâtre, et se fait dès l'aurore,
Rapporter par le vent qui, la nuit, l'enleva,
Et fait ses volontés dans la montagne, et va,
Vient, soumettant le marbre à ses lois triomphantes,
Et passe entre deux plans, et glisse entre deux fentes,
Et démolit et sculpte, infatigable main.
Urne hier, aujourd'hui réservoir, lac demain,
L'œuvre augmente et s'enfonce, et l'œil qui veut la suivre
Croit voir un trou qu'un ver fait aux pages d'un livre.
Penche-toi: devant nous, comme si nous rêvions,
Forant ce monstrueux monceau d'alluvions,
D'une lame percée allant à l'autre lame,
Obéissant au poids qui d'en bas la réclame,
Hydre, outil, vilbrequin, pioche, trompe, suçoir,
Commençant le matin, recommençant le soir,
Descendant l'escalier de l'épaisseur des couches,
Polissant leurs largeurs en murailles farouches,
Élargissant le haut, baissant l'âpre fond noir,
Évasant et fouillant sans cesse l'entonnoir,
Cognant partout, toujours, hiver, printemps, automne,
Son petit marteau sombre, effrayant, monotone,
Usant le mont, coupant le roc, sciant le grès,
Complétant sa ruine et faisant son progrès,
Et profitant d'un creux pour creuser davantage,
Et d'une argile à l'autre, et d'étage en étage,
Du haut en bas, de bloc en bloc, de banc en banc,
Errant, roulant, brisant, sapant, taillant, courbant,
La goutte d'eau travaille, et, terrible ouvrière,
Tord en cercles profonds l'énorme fondrière.

Returns and immerses itself, piercing and mining like an
Adamantine drill, and the interior of the fearsome mountain
Becomes visible, stratification by stratification; and see! up there,
The droplets being spherical, the dawn lights up a circular basin.
A pond, which the gilded, azure sky makes crimson,
Spreads and widens on the deserted plateau.
Again and yet again the droplet returns, unflagging,
And at dawn, makes the wind, which at night had
Carried it off, carry it back. It acts according to its fancy
In the mountain, coming and going, subjecting the
Marble to its triumphant laws, passing between two
Planes here, and slipping between two fissures there.
It demolishes and sculpts, a tireless hand.
An urn yesterday, today a reservoir, tomorrow a lake, the work
Grows larger and deeper, and the eye wishing to follow it
Believes it a hole a worm makes in the pages of a book.
Lean forward: before us, as in a dream,
Boring this monstrous pile of alluvia,
Moving from one pierced layer to another,
Obeying the weight which from below lays claim to it,
Monster, implement, drill, pickaxe, trunk, proboscis,
Beginning in the morning, resuming again at night,
Descending the staircase of thick layers,
Burnishing the breadth of fierce high walls,
Enlarging the top, lowering the bitter, black bedrock,
Widening and searching ceaselessly the funnel,
Banging everywhere, always, winter, spring, autumn,
Its small, dark, terrible, monotonous hammer,
Corroding the mountain, cutting the rock, sawing the sandstone,
Progressing through its act of destruction,
And taking advantage of a hollow in order to hollow out more,
From one clay and one level to another,
From top to bottom, block after block, stratum after stratum,
Wandering, tumbling, breaking, undermining, cutting, bending,
The droplet works, and, terrible worker,
Cuts in deep circles the enormous rut.

Le vaste mont, battu des aquilons sifflants,
Frémit de voir creuser dans ses ténébreux flancs
Ce puits prodigieux par cette vrille infime,
Et de sentir l'atome en lui créer l'abîme.

Sur ce qui s'édifie et ce qui se détruit,
Laissons rouler du temps, du gouffre et de la nuit.

Et maintenant regarde:

Un cirque! un hippodrome,
Un théâtre où Stamboul, Tyr, Memphis, Londres, Rome,
Avec leurs millions d'hommes pourraient s'asseoir,
Où Paris flotterait comme un essaim du soir!
Gavarnie! un miracle! un rêve!

Architectures
Sans constructeurs connus, sans noms, sans signatures,
Qui dans l'obscurité gardez votre secret,
Arches, temples qu'Aaron ou Moïse sacrait,
O champ clos de Tarquin où trois cent milles têtes
Fourmillaient, où l'Atlas hideux vidait ses bêtes,
Casbahs, At-meïdans, tours, Kremlins, Rhamséions,
Où nous, spectres, venons, où nous nous asseyons,
Panthéons, parthénons, cathédrales qu'ont faites
De puissants charpentiers aux âmes de prophètes,
Monts creusés en pagode où vivent des airains,
Aux plafonds monstrueux, sombres ciels souterrains,
Cirques, stades, Élis, Thèbe, arènes de Nîmes,
Noirs monuments, géants, témoins, grands anonymes,
Vous n'êtes rien, palais, dômes, temples, tombeaux,
Devant ce colysée inouï du chaos!
Vois: l'homme fait ici le bruit de l'éphémère.
C'est l'apparition, l'énigme, la chimère
Taillée à pans coupés et tirée au cordeau.
L'aube est sur le fronton comme un sacré bandeau,

The vast mountain, beaten by the whistling north winds,
Trembles while it views, on its dark sides, the digging
Of this prodigious well by this tiny tendril,
Feeling the atom, within, creating the abyss.

Let us allow time, chasm, and night to pass
Over what is being created and what is being destroyed.

And now look:

An arena! A hippodrome,
A theater where Istanbul, Tyre, Memphis, London, Rome,
With their throngs of millions, could sit,
Where Paris would float like an evening crowd!
Gavarnie! A miracle! A dream!

Architectures
Without known builders, nameless, without signatures,
You who preserve your secrets in the gloom,
Arches, temples which Aaron or Moses consecrated,
O enclosed field of Tarquin where three hundred thousand
Beings teemed, where hideous Atlas exhausted his beasts,
Casbahs, At-meidans, towers, Kremlins, Ramesseums,
Where we ghosts come, where we sit,
Pantheons, parthenons, cathedrals wrought
By stout carpenters with the souls of prophets,
Mounts hollowed out as pagodas where bronzes endure,
With monstrous ceilings, somber subterranean skies,
Circuses, stadiums, Elis, Thebes, arenas of Nimes,
Black monuments, giants, witnesses, great nameless things,
You are nothing, palaces, domes, temples, mausoleums,
Beside this incredible coliseum of chaos!
See: here Man makes the sound of the ephemeral.
This is the ghost, the enigma, the chimera
Hewn into perfectly straight, separate faces of stone.
The dawn glows on the pediment like a sacred diadem,

Et cette énormité songe, auguste et tranquille.
Morceau d'Olympe; reste étrange d'une ville
De l'infini, qu'un être inconnu démembra;
Cour des lions d'un vague et sinistre Alhambra;
Gageure de Dédale et de Titan; démence
Du compas ivre et roi dans la montagne immense;
Stupeur du voyageur qui suspend son chemin;
Exagération du monument humain
Jusqu'à la vision, jusqu'à l'apothéose;
Monde qui n'est pas l'homme et qui n'est plus la chose;
Entrée inexprimable et sombre du granit
Dans le rêve, où la pierre en prodige finit;
Problème; précipice édifice; sculpture
Du mystère; œuvre d'art de la fauve nature;
Construction que nie et que voit la raison,
Et qu'achève, au delà du terrestre horizon,
Sur le mur de la nuit, la fresque de l'abîme;
C'est Vignole à la base et l'éclair sur la cime;
C'est le spectre de tout ce que l'homme bâtit,
Terrible, raillant l'homme, et le faisant petit.

La grande pyramide ici serait la borne
Où le taureau courbé vient aiguiser sa corne,
Et tu demanderais: quel est donc ce caillou?
Plante dans le pavé du cirque d'Arle un clou,
Et ce clou jettera dans l'herbe qui se fane
La même ombre qu'ici la colonne trajane.
Quel joueur gigantesque a laissé là ce dé?
Un mont dort dans un angle, un autre est accoudé,
Et la brume à son cou s'enfle et pend comme un goître.
Vois croître vers la cime et vers le bas décroître,
Écaillant de lichens leurs lourds granits vermeils,
Ces grands cercles de bancs superposés, pareils
A des boas roulés l'un au-dessus de l'autre.
Avec on ne sait quelle attitude d'apôtre,
Un rocher rêve au seuil, et, le long des degrés,

And this enormity muses, august and quiet.
A piece of Olympus, the strange remains of a city
Of the infinite, which an unknown being dismembered;
Court of lions of a vague and sinister Alhambra;
A wager between Dædalus and Titan; insanity
Of the mad compass and king in the immense mountain;
The lethargy of the traveler who interrupts his journey;
A human monument exaggerated
To the point of vision, to the point of apotheosis;
World which is not Man and which is no longer thing;
Unspeakable and somber entry of the granite
Into the dream, where the stone becomes marvel;
A riddle; precipitous edifice; sculpture
Of mystery; artwork of wild nature;
Construction which reason denies and yet sees,
And which, beyond the terrestrial horizon,
On the wall of night, the fresco of the abyss completes;
It is Vignola at the base and lightning on the summit.
It is the specter of all that Man builds,
Terrible, mocking Man, and diminishing him.

Here the Great Pyramid would be but a boundary-stone,
Where the bull stoops to sharpen his horn,
And you would ask: what is this rock?
Plant a nail in the pavement of the Circus of Arle,
And this nail will cast in the withering grass
As tiny a shadow as would the Trajan column here.
What gigantic player left that die there?
One mountain sleeps askew, another one is leaning,
And the mist on its neck swells and hangs like a goiter.
See growing towards the top and diminishing towards the base,
Scaling with lichens their heavy ruby granites,
These great circles of superimposed strata, like
Boas coiled one atop the other.
With some unfathomed attitude of an apostle,
A rock dreams at the threshold, and, along the steps,

D'autres blocs stupéfaits, voilés, désespérés,
Semblent des Niobés, des Rachels, des Hécubes.
Vois ces pavés; le moindre a dix mille pieds cubes.

La forme est simple, c'est le cirque; mais le mur,
A force de grandeur et de vie, est obscur;
Qu'est-ce que c'est qu'un mur vertical, rouillé, fruste,
Où, comme un bas-relief, le glacier blanc s'incruste?
Des albâtres, des gneiss, des porphyres caducs
Mêlent à ses créneaux des arches d'aqueducs,
Et là-bas la vapeur sous des frontons estompe
Des éléphants portant des blocs, baissant leur trompe;
Ces tours sont les piliers angulaires; de quoi?
Du vide, de l'éther, du souffle, de l'effroi.
L'impossible est ici debout; l'aigle seul brave
Cette incommensurable et farouche architrave.
Comme, lorsque la terre a tremblé, sont confus
Dans l'herbe, les claveaux, les chapiteaux, les fûts,
Tout se mêle, l'art grec avec l'art syriaque.
Sous les portes croupit l'ombre hypocondriaque.
Vois: tours où l'on dirait que chante Beethoven,
Pylône, imposte, cippe, obélisque, peulven,
Tout en foule apparaît; soubassements, balustres
Où l'eau nacrée étale au jour ses vagues lustres;
Crevasses où pourraient tenir des bataillons;
Sur les parois des creux pareils à ces sillons
Qu'aux temps diluviens faisaient aux seuils des antres
Et dans les grands roseaux des passages de ventres;
Là, des courbes, des arcs, des dômes; par endroits
Des murs carrés, des plans égaux, des angles droits;
Partout la symétrie inconcevable et sûre;
Des gradins dont on semble avoir pris la mesure
Aux angles des genoux des archanges assis!
Des pinacles géants portent des oasis;
Ordre et gouffre; les pines semblent sous les arcades
L'herbe; et l'arc-en-ciel s'envole des cascades.

Other astounded, veiled, desperate blocks,
Seem Niobes, Rachels, Hecubas.
See these facings; the slightest is ten thousand cubic feet!

The shape is simple, it is the cirque; but the wall,
By dint of its size and vitality, is hidden.
What is a vertical, impaired, defaced wall,
Where, like a bas-relief, the white glacier is encrusted?
Alabasters, gneisses, decaying porphyries
Merge aqueduct arches onto its battlements,
And lower down the haze under some pediments obscures the
View of elephants carrying blocks of stone, lowering their trunks.
These towers are oblique pillars; of what?
Of space, of æther, of breath, of dread.
The unheard-of is standing here; only the eagle braves
This immense and fierce epistyle.
Just as the arch-stones, the capitals, the shafts of columns
Are disordered in the grass when the earth has quaked,
So everything is mixed, Greek art with Syriac art.
The bilious shade lies wallowing under the arches.
Look: towers where it might be said that Beethoven sings,
Pylon, impost, cippus, obelisk, peulvan,
All appear in great numbers; bases, balusters
Where the pearly water displays to the daylight its vague
Lustrums; fissures which could hold battalions;
On the walls, hollows similar to those furrows
That, in diluvial times, passing bellies made at the thresholds of caves
And in the tall reeds of the passes;
There, curbs, arches, domes; in other places
Squared walls, smooth planes, right angles;
Everywhere an undreamt of and sure symmetry;
Terraces whose proportions seem to have been taken
From the bent knees of seated archangels!
Giant pinnacles support oases.
Order and chasm. The pines appear to be grass under the
Archways. And the rainbow flies off from the waterfalls.

Tout est cyclopéen, vaste, stupéfiant;
Le bord fait reculer le chamois défiant;
L'édifice, étageant ses marches que l'œil compte,
Blanchit de plus en plus à mesure qu'il monte,
Et, de tous les reflets de l'heure s'empourprant,
Passe du roc calcaire au marbre pur, et prend,
Comme pour consacrer sa forme solennelle,
Sa dernière corniche à la neige éternelle.
Combien a-t-il de haut? demande au ciel profond,
Au vent, à l'avalanche, aux vols d'oiseaux qui vont,
Aux douze chutes d'eau que l'ombre entend se plaindre
Dans cet épouvantable et tournoyant cylindre,
Aux gaves, épuisés d'écume et de combats,
Qui s'écroulent, torrent en haut, fumée en bas!

Piranèse effaré, maçon d'apocalypses,
Seul comprendrait ce nœud d'angles, d'orbes, d'ellipses;
Pourtant l'œil peut encore en mesurer, le jour,
La forme inexprimable et l'effrayant contour,
Mais sitôt qu'effaçant le bord, le fond, le centre,
Le soir dans l'édifice ainsi qu'un brouillard entre,
La forme disparaît; c'est sous le firmament
Une espèce d'étrange et morne entassement
De brèches, de frontons, de cavernes, de porches
Où les astres hagards tremblent comme des torches,
Et, dans on ne sait quel cintre démesuré,
De l'étoilé qui flotte avec de l'azuré.
Entre encor plus avant dans la chose géante:

Ce cirque, ce bassin, embouchure béante,
Imprime un mouvement de roue à l'aquilon,
Et fait de tout le vent qui passe un tourbillon;
La bise habite là, traître et battant de l'aile,
Et la trombe y tournoie en spirale éternelle.
Embûche formidable à prendre l'ouragan!
Le précipice s'ouvre en gueule de volcan,

Everything is Cyclopean, vast, stunning;
The brink makes the wary chamois recoil;
The edifice, staging its steps which the eye counts,
Turns more and more pale as it rises,
And, turning crimson from all the hour's play of colors,
Passes from calcareous rock to pure marble.
It derives, as if to consecrate its solemn form,
Its last cornice from the eternal snow.
How high is it? Ask the deep sky,
The wind, the avalanche, the birds in flight,
The twelve waterfalls that the shadow hears moaning
In this dreadful and swirling cylinder, with its mountain
Torrents, exhausted from foaming and struggling,
Falling, their floods at the top, their mist below!

A frightened Piranesi, mason of apocalypses, alone
Would understand this knot of angles, orbs, ellipses.
Nevertheless, the eye can still take the measure, during the day,
Of the unspeakable shape and the terrible contour;
But as soon as night rolls into the edifice
Like a fog, obscuring its outline, its base and middle,
It disappears. It is hidden under the firmament, a kind
Of strange and mournful heap of breaches, pediments,
Caves, and porticos, where haggard stars flicker like torches,
Something studded with stars drifting with
Something azure-tinged, in some unknown,
Measureless round archway.
Enter still further this giant object:

This cirque, this basin, a gaping mouth,
Stamps a whirling motion on the north wind,
And makes of every gust that blows a whirlwind;
The black wintry tempest lives there, treacherous, beating its
Wings, and the waterspout swirls there in an eternal spiral,
A formidable trap to capture the hurricane!
The precipice opens into the mouth of a volcano,

Et malheur au nuage errant qui se hasarde
A venir regarder par quelque âpre lézarde!
Sitôt qu'il y pénètre, il ne peut plus sortir;
Il a beau reculer, trembler, se repentir,
Le tourbillon le tient. C'est fini. Le nuage
Lutte, et bat le courant comme un homme qui nage;
Il roule. Il est saisi! Vois, entends-le gronder.
Il fait de vains efforts, il cherche à s'évader;
On dirait que le gouffre implacable le raille;
Il monte, il redescend; le long de la muraille,
Fauve, il quête une issue, un soupirail, un trou;
Étreint par la rafale, égaré, fuyant, fou,
Il vomit ses grêlons, crache sa pluie, et crible
D'aveugles coups d'éclair l'escarpement terrible;
Et le vieux mont s'émeut, car les rocs convulsifs
Tremblent quand, s'accrochant aux pitons, aux récifs,
Du haut de l'azur vaste où toujours elle rôde,
Libre et sans soupçonner l'immensité de fraude,
A ce sombre entonnoir trébuchant brusquement,
Et de son épouvante et de son hurlement
Ébranlant la paroi, les tours, la plate-forme,
La tempête, ce loup, tombe en ce piège énorme!
Voisinage effrayant pour les arbres, tordus
Par le vent ou roulés dans l'abîme, éperdus!
Du brin d'herbe au rocher, du chêne à la broussaille,
Tout l'horizon autour du cirque noir tressaille,
Le gave a peur, le pic, par l'orage mouillé,
A le frisson dans l'ombre, et le pâtre éveillé,
Pâle, écoute, parmi les sapins centenaires,
Rugir toute la nuit cette fosse aux tonnerres!

Et ce cirque qui met, au lieu de loups et d'ours,
Les ouragans aux fers dans ses cabanons sourds,
Ce large amphithéâtre au mur inaccessible,
Cet édifice fou, redoutable, impossible,
Fait à l'esprit, et même au delà des titans,

And woe unto the wandering cloud that risks
Coming to look through some bitter cranny!
As soon as it enters there, it can no longer leave;
Try as it may to retreat, to tremble, to rue the day,
The whirlwind holds fast. It is finished. The cloud
Struggles, like a swimmer fighting the current;
It redoubles its efforts, but is seized! Listen, hear it roar.
It tries to escape, but its efforts are in vain;
It looks like the merciless abyss is mocking it.
It climbs, it descends; along the wall,
Desperate, seeking an exit, an air-hole, a gap;
Embraced by the squall, led astray, flying, frantic,
It vomits its hailstones, spits its rain, and blindly
Riddles the terrible steep slope with strikes of lightning.
And the old mountain is moved, because the convulsive rocks
Tremble when, hanging on to the peaks, to the cliffs,
Down from the heights of the vast azure where it usually roams,
Free and without suspecting the immensity of deception,
Suddenly stumbling into this dark funnel,
And with its horror and its roaring
Shaking the walls, the towers, the level stretches of rock,
The storm, this wolf, falls into this enormous trap!
Terrifying surroundings for the trees, twisted
By the wind, or rolled into the abyss, frantic!
From the blade of grass to the rock, from the oak to the bush,
Every horizon surrounding the black cirque quivers, the mountain
Torrent is afraid, the woodpecker, sodden from the storm,
Shivers in the darkness, and the shepherd awakens,
Pale, listening, and, among the hundred-year-old fir trees,
Hears every night this thundering pit roar!

And instead of wolves and bears, this arena
Enchains hurricanes in its soundless sheds,
This wide amphitheater with the impervious wall,
This insensate, redoubtable, unfeasible edifice,
Makes the spirit dream of such more-than-Titanic

Rêver de tels combats et de tels combattants,
Qu'on le croirait bâti, qui sait? pour la mêlée
Des hydres que d'en bas la terre humble et troublée
Entrevoit dans l'horreur du taillis sidéral;
Qu'il semble en ce champ clos étrange et sépulcral,
Que, sous cette splendide et sublime falaise,
Les constellations pourraient se tordre à l'aise;
Et que, dans cette arène inouïe, on a peur
Parfois d'y voir descendre à travers la vapeur,
Pour s'entre-dévorer, les bêtes des étoiles;
Et d'entendre lutter, là, sous de sombres voiles,
Et hurler et rugir le taureau, monstre ailé,
L'effrayant capricorne aux nuages mêlé,
Le lion flamboyant, tout semé d'yeux funèbres,
Bâillant de la lumière et mâchant des ténèbres,
Le scorpion tenant dans ses pattes le soir,
Et, se ruant sur tous, le sagittaire noir,
Ce chasseur au carquois rempli de météores,
Dont par moments on voit, ainsi que des aurores
Qui passent et s'en vont et qu'un sillon d'or suit,
Les flèches d'astres luire et tomber dans la nuit!

Immensité! l'esprit frissonne. Quel Vitruve
A bâti ce vertige et creusé cette cuve?
Quel Scopas, quel Sostrate ou quel Eutinopus
A construit cet attique avec des monts rompus?
Quel Phidias du ciel a fait à sa stature
L'âpre sérénité de cette architecture?
Qui forgea les crampons? qui broya les ciments?
O nature, qui donc à ces escarpements
A lié les torrents, ces chevaux dont les queues
Pendent en crins d'argent dans les cascades bleues?
Du haut de quel zénith tomba le fil à plomb?
Qui mesura, toisa, régla, tailla? le long
De quel mur idéal a-t-on tracé l'épure?
De quelle région de la vision pure

Combats and combatants, that it would
Seem to have been built, who knows, for the battle
Of the hydras which the humble and disturbed
Earth, below, glimpses in the horror of the sidereal copse;
That it seems, in this strange and sepulchral battleground,
Under this magnificent and sublime cliff,
The constellations could writhe at their ease;
And that, in this incredible arena, one is afraid
Sometimes of seeing, descending through the haze,
In order to devour one another, the bestial stars;
And of hearing clash, and scream out and roar,
Under dark veils, the Bull, that wingèd monster,
The frightening Capricorn in amongst the clouds,
The blazing Lion, all strewn with mournful eyes,
Yawning light and chewing gloom,
The Scorpion grasping in its claws the evening,
And, hurling itself at everything, the black Sagittarius,
That hunter with the quiver full of meteors,
Whose arrows of stars one sometimes sees, gleaming
And falling into the night, like dawns
Which pass and disappear, leaving behind but a gilded trail!

Immensity! The spirit shudders. What Vitruvius
Built this vertigo and dug this cistern?
What Scopas, what Sostratus or what Entinopus
Constructed this attic with its worn-out mountains?
What Phidias from the heavens raised to these heights
The bitter serenity of this architecture?
Who forged the cramp irons? Who crushed the cements?
O nature, who on these steep slopes
Bound the torrents, these horses whose tails
Hang, silvery, in the cyanic chutes?
From the height of what zenith fell the plumb line?
Who measured, surveyed, adjusted, carved?
On the length of what ideal wall was the blueprint traced?
From which region of pure vision

Est sorti le rêveur de ce rêve inouï?
Quel cyclope savant de l'âge évanoui,
Quel être monstrueux, plus grand que les idées,
A pris un compas haut de cent mille coudées,
Et, le tournant d'un doigt prodigieux et sûr,
A tracé ce grand cercle au niveau de l'azur,
Rondeur sinistre ayant le gouffre pour fenêtre,
Puits qui, lorsque le soir le noircit, pourrait être
L'énorme coupe d'ombre où vient boire la nuit?
Aux temps où, rien n'étant complètement construit,
Du chaos encor proche on sentait le mélange,
Quand la montagne était encore un tas de fange,
Quelque étrange géant, fils de Cham ou de Bel,
A-t-il pris brusquement et retourné Babel,
Et l'a-t-il appuyée à ce mont, comme on scelle
Un cachet sur la cire ardente qui ruisselle,
De sorte que, léguant, dans le mont affaissé,
Sa forme renversée au trou qu'elle a laissé,
La tour s'est dans le roc imprimée en citerne,
Avec sa rampe où l'ombre après le jour alterne,
Et ses escaliers noirs et ses étages ronds,
Et ses portails s'ouvrant en bouches de clairons;
Si bien que maintenant l'œil voit ce moule horrible,
Et le creux dont Babel fut le relief terrible!

L'auteur, je te l'ai dit, c'est l'atome; l'auteur,
C'est ce fil brun rayant l'azur sur la hauteur,
C'est un peu de brouillard d'où tombe un peu de pluie,
C'est le grain de cristal qu'un souffle tiède essuie,
C'est, au jour ou dans l'ombre, au matin comme au soir,
La molécule d'eau qui coule du ciel noir,
C'est la larme échappée aux cils de la nuée;
C'est ce qui tremble au bout de l'herbe remuée,
Ce qui n'a pas de nom, ce qui ressemble aux pleurs;
C'est ce que la lumière, en traversant les fleurs,
Prend et roule en son vol sans en être chargée,

Came the dreamer of this unheard-of dream?
What cyclopean savant from what vanished age,
What monstrous creature, grander than the ideas,
Took a compass one hundred thousand cubits high
And, turning it with a prodigious and sure hand,
Drew this large circle at the level of the azure,
A sinister curvature having the abyss for a window,
A well which, when the evening darkens it, could be
The enormous cup of gloom where the night comes to drink?
In the days when, nothing having been completed,
One sensed the melange of chaos still near to hand,
When the mountain was still a heap of mud,
Did some unknown giant, son of Ham or Bel,
Suddenly seize and bring back Babel,
And did he press it onto this mountain, as one stamps
A seal on steaming, hot wax,
Thus bequeathing to the sagging mountain
This reversed shape left behind in the hole?
The tower was imprinted in the rock as a cistern,
With its incline where darkness and daylight alternate,
And its black staircases and its round floors,
And its portals opening like the mouths of clarions,
So that now the eye sees this horrible mold,
This hollow, of which Babel was the terrible relief!

The author, I have told you, is the atom; the author,
Is this dark thread streaking the azure up on the heights.
It is a little fog from whence falls a little rain,
It is the grain of crystal which a tepid wind caresses,
It is, in the day or in the dark, in the morning as in the evening,
The water molecule which falls from the black sky,
It is the teardrop escaped from the lashes of the thick cloud;
It is what trembles on the tips of the stirred grass,
What has no name, what resembles tears;
It is what the light, passing across the flowers,
Captures and tumbles in its flight without being burdened,

Ce qu'un petit oiseau boit dans une gorgée!
Oui, ce cirque et ses tours, édifice sacré
Où le drapeau d'azur du gouffre est arboré,
Ce théâtre où le vent combat la trombe enfuie,
Voilà ce qu'a construit un atome de pluie.
Quel besoin as-tu donc d'un Vishnou, d'un Allah,
D'un Bouddha, d'un Ammon cornu, pour tout cela?
Pourquoi sortir du cercle où le réel t'enferme?
A quoi bon détrôner l'élément et le germe?
Pourquoi donc à la chose ôter sa mission?
Pourquoi forcer l'atome à l'abdication?
Pourquoi destituer, homme, le grain de sable?
Quelqu'un qui dise moi t'est-il indispensable?
Tu mets en haut de tout un pronom personnel!
Quelle rage as-tu donc d'un faiseur éternel?
Ne peux-tu faire un pas sans un Très-Haut quelconque?
L'océan se va-t-il ruer hors de sa conque,
Tout mordre et tout ronger si ton Zéus n'est là
Pour le saisir aux crins et mettre le holà?
Tout n'est-il qu'une grotte à loger ce druide?
Crois-tu que le solide étreindra le fluide,
Que la mer manquera d'onde et de gonflement,
Que le soleil fuira, s'éteignant et fumant,
Que le germe oubliera le secret de la vie,
Que la terre prendra la route qui dévie,
Ou que la lune va perdre un de ses quartiers,
Si tu n'as dans un coin, pilant dans les mortiers,
Forgeant, créant, sculptant les os, broyant les poudres,
Un fantôme forgé d'étoiles et de foudres?
Dis, sans cet arrangeur, vivant, perpétuel,
Soulignant ce qu'il faut changer au rituel,
Dont tu doutes, songeur, même quand tu l'implores,
Les lys pâliront-ils sur les robes des flores,
Les violettes, dis, perdront-elles la clé
De la boîte aux parfums dans l'herbe et dans le blé?
Entre l'ombre passée et la flamme future,

What a small bird drinks in a mouthful!
Yes, this cirque and its towers, sacred edifice
Where the azure flag of the abyss is raised,
This battle scene where the wind fights the fleeing whirlwind,
This is what an atom of rain built.
What need have you, therefore, of a Vishnu, an Allah,
A Buddha, a horned Ammon, for all this?
Why leave the circle where reality encloses you?
What is the good of dethroning the element and the seed?
Why, therefore, take away from matter its mission?
Why force the atom to abdicate?
Why dismiss the grain of sand?
Is somebody who says "I" indispensable to you?
You place at the top of everything a personal pronoun!
What mania have you thus for an eternal maker?
Can't you take a step without some Almighty?
Is the ocean going to dash from its conch,
To bite and chew everything if your Zeus is not
There to seize it by the hair and put a stop to it?
Is everything only a grotto to accommodate this druid?
You believe that the solid will embrace the fluid,
That the sea will lack a wave and a swell,
That the sun will flee, burning up, smoking,
That the seed will forget the secret of life,
That the earth's orbit will lead it astray,
Or that the moon is going to lose one of its quarters,
If you do not have in place, mixing mortars,
Forging, creating, carving bones, pulverizing powders,
A phantom formed from stars and thunderbolts?
Tell me, without this arranger, active, perpetual, stressing
What must be altered in the ritual, about which
You have misgivings, dreamer, even when you implore it,
Tell me, will the lilies go pale on the robes of the florae,
Will the violets lose in the grass and
Wheat the key to the perfume box?
Between the past shadow and the future flame,

Dis, l'homme sera-t-il, en sa sombre aventure,
Englouti par hier ou détruit par demain,
Si tu n'as, pour sauver le triste germe humain,
Quelque Janus bifront, faisant face aux deux hydres?
La minute va donc figer dans les clepsydres,
Le temps, cet ouvrier mystérieux qui court,
Au cabestan du ciel va donc s'arrêter court,
La lumière, l'aimant, la sève, l'atmosphère,
Vont se déconcerter et ne savoir que faire,
Tout le mouvement va s'interrompre transi
Si ton Brahma ne vient leur crier: par ici!
Avril a-t-il besoin d'un mot d'ordre? Un tonnerre
Est-il un frissonnant et noir fonctionnaire
Attendant que quelqu'un lui fixe son emploi?
Faut-il donc un veilleur toujours présent, sans quoi
Les astres manqueraient les heures des aurores?
Le monde est une tour pleine de bruits sonores;
Faut-il un horloger derrière le cadran,
Réglant les poids dans l'ombre et tant de fois par an,
Mettant de l'ordre au ciel, versant l'huile aux rouages
Des globes, des saisons, des vents et des nuages;
Disant: Vesper, Vénus, rentrez! sors, Jupiter!
Donnant à chaque sphère à son tour dans l'éther
Ou la note qui chante ou la note qui prie,
Et remontant la vaste et sombre sonnerie?
Prends-tu pour des pantins et pour des jacquemards
Orion, Sirius, Vesta, Saturne et Mars?
Et la création est-elle une fontaine
A mécanique ainsi que la Samaritaine?
As-tu donc peur de voir le monde aller tout seul?
Faut-il que la forêt dise:—Père, un tilleul!
Un chêne! et maintenant donnez-moi de la mousse
Pour que le bruit du vent dans mes antres s'émousse!—
Quoi! cet échange vaste et saint d'attraction,
Ce flux et ce reflux de la création
Qui jette dehors l'être et sans fin le résorbe,

Tell me, will Man be, in his somber adventure,
Gobbled up by yesterday or destroyed by tomorrow,
If you do not have, to save the sad human seed,
Some two-headed Janus, facing both hydras?
The minute is thus going to congeal in water clocks,
Time, this mysterious worker always passing,
Is thus going to stop short in the capstan of the sky,
The light, the magnet, the sap, the atmosphere,
Are going to feel disconcerted and know not what to do,
All movement is going to be interrupted, transfixed,
If your Brahma does not come to shout at them: Through here!?
Does April need a watch-word? Is thunder
A shivering, dark functionary
Waiting for someone to employ it?
Must one keep constant vigil, to assure that
The stars not miss the hours of the dawns?
This world is a tower full of sonorous sounds;
Is a clockmaker needed behind the dial,
Adjusting the weights in the darkness and, so many times a year,
Tidying up the heavens, oiling the cogs of
The spheres, the seasons, the winds and clouds;
Saying: Vesper, Venus, return! Depart, Jupiter!
Giving each sphere his turn in the æther,
Either the note that sings, or the note of prayer,
And rewinding the vast, dark set of bells?
You take for marionettes and for jaquemarts,
Orion, Sirius, Vesta, Saturn and Mars?
And Creation is a mechanical
Fountain like the Samaritan one?
Are you afraid, then, to see the world working by itself?
Must the forest say:—Father, a lime tree!
An oak! And now give me some moss
To quiet the sound of the wind in my lairs!—
What! This vast and holy interchange,
This ebb and flow of Creation
Which casts out Existence and endlessly reabsorbs it,

L'univers, ne peut-il rouler, cercle, flamme, orbe,
Sans que ta terreur crie: il nous faut des étais!
Sans que l'homme, appelant à l'aide Teutatès,
Irmensul, Bhagavan, Chronos, Théos, échine
Un travailleur divin à tourner la machine?
Fais ce rêve, homme! et marche où l'erreur te conduit.
Quant à moi, qui suis l'ombre et qui vais dans la nuit,
Je n'accepterais pas, pour faire des prodiges,
Pour creuser un puits sombre et l'emplir de vertiges,
Pour soulever un monde, effroyable fardeau,
L'échange de ton Dieu contre ma goutte d'eau.

—Oui, mais la goutte d'eau, criai-je, qui l'a faite?

XIII
UNE AUTRE VOIX

Swedenborg prit un jour la coupe de Platon,
Et, pensif, s'en alla boire à l'azur terrible.
Il entra sous le porche obscur de l'invisible
Et disparut. Où donc alla-t-il? Qui le sait?
Peut-être aux lieux sacrés où Socrate pensait,
Où, dans l'ombre, effleuré de l'urne des Homères,
Le vin de l'idéal sort du puits des chimères.
Peut-être égara-t-il ses pas plus haut encor;
Jusqu'au gouffre inconnu, jusqu'aux pléiades d'or,
Jusqu'au ruissellement des fontaines d'aurore,
Jusqu'à l'ombre où l'on voit l'inexprimable éclore;
Là sont les cuves: sève, esprit, immensité;
Là vit, abonde et croît la vigne de clarté
Où l'on ne trouve pas un seul aster qui dorme,
Où les créations font leur vendange énorme;
Où la grappe de vie à flots ruisselle, ayant
La pierre du tombeau pour pressoir effrayant;
Là sont les infinis, la cause, le principe,
L'être qui s'évapore en mondes, se dissipe

In a word, the Universe, it can not run, circle, flame, orbit,
Without your fear shouting: We need props!
Without Man, calling to his aid Teutates,
Irmensul, Bhagavan, Chronos, Theos, and tiring out
A divine worker to turn the machine?
Create this dream, Man! and walk wherever error leads you.
As for me, who is darkness and who recedes into the night,
I would not accept, in order to create miracles,
In order to dig a dark well and fill it with vertigo,
In order to arouse a world, a terrible burden,
The exchange of your God for my droplet of water.

—But this drop of water, I cried, who created it?

XIII
ANOTHER VOICE

One day, Swedenborg took up the cup of Plato,
And, in a melancholy mood, went away to drink in the terrible
Azure. He entered the dark portico of the invisible,
And disappeared. Whither did he go? Is it known?
Perhaps to the sacred places where Socrates mused,
Where, in the shadows, skimmed from the urn of the Homers,
The wine of the ideal is drawn from the well of dreams.
Perhaps he lost his way higher up still;
Up in the unknown deep, up amongst the golden Pleiades,
Amidst the streaming fountains of dawn,
Up as far as the darkness where we see the unspeakable born;
Up there are found the cisterns: sap, spirit, immensity;
Up there lives, abounds, and grows, the vine of illumination
Where one finds nary a single, sleeping star,
Where the creations reap their enormous harvest of grape;
Where the clusters of life stream in torrents, having
The gravestone for a terrible press; and there he
Found the Infinite, Cause, Principle, and very Existence
Itself which dissolves into worlds, dissipates

En astres, et s'épanche en ciel démesuré:—
Il revint éperdu, chancelant, effaré,
Ployant sous la lueur farouche des étoiles;
Voyant l'homme à travers des épaisseurs de voiles
Et de tremblants rideaux de lumière où, sans fin
Multipliés, flottaient l'ange et le séraphin;
Ayant dans son cerveau l'ombre et tous ses délires,
De ses doigts écartés cherchant de vagues lyres,
Nu, bégayant l'abîme, et balbutiant Dieu;
Rapportant cette joie étrange du ciel bleu
Qui fait peur à la terre et trouble les fils d'Ève,
Et laissant voir, ainsi que le monde du rêve,
Dans de blêmes rayons tombés on ne sait d'où,
Un paradis sinistre au fond de son œil fou.
La raison l'attendait, grave, et lui dit: Ivrogne!

Esprit, fais ton sillon, homme, fais ta besogne.
Ne va pas au delà. Cherche Dieu. Mais tiens-toi,
Pour le voir, dans l'amour et non pas dans l'effroi.

APRÈS LES VOIX

... Une troisième fois, dans l'effrayant ciel noir
On éclata de rire, et muet, sans pouvoir
Deviner d'où venait cette gaieté terrible,
Je regardai, lutteur frémissant, l'ombre horrible.

—Qui donc a ri? criai-je égaré. Quel qu'il soit,
Qu'il se montre.

Alors, blême et se tenant tout droit,
Je vis monter du fond de l'abîme un suaire.
Ses plis vagues jetaient une odeur d'ossuaire;
Et sous le drap hideux et livide on sentait
Un de ces êtres noirs sur qui la nuit se tait.

Into stars, and pours into the unbounded heavens.—
He returned dazed, bewildered, staggered,
Tamed by the fierce glare of the stars;
Seeing Man through layers of veils
And trembling curtains of light where, endlessly
Multiplied, the angels and the seraphim floated;
Bearing in his mind the darkness and all its frenzies,
With outstretched fingers seeking indistinct lyres,
Naked, stuttering the abyss and stammering God;
Bringing back from the blue firmament this strange ecstasy
Which terrifies the world and makes tremble the sons of Eve,
And allowing one to see, as well as the realm of dreams,
In the pale light fallen from who knows where,
A sinister paradise deep within his mad eye.
Grave Reason awaited him and exclaimed: Drunkard!

Spirit, plow your furrow, Man, do your job.
Do not go beyond. Look for God. But be content
To see him in love and not fear.

AFTER THE VOICES

... For a third time, in the frightful black sky
There again burst forth laughter, and speechless, without being
Able to guess whence came this terrible gaity,
I looked, shuddering struggler, at the horrible darkness.

— Who laughed thus? I shouted, distraught. Whoever he is,
He must show himself.

Then, pale, erect, there emerged
A shroud from the bottom of the abyss.
Its pallid folds emitted an odor of the ossuary;
And under the hideous and livid cloth one sensed one of those
Dark Beings about which the night, itself, keeps silent.

C'était de ce linceul qu'était sorti le rire.
Sans que la sombre voix s'élevât pour le dire,
Je le compris; ma chair frémit; mon front pâlit.
L'être voilé, debout, comme quelqu'un qui lit
En tournant gravement les pages d'un registre,
Se mit à me parler, calme, lent et sinistre:...

From this shroud had come the laughter.
Without its raising its voice to say so, I understood;
My flesh quivered; my brow turned pale.
The veiled Being, standing as if reading
While gravely turning the pages of a register,
Began speaking to me, calm, slow and sinister:...

Victor Hugo, *Souvenir de Burscheid* (Remembrance of Burscheid), detail, July 1871, Bibliothèque nationale de France

L'océan d'en haut

I LA CHAUVE-SOURIS

[L'athéisme. *Nihil.*]

Et je vis au-dessus de ma tête un point noir.

Et ce point noir semblait une mouche du soir
Volant à l'heure où l'ombre à prier nous invite.
Et, l'homme, quand il pense, étant ailé, j'eus vite
Franchi l'éther qui s'ouvre à l'essor des esprits!
Et cette mouche était une chauve-souris.

Et ce lugubre oiseau volait seul dans l'espace
Et disait:—C'est énorme et hideux. Ce qui passe
Devant mes yeux me fait trembler. C'est effrayant.
Quand donc serai-je hors de l'ombre?—Et, me voyant,
Il cria:

The Ocean of the Heights

I THE BAT

[Atheism. *Nihil.*]

And I saw, above my head, a black speck.

And this black speck seemed a fly winging its way
At dusk, when darkness invites us to pray.
And since Man, himself, dons wings when he reflects,
I quickly crossed the æther which embraces
Soaring spirits! And I saw that this fly was a bat.

And this dismal creature, flying alone in the firmament,
Was saying:—It is vast and hideous. What passes
Before my eyes makes me tremble. It is frightful.
When shall I ever get beyond this darkness?—And, seeing me,
He exclaimed:

*

—Que veux-tu de moi, passant rapide?
Je regarde, éperdu, la matière stupide.
Homme, écoute: je suis l'oiseau noir que trouva
Démogorgon en Grèce et dans l'Inde Shiva.
Je contemple l'horreur de la sombre nature.
Homme, quel est le sens de l'affreuse aventure
Qu'on appelle univers? Je le cherche et j'ai peur.
J'interroge ce bloc qui n'est qu'une vapeur;
J'observe l'infini monstrueux, et je scrute
La taupe et le soleil, l'homme, l'arbre et la brute.
Je suis triste. O passant, comprends-tu ce mot: Rien!
Ce qu'on nomme le mal est peut-être le bien.
Quand un gouffre se comble, un autre puits se creuse.
Tourment, volupté, rire et clameur douloureuse,
Flux et reflux, le juste et l'injuste, le bon,
Le mauvais, blanc et noir, diamant et charbon,
Vrai, faux, pourpre et haillon, le carcan, l'auréole,
Jour et nuit, vie et mort, oui, non; navette folle
Que pousse le hasard, tisserand de la nuit!
Connaît-on ce qui sert, et sait-on ce qui nuit?
Tout germe est un fléau, tout choc est un désastre;
La comète, brûlot des mondes, détruit l'astre;
Le même être est victime et bourreau tour à tour,
Et pour le moucheron l'hirondelle est vautour.
Les cailloux sont broyés par la bête de somme,
L'âne paît le chardon, l'homme dévore l'homme,
L'agneau broute la fleur, le loup broute l'agneau.
Sombre chaîne éternelle où l'anneau mord l'anneau!
Et ce qu'on voit n'est rien: les fils tuant les pères,
Les requins, les Nérons, les Séjans, les vipères,
Cela n'est que peu d'ombre et que peu de terreur;
L'infiniment petit contient la grande horreur;
L'atome est un bandit qui dévore l'atome;
L'araignée a sa toile et le ver son royaume;

*

—What do you want of me, fleet passer-by?
Man, listen: I am the black creature found by
Demogorgon in Greece and Shiva in India.
Bewildered, I gaze at insensate matter.
I contemplate the horror of dark nature.
Man, what is the meaning of this frightful venture
Called Universe? I search it, fearful.
I question this vaporous mass;
I observe monstrous infinity, and I study
The mole and the sun, Man, tree, and the brute beast.
I am sad. O passer-by, do you understand this word: Nothing!
What is called evil may be good.
When one abyss is closed, yet another opens up.
Agony, exquisite delight, laughter and heart-rending outcry,
Ebb and flow, right and wrong, good,
Bad, white and black, diamond and coal,
True, false, royal robes and rags, the iron collar, the halo,
Day and night, life and death, yes, no—a mad pendulation
Impelled by Chance, Night's weaver!
Do we understand what helps, do we know what harms?
Every seed is a scourge, every impact a disaster;
The comet, blazing flame of the worlds, destroys the star,
The same creature is both victim and executioner by turns,
And for the midge the swallow is a vulture.
Stones are crushed by the beast of burden,
The donkey grazes the thistle, man devours man,
The lamb feeds on the flower, the wolf on the lamb:
'Tis an eternal darksome chain where link bites link!
And what you see is nothing: sons killing fathers,
Sharks, Neros, Sejanuses, vipers,
Are but rudimentary aspects of the darkness and terror;
The infinitely small contains the true horror;
The atom is a bandit that devours the atom;
The spider has its web and the worm its kingdom;

Les fourmilières sont des Babels; l'animal
En se rapetissant se rapproche du mal;
Plus la force décroît, plus la bête est difforme;
Et, quand il les regarde avec son œil énorme,
Homme, les gouttes d'eau font peur à l'océan;
La rosée en sa perle a Typhon et Satan;
Ils s'y tordent tous deux à jamais; l'éphémère
Est Moloch; l'infusoire, effroyable chimère,
Grince, et si le géant pouvait voir l'embryon,
Le béhémoth fuirait devant le vibrion.
Le moindre grain de sable est un globe qui roule
Traînant comme la terre une lugubre foule
Qui s'abhorre et s'acharne et s'exècre, et sans fin
Se dévore; la haine est au fond de la faim.
La sphère imperceptible à la grande est pareille;
Et le songeur entend, quand il penche l'oreille,
Une rage tigresse et des cris léonins
Rugir profondément dans ces univers nains.
Toute gueule est un gouffre, et qui mange assassine.
L'animal a sa griffe et l'arbre a sa racine;
Et la racine affreuse et pareille aux serpents
Fait dans l'obscurité de sombres guets-apens;
Tout se tient et s'embrasse et s'étreint pour se mordre;
Un crime universel et monstrueux est l'ordre;
Tout être boit un sang immense, ruisselant
De la création comme d'un vaste flanc.
On lutte, on frappe, on blesse, on saigne, on souffre, on pleure.
Tout ce que vous voyez est larve; tout vous leurre,
Et tout rapidement fond dans l'ombre; car tout
Tremble dans le mystère immense et se dissout;
La nuit reprend le spectre ainsi que l'eau la neige.
La voix s'éteint avant d'avoir crié: Que sais-je?
Le printemps, le soleil, les bêtes en chaleur,
Sont une chimérique et monstrueuse fleur;
A travers son sommeil ce monde effaré souffre;
Avril n'est que le rêve érotique du gouffre,

Anthills are Babels; by shrinking,
The animal draws near the essence of evil; the more
Diminished the power, the more deformed the beast;
And when the sea views mere drops of water
With its enormous eye, it is afraid;
The dewdrop contains Typhon and Satan;
It is there that they both writhe about, together, forever;
The mayfly is Moloch; the infusorian, frightful chimera,
Gnashes its teeth, and if the giant could see the embryo,
The behemoth would flee before the vibrio.
The least grain of sand is a spinning world
Drawing in its wake, like the earth, a mournful throng
That abhors itself, hounds itself, detests itself, and endlessly
Devours itself; hatred lies at the base of hunger.
The imperceptible sphere is the same as the immense;
And the dreamer hears, when he turns his ear,
A tigrine fury and leonine roars
Resounding deeply in these dwarfish universes.
Every maw is an abyss, and he who feasts, a murderer.
The animal has its claw and the tree its root;
And this frightful root, like the serpent,
Waits in grim ambush in the dark; all things cling together,
Embracing and grasping, in order to bite into each other;
Universal and monstrous crime is in the nature of things;
Every Being drinks mighty sheddings of blood, streaming
From Creation as from a giant flank. They fight, they strike,
They wound, they bleed, they suffer, they weep.
All that you see are larvae; everything deceives you
And quickly disappears into the gloom; for everything
Trembles and dissolves in the immense mystery;
Night reclaims the shadow as does water the snow.
The voice dies before it can cry out: what do I know?
The Spring, the Sun, the animals in heat,
Are but a fanciful and monstrous flower;
While it sleeps this frightened world suffers;
April is but the erotic dream of the abyss,

Une pollution nocturne de ruisseaux,
De rameaux, de parfums, d'aube et de chants d'oiseaux.
L'horreur seule survit, par tout continuée.
Et par moments un vent qui sort de la nuée
Dessine des contours, des rayons et des yeux
Dans ce noir tourbillon d'atomes furieux.
O toi qui vas! l'esprit, le vent, la feuille morte,
Le silence, le bruit, cette aile qui t'emporte,
Le jour que tu crois voir par moments, ce qui luit,
Ce qui tremble, le ciel, l'être, tout est la nuit!
Et la création tout entière, avec l'homme,
Avec ce que l'œil voit et ce que la voix nomme,
Ses mondes, ses soleils, ses courants inouïs,
Ses météores fous qui volent éblouis,
Avec ses globes d'or pareils à de grands dômes,
Avec son éternel passage de fantômes,
Le flot, l'essaim, l'oiseau, le lys qu'on croit béni,
N'est qu'un vomissement d'ombre dans l'infini!
La nuit produit le mal, le mal produit le pire.
Écoute maintenant ce que je vais te dire:

L'oiseau noir s'arrêta, d'épouvante troublé,
Puis, sombre et frémissant, reprit:

Je suis allé
Jusqu'au fond de cette ombre, et je n'ai vu personne.

*

Je tressaillis. L'oiseau poursuivit:

J'en frissonne
A jamais, dans ce gouffre où j'erre plein d'effroi!
Dans cette obscurité, personne ne dit: moi!
Noire ébauche de rien que personne n'achève!
L'univers est un monstre et le ciel est un rêve;

A nocturnal emission of brooks,
Branches, perfumes, dawn and bird-songs.
Horror, alone, survives, persisting through everything.
And, from time to time, a wind which issues from the thick cloud
Traces forms, light beams and eyes
In this black whirlwind of furious atoms.
O you who pass! spirit, wind, dead leaf,
Silence, sound, this wing which carries you,
The daylight you believe you see at times, that which gleams,
That which trembles, Heaven, Existence—all is Night!
And all of Creation, with Man,
With what the eye sees and what the voice names,
Its worlds, its suns, its rare currents,
Its dazzling, streaking, mad meteors,
With its golden globes like great domes,
With its eternal passage of phantoms, waters,
Swarms, birds, the lily that we believe blessed,
Is only a vomiting of darkness into the Infinite!
Night produces evil, evil produces the worst.
Listen, now, to what I have to tell you:

The black creature paused, full of dread,
Then, somber and trembling, resumed:

I went
To the heart of this darkness, and I saw no one.

*

I gave a start. The wingèd creature continued:

I shudder from this
Forever, in this abyss where I wander, fearful!
In this gloom, no one says: I!
Black, rough-hewn sketch of nothingness that no one completes!
The universe is a monster and heaven a conceit;

Ni volonté, ni loi, ni pôles, ni milieu;
Un chaos composé de néants; pas de Dieu.
Dieu, pourquoi? L'idéal est absent. Dans ce monde,
La naissance est obscène et l'amour est immonde.
D'ailleurs, est-ce qu'on naît? est-ce qu'on vit? quel est
Le vivant, le réel, le certain, le complet?
Les penseurs, dont la nuit je bats les fronts moroses,
Questionnent en vain la surdité des choses;
L'eau coule, l'arbre croît, l'âne brait, l'oiseau pond,
Le loup hurle, le ver mange; rien ne répond.
La profondeur sans but, triste, idiote et blême;
Quelque chose d'affreux qui s'ignore soi-même;
C'est tout: sous mon linceul voilà ce que je sais.
Et l'infini m'écrase, et j'ai beau dire: assez!
C'est horrible. Toujours cette vision morne!
Jamais le fond, jamais la fin, jamais la borne!
Donc je te le redis, puisque tu passes là:
J'entends crier en bas, Jéhovah, Christ, Allah!
Tout n'est qu'un sombre amas d'apparitions folles;
Rien n'existe; et comment exprimer en paroles
La stupéfaction immense de la nuit?
L'invisible s'efface et l'impalpable fuit;
L'ombre dort; les fœtus se mêlent aux décombres;
Les formes, aspects vains, se perdent dans les nombres;
Rien n'a de sens; et tout, l'objet, l'espoir, l'effort,
Tout est insensé, vide et faux, même la mort;
L'infini sombre au fond du tombeau déraisonne;
La bière est un grelot où le cadavre sonne;
Si quelque chose vit, ce n'est pas encor né.
Muet, quoique béant, sourd, lugubre, étonné,
Les ténèbres en lui, hors de lui les ténèbres,
Sans qu'un rayon, éclos dans ces brumes funèbres,
Vienne jamais blanchir l'horizon infini,
Pas même criminel, et pas même puni,
Le monde erre au hasard dans la nuit éternelle,
Et, n'ayant pas d'aurore, il n'a pas de prunelle.
Le monde est à tâtons dans son propre néant.

No will, no law, no poles, no center;
A chaos consisting of emptiness; no God.
God, why? The ideal is absent. In this world,
Birth is obscene and love unclean.
Besides, are we born? Is one alive? What is
The living, the real, the certain, the complete?
Thinkers, whose morose brows I beat at night,
Question in vain the deafness of things;
Water flows, the tree grows, the donkey brays, the bird lays,
The wolf howls, the worm eats. Nothing responds.
Just some hideous thing unaware of itself,
Some aimless, sad, senseless chasm, deathly pale,
That is all. Under my shroud, that is what I know.
And infinity crushes me, and I say in vain: Enough!
It is frightful. Always this bleak vision!
Fathomless, endless, boundless!
So I repeat, since you pass by here:
I hear shouting down below: Jehovah, Christ, Allah!
Everything is just a dark mass of mad apparitions;
Nothing exists; and how express in words
The immense bewilderment of Night?
The invisible fades and the impalpable flees;
Darkness sleeps; fetuses are mixed with rubble;
Forms, vain aspects, lose themselves in the array;
Nothing has meaning, and everything—purpose, hope, effort—
Is senseless, empty, and false, even death.
The somber infinite raves in the depths of the unreasoning grave,
The coffin is a small bell that the corpse rings.
If something lives, it is not yet born.
Mute—though agape—deaf, dismal, shaken,
Darkness within, darkness without,
Devoid of a ray of light, hatched in these funereal mists,
Never illuminating the limitless horizon,
Not even criminal, let alone punished,
The world wanders blindly in eternal Night,
And, having no dawn, it has no eye.
The world is groping in its own Emptiness.

La nuit triste emplissait le ciel comme un géant;
Et la chauve-souris rentra dans l'ombre horrible;
Et j'entendis l'oiseau, disparu, mais terrible
Qui criait:—Dieu n'est pas! Dieu n'est pas! désespoir!—

. : . : . : . : . : . : . : . : . : . : .

VI LE GRIFFON

[Le Christianisme. *Triplex.*]

Et je vis au-dessus de ma tête un point noir;
Et ce point noir semblait une mouche dans l'ombre.
J'y volai.
L'âpre nuit mourait, mais sa pénombre
Masquait encor le jour qu'on voyait poindre aux cieux.

Et cette mouche était un griffon monstrueux
Qui faisait trembler l'ombre avec son aile énorme.
Et le griffon cria:

*

—Que l'aigle d'en bas dorme!
Je veille. Dieu plus haut que l'aigle m'emporta.
Tu viens du Sinaï, je viens du Golgotha;
Aigle, la foudre emplit ton œil visionnaire;
Moi, j'ai vu le gibet plus grand que le tonnerre!
Quand les bourreaux dressaient la croix, j'étais dessus;
J'ai frissonné sur l'arbre où l'on cloua Jésus;
J'ai vu cette agonie immense et solennelle;
Marc a pris pour l'écrire une plume à mon aile;
J'ai regardé Jésus saigner et s'assoupir;
Je sais tout; je suis plein de son dernier soupir.
Je sème sa parole au souffle de la bise.

Sorrowful Night began to fill the heavens, like a giant;
And as the bat returned to the frightful darkness,
I heard it, disappearing, but terrible,
Crying:—There is no God! There is no God! despair!—

.:.:.:.:.:.:.:.:.:.

VI THE GRIFFIN

[Christianity. *Threefold.*]

And I saw above my head a black speck;
And this black speck seemed like a fly in the darkness.
I flew towards it.
The bitter night was dying, but her half-light
Still concealed the day that was dawning in the heavens.

And this fly was a monstrous griffin
Who made the darkness tremble with his enormous wing.
And the griffin shouted:

*

—How the eagle, below, sleeps! I am awake
And watchful, and God shall carry me higher than the eagle.
You hail from Sinai, but I come from Golgotha;
Eagle, the lightning blinds your visionary eye.
As for me, I saw the gibbet looming larger than thunder!
I was there, above, when the executioners raised the cross.
I shuddered on the tree where they nailed Jesus;
And I saw the immense and solemn agony.
Mark took a plume from my wing, that he might write about it.
I watched Jesus bleeding and dying; and
I know everything; I am full of his dying breath.
I scatter his word in the winds of winter.

Aigle, Christ en sait plus que Moïse, Moïse
N'ayant que les rayons, et Christ ayant les clous.
Non, Dieu n'est pas vengeur! non, Dieu n'est pas jaloux!
Non, Dieu ne s'endort pas, portant toute la voûte!
Non, l'homme ne meurt pas tout entier!

Aigle, écoute:

*

Dieu, le monde étant fait, reconnut que cela
N'était rien, puisque rien n'y disait: me voilà;
Puisque rien n'y pensait et n'y parlait; de sorte
Que la création en naissant était morte;
Or l'incréé voulut engendrer l'immortel.
Il fit l'âme, et la mit dans l'homme, son autel.
L'homme seul reçut l'âme en l'univers visible.
Dieu créa pour Adam ce faîte inaccessible.
Au-dessous de l'homme, âme, intelligence, esprit,
La matière roula dans la pierre, fleurit
Dans la plante, et hurla dans la bête, sans vivre.
Voyant qu'il avait seul une âme, Adam fut ivre;
Il voulut la science et déroba le fruit.
C'est pourquoi Dieu jeta les hommes dans la nuit.
Et, depuis ce jour-là, l'urne amère est remplie.
Sous la faute d'Adam tout le genre humain plie.
Le labeur est ingrat et le sillon est dur;
L'homme naît mauvais, triste, inexorable, impur;
L'enfantement du mal déchire le flanc d'Ève.
La guerre et l'échafaud, ces deux tranchants du glaive,
Vont fauchant l'ignorant, le faible et l'innocent;
Le fratricide affreux, qui croit le père absent,
Fait peur aux cieux avec le sang qu'on lui voit boire;
Hélas! dans la forêt de l'humanité noire,
Un éternel Caïn tue à jamais Abel.
L'homme adore Moloch, Dagon, Teutatès, Bel;

Eagle, Christ is more knowing than Moses, for Christ had
Nails, and Moses only beams of light.
No, God is not vengeful! No, God is not jealous!
No, God does not fall asleep, supporting the entire celestial
Vault. No, Man does not wholly die!

Eagle, listen:

*

When the world was created, God acknowledged that it
Was nothing, since nothing had said to him: Here I am.
Since nothing had thought or spoken, thus
Had Creation died at birth.
Now the divine Increate wished to create the immortal.
He forged the soul, and placed it in Man, his altar, and
Man, alone, received it in the visible universe.
God created for Adam this inaccessible pinnacle.
Below Man and his soul, spirit, and intelligence,
There was only matter, rolling in the stone, blooming
In the plant, and roaring in the beast, without living.
Seeing that he, alone, had a soul, Adam was voracious;
He desired knowledge and stole the fruit;
And that is why God cast him into the night.
And, since that day, the bitter urn is full.
For Adam's mistake the entire human race suffers.
Labor is thankless and the furrow, unyielding;
Man is born wicked, sad, inexorable, impure;
The birth of evil rends Eve's flank.
War and the scaffold, those two sharp edges of the sword,
Cut down the ignorant, the weak and the innocent;
Hideous fratricide, who believes the absent father,
Frightens the heavens with the blood that they see him drinking;
Alas! In the forest of dark humanity,
An eternal Cain kills Abel forevermore.
Man worships Moloch, Dagon, Teutates, Bel;

Et sur les crimes rois les monstres dieux flamboient.
Les vices, meute infâme, autour de l'âme aboient.
Toute l'humanité tinte comme un beffroi.
Partout l'horreur, le râle et le rire, et l'effroi.
Toute bouche est ulcère et tout faîte est cratère.
Un bruit si monstrueux sort de toute la terre
Que la nuit, veuve en deuil, dit au jour qui rougit:
C'est le tigre qui parle ou l'homme qui rugit!
Satan à l'entour vole et plane, oiseau de proie
Des âmes. La douleur formidable est sa joie.

Et plein de feux, de pleurs, de tourments éperdus,
Et de bustes vivants dans les flammes tordus,
Plein de cris qui s'en vont au bronze de la voûte
Et que la surdité de l'impossible écoute,
Coupole de l'abîme ayant pour pendentifs
D'affreux écroulements d'êtres noirs et plaintifs,
Geôle sans fond, sans jour, sans espoir, sous la foule
Des vivants, sous ce tas de vanité qui roule,
Sous le flot des passants de la vie et du bruit,
Sous le penseur, captif du rêve qu'il construit,
Sous les guerriers casqués et sous les femmes nues,
Sous les larges festins qui chantent jusqu'aux nues,
Sous tout ce qui s'allume et tout ce qui s'éteint,
Sous tous les pas de l'homme, orgueil, science, instinct,
Sous tout être qui marche, ou chancelle, ou trébuche,
L'enfer éternel guette et s'ouvre, vaste embûche.

Noir sillon composé de tous les vils limons,
Qui reçoit des esprits et qui rend des démons,
Qui produit des moissons de spectres, et des gerbes
De monstres flamboyants, lugubres et superbes,
D'où sort tout ce qui tue, où croît tout ce qui ment,
Et qui tressaille, ému d'un long frémissement,
Chaque fois qu'il entend l'affreux cri de la chute,
Chaque fois qu'en sa nuit descend, essaim qui lutte,

And on crimes and kings, the monsters and gods blaze.
The vices, that infamous pack, bay at the soul, and
All humanity rings out as from a belfry.
Everywhere the horror, the gasp, and laughter, dismay him.
Every mouth is an ulcer and every summit a crater.
A sound erupting from the entire world is so monstrous
That the night, grieving widow, says to the blushing day:
It is the tiger that speaks, or the man that roars!
Satan flies and soars hither and yon, a bird of prey of
Souls; and great pain is his joy.

Full of fires, tears, desperate torments,
And living torsos in raging flames,
Full of cries which dissipate in the bronze vault
And which the deafness of the impossible hears,
The dome of the abyss having for pendentives
Hideous ruins of dark, plaintive beings,
A bottomless gaol, without day, hopeless, below the throng
Of the living, below this unbound heap of vanity,
Below the stream of passers-by of life and sonority,
Below the thinker, captive of the dream he himself has created,
Below the helmeted warriors and the naked women,
Below the great feasts which sing to the heavens,
Below all that catch fire and all that burn out,
Below all the steps of Man, pride, knowledge, instinct,
Below every being who walks, or hesitates, or stumbles,
Eternal Hell watches and opens, a vast trap.

This black furrow is composed entirely of vile silt,
Which swallows spirits and regurgitates demons,
Which produces harvests of phantoms, and sheaves
Of flaming monsters, mournful and magnificent,
Whence all who kill emerge, where all who lie germinate,
And which thrills, stirred by a prolonged trembling,
Each time that it hears the hideous cry of the Fall,
Each time that its night descends—a contentious swarm,

Quelque tourbillon sombre et triste où l'âme luit,
Et qu'il voit au-dessus de lui, noire et sans bruit,
S'ouvrir l'immense main de son semeur sinistre!

*

Mais le livre de vie est là, divin registre,
L'homme, c'est l'âme; l'homme en lui porte un rayon,
Et la matière seule est la damnation.
Dieu pense, et la douleur lentement le désarme.
Dieu s'appelle pardon, l'homme se nomme larme;
Dieu créa la pitié le jour où l'homme est né.
Devant les actions de l'homme infortuné
Souvent la pureté des firmaments s'indigne;
Souvent l'astre aux yeux d'aigle et l'ange au vol de cygne
S'étonnent de cette ombre et de cette noirceur;
Dieu, voyant l'homme fourbe, implacable, oppresseur,
Est triste; et quand, sortant de la nuit, la Colère
Apparaît, face sombre et que la foudre éclaire,
Rappelant au Seigneur ce que l'homme lui doit,
Prête à maudire, il met sur cette bouche un doigt.
Ce doigt mystérieux et doux, c'est la clémence.

Le pardon dit tout bas à l'homme: recommence!
Redeviens pur. Remonte à ta source. Essayons.
Rentre au creuset. Ton Dieu t'offre dans les rayons,
Pour refaire ton âme obscurcie et difforme,
Le cercueil, ce berceau de la naissance énorme.

Clémence, c'est le fond de Dieu. Dieu boit le fiel.
Dieu ne venge pas Dieu devant l'azur du ciel.
Il ne revomit rien sur l'homme. Secourable,
Tendre, il chasse du pied le mal, ce misérable.
Dieu, que l'homme coupable appelait, s'est penché,
Et, voyant l'univers sanglant, mort, desséché,
Et songeant, pour lui-même et pour lui seul sévère,

A dark, sad whirlwind where the soul dawns—
And each time it sees opening above it, black and soundless,
The immense hand of its sinister sower!

*

But the book of life is there, a divine register;
Man is the soul; he carries a beam of light within him,
And the lone subject is damnation.
God thinks, and pain slowly disarms him.
God calls himself forgiveness, Man is named tear;
God created pity the day Man was born.
Given the actions of this unfortunate, the purity of
The firmaments often becomes indignant; often the star
With the eyes of an eagle, and the angel with the flight of
The Swan, wonder at this dark and gloom.
God is sad, seeing deceitful, merciless man,
The oppressor; and when, from out the night, Wrath
Appears, the dark face illuminated by lightning,
Ready to condemn to eternal punishment, reminding the
Lord that Man is indebted to him, God puts a finger to his lips;
And this mysterious and gentle finger is called Mercy.

Forgiveness whispers to Man: Begin anew!
Become pure once more. Try to return to your beginnings,
To the crucible. Your God offers you the coffin,
This cradle of enormous birth suffused in light,
That you may recreate your darkened and deformed soul.

The substance of God is Mercy. He drinks the gall,
And does not avenge Himself before the azure of the sky.
He regurgitates nothing back on Man. Willing to help,
Tender, he chases away evil, the miserable one.
He, whom guilty Man summoned, leaned down,
And, seeing the universe bloody, dead, desiccated,
And imagining, for himself and for him alone, austere,

Que pour sauver un monde il suffit d'un calvaire,
Il a dit: Va, mon fils! Et son fils est allé.

Rédemption! mystère! O grand Christ étoilé!
Soif du crucifié, d'amertume assouvie!
Linceul dont tous les plis font tomber de la vie!
O gibet qui bénit Judas et Barabbas!
Qui verse à flots la sève et l'espérance en bas,
Croix, à tous les esprits, arbre, à toutes les plantes!
Sublime embrassement des grandes mains sanglantes!
Œil mourant de Jésus dont l'éternité luit!
O pardon! ô pitié de l'azur pour la nuit!
Paix céleste qui sort de toutes les clémences!
O mont mystérieux des oliviers immenses!
Après le créateur, le sauveur s'est montré.
Le sauveur a veillé pour tous les yeux, pleuré
Pour tous les pleurs, saigné pour toutes les blessures.
Les routes des vivants, hélas! ne sont pas sûres,
Mais Christ, sur le poteau du fatal carrefour,
Montre d'un bras la nuit et de l'autre le jour!

Après lui sont venus les apôtres, ces têtes
Flamboyantes; les saints; martyrs jetés aux bêtes,
Vierges louant Jésus dans le noir tombereau,
Femmes grosses chantant pendant que le bourreau,
Effroyable, arrachait leurs enfants de leurs ventres,
Et les pères des bois, et les docteurs des antres,
Et les voix des déserts et des cloîtres, criant
A l'homme en sa nuit froide: Orient! Orient!

*

Oh ! vous l'avez cherché sans l'entrevoir, sibylles,
Ce Dieu mystérieux des azurs immobiles!
Filles des visions, toi, sous l'arche d'un pont,
Daphné; toi, guettant l'œuf que la chouette pond,

That in order to save a world a Calvary would suffice,
Said: Go, my son! And his son went.

Redemption! Mystery! O great star-studded Christ!
Thirst of the crucified, quenched by bitterness!
Shroud whose every fold makes some life diminished!
O gibbet which blesses Judas and Barabbas!
Which pours sap and hope in torrents below,
A cross to every soul, a tree to every plant!
Sublime embrace of the great bloody hands!
Dying eye of Jesus whose eternity shines forth!
O Forgiveness! O pity of the azure for the night!
Heavenly peace which comes from all mercies!
O immense, mysterious Mount of Olives!
After the Creator, the Savior appeared,
And He saw for every eye, wept
For every tear, bled for every wound.
The paths of the living, alas! are not safe,
But Christ, on the post of the fateful crossroads,
Points out with one arm, night, and with the other, day!

After him came the apostles, those blazing beings;
The saints; martyrs thrown to the beasts,
Virgins praising Jesus in the black tumbrel,
Pregnant women singing whilst the executioner,
Horrifying, tears their children from their wombs,
And the fathers from the woods and the priests from the caves,
And the voices from the deserts and convents, shouting
To Man in his cold night: East! East!

*

Oh! You sought him, without catching a glimpse of him, sibyls,
This mysterious God of the quiescent azures!
Daughters of visions, you, Daphne, under the arch of
A bridge; you, Albunea, watching for the egg which

Albunée, et brûlant une torche de cire;
Toi, celle de Phrygie, épouvante d'Ancyre,
Parlant à l'astre et, pâle, écoutant s'il répond;
Celle d'Imbrasia; celle de l'Hellespont
Qui se dresse déesse et qui retombe hyène;
Toi, Tiburtine; et toi, la rauque Libyenne,
Criant: Treize! essayant la loi du nombre impair;
Toi dont le regard fixe inquiétait Vesper,
Larve d'Endor; et toi, les dents blanches d'écume,
Les deux seins nus, ô folle effrayante de Cume;
Chaldéenne, filant un invisible fil;
Sardique à l'œil de chèvre, au tragique profil;
Toi, maigre et toute nue au soleil, Érythrée,
D'azur et de lumière et d'horreur pénétrée;
Toi, Persique, habitant un sépulcre détruit,
O face à qui parlaient les passants de la nuit
Et les échevelés qui se penchent dans l'ombre;
Toi, mangeant du cresson dans ta fontaine sombre,
Delphique; âpres esprits, toutes, vous eûtes beau
Hurler, frapper le vent, remuer le tombeau,
Rouler vos fauves yeux dans la profondeur noire,
Nulle de vous n'a vu clairement dans sa gloire
Ce grand Dieu du pardon sur la terre levé.
Sainte-Thérèse, avec un soupir, l'a trouvé.

*

Le pardon est plus grand que Caïn, et le couvre.
La clémence de Dieu de tous les côtés s'ouvre,
Et c'est la seule embûche où l'on tombe toujours.
La langue des muets et l'oreille des sourds,
C'est le pardon. La grâce aide qui s'abandonne;
C'est ce qui manque à tous et ce qu'à tous Dieu donne.
Père, il sourit aux fils qui lui montrent le poing.
Dieu serait le puni s'il ne pardonnait point.
Son ciel est un regard clément. Toutes les grâces

The owl lays, and burning a waxen torch;
You, the one from Phrygia, terror of Ancyra,
Speaking to the star and, pale, listening to hear if it responds;
The one from Imbrasus; the one from the Hellespont
Who rises up a goddess and returns a hyena;
You, Tiburtine; and you, the hoarse Libyan,
Shouting: Thirteen! trying out the law of the uneven number;
You whose fixed gaze worried Vesper,
Ghost of Endor; and you, teeth white with foam,
Both breasts bare, O terrible madwoman of Cumæ;
Chaldean, spinning an invisible thread;
Sardica with the eye of a goat, with the tragic profile;
You, Eritrea, lean and stark naked in the sun,
Full of azure and light and horror;
You, Persian, living in a ruined tomb,
O countenance to whom spoke the passers-by of night
And the disheveled who brood in the darkness;
You, Delphica, eating watercress in your dark
Fountain; bitter spirits, all, try as you may to
Roar, to strike the wind, to stir the grave,
To roll your wild eyes in the black depths,
None of you saw clearly, in his glory,
This great God of forgiveness arisen on the earth.
Saint Theresa, with a sigh, found him.

*

Forgiveness is greater than Cain, and protects him.
The mercy of God opens its heart far and wide,
And it is the only trap into which one always falls.
The speech of mutes and the hearing of the deaf,
That is forgiveness. Grace helps those who have lost heart;
It is what is wanting to all and that which God gives to all.
Father, he smiles at the sons who raise their fist to him.
God would be the punished one if he did not forgive.
His heaven is a clement glance, and all the graces

Qu'il fait à chaque instant s'envolent, jamais lasses,
Se dispersent au loin dans tous les univers,
Et, du faible au méchant, du farouche au pervers,
Errent, abeilles d'or, et butinent les âmes,
Puis reviennent, mêlant baumes, encens, dictames,
Rapportant les parfums extraits des cœurs maudits,
Emplir du miel pardon la ruche paradis.
Clémence! mot formé de toutes les étoiles!
Dieu! ciel de tous les yeux! port de toutes les voiles!
Jamais, brume ou tempête, et quel que soit le vent,
L'asile n'est fermé tant que l'homme est vivant;
Toute lèvre est reçue au céleste ciboire;
Le sang du sauveur coule et toute âme y peut boire;
Si ténébreux que soit l'homme qui va partir,
A l'heure de la mort un cri de repentir,
Un appel de la foi que le tombeau recrée,
Un regard attendri vers la lueur sacrée,
Vers ce qu'on insultait et ce qu'on dénigrait,
Un sanglot, moins encore, un soupir, un regret
De l'âme détestant sa tache originelle,
Suffit pour qu'elle échappe à la peine éternelle,
A l'enfer qui, voyant ce que les hommes font,
Tord les chaînes sans fin dans les gouffres sans fond.
Qui que tu sois, esquif, tourne vers Dieu ta proue.
Le châtiment sans terme et sans espoir écroue,
Sous les éternités plus lourdes que les monts,
Les démons seuls et ceux qui deviennent démons.
Pour que la peine tombe immuable et tardive,
Il faut du dernier cri l'horrible récidive;
Dans l'éternité sombre, Achab, Caligula,
Borgia qu'entre tous la tiare étoila,
Philippe deux, Timour, Phalaris, Louis onze,
Néron, sont au carcan sur des trônes de bronze.
Pourquoi? parce qu'ils ont dit non! au grand moment,
Que leur âme est sortie en un vomissement!
L'homme n'a qu'à pleurer pour retrouver son père.

That he bestows at each moment, take flight, never tire,
Scatter in the distance into every universe,
And, from the weak to the wicked, the wild to the debased,
Wander, golden bees, to gather souls,
Then return, mixing balms, incense, dittanies,
Bearing perfumes extracted from accursed hearts,
To fill the bee hive, paradise, with honey, forgiveness.
Mercy! A word formed from all the stars!
God! A heaven for every eye! A harbor for every sail!
Whether fog or storm, no matter what the wind,
Never is the sanctuary closed as long as Man is living;
Any lip is received on the celestial chalice;
The blood of the savior flows, and any heart may drink of it;
No matter how dark the soul of the man about to die,
At the time of death a cry of repentance,
An appeal of faith which the tomb recreates,
A glance towards the sacred light,
Towards what was offended and what was denigrated,
A sob, even less, a sigh, a regret
Of the soul hating its stain of original sin,
Is enough to escape eternal punishment
In the Hell which, seeing what men do,
Winds endless chains in the bottomless gulfs.
Whoever you might be, skiff, turn your bow towards God.
Endless punishment and hopeless imprisonment,
Under eternities more ponderous than mountains,
Are for devils, alone, and for those who become devils.
For the punishment to fall immutable and belated,
The horrible recurrence of the last cry is required;
In dark eternity, Achab, Caligula,
Borgia, whom the tiara spangled most of all,
Philip the Second, Timur, Phalaris, Louis the Eleventh,
Nero, are in the pillory on the thrones of bronze.
Why? Because they said No! at the great moment
Their soul was released in vomit!
Man has only to weep to rediscover his father, and

Le malheur lui dit: crois. La mort lui crie: espère!
Qu'il se repente, il tient la clef d'un sort meilleur.
Dieu lui remplace, après l'épreuve et la douleur,
Le paradis des fleurs par l'éden des étoiles.
Ève, à ta nudité Marie offre ses voiles;
L'ange au glaive de feu rappelle Adam proscrit;
L'âme arrive portant la croix de Jésus-Christ;
L'éternel près de lui fait asseoir l'immortelle.
Aigle, la sainteté de l'âme humaine est telle
Qu'au fond du ciel suprême où la clarté sourit,
Où le Père et le Fils se mêlent dans l'Esprit,
Il semble que l'azur égalise et confonde
Jésus, l'âme de l'homme, et Dieu, l'âme du monde!—

*

Et, l'œil au firmament, ne regardant plus rien,
Comme ivre de rayons, le monstre aérien,
Lion par la crinière et l'ongle, aigle par l'aile,
Chanta:
            Paix, vie et gloire à la voûte éternelle!
Il est le véritable! Il vit. Il est présent.
Comme il est l'invisible, il est l'éblouissant;
Il a créé d'un mot la chose et le mystère,
Tout ce qu'on peut nommer et tout ce qu'il faut taire.
Quand l'homme juste meurt, il lui ferme les yeux;
Le beau jardin Azur est plein d'esprits joyeux;
Ils entrent à toute heure et par toutes les portes;
Dieu fait évanouir les gonds des villes fortes;
Entre ses doigts distraits il tord le pâle éclair;
Le grand serpent lui semble un cheveu dans la mer.
Il est le grand poëte, il est le grand prophète.
Il est la base, il est le centre, il est le faîte;
Il est celui qui songe, il est celui qui voit;
Il connaît l'avenir auquel tout homme a droit,
L'Éden soleil, l'abîme et ses chambres funèbres.

Misfortune says to him: Believe! Death shouts to him: Hope!
And if he repents, he holds the key to a better fate.
After the trial and the pain, God supplants
The Eden of stars with the Paradise of flowers.
Eve, for your nakedness Mary offers you her veils;
The angel with the sword of fire calls back banned Adam;
And the soul arrives carrying the cross of Jesus Christ.
The Eternal makes the Immortal sit beside him.
Eagle, the sanctity of the human soul is such
That at the heart of supreme heaven where resplendence smiles,
Where the Father and the Son come together in the Spirit,
It seems that the azure renders equal, and unites,
Jesus, the soul of Man, and God, the soul of the world!—

*

And, the eye in the firmament no longer able to see,
As if intoxicated by shafts of light, the monster overhead—
A lion, judging by its mane and claws, or an eagle, judging
By its wings—sings:
Peace, life and glory in the eternal vault!
He is the true one! He lives. He is present.
Just as he is the invisible one, he is also the dazzling countenance;
He has created, from one word, matter and mystery,
All that we can name and all that about which we must remain
Silent. When the just man dies, he closes his eyes;
The beautiful Azure garden is full of joyful spirits;
They enter at every hour and by every entryway;
God makes the hinged gates of fortified towns disappear;
Between bemused fingers he twists pale lightning;
The great serpent seems to him but a thread in the sea.
He is the great poet, he is the great prophet.
He is the base, he is the center, he is the summit;
He is the one who dreams, the one who sees;
He knows the future to which every man is entitled,
The Eden sun, or the abyss and its dismal chambers.

Ceux qui marchent sans lui s'en vont dans les ténèbres.
Il ordonne à la nuit d'envelopper le jour.
Il met la mort, archer, au créneau de la tour.
Les cèdres du Liban, pareils à de vieux prêtres,
Parlent de lui tout bas; l'ombre de tous les êtres
S'incline devant lui les matins et les soirs.
Les vierges, à ses pieds, dans de purs encensoirs,
Font brûler un parfum composé des prières
De tous ceux que le monde appelle ses lumières,
De tous les saints qui sont sur terre et dans le ciel;
Cette blanche fumée enveloppe l'autel,
Et l'Incréé, caché sous des voiles de flammes,
Se penche, respirant la douce odeur des âmes.
Les colonnes des cieux s'étonnent devant lui;
Ces hauts piliers, chargés de ce dôme inouï,
Frissonnent éperdus à son souffle, et ressemblent
A leur propre reflet dans des ondes qui tremblent.
O Dieu! roi! père! asile! espoir du criminel!
Éternel laboureur! moissonneur éternel!
Maître à la première heure et juge à la dernière!
C'est lui qui fit le monde avec de la lumière!
Le firmament est clair de sa sérénité.
Par moments, dans l'azur splendide et redouté,
O mystère! il se fait des silences d'une heure;
Personne en haut ne chante et nul en bas ne pleure;
L'ange abaisse, pensif, son clairon éclatant;
Dieu médite; le ciel rêve; l'enfer attend.

Et c'est ce mot qui sort de l'ombre: Je pardonne.

Le griffon s'effaça, comme l'éclair qui tonne,
Dans une brume où rien ne semblait se mouvoir.

Those who walk without him depart in darkness.
He orders the night to envelope the day.
He places Death, the archer, in the battlement of the tower.
Cedars of Lebanon, like old priests,
Speak of him in whispers; the shade of every Being
Bows before him morning and night.
The virgins at his feet, in their pure censers,
Burn an incense consisting of the prayers
Of all those whom the world calls its splendors,
Of all the saints on earth and in Heaven;
This white smoke envelopes the altar,
And the Uncreated, hidden under veils of flames,
Stoops down, inhaling the sweet smell of souls.
The columns of the heavens are astonished before him;
These high pillars, bearing this incredible dome,
Quiver visibly at his every breath, and resemble
Their own reflection in trembling waves.
O God! King! Father! Sanctuary! Hope of the criminal!
Eternal laborer! Eternal harvester!
Master from the very first hour and judge till the last!
It is he who created the world out of light, and
The firmament is bright with his serenity!
From time to time, in the magnificent and dreaded azure,
O mystery! hour-long silences occur—
No one, on high, sings and no one, below, weeps.
The pensive angel lowers his brilliant clarion;
God meditates; Heaven dreams; Hell abides.

And these are the words that flow out of the darkness: I forgive.

The griffin faded, like thunder and lightning,
Into a mist where all was still.

.:.:.:.:.:.:.:.:.:.:.

VIII LA LUMIÈRE

[Ce qui n'a pas encore de nom. *Dies.*]

Et je vis au-dessus de ma tête un point noir.
Et ce point noir semblait une mouche dans l'ombre.

Comme un vert rejeton sort d'une souche sombre,
Des profondeurs sortait le jour éblouissant.

Je me précipitai vers le point grandissant,
Plus prompt que les oiseaux envolés hors des branches;
C'était une lumière avec deux ailes blanches;
Et qui m'avait semblé, lorsque je l'aperçus,
Obscure, tant le ciel rayonnait au-dessus.

Cette clarté disait:

*

—Pas de droite et de gauche;
Pas de haut ni de bas; pas de glaive qui fauche;
Pas de trône jetant dans l'ombre un vague éclair;
Pas de lendemain, pas d'aujourd'hui, pas d'hier;
Pas d'heure frissonnant au vol du temps rapace;
Point de temps; point d'ici, point de là; point d'espace;
Pas d'aube et pas de soir; pas de tiare ayant
L'astre pour escarboucle à son faîte effrayant;
Pas de balance, pas de sceptre, pas de globe;
Pas de Satan caché dans les plis de la robe;
Pas de robe; pas d'âme à la main; pas de mains;
Et vengeance, pardon, justice, mots humains.

Qui que tu sois, écoute: Il est.
Qu'est-il? Renonce!

VIII THE LIGHT

[That which has yet no name. *Day*.]

And I saw above my head a black speck.
And this black speck seemed a fly in the shadows.

As a green shoot emerging from a dark stem,
From the depths came brilliant daylight.

I rushed towards this growing speck,
Quicker than birds that take flight from the boughs of trees;
It was a luminescence, adorned with two white wings,
And yet which seemed, upon sight, dark to me,
So radiant shone the sky above.

This brightness said:

*

—No right or left;
No high or low, no sword laying waste;
No throne hurling spectral lightning in the darkness;
No tomorrow, no today, no yesterday;
No hour quivering on the wing of rapacious time;
No time at all; no here or there; no space at all;
No dawn and no dusk; no tiara with
The star a garnet at its terrible peak;
No balance, no sceptre, no globe;
No Satan hidden in the folds of the vestment;
No vestment; no soul in hand; no hands;
And revenge, forgiveness, justice—mere human words.

Whoever you are, listen: He is.
What is he? Do not question!

*

L'ombre est la question, le monde est la réponse.
Il est. C'est le vivant, le vaste épanoui!
Ce que contemple au loin le soleil ébloui,
C'est lui. Les cieux, vous, nous, les étoiles, poussière!
Il est l'œil gouffre, ouvert au fond de la lumière,
Vu par tous les flambeaux, senti par tous les nids,
D'où l'univers jaillit en rayons infinis.
Il regarde, et c'est tout. Voir suffit au sublime.
Il crée un monde rien qu'en voyant un abîme.
Et cet être qui voit, ayant toujours été,
A toujours tout créé, de toute éternité.
Quand la bouche d'en bas touche à ce nom suprême,
L'essai de la louange est presque le blasphème.
Pas d'explication donc! Fais mettre à genoux
Ta pensée, et deviens un regard, comme nous.
Pourquoi chercher les mots où ne sont plus les choses?
Le vil langage humain n'a pas d'apothéoses.
Ce qu'il est, est à peine entrevu du tombeau.
Il échappe aux mots noirs de l'ombre. On aurait beau
Faire une strophe avec les brises éternelles,
Et, pour en parfumer et dorer les deux ailes,
Mettre l'astre dans l'une et dans l'autre la fleur,
Et mêler tout l'azur à leur splendide ampleur,
On ne peindrait pas Dieu. Songeur, qu'on le revête
De bruit et d'aquilon, de foudre et de tempête;
Qu'on le montre éveillé, qu'on le montre dormant,
Sa respiration soulevant doucement
Toutes les profondeurs de toute l'étendue,
Remuant la comète au fond des cieux perdue,
Le vent sur son cheval, la mort sur son éclair,
Et le balancement monstrueux de la mer,
On ne le peindra pas! Lui! Lui! l'inamissible,
L'éternel, l'incréé, l'imprévu, l'impossible,
Il est. La taupe fouille et creuse, et l'aperçoit;

*

Darkness is the question, the world the reply.
He is. He is the living, the vast, in full bloom!
That which the dazzled sun contemplates afar,
Is he. The heavens, you, we, the stars—only dust!
He is the abyssal eye open at the heart of light,
Seen by every torch, sensed by every nest,
Whence the universe springs forth in infinite light beams.
He gazes, and that is all. Merely to see, suffices the sublime.
He creates a world by simply viewing an abyss.
And this seer, having always been,
Has created everything, for all everlastingness.
When the mouth from below touches on this supreme name,
The attempt at praise is near blasphemy.
So, no explanation! Persuade your thought to
Kneel, and become a gaze, like us.
Why seek words with nothing to name?
The contemptible human language has no apotheoses.
What he is, can scarcely be glimpsed from the tomb.
He evades dark words come forth from the shadows.
Try as you may to create a strophe with breezes eterne,
And, in order to perfume and gild both its wings,
Enflowering the one and starring the other,
And suffusing the entire azure with their magnificent breadth,
You would not portray God. Dreamer, whether you
Dress him in sonorousness and north wind, thunder
And storm; whether you reveal him awake or asleep,
His breath gently lifting
All the deeps of the entire expanse,
Stirring the comet at the heart of the lost heavens,
The wind astride his horse, death astride his lightning bolt,
And the sea astride her monstrous swells,
You would not portray him. He! He! The inalienable,
The eternal, the uncreated, the unforeseen, the impossible,
Is he. The mole excavates and digs, and sees him;

L'ombre dit à la taupe: es-tu sûre qu'il soit?
La taupe répond: Dieu! Dieu de l'aigle est la proie.
Suppose que sur terre un seul être en Dieu croie,
Cet être, si jamais le soleil s'éclipsait,
Remplacerait l'aurore. Et sais-tu ce que c'est
Que le fauve ouragan, tonnant et formidable?
C'est, dans les profondeurs du gouffre inabordable,
L'infini murmurant: je l'aime! à demi-voix;
Quand l'étoile rayonne, elle dit: je le vois!
Tout le cri, tout le bruit et tout l'hymne de l'homme
Avorte à dire Dieu! Le baiser seul le nomme.

J'aime!

*

Ici la clarté me dit:
—Si tu m'en crois,
Va-t'en. Car les rayons brûlants dont tu t'accrois
Pourraient te consumer, frémissant, avant l'heure.
L'homme meurt d'un excès de flamme intérieure;
L'ange qui va trop loin dit: Ne restons pas là.
En voulant trop voir Dieu, Moïse chancela;
Un peu plus, il tombait du haut de cette cime,
L'œil plein des tournoiements terribles de l'abîme.

—Parle! oh! parle! criai-je à la forme de feu.

—O curieux du gouffre, Empédocle de Dieu,
Je parlerai, dit l'être, et même ton langage;
Car, lorsqu'en l'infini près de vous on s'engage,
Hommes, on ne peut plus toucher à ses rameaux
Sans en faire tomber vos misérables mots.

The darkness says to the mole: are you certain that he exists?
The mole answers: God! God is the eagle's prey.
Suppose that one person alone on earth believes in God,
This being, were the sun eclipsed,
Would replace the dawn. And do you know what is
The wild hurricane, thundering and formidable
In the depths of the inaccessible abyss? It is
The Infinite, murmuring under his breath: I love him!
When the star twinkles, she is declaring: I see him!
Every cry, every sound and every hymn of Man
Fails to say the name of God! The kiss alone names him.

I love!

*

Here the brightness said to me:
—If I am to be believed,
Then go away. For the burning rays of light, about which
You delude yourself, could consume you, trembling,
Before your time. Man dies from an excess of inner flame;
Angels who go too far say: let us not remain here.
By desiring too much to see God, Moses was unnerved;
A bit further, he fell from this high summit,
His eyes full of the dire whirl of the abyss.

—Speak! oh! speak! I cried to the candent form.

—O curious one from the abyss, God's Empedocles,
I shall speak, said the being, and in your very language;
For when we enter the infinite near to you,
Men, we can no longer touch its boughs
Without causing to fall your wretched words.

*

Le tout éternel sort de l'éternel atome.
De l'équation Dieu le monde est le binôme.
Dieu, c'est le grand réel et le grand inconnu;
Il est; et c'est errer que dire: Il est venu.
Quoique l'impénétrable énigme le vêtisse,
Quoiqu'il n'ait ni lever, ni coucher, ni solstice,
Êtres bornés, il marque, au fond du ciel sans bord,
Vos quatre angles, levant, occident, midi, nord;
Il est X, élément du rayonnement, nombre
De l'infini, clarté formidable de l'ombre,
Lueur sur le coran comme sur le missel,
Éternelle présence à l'œil universel!
C'est lui l'autorité d'où jaillit l'âme libre;
C'est lui l'axe invisible autour duquel tout vibre,
Et l'oscillation dans l'immobilité;
Oscillation sombre au cercle illimité,
Qui va, prodigieuse, une, inouïe, étrange,
Des oreilles de l'âne aux ailes de l'archange.
L'être sans cesse en lui se forme et se dissout;
Il est la parallèle éternelle de tout;
Il est précision, loi, règle, certitude,
Justesse, abstraction, rigueur, exactitude,
Et toute cette algèbre en tendresse se fond.
Et dans l'indéfini, l'obscur et le profond,
A travers ce qu'on nomme air et terre, flamme, onde,
Cet X a quatre bras pour embrasser le monde,
Et, se dressant visible aux yeux morts ou déçus,
Il est croix sur la terre et s'appelle Jésus.

Hors de la terre il est l'innommé.

Chaque sphère
Le nomme en frissonnant du nom qu'elle préfère,
Mais tous les noms sur Dieu sont des flots insensés.

*

The eternal entire emerges from the eternal atom.
In the equation God, the world is the binomial.
God is the great reality and the great unknown;
He is; and to say: He has come—is to err.
Although the impenetrable enigma clothes him,
Although he has neither sunrise, nor sunset, nor solstice,
He marks, at the bottom of the boundless sky,
Your four quarters, east, west, south, north;
He is X, lustrous element, number
Of the infinite, fearsome brilliance from the dark,
Glow upon the Koran as upon the Missal,
Eternal presence with a universal eye!
He is the authority from which springs the unbridled soul;
He is the invisible axis about which everything vibrates,
And the fluctuation within the stillness;
Dark oscillation within the boundless circle,
Which shifts, prodigious, indivisible, unheard-of, strange,
From the ears of the donkey to the wings of the archangel.
Existence ceaselessly takes form and dissolves within him;
He is the eternal parallel of everything;
He is precision, law, rule, certainty,
Accuracy, abstraction, rigor, exactitude,
And all this algebra is interwoven in tenderness.
And within the undefined, the dark and the deep,
Across what is called air and earth, fire and water,
This X has four arms in order to embrace the world,
And, arising erect, visible to dead or repining eyes,
He is the cross on earth, and is called Jesus.

Beyond the earth, he is the unnamed.

Each sphere
Names him, yet shuddering from the name that it has chosen;
But all names are senseless tides drifting o'er God.

*

Quant au globe chétif et morne où vous passez,
Hommes, l'ange a parlé d'une façon sévère;
L'homme est l'être sacré que la terre révère;
Mais l'arbre est quelque chose et la bête est quelqu'un;
La pierre et son silence, et l'herbe et son parfum,
Vivent; l'homme, rayon, doit plaindre la poussière.
L'être est une famille où l'homme est le grand frère;
Et lui, l'âme d'en haut, il doit, dans leurs combats,
Verser tout son azur sur les âmes d'en bas;
L'homme, malgré sa haine et malgré sa démence,
Est le commencement de la lumière immense.
L'égalité dans l'ombre ébauche l'unité;
L'unité, c'est le but de la route clarté.

*

Âme! être, c'est aimer.
                                        Il est.

*

                                                  C'est l'être extrême.
Dieu, c'est le jour sans borne et sans fin qui dit: j'aime.
Lui, l'incommensurable, il n'a point de compas;
Il ne se venge pas, il ne pardonne pas;
Son baiser éternel ignore la morsure;
Et quand on dit: justice, on suppose mesure.
Il n'est point juste; il est. Qui n'est que juste est peu.
La justice, c'est vous, humanité; mais Dieu
Est la bonté. Dieu, branche où tout oiseau se pose!
Dieu, c'est la flamme aimante au fond de toute chose.
Oh ! tous sont appelés et tous seront élus.

*

Humans, as for the pitiful and mournful globe whereon you
Pass, the angel has spoken in a stern manner.
Man is the sacred being whom the earth reveres,
But the tree is of some account, as is the animal.
The stone and its silence, the grass and its scent,
Are alive; Humankind, beam of light, must pity the dust.
Existence is a family where Humanity is the elder brother,
And he, the higher soul, must shed all his azure
On the lower souls, in their struggles;
Humankind, despite its hatred and despite its madness,
Is the beginning of the immense light.
Equality in the shadow first gives shape to unity,
And unity is the objective of the way towards luminescence.

*

Soul! To be, is to love.
He is.

*

He is the height of being.
God is the boundless and endless day that says: I love.
He, the incommensurable, cannot be measured;
He does not take revenge, he does not forgive;
His eternal kiss ignores the bite;
And when you say justice, you assume a norm.
He is not just at all; he is. He who is only just is trivial.
Justice is you, Mankind; but God
Is Goodness. God, bough where every bird alights!
God is the loving flame at the very heart of everything.
Oh! all are called and all shall be chosen.

Père, il songe au méchant pour l'aimer un peu plus.
Vivants, Dieu, pénétrant en vous, chasse le vice.
L'infini qui dans l'homme entre, devient justice;
La justice n'étant que le rapport secret
De ce que l'homme fait à ce que Dieu ferait.
Bonté, c'est la lueur qui dore tous les faîtes;
Et, pour parler toujours, hommes, comme vous faites,
Vous qui ne pouvez voir que la forme et le lieu,
Justice est le profil de la face de Dieu.
Vous voyez un côté, vous ne voyez pas l'autre.
Le bon, c'est le martyr; le juste n'est qu'apôtre;
Et votre infirmité, c'est que votre raison
De l'horizon humain conclut l'autre horizon.
Limités, vous prenez Dieu pour l'autre hémisphère.
Mais lui, l'être absolu, qu'est-ce qu'il pourrait faire
D'un rapport? L'innombrable est-il fait pour chiffrer?
Non, tout dans sa bonté calme vient s'engouffrer.
On ne sait où l'on vole, on ne sait où l'on tombe,
On nomme cela mort, néant, ténèbres, tombe,
Et, sage, fou, riant, pleurant, tremblant, moqueur,
On s'abîme éperdu dans cet immense cœur!
Dans cet azur sans fond la clémence étoilée
Elle-même s'efface, étant d'ombre mêlée!
L'être pardonné garde un souvenir secret,
Et n'ose aller trop haut; le pardon semblerait
Reproche à la prière, et Dieu veut qu'elle approche;
N'étant jamais tristesse, il n'est jamais reproche,
Enfants; et maintenant, croyez si vous voulez!

Devant le sacrifice et les cieux constellés,
Devant l'aigle effaré, devant les forêts vertes,
Devant les profondeurs dans tout être entr'ouvertes,
Hommes, on peut nier, mais l'inconvénient
C'est que l'esprit décroît et noircit en niant.
L'être fait pour l'extase et la soif infinie
Devient sarcasme, rire, ignorance, ironie;

As father, he thinks of the wicked, that he may love them even more.
Living beings, God, penetrating you, dispels vice.
The infinite which enters Man, becomes justice,
Justice being merely the secret relationship
Of what Man does to what God would do.
Goodness is the glow that gilds all summits;
And, Mankind, still speaking as you do,
You who can see only shape and place,
Justice is the profile of God's countenance.
You see one side, but not the other.
The good man is the martyr; the just man is only the apostle;
And your frailness consists of your reason
Inferring, from the human horizon, the other horizon.
Limited, you take God for the other hemisphere.
But he, the absolute being, what could he do
In a relationship? Can the uncountable be quantified?
No, all things come and are swept up in his calm goodness.
You do not know whereto you fly, you do not know whereto you fall,
You call it death, nothingness, darkness, tomb,
And—wise, foolish, laughing, weeping, quavering, mocking—
Overwhelmed, you become engulfed in this immense heart!
Star-studded mercy, herself, in this fathomless azure,
Fades away, becoming mixed with darkness!
The forgiven being keeps a secret memory,
And dares not climb too high; forgiveness would seem
Reproof to prayer, and God wishes that she approach;
Never being sadness, he never casts blame, children.
And now, believe it if you so desire!

Before the sacrifice and the constellated heavens,
Before the frightened eagle, before the verdant forests,
Before the half-opened depths in every being,
Humans, you can deny, but the drawback thereby
Becomes that the spirit decreases and darkens.
The being designed for ecstasy and boundless thirst
Becomes sarcasm, laughter, ignorance, irony;

Il n'a plus rien de saint, il n'a plus rien de cher;
Et sa tête de mort apparaît sous sa chair.
Votre terre niant ne serait qu'une infâme,
Et sa nuit grandirait; car retirer cette âme
A l'univers, c'est faire un abîme au milieu.
Oui, du centre de l'être insondable, ôte Dieu,
Ote l'Idée avec tous ses aspects, puissance,
Vérité, liberté, paix, justice, innocence;
Ote aux êtres le droit, ôte aux forces l'aimant,
Ote la clef de voûte, et vois l'écroulement!

*

Je t'ai parlé ta langue, homme que je rencontre.
Et que veux-tu de plus? faut-il qu'on te le montre?
O regardeur aveugle et qui te crois voyant,
Comment te montrer Dieu, cet informe effrayant?
Comment te dire: ici finit, ici commence?
Fin et commencement sont des mots de démence.
Fin et commencement sont vos deux grands haillons.
Homme, chante ou blasphème à travers tes bâillons,
Tu mêleras, sans dire un mot de la grande âme,
Ton blasphème à la nuit et ton hymne à la flamme.
L'idée à peine éclôt que les mots la défont.
Comment se figurer la forme du profond,
Le contour du vivant sans borne, et l'attitude
De la toute-puissance et de la plénitude?
Est-ce Allah, Brahma, Pan, Jésus, que nous voyons?
Ou Jéhovah? Rayons! rayons! rayons! rayons!

*

La clarté s'arrêta, comme tout éblouie.
Je m'évanouissais, et la vue et l'ouïe,
Et jusqu'aux battements du cœur s'interrompant,
S'en allaient hors de moi comme une eau se répand.

It no longer holds anything sacred, or dear;
And its skull appears beneath its flesh.
Your earth, if it denied, would become but squalid,
Still more benighted; for to remove this soul
From the universe, would be to create an abyss in its midst.
Yes, remove God from the heart of the unfathomable being,
Remove the Idea with all its aspects—power,
Truth, liberty, peace, justice, innocence—remove the righteous
One from his creatures, remove the loving one from his powers,
Remove the keystone from its arch, and see the collapse!

*

I have spoken your language, Man whom I have happened upon.
What further do you desire? must I show you him?
O blind watcher who, yet, believe you see,
How do I show you God, this frightening, formless one?
How do I tell you: here he ends, here he begins?
Beginning and end are words of madness.
Beginning and end are your two great ragged garments.
Man, were you to sing or blaspheme through your muzzled
Mouths, without a word of the great soul, your blasphemy
Would merely be absorbed by night and your hymn by flame.
The idea hardly emerges when words undo it.
How can one imagine the shape of the profound,
The contour of the boundless living being, and the bearing
Of omnipotence and plenitude?
Is it Allah, Brahma, Pan, Jesus, whom we see?
Or Jehovah? Rays of light! rays! rays! rays!

*

The luminescence paused, as if quite bedazzled.
I was on the point of swooning, and sight and hearing
And the very beatings of my heart, which faltered,
Were spreading from me like spilt water.

Et la clarté cria dans la profondeur noire
Où flottaient vaguement sous la brume illusoire
Ces faces de néant qu'on voit dans le trépas:

*

O Ténèbres, sachez ceci: la nuit n'est pas.

Tout est azur, aurore, aube sans crépuscule,
Et fournaise d'extase où l'âme parfum brûle.
Le noir, c'est non; et non, c'est rien. Tout est certain.
Tout est blancheur, vertu, soleil levant, matin,
Placide éclair, rayon serein, frisson de flamme.
Un ange qui dirait: la nuit, dirait: je blâme.
Les astres ne sont pas. Ces lueurs des tombeaux
Sont fausses, et le jour ignore les flambeaux.
La constellation dans l'illusion rampe;
Le plein midi n'aurait que faire d'une lampe;
Tout rayonnement vient du centre et du milieu;
Comme il n'est qu'une aurore, il n'est qu'un soleil, Dieu,
Qui pour les yeux de chair, couverts de sombres voiles,
Pleut le jour en rayons et la nuit en étoiles.
L'âme est l'œil, il est l'astre. Elle ne voit que lui.
Tout est clarté. Le ver rampant, l'ange ébloui,
Tout, les immensités où se perdent les sondes,
Tout, ces vagues de Dieu que vous nommez les mondes,
L'apparent, le réel, le lever, le déclin,
Homme, enfant, cieux et mers, espaces, tout est plein
D'un resplendissement d'éternité tranquille.
Comptez les milliards de siècles par cent mille,
Vous n'aurez pas dit un devant l'éternité.
Jetez toute votre ombre, ô nuits, à la clarté,
Au gouffre de splendeur que Dieu profond anime,
Et vous ne ferez pas une tache à l'abîme.
Vous n'êtes point. Au bas des cieux où nous montons,
On voit vos grandes mains qui cherchent à tâtons,

And the light cried out in the dark depths
Where dimly floated, in the illusory mist,
These faces of nothingness that we see in death:

*

O Darknesses, know this: night exists not.

Everything is azure, golden, dawn without dusk,
And furnace of ecstasy where the soul-incense is alight.
Blackness is a 'no,' and a 'no' is nothing. Everything is assured.
Everything is purity, virtue, sunrise, morning,
Tranquil lightning, serene light, quivering flame.
Were an angel to say: 'Night,' it would be censure.
The stars exist not. Those lights from the tombs
Are false, and day knows nothing of torches.
The constellation crawls within the illusion;
Broad daylight would have no use for a lamp.
All radiance comes from the center, the middle;
Just as there is but one dawn, there is but one sun:
God, who, for eyes of flesh vested in dark veils,
Rains down light beams by day, and stars by night.
The soul is the eye, he is the Sun. It sees only him.
All is brightness. The crawling worm, the dazzled angel,
Everything, the immensities where sounding leads are lost,
God's waves that you call worlds,
The apparent, the real, the rising sun, the close of day,
Man, child, skies and seas, space—everything is full
Of a resplendence of tranquil eternity.
Count the billions of centuries by the hundreds of thousands,
You will not have said One before eternity.
Cast all your darkness, O nights, into the light,
Into the chasm of splendor that profound God quickens,
And you will not make one mark in the abyss.
You do not exist at all. In the lower reaches of the heavens
Where we ascend, we see your mighty hands groping,

O nuits, spectres! on voit vos formes de nuées
S'approcher et grandir ou fuir diminuées,
Et le grand gouffre bleu, plein d'éblouissements,
O brumes, ne sait rien de vos écroulements,
Et le rayonnement formidable flamboie.
Ombres, vous n'êtes point. Pour être il faut qu'on voie.
Ténèbres, il n'est pas, devant les firmaments,
De ténèbres; il n'est que des aveuglements.

Des aveugles! Pourquoi?

*

Pourquoi la loi, la règle,
Le gland avant le chêne, et l'œuf sombre avant l'aigle?
L'aveugle est l'embryon du voyant; le voyant
Se change en lumineux, qui devient flamboyant;
C'est la loi. Vous verrez, vous rayonnerez, ombres!
Vous serez les frontons éternels, ô décombres!
Limbes, vous serez ciel! Vous l'êtes déjà, nuit!
De même que déjà le germe, c'est le fruit;
Que déjà dans le gland, monde que l'herbe ignore,
Avec toute sa feuille éclatante d'aurore,
Avec son noir branchage où la lune blêmit,
Solide et frissonnant, le grand chêne frémit,
Plein de cris, de chansons, d'hymens et de querelles;
Et que dans l'œuf profond déjà tremblent les ailes!
Devoir être, c'est être. Oui, la fange est cristal.
Chrysalide du bien qu'on appelle le mal,
Ne te plains pas; un fil à Dieu même te noue.
Le réel, c'est la roue, et non le tour de roue.
O larves, vous serez. Attendez votre tour.
Puisque le papillon qu'elle doit être un jour
Est là-haut, ouvrant l'aile, et, joyeux, tourbillonne,
Puisque le paradis qu'il doit être rayonne,
La chenille n'est pas, l'enfer n'existe point.

O nights, specters! we see your cloud-forms
Approach and expand, or flee, diminished.
And the great dazzling, blue gulf,
Knows nothing of your collapses, O mists,
And the great brilliance blazes on.
Shadows, you exist not at all. For to exist, one must see.
Shadows, I tell you, there are no darknesses before
The Firmaments, there are only blindnesses.

Blind! Why?

*

Why the law, the rule,
The acorn before the oak, and the dull egg before the eagle?
The blind man is the embryo of the seer; the seer
Transforms into light, which becomes brilliant;
It is the law. Shadows, you will see. You, too, shall radiate!
You shall be the eternal pediments, O ruins!
Limbo, you shall be Heaven! Night, you are it already!
Just as already the seed is the fruit,
As already within the acorn, world that the grass knows not,
With its entire, brilliant foliage of dawn,
With its black branchwork when the moon grows wan,
Full of cries, songs, matings and quarrels,
Thickset and shuddering, the great oak trembles;
And as deep within the egg already tremble the wings!
That which is compelled to exist, does so. Yes, mud is crystal.
Chrysalis of the good, which is called evil,
Do not complain; a thread ties you to God himself.
Reality is the wheel, not its spin.
O embryos, you will come to be. Await your turn.
Since the butterfly that she must become one day
Is on high, opening her wing and fluttering, joyous,
Since the paradise that it must become is shining,
The larva and Hell do not exist at all.

A la vie à venir le sort présent se joint.
L'être, qui n'est vivant que complet, se déploie
Composé d'aucune ombre et de toute la joie,
Ne gardant du passé que l'extase, et rempli
D'un souvenir céleste et d'un divin oubli.

*

L'univers, c'est un livre, et des yeux qui le lisent.
Ceux qui sont dans la nuit ont raison quand ils disent:
Rien n'existe! Car c'est dans un rêve qu'ils sont.

Rien n'existe que lui, le flamboiement profond,
Et les âmes, les grains de lumière, les mythes,
Les moi mystérieux, atomes sans limites,
Qui vont vers le grand moi, leur centre et leur aimant;
Points touchant au zénith par le rayonnement,
Ainsi qu'un vêtement subissant la matière,
Traversant tour à tour dans l'étendue entière
La formule de chair propre à chaque milieu,
Ici la sève, ici le sang, ici le feu;
Blocs, arbres, griffes, dents, fronts pensants, auréoles;
Retournant aux cercueils comme à des alvéoles;
Mourant pour s'épurer, tombant pour s'élever,
Sans fin, ne se perdant que pour se retrouver,
Chaîne d'êtres qu'en haut l'échelle d'or réclame,
Vers l'éternel foyer volant de flamme en flamme,
Juste éclos du pervers, bon sorti du méchant;
Montant, montant, montant sans cesse, et le cherchant,
Et l'approchant toujours, mais sans jamais l'atteindre,
Lui, l'être qu'on ne peut toucher, ternir, éteindre,
Le voyant, le vivant, sans mort, sans nuit, sans mal,
L'idée énorme au fond de l'immense idéal!

La matière n'est pas et l'âme seule existe.

Current fate joins with the life to come.
The being who is alive only when complete, unfolds,
Composed not of darkness but entirely of joy,
Retaining only the ecstasy of the past, full
Of a celestial memory and a divine forgetfulness.

*

The universe is a book, and the eyes that read it.
Those who reside in the night are correct when they say:
Nothing exists! For they are in a dream.

Nothing exists but he, the profound flame,
And souls, the specks of light, myths,
Mysterious selves, limitless atoms that move
Towards the great self, their center and magnet;
Points touching the zenith with their radiance,
Tolerating matter like a garment,
Spanning, by turns, the entire range
Of flesh befitting each milieu,
Here sap, here blood, here fire;
Blocks, trees, claws, teeth, thoughtful brows, haloes;
Returning to coffins as to honeycomb cells;
Dying in order to be purified, falling in order to rise up,
Endlessly, losing one's bearings only to find them anew,
A chain of beings that the golden ladder, on high, summons,
Flying, flame to flame, towards the eternal hearth,
The righteous hatched from the depraved, good issuing from evil;
Rising, rising, ever rising, and seeking him,
Always approaching him, but never reaching him,
He, the being that can be neither touched, sullied, nor destroyed,
The seer, living, deathless, nightless, devoid of evil,
The enormous idea at the core of the immense ideal!

Matter exists not; the soul alone exists.

Rien n'est mort, rien n'est faux, rien n'est noir, rien n'est triste;
Personne n'est puni, personne n'est banni.
Tous les cercles qui sont dans le cercle infini
N'ont que de l'idéal dans leurs circonférences.

Astres, mondes, soleils, étoiles, apparences,
Masques d'ombre ou de feu, faces des visions,
Globes, humanités, terres, créations,
Univers où jamais on ne voit rien qui dorme,
Points d'intersection du nombre et de la forme,
Chocs de l'éclair puissance et du rayon beauté,
Rencontres de la vie avec l'éternité,
O fumée, écoutez! Et vous, écoutez, âmes,
Qui seules resterez étant souffles et flammes,
Esprits purs qui mourez et naissez tour à tour :
Dieu n'a qu'un front: Lumière! et n'a qu'un nom: Amour!

*

Je tremblais; comme si, prêt à changer de forme,
J'eusse été foudroyé par un baiser énorme.
La clarté flamboyait, transparente et debout.
Et je criai: lumière, ô lumière, est-ce tout?

Et la clarté me dit: silence! Le prodige
Sort éternellement du mystère, te dis-je.
Aveugle qui croit lire et fou qui croit savoir!

IX

[Ce qui n'a pas encore de nom. *Deus.*]

Et je vis au-dessus de ma tête un point noir......................

Nothing is dead, nothing false, nothing dark,
Nothing sad; no one is punished, no one exiled.
All circles within the infinite circle
Have only the ideal within their circumferences.

Heavenly bodies, worlds, suns, stars, semblances,
Masks of shadow or fire, faces of visions,
Globes, humanities, earths, creations,
Realms where nothing ever sleeps,
Places where number and form meet,
Collisions of lightning's power and light beam's grace,
Encounters of life with eternity,
O vapors, listen! And you, souls, listen, you
Who, being breaths and flames, alone shall remain,
Dying and being born as pure spirits by turns:
God has only one countenance: Light! and only one name: Love!

*

I trembled, as if, about to be transformed,
I had been struck down by a mighty kiss.
The luminosity blazed, translucent and standing erect.
And I cried out: light, O light, is that all?

And the luminosity said: silence! Blind man who thinks
He reads, fool who thinks he knows! I tell you:
For all eternity does the wondrous emerge from the mysterious!

IX

[That which has yet no name. *God.*]

And I saw above my head a black speck......................

Épilogue

Le spectre reparaît et me dit:

Écoute. Tu n'as vu jusqu'ici que des songes,
Que de vagues lueurs flottant sur des mensonges,
Que les aspects confus qui passent dans les vents
Ou tremblent dans la nuit pour vous autres vivants.
Mais maintenant veux-tu d'une volonté forte
Entrer dans l'infini, quelle que soit la porte?
Ce que l'homme endormi peut savoir, tu le sais.
Mais, esprit, trouves-tu que ce n'est pas assez?
Ton regard, d'ombre en ombre et d'étage en étage,
A vu plus d'horizon...—en veux-tu davantage?
Veux-tu, perçant le morne et ténébreux réseau
T'envoler dans le vrai comme un sinistre oiseau?
Veux-tu derrière toi laisser tous les décombres,
Temps, espace; et, hagard, sortir des branches sombres?
Veux-tu, réponds, aller plus loin qu'Amos n'alla,

Epilogue

The specter reappeared and said to me:

Listen—Up to now you have seen only dreams,
Only vague glimmers floating on falsehoods,
Merely the muddled appearances which pass in the winds
Or tremble in the night for you living creatures.
But now, do you greatly desire, willingly,
To enter the infinite, no matter what the gate?
That which somnolent Man can know, you know.
But, spirit, do you find that it is not enough?
Your glance, from shadow to shadow and tier to tier,
Has seen no horizon—do you desire still more?
Do you wish to break through the bleak, dark net
And fly away into truth like a sinister bird?
Do you wish to leave behind you all forms of debris,
Time, space; and, wild of countenance, abandon these somber
Branches? Respond. Do you wish to journey out further than

Et plus avant qu'Esdras et qu'Élie, au delà
Des prophètes pensifs et des blancs cénobites,
Percer l'ombre, emporté par des ailes subites?
O semeur du sillon nébuleux, laboureur
Perdu dans la fumée horrible de l'erreur,
Front où s'abat l'essaim tumultueux des rêves,
Doutes, systèmes vains, effrois, luttes sans trêves,
Te plaît-il de savoir comment s'évanouit
En adoration toute cette âpre nuit?
Veux-tu, flèche tremblante, atteindre enfin la cible?
Veux-tu toucher le but, regarder l'invisible,
L'innommé, l'idéal, le réel, l'inouï?
Comprendre, déchiffrer, lire? être un ébloui?
Veux-tu planer plus haut que la sombre nature?
Veux-tu dans la lumière inconcevable et pure
Ouvrir tes yeux, par l'ombre affreuse appesantis?
Le veux-tu? Réponds.—Oui!—criai-je. Et je sentis
Que la création tremblait comme une toile;
Alors, levant un bras et, d'un pan de son voile,
Couvrant tous les objets terrestres disparus,
Il me toucha le front du doigt, et je mourus.

(*Puis le réveil*)

APRÈS LA MORT

Spectre, tu m'as trompé, je ne sais rien encore.

(Dieu, c'est l'infini. Il recule toujours—
aucune transformation de la vie ne
l'atteint.—Seulement on avance dans
la lumière.)

Amos, to travel further ahead than Ezra and Elijah,
Beyond the pensive prophets and the pure cenobites,
To pierce the darkness, borne off on swift wings?
O sower of the nebulous furrow, ploughman
Lost in the frightful smoke of error,
Facing the tumbling, tumultuous swarm of dreams,
Doubts, vain systems, fears, battles without respite,
Would it please you to know how all this
Bitter night disappears in adoration?
Do you desire, trembling arrow, to reach the target at last?
Do you wish to attain the goal, to look at the invisible,
The unnamed, the ideal, reality, the unheard-of;
To understand, decipher, read? To be overwhelmed?
Do you wish to soar higher than dark nature?
Do you want to open your eyes, weighed down
By dread darkness, in the inconceivable pure light?
Is that what you wish? Answer me.—Yes!—I shouted.
And I felt that creation trembled like a fabric;
Then, raising an arm and covering all the vanishing
Terrestrial objects with a fold of his veil,
He touched my brow with his finger, and I died.

(*Then the awakening*)

AFTER DEATH

Specter, you misled me, I still know nothing.

(God is infinite. He keeps withdrawing perpetually—
No transformation of life ever reaches
him.—One only advances into the
light.)

Fragments

LES VOIX.

Soudain je crus entendre quelque chose,
Et, stupéfait, sondant les cieux, penchant mon front
Dans le plus ténébreux et dans le plus profond,
Dans l'espace impalpable et blême qui refuse
La forme et la dissout en vision confuse,
Je vis, avec le bruit vague et presque vivant
Que feraient des feuillets remués par le vent,
Je ne sais quoi d'obscur qui flottait dans les ombres,
Et qui semblait un livre en proie aux souffles sombres.

Tel dut être, ô Colomb, ton morne étonnement,
Quand face à face avec l'éternel firmament,
Depuis déjà vingt jours ayant quitté la terre,
Te croyant dans un flot farouche et solitaire
Que n'avait avant toi franchi nul nautonier,
Tu vis passer sous l'onde un débris de hunier.

(Sur ce livre, un nom: Swedenborg.)

Fragments

THE VOICES.

Suddenly I thought I heard something,
And, stunned, sounding the heavens, leaning my brow
Into the most dark and into the most deep,
Into the impalpable and pallid expanse which rejects
Form and dissolves it in confused vision,
I spied, accompanied by the vague yet nearly vivid sound
That pages would make stirred by the wind,
I know not what obscure thing floating in the dark,
Which seemed a book in the grip of somber winds.

O Columbus, such had to be your sad astonishment,
When, face to face with the eternal firmament,
Already twenty days out from land,
Believing yourself on a savage and solitary flood
That no mariner before you had crossed,
You saw pass beneath the wave a fragment of topsail.

(On this book, one name: Swedenborg)

Mais les mages hagards, les sages inquiets,
Les noirs explorateurs des mystérieux faîtes,
Les contempteurs soudain transformés en prophètes,
Comment ont-ils été par l'être terrassés,
Comment ont-ils crié sous l'évidence: Assez!
Demande à l'ineffable, au gouffre, au phénomène!
Qui peut le raconter dans votre langue humaine?
Ils méditaient, sondant l'inconnu, regardant.
L'espace, ici fumée et là cratère ardent,
Le grand fond immobile et sourd, la violence
Des visions mêlée à l'éternel silence,
Rien et Tout, le roulis démesuré des cieux
Dans on ne sait quel vent lugubre et monstrueux,
Des tours d'ombre dont l'œil ne peut compter les marches,
Des déluges roulant d'inexprimables arches,
La pluie immense au loin rayant les infinis,
Des lueurs éclairant des masques d'Erynnis,
Des passages subits de méduses, frappées
D'une clarté pareille à des reflets d'épées,
Des ponts difformes, noirs, allant hors du réel,
Sinistres, bleuissant vaguement près du ciel,
Des tourbillons sans but, des profondeurs sans bornes;
Voilà ce que voyaient les contemplateurs mornes,
Et tristes, ils disaient:—Cette ombre n'est pas Dieu.—
Par moments des fléaux, sur des ailes de feu,
Survenaient, et faisaient, comme un esquif sans voiles,
Sombrer un monde au fond d'une écume d'étoiles,
La vague des chaos montait engloutissant
Quelque éden encor plein d'un sourire innocent,
Comme un groupe ennemi qui gronde et qui s'insulte,
Les éléments passaient avec un grand tumulte,
Tout croulait dans l'horreur où nul regard n'atteint,
Et rien ne vivait plus dans l'univers éteint;
Or, à l'heure où, devant ces sombres catastrophes,

But the distraught magi, the anxious sages,
The forlorn explorers of mysterious summits,
The despisers suddenly turned prophets,
How overwhelmed they were by existence,
How they shouted before the evidence: enough!
Ask the intangible, the abyss, the phenomenon!
Who can say it in your human tongue?
They meditated, staring, probing the unknown.
Space—here smoke and there burning crater—
The great motionless and mute foundation, the violence
Of visions mixed with eternal silence, nothing and
Everything, the measureless pitching of the heavens
In we know not what mournful and monstrous wind,
Towers of darkness with their countless steps,
Floods surging under unutterable arches,
The immense rain far off streaking the infinities,
Lights illuminating masks of Erynnes,
Sudden passings of Medusas, struck
By a brightness like the glintings of swords,
Formless, black bridges, stretched beyond reality,
Sinister, turning vaguely blue approaching the firmament,
Aimless whirlwinds, boundless deeps;
That is what the sad contemplators saw,
And sorrowful, they said:—This darkness is not God.—
At times, plagues, on wings of fire,
Arose, and caused a world, like a wherry without sails,
To sink to the bottom of a spume of stars,
The wave of chaoses soared, engulfing
Some Eden still beaming an innocent smile,
The elements passed with a great tumult
Like a hostile mass that mutters and scolds,
All collapsed into the horror that no glance reaches,
And nothing more lived in the extinct universe;
Now, when, before these somber catastrophes,

Voyants aveugles, saints tremblants, vains philosophes,
Ils crispaient dans le vide horrible leur poignet,
A l'heure où la stupeur du doute les gagnait,
Éperdus, ils voyaient subitement des astres
De confirmation poindre dans les désastres,
Ou sortir brusquement du nuage ébloui
Une foudre hurlant dans les gouffres:—C'est lui!—

Parmi les visions, parmi les paraboles,
Ils vont, ils vont, ils vont. Et ces sagesses folles
Cherchent Dieu, le front pâle et baigné de sueurs;
Et tout ce qu'on peut voir de farouches lueurs,
Tous les éclairs d'été d'une chaude soirée,
La trombe, tous les yeux d'une meute effarée,
Les passages subits d'astres dans la vapeur,
N'expriment pas l'effroi, le trouble, la stupeur,
De toutes ces raisons, de toutes ces pensées,
Dans cette poursuite âpre et terrible lancées.

L'ANGE.

Je commence par toi, Légion. Tu te trompes.

Légion dit qu'il faut rester dans le réel,
Et tendre au bien terrestre et ne pas tendre au ciel;
Légion veut que l'homme ait pour labeur unique
De mettre à son sépulcre une verte tunique,
De vêtir de moissons la terre, abîme obscur,
De bêcher le sillon sans regarder l'azur;
Légion, sur la fosse où voltige une flamme,
Voit éclore la fleur; j'y vois éclore l'âme.
Quoi! la vie est ton but! la terre est ton effort!
Qu'est-ce qu'un but ayant derrière lui la mort?
Ah! tu veux te refaire un Eden de matière!

Blind seers, trembling saints, vain philosophers
Clenched their fists in dreaded space,
When the bewilderment of doubt overwhelmed them,
Distraught, they suddenly saw stars
Of affirmation appear amidst the disasters,
Or abruptly emerge from the dazzled cloud,
A thunderbolt roaring in the pits:—It is he!—

Amongst the visions, amongst the parabolas,
They go, they go, they go. And these mad wisdoms
Seek God, their brows pale and bathed in sweat;
And all that one can see of wild lights,
All the flashes of summer lightning on a warm evening,
The whirlwind, all the eyes of a frightened pack,
The sudden passing of stars into the mist,
Do not express the fear, the confusion, the bewilderment,
Of all these reasons, all these thoughts,
Launched in this bitter and terrible pursuit.

THE ANGEL.

I begin with you, Legion. You are mistaken.

Legion says that one must remain within reality,
And direct oneself towards earth and not towards Heaven;
Legion wishes that Man's sole labor be
Placing at his tomb a green tunic,
Dressing the earth, the dark abyss, in harvests,
Digging the furrow without beholding the azure;
Legion discerns the flower opening above the pit
Where a flame flutters; I see there the soul opening.
What! Life is your purpose! The earth your endeavor!
What is a purpose having after it only death?
Ah! You wish to recover a tangible Eden!

Qu'est-ce qu'un paradis troué d'un cimetière?
Qu'est-ce qu'un bonheur doux, charmant, splendide et beau,
Ayant cette ouverture affreuse, le tombeau;
Ayant ce gouffre, ayant sur l'abîme une voie
D'infini, par où vient l'ombre et s'en va la joie!

Oui, cherche le bien-être! Après la Vérité!
Tu ne vois du devoir que le moindre côté.
Tu te trompes, esprit. Passons.

Du haut des cieux sereins dont les chastes azurs
Ne gardent que les saints, les justes et les purs,
Tous les esprits déchus qui deviennent matière
Neigent sur votre globe, horrible cimetière;
Ils y trouvent le sang, le squelette, les os,
Naissent, et l'on entend leurs cris dans les berceaux.
Car le spectre terrestre, affreux, pesant, funeste,
Est comme le flocon du fantôme céleste;
Le lourd être charnel naît de l'être aromal;
La chair est un glaçon; sous le vent froid du mal
La condensation de l'ange produit l'homme.

Je ne t'ai jusqu'ici parlé que de la terre;
Et je t'ai fait pâlir rien qu'avec ton mystère;
Mais que deviendrais-tu si j'entrais tout à coup,
Homme, dans le fermé, dans l'inconnu, dans tout!
Si je noyais ta soif de voir et de connaître,
Si je te jetais nu dans l'océan de l'être,
Si je te criais:—Viens! viens, puisque tu le veux!—
Et si je m'envolais te tenant aux cheveux,
Dans l'âpre vision qu'aucun songe n'invente,
Dans toute la nuée et toute l'épouvante!

What is a paradise pierced by a cemetery? What is a gentle,
Charming, magnificent and beautiful happiness having this
Strange opening, the grave; having this abyss, having above
The abyss an infinite passageway, through which
Arrives darkness, but through which departs joy!

Yes! Search for well-being! After the Truth!
You see of duty only the slightest side.
You are mistaken, spirit. Let us pass.

From the height of the serene heavens where chaste azures
Retain only the holy, the just, and the pure,
All the fallen spirits who become matter
Snow on your sphere, horrible cemetery;
There they discover blood, skeleton, bones,
Are born, and we hear their cries from the cradles.
Because the terrestrial, hideous, ponderous, disastrous specter,
Is like the flake of the celestial phantom;
The sluggish carnal being arises from the aromal being;
The flesh is an ice floe; beneath the cold wind of evil
The condensation of the angel produces Man.

Till now, I have spoken to you only of the earth;
And I have made you go pale merely with your mystery;
But Man, what would become of you if I were, of a
Sudden, to enter the forbidden, the unknown, everything!
If I flooded your thirst to see and know,
If I cast you, naked, into the ocean of Existence,
If I shouted to you:—Come! Come, since you wish it!—
And if I flew off, dragging you by the hair,
Into the bitter vision that no dream invents,
Into the very fullness of the cloud-mass and the terror!

PAROLES DE L'ARCHANGE.

. . . .
Une étoile est un astre entouré d'autres astres,
Terres, lunes, Vénus, Saturnes, Jupiters;
Tout cela tourne au fond des sublimes éthers;
Et ces mondes portés par rien jamais ne croulent;
Et la rapidité des planètes qui roulent
Dans l'empyrée autour de leur centre vermeil,
Est telle que pour Dieu rêveur, chaque soleil
Semble avoir des colliers de perles lumineuses...

APRÈS LA MORT.

Je vis là les docteurs du gouffre, les voyants,
Les immenses songeurs aux sourcils flamboyants,
Les fauves inspirés, les orageux prophètes,
Qui ne changent jamais de place, dont les têtes
Rêvent, et qui, penchés sur l'infini sans bords,
Font encore à présent ce qu'ils faisaient alors.
Un crépuscule affreux jette des reflets louches
Sur leur maigreur livide et leurs barbes farouches;
Des suaires de brume et d'astres font des plis
Sur leurs fronts, de pensée et de lueur remplis;
On voit à nu leurs os, leurs côtes, leurs vertèbres;
Engloutis dans la vue étrange des ténèbres,
Ils ont l'immensité lugubre au-dessous d'eux,
Et la tragique horreur des mystères hideux.
Leur contemplation de l'être est si profonde
Que ces hommes, plus grands que l'ombre et que le monde,
En sont venus, puisant presque à l'éternité,
A s'emplir de prodige et de divinité.
Ils sont devenus dieux à force d'être prêtres.
Avec des plumes d'aigle ou de griffon, ces êtres
Traçaient, à la clarté d'un jour qui s'amoindrit,

WORDS OF THE ARCHANGEL.

. . . .

A star is a celestial body surrounded by other celestial bodies,
Earths, moons, Venuses, Saturns, Jupiters;
The whole system turns at the heart of the sublime æthers;
And these worlds, brought forth by nothing, never collapse;
And the speed at which each planet revolves
About its ruby axis in the Empyrean,
Is such that for God, musing, every sun
Seems bestrewn with luminous necklaces of pearl...

AFTER DEATH.

There I saw the doctors of the abyss, the seers,
The immense thinkers with blazing eyebrows,
The inspired wild ones, stormy prophets,
Who never move, whose heads are full of
Dream, and who, leaning o'er the boundless infinite,
Still do now what they did then.
A hideous twilight casts dark reflections
Upon their pale thinness and their savage beards;
Shrouds of mist and stars create, upon their brows,
Wrinkles brimming with thought and starlight;
We see their bare bones, ribs, their vertebrae;
Engulfed within the strange sight of darkness,
They have the lugubrious vastness below them,
And the tragic horror of hideous mysteries.
Their contemplation of existence is so profound
That these men, greater than the darkness and the world,
Came from there, nearly drawing on eternity,
To become full of miracle and divinity.
They became deities because they were priests.
With plumes of an eagle or griffin, these beings
Drew, in the diminishing daylight,

En frissonnant d'eux-mêmes et de leur propre esprit,
Des caractères noirs sur d'horribles registres;
Le vent triste soufflait dans les feuilles sinistres,
Si bien que, par moments, ces mages dont l'œil luit,
Mécontents, regardaient l'ouragan dans la nuit.
Oh, comme avec terreur, le spectre et moi, nous lûmes
Les choses qu'écrivaient ces redoutables plumes!
Une race mourait, ou, sur quelque sommet,
Un soleil s'éteignait, un volcan s'allumait,
Un fléau frémissant sortait de la nature,
Chaque fois que leur main faisait une rature.

DÉNOUEMENT.

Alors, sur le sommet du monde, l'ange et moi,
Silencieux, nous nous assîmes.
Nous voyions sous nos pieds, forêts, cités, châteaux,
L'Atlas, le Sinaï, le Caucase, l'Athos,
Et le Liban, groupe de cimes.

... Et comme je songeais,
Éperdu, me sentant devenir presque horrible,
Je vis paraître et fuir un tourbillon terrible,
Plus rouge qu'un soleil d'automne à son déclin,
Rugissant, traversé de mille éclairs, et plein
De bouches d'aquilon qui soufflaient de la neige.
—O prophète! est-ce toi qui passes, m'écriai-je?
Est-ce toi qui dans l'ombre affreuse t'engloutis?
Est-ce toi, charpentier du gouffre qui bâtis
Et clouas ce grand char des routes inconnues,
Bondissant sur la terre et volant dans les nues,
Et qui, pour le traîner dans l'abîme, attelas
Les aigles du Liban aux lions de l'Atlas?

While shuddering from themselves and their own spirit,
Black letters on horrible registers;
The mournful wind blew within these sinister pages,
So that, at times, these vexed Mages with
Gleaming eyes spied the hurricane in the night.
Oh, terrified, the specter and I read
The things that these frightening pens wrote!
A race vanished, or, on some summit,
A sun died out, a volcano erupted,
A quivering plague emerged from out nature,
Each time their hand made an erasure.

DENOUEMENT.

Then, the angel and I sat, silent, on the top of
        The world, and
We saw below our feet, forests, cities, castles,
Atlas, the Sinai, the Caucasus, Athos,
        And Lebanon, a range of summits.

...And as I dreamt,
Distraught, sensing myself becoming well-nigh monstrous,
I saw appear and flee a terrible whirlwind,
More red than an autumn sun sinking, howling,
Pierced by a thousand flashes of lightning, and replete
With mouths of the North Wind blowing snow.
O prophet! Is it you who passes? I exclaimed,
Is it you, gobbled up by this hideous darkness?
Is it you, carpenter of the abyss who built and
Nailed together this great chariot of the unknown byways,
Springing upon the earth and soaring into the clouds,
And who, in order to draw it into the abyss, harnessed
The eagles of Lebanon to the lions of Atlas?

Tu regardes le ciel, l'être, l'éternité,
Et tu ne comprends pas, et tu dis, dépité:
—La lumière ici bas manque, et c'est Dieu qui l'ôte.
Dieu veut n'être pas vu par l'homme.—Est-ce la faute
De l'océan s'il est trop grand pour le nocher?
Dis, crois-tu que Dieu prend la peine de cacher
Dans les immensités sa gloire et sa puissance?
Crois-tu que l'univers est une réticence?
C'est à toi d'en trouver le sens, si tu le peux.

Et j'ai dit à l'esprit:—Crois-tu donc que je crains
La flamme qui pâlit devant les fronts sereins,
L'océan effaré, pauvre bête hagarde?
Ou l'éclair qui s'enfuit sitôt qu'on le regarde,
Ou l'écueil qui se cache au milieu des roseaux?
Ou que je crains les vents, cette troupe d'oiseaux?
Ou que je crains la vague, ou que je crains l'écume?
Ou que je crains la nuit, spectre assis dans la brume,
Mêlant dans son néant l'être, le temps, le lieu?
Ou que je crains la mort pâle? Non, je crains Dieu.
Je crois en lui. Croyant, je le cherche.

Alors je dis:—Visage impassible et glacé,
Qui jettes tant d'horreur sur mon front hérissé,
Qu'es-tu, toi dont l'haleine effrayante m'effleure?
N'es-tu, comme celui qui parlait tout à l'heure
Dans cette redoutable et pâle région,
Qu'une des sombres voix de l'esprit Légion?
Es-tu distinct de lui dans ce vague royaume?—

Il me répondit:—Tout est le même fantôme.—

You look at heaven, existence, eternity,
And you do not understand. Offended, you say
—Light down here is missing, and it is God who removes it.
God wishes not to be seen by Man.—Is it the fault
Of the ocean if it be too vast for the mariner?
Tell me, do you believe that God takes pains to hide
His glory and power in the unlimitedness?
Do you believe the universe a reticence?
It is for you to discover its meaning, if you can.

And I said to the spirit:—You believe, thus, that I fear
The flame that fades before the serene brows,
The fearful sea, poor distraught beast?
Or the lightning bolt that flees as soon as it is glimpsed,
Or the reef that hides amidst the reeds?
Or that I fear the winds, this flock of birds?
Or that I am afraid of the wave, or of the spume?
That I fear the night, that specter seated in the mist,
Stirring into his nothingness, existence, time, place?
Or that I am afraid of pale death? No, I am afraid of God.
I believe in him. Believing, I seek him.

Then I said:—Impassive and ice-cold visage,
Who casts so much horror on my bristly brow,
Who are you, you whose terrible breath touches me?
Aren't you, like the one who spoke just now
In this deadly and pale region,
One of the somber voices of the spirit Legion?
Are you separate from him in this vague kingdom?—

He answered me:—Everything is the same phantom.—

Et je repris:—Qu'es-tu? réponds! suis-je vivant?
Ne m'abandonne pas dans ce désert du vent.
Qu'es-tu? parle! je tremble à ton souffle tranquille—

Et le spectre me dit:—Je demeure à la ville
Éternité, maison Ténèbres, porte Nuit.—

(...Mais je te quitte, dit l'esprit.)

...Voici l'aube. C'est l'heure
Des vagues chants du coq dans le lointain décrus,
Et de l'effacement des spectres disparus,
Remportés dans l'obscur, repris par l'ombre épaisse
Ainsi que des poissons par une mer qui baisse,
Et fuyant pêle-mêle à travers les plis noirs
Que la nuit sombre prête aux matins comme aux soirs.

Je sentis une main qu'on posait sur ma bouche,
Et je fus emporté dans la brume farouche.

. . . .
Il me dit:—Dans ce temple où vit l'être très haut,
Ne crains rien, tu seras prêtre un jour; mais il faut
Que la porte, ô vivant, te soit d'abord ouverte.
—Quand?—lui dis-je.—L'esprit baissa sa palme verte
Et répondit:—Plus tard.—Et je criai:—Rayon,
Oh! dis-moi seulement la première action
Qu'il faut faire ici-bas pour que la porte s'ouvre.—
Alors, comme au matin l'horizon se découvre,
Il me montra du doigt l'orient qui rougit,
Et j'y lus ces deux mots dans la clarté: CI-GÎT.

And I began anew:—Who are you? Answer! Am I alive?
Do not abandon me in this desert of the wind.
Who are you? Speak! I tremble at your quiet breath.—

And the specter said to me:—I live in the city,
Eternity, within the house, Darkness, through the entryway, Night.—

(...But I am leaving you, says the spirit.)

...Here is the dawn. It is the hour when the
Indistinct songs of the cock fade away in the distance,
And when the vanishing specters disappear,
Borne off into the dark, retrieved by the dense shadow
Just as are fish by an ebbing tide,
And fleeing pell-mell through the black folds
That melancholy night imparts to the mornings as to the evenings.

I felt a hand placed upon my mouth,
And I was taken into the savage mist.

. . . .
He says to me:—In this temple where dwells the Most High,
Be afraid of nothing, you shall be a priest one day; but it is
Necessary that the door, O living one, be first opened to you.
—When?—I said to him.—The spirit lowered his green palm
And answered:—Later.—and I cried:—Ray of light,
Oh! Tell me only what I must first do
Down here, that the portal may open.—
Then, just as in the morning the horizon is revealed,
He pointed out to me the East which was growing crimson,
And I read there these two words in the light: HERE LIES.

L'ange montra du doigt le ciel, et je vis Dieu.

L'ESPRIT NOIR.

Tous les sages sont morts. Iras-tu les rejoindre
Dans le gouffre où l'on voit le crépuscule poindre?
Qu'oseras-tu leur dire? Est-ce que tu connais
Pythagore, Bouddha, Confucius, Manès?
Pourras-tu pénétrer à des profondeurs telles
Que tu verras passer ces ombres immortelles,
Des fleurs de l'idéal exhalant le parfum,
Et que tu leur pourras demander à chacun
Ce qu'il sait de l'abîme et ce qu'il sait de l'être,
Si Dieu vit, si l'on meurt pour mourir ou pour naître
Et si c'est de la nuit ou de l'aube qu'ils ont
Mêlée à la lueur étrange de leur front?

*

Que savez-vous de l'être et de ses facultés,
Et des forces qui sont de sombres volontés?
...Vous ne comprenez pas ce que fait la nature;
Vous ne comprenez pas ces bruits mystérieux
Qui grondent sous la terre ou flottent dans les cieux;
La mer mordant l'esquif comme un loup la gazelle;
Pourquoi l'ouragan court, pourquoi le mont ruisselle;
Ce que le flot poursuit, ce que l'écueil attend;
Vous ne devinez rien dans cette ombre; et pourtant
Vous avez sous vos yeux, sous vos pieds, sur vos têtes,
Ces égoïsmes noirs des vents et des tempêtes.

The angel pointed to Heaven, and I saw God.

THE BLACK SPIRIT.

All the sages have died. Will you go to join them
In the abyss where we see the dawn breaking?
What will you dare say to them? Do you know
Pythagoras, Buddha, Confucius, Manes?
Can you penetrate the depths such that
You will see, crossing, these immortal shades,
Flowers of the ideal exhaling perfume,
And so that you may ask of each what he knows
Of the abyss and what he knows of existence,
If God lives, if we die just to die, or to be reborn,
Or whether it be night or dawn that has merged
With the strange light emanating from their brows?

*

What do you know of existence and of its powers,
And of the forces that are somber wills?
...You do not understand what nature creates;
You do not understand these mysterious sounds
Muttered under the earth or floating in the heavens;
The sea biting the skiff as does a wolf the gazelle;
Why the hurricane roams, why the mountain streams;
What the flood pursues, what the reef awaits;
You guess nothing in this darkness; and nevertheless
You have beneath your eyes, beneath your feet, upon your heads,
These black egoisms of winds and tempests.

L'ENFER.—SATAN.

. . . .

—Ah! Ta religion veut un souffre-douleurs?
Il te faut un Satan? Eh bien, soit. Je l'accepte.
Le mal est un principe et l'enfer un précepte;
Satan va résumer dans son être fatal
Tout ce qu'on peut garder de divin dans le mal;
Maintenant, pour punir ce brigand de ton rêve,
Faut-il que l'univers soit ta place de Grève?
Te plaît-il d'employer les cieux éblouissants
A l'exécution du monstre? J'y consens;
Et l'expiation sera si grandiose
Que l'échafaud aura l'air d'une apothéose.
On entendra hurler d'effroi les éléments;
Pour la répandre au fond des mornes firmaments,
L'ombre, avec tout l'espace et toute la durée,
Fera je ne sais quelle horreur démesurée;
La torture sans fin du coupable infini
S'emparera; l'éclair mordra le grand puni;
Le jour, ange indigné, vaincra l'incendiaire;
Dieu fera châtier Satan par la lumière;
Au delà des chaos où parfois nous fuyons,
On ira le saisir dans l'enfer; les rayons
De l'aurore seront les barres de fer rouge
Dont on lui brisera les membres dans ce bouge;
On l'exposera nu sur les azurs vermeils;
La grande Ourse des nuits, faite de sept soleils,
Traînera le mourant éternel sur des claies
D'astres dont les clous d'or déchireront ses plaies;
Les constellations l'une après l'autre auront
L'une un peu de son flanc, l'autre un peu de son front;
Des morceaux de sa chair pendront aux sacrés voiles;
Les gouttes de son sang tacheront les étoiles;
Et de ce grand supplice où, criant: Anankè!

HELL. — SATAN.

. . . .

—Ah! Your religion desires a scapegoat?
You need a Satan? Well, so be it. I accept.
Evil is a principle and Hell a precept;
Satan shall encapsule in his fateful being
All that one can maintain of the divine in evil;
Now, in order to punish this brigand of your dream,
The universe has to be your Place de Grève?
It pleases you to use the garish heavens
In the execution of this monster? I consent;
And the atonement of sin shall be so imposing
That the scaffold will appear an apotheosis.
One will hear the elements roar with dismay;
In order to spread it to the heart of the sad firmaments,
The darkness shall create I know not what measureless
Horror out of all space and time;
Endless torture shall possess itself of shameful infinity;
Lightning shall bite the great punished one;
Day, the indignant angel, shall defeat the arsonist;
God shall have Satan punished by the light;
Beyond the chaoses where sometimes we flee,
You shall seize him in Hell; light beams
Of the dawn shall be the bars of red iron
With which you shall break his limbs in this hovel;
You shall expose him naked above ruby azures;
The Great Bear of the nights, made of seven suns,
Shall drag the eternal dying one athwart execution machines
Of stars whose golden points shall tear his wounds;
One constellation shall have a piece from his side,
Another a piece from his brow;
Scraps of his flesh shall hang from the sacred veils;
Drops of his blood shall stain the stars;
And of this great torture where, shouting: Anagke!

Il râlera, laissant de son corps disloqué
Tomber l'ombre, le sang, la douleur et la boue,
Le zodiaque énorme et noir sera la roue!

L'ENFER.

Au plus bas de la fosse aveugle où tout est noir
Le châtiment habite avec le désespoir;
Là pèse l'ombre, inerte, opaque, indivisible.

Sous l'implacable Dieu gît l'enfer impassible.
La géhenne subit en silence son deuil;
L'enfer, ce mort vivant, accepte le cercueil;
Jamais il ne se plaint, ce regardeur terrible
Du dedans de l'abîme et de la nuit horrible;
Ce voyant du néant, ce noir témoin puni
Du vide impénétrable et du rien infini,
Jamais il ne gémit, jamais il ne réclame.
Tu t'étonnes, tu dis:—Quoi! souffrir l'ombre infâme
Sans un cri! quoi! toujours! hier, aujourd'hui, demain!—
T'imagines-tu donc la nuit tendant la main,
Frémissant sous la brume éternelle qui rampe,
Espérant une grâce, implorant une lampe?
Te figures-tu donc la malédiction
Demandant à l'horreur l'aumône d'un rayon,
Pleurant le jour au fond des ténèbres suprêmes?
Crois-tu donc que l'enfer, enviant aux cieux blêmes
La lueur qui s'allume et s'éteint devant eux,
Espèce de bon pauvre et d'indigent honteux,
Tâche d'attendrir Dieu, l'avare de l'aurore,
Et mendie une étoile ou gueuse un météore?
Non! jamais de clarté! non! jamais de sursis!
Le mal rayonne mieux dans des yeux obscurcis;
Tout ce qui veut rester mauvais, doit rester sombre,
Songeur, et le regard de la haine est fait d'ombre.

He shall emit the death rattle, letting fall from his broken
Body the darkness, the blood, the pain and the filth,
The enormous and black zodiac shall be the breaking wheel!

HELL.

At the lowest point of the blind pit where all is black,
Punishment resides alongside despair;
There darkness weighs heavy, sluggish, opaque, inseparable.

Beneath merciless God lies impassive Hell.
The Gehenna silently suffers its mourning;
Hell, this living death, accepts the coffin;
Never does it complain, this terrible watcher
From inside the abyss and within peccant night;
This seer of nothingness, this black, punished witness
Of impenetrable space and infinite nullity,
Never does it moan, never does it lament.
You are astonished; you say:—What! to suffer vile darkness
Without a cry! What! Always! Yesterday, today, tomorrow!—
You thus imagine yourself at night extending your hand,
Shivering under the eternal, lingering mist,
Hoping for mercy, imploring a lamp?
You thus imagine malediction
Beseeching horror for the charity of a ray of light,
Weeping for daylight at the heart of supreme darkness?
You thus believe Hell a kind of virtuous and proud indigent,
Envying the light that kindles and burns
Out before the pallid heavens,
Trying to move God, the miser of the dawn, to pity,
Begging for a star or pleading for a meteor?
No! Never light! No! Never a reprieve!
Evil shines better in darkened eyes;
All that wishes to remain bad, must remain dismal,
Dreamer, and the glance of hatred consists of darkness.

Victor Hugo, *Ma destinée* (My Fate), detail,
1857, Musée Maison de Victor Hugo

from

THE END OF SATAN

---

from

LA FIN DE SATAN

Hors de la terre I

ET NOX FACTA EST

I

Depuis quatre mille ans il tombait dans l'abîme.

Il n'avait pas encor pu saisir une cime,
Ni lever une fois son front démesuré.
Il s'enfonçait dans l'ombre et la brume, effaré,
Seul, et derrière lui, dans les nuits éternelles,
Tombaient plus lentement les plumes de ses ailes.
Il tombait foudroyé, morne, silencieux,
Triste, la bouche ouverte et les pieds vers les cieux,
L'horreur du gouffre empreinte à sa face livide.
Il cria:—mort!—les poings tendus vers l'ombre vide.
Ce mot plus tard fut homme et s'appela Caïn.
Il tombait. Tout à coup un roc heurta sa main;
Il l'étreignit, ainsi qu'un mort étreint sa tombe,
Et s'arrêta.

Beyond the Earth I

AND THEN THERE WAS NIGHT

I

For four thousand years he was falling into the abyss.

He had not yet been able to seize an outcropping,
Nor once raise his massive brow.
He plunged into the darkness and mist, frightened,
Alone; and behind him, into the eternal nights,
Fell more slowly the feathers of his wings.
He plummeted, thunderstruck, full of gloom, silent,
And mournful, his mouth open and his feet towards the
Heavens, the horror of the gulf imprinted on his livid face.
He cried:—Death!—his fists outstretched toward the empty
Darkness. This word later became 'Man' and was named Cain.
He was falling. Suddenly a rock struck his hand;
He held to it, as a dead man embraces his tomb,
And stopped.

Quelqu'un, d'en haut, lui cria:—tombe!
Les soleils s'éteindront autour de toi, maudit!—
Et la voix dans l'horreur immense se perdit.
Et, pâle, il regarda vers l'éternelle aurore.
Les soleils étaient loin, mais ils brillaient encore.
Satan dressa la tête et dit, levant ses bras:
—Tu mens!—Ce mot plus tard fut l'âme de Judas.
Pareil aux dieux d'airain debout sur leurs pilastres,
Il attendit mille ans, l'œil fixé sur les astres.
Les soleils étaient loin, mais ils brillaient toujours.
La foudre alors gronda dans les cieux froids et sourds.
Satan rit, et cracha du côté du tonnerre.
L'immensité qu'emplit l'ombre visionnaire,
Frissonna. Ce crachat fut plus tard Barabbas.
Un souffle qui passait le fit tomber plus bas.

II

La chute du damné recommença.—Terrible,
Sombre, et percé de trous lumineux comme un crible,
Le ciel plein de soleils s'éloignait, la clarté
Tremblait, et dans la nuit le grand précipité,
Nu, sinistre, et tiré par le poids de son crime,
Tombait, et, comme un coin, sa tête ouvrait l'abîme.
Plus bas! plus bas! toujours plus bas! Tout à présent
Le fuyait; pas d'obstacle à saisir en passant,
Pas un mont, pas un roc croulant, pas une pierre,
Rien, l'ombre, et d'épouvante il ferma sa paupière.
Quand il rouvrit les yeux, trois soleils seulement
Brillaient, et l'ombre avait rongé le firmament.
Tous les autres soleils étaient morts.

Someone, from on high, cried out to him:—Fall!
The suns will die out around you, accursed one.—
And the voice was lost in the immense horror.
And, turning pale, he looked toward the eternal dawn.
The suns were distant, but shone still.
Satan lifted his head and said, raising his arms:
—Liar!—This word later became the soul of Judas.
Like bronze gods upright upon their pilasters,
He waited a thousand years, his eyes fixed upon the stars.
The suns were distant, but were shining as ever.
A thunderbolt then roared in the cold and voiceless heavens.
Satan laughed, and spat at the thunder.
The cosmos, filled by the visionary darkness,
Shuddered. This spittle later became Barabbas.
Then, a passing wind made him fall further.

II

The fall of the damned one began once again—Terrifying,
Overcast, and pierced with luminous holes like a sieve,
The sky full of suns vanished, the light
Trembled, and into the night this giant plummeted headlong,
Naked, sinister, and dragged down by the weight of his crime;
And like a wedge, his head opened the abyss.
Lower! Lower! Ever lower! All, at his approach,
Fled him; no obstacle could he seize in passing,
Neither a mountain, nor a crumbling rock, nor a stone,
Nothing but darkness. Terrified, he closed his eyes.
When he reopened them, only three suns
Shone, and the darkness had eroded the firmament.
All the other suns were dead.

III

Une roche
Sortait du noir brouillard comme un bras qui s'approche.
Il la prit, et ses pieds touchèrent des sommets.

Alors l'être effrayant qui s'appelle Jamais
Songea. Son front tomba dans ses mains criminelles.
Les trois soleils, de loin, ainsi que trois prunelles,
Le regardaient, et lui ne les regardait pas.
L'espace ressemblait aux plaines d'ici-bas,
Le soir, quand l'horizon qui tressaille et recule,
Noircit sous les yeux blancs du spectre crépuscule.
De longs rayons rampaient aux pieds du grand banni.
Derrière lui son ombre emplissait l'infini.
Les cimes du chaos se confondaient entre elles.
Tout à coup il se vit pousser d'horribles ailes;
Il se vit devenir monstre, et que l'ange en lui
Mourait, et le rebelle en sentit quelque ennui.
Il laissa son épaule, autrefois lumineuse,
Frémir au froid hideux de l'aile membraneuse,
Et croisant ses deux bras, et relevant son front,
Ce bandit, comme s'il grandissait sous l'affront,
Seul dans ces profondeurs que la ruine encombre,
Regarda fixement la caverne de l'ombre.
Les ténèbres sans bruit croissaient dans le néant.
L'opaque obscurité fermait le ciel béant;
Et, faisant, au-delà du dernier promontoire,
Une triple fêlure à cette vitre noire,
Les trois soleils mêlaient leurs trois rayonnements.
Après quelque combat dans les hauts firmaments,
D'un char de feu brisé l'on eût dit les trois roues.
Les monts hors du brouillard sortaient comme des proues.
—Eh bien, cria Satan, soit! je puis encor voir!
Il aura le ciel bleu, moi j'aurai le ciel noir.
Croit-il pas que j'irai sangloter à sa porte?

III

A rock
Emerged from the black fog, like an arm drawing near.
He took hold, and alighted on the mountain peaks.

Then the dreadful Being, who is called Never,
Began to think, lowering his brow to his criminal hands.
Like three eyes, the three suns watched him from afar;
But he did not return their gaze.
Space resembled the plains on earth in the evening,
When the horizon that sinks and recedes
Darkens under the white eyes of the spectral twilight.
Long beams crawled to the feet of this great exile.
Behind him, his shadow filled the infinite.
The summits of chaos merged.
Suddenly he found himself sprouting horrible wings;
He saw himself becoming a monster, the angel in him
Dying, as the rebel in him felt growing trepidation.
He let his shoulder, once luminous,
Tremble with the hideous cold of the membranous wing,
And crossing his arms and raising his head,
This outlaw, as if growing taller in the face of this insult,
Alone in these depths congested by his ruin,
Looked fixedly at the cavern of darkness.
The gloom began to slowly spread in this nothingness.
The opaque shadow closed the gaping sky;
And, beyond the last headland,
The three suns merged their radiances,
Making a threefold fissure in this dark window.
It appeared to be the three wheels of a chariot of fire
Shattered after some battle in the high firmaments.
And the mountains emerged from the fog like the prows of ships.
—Very well, shouted Satan, so be it! I can still see!
He shall have the blue sky, and I, myself, the black.
Does he believe I shall go weeping to his gate?

Je le hais. Trois soleils suffisent. Que m'importe!
Je hais le jour, l'azur, le rayon, le parfum!—

Soudain il tressaillit; il n'en restait plus qu'un.

IV

L'abîme s'effaçait. Rien n'avait plus de forme.
L'obscurité semblait gonfler sa vague énorme.
C'était on ne sait quoi de submergé; c'était
Ce qui n'est plus, ce qui s'en va, ce qui se tait;
Et l'on n'aurait pu dire, en cette horreur profonde,
Si ce reste effrayant d'un mystère ou d'un monde,
Pareil au brouillard vague où le songe s'enfuit,
S'appelait le Naufrage ou s'appelait la Nuit;
Et l'archange sentit qu'il devenait fantôme.
Il dit:— Enfer!—Ce mot plus tard créa Sodome.

Et la voix répéta lentement sur son front:
—Maudit! autour de toi les astres s'éteindront.—

Et déjà le soleil n'était plus qu'une étoile.

V

Et tout disparaissait par degrés sous un voile.
L'archange alors frémit; Satan eut le frisson.
Vers l'astre qui tremblait, livide, à l'horizon,
Il s'élança, sautant d'un faîte à l'autre faîte.
Puis, quoiqu'il eût horreur des ailes de la bête,
Quoique ce fût pour lui l'habit de la prison,
Comme un oiseau qui va de buisson en buisson,
Hideux, il prit son vol de montagne en montagne,
Et ce forçat se mit à courir dans ce bagne.

I despise him. Three suns, that is enough. What does it matter to
Me! I hate the day, the azure, the sunlight, the perfume!—

Suddenly he gave a start, for now there remained but one sun.

IV

The abyss was becoming obliterated. There were no more forms.
The obscurity seemed to expand in an enormous wave,
Creating a vague feeling of being submerged. It became
That which is no longer, that which disappears, becomes hidden;
And one could not have said, in this deep horror,
Whether this was the frightening vestige of a mystery or of a
World, like a hazy fog where the dream flees,
Or whether it called itself Shipwreck or Night;
And the archangel felt that he was becoming a phantom.
He said:—Hell!—This word later created Sodom.

And the voice from above slowly repeated:
—Accursed one! Around you the suns shall die out.—

And already the sun was nothing but a star.

V

And everything was slowly disappearing under a veil.
The archangel became faint-hearted; Satan shuddered.
He sprang towards the star that flickered, pale, on the horizon,
Leaping from one peak to another.
Then, though he detested these bestial wings,
Which were for him the dress of prison,
Just as a bird flies from bush to bush,
So this wretched convict took wing from mountain to mountain,
And began to hasten towards this punition.

Il courait, il volait, il criait:—Astre d'or!
Frère! attends-moi! j'accours! ne t'éteins pas encor!
Ne me laisse pas seul!—

Le monstre de la sorte
Franchit les premiers lacs de l'immensité morte,
D'anciens chaos vidés qui croupissant déjà,
Et dans les profondeurs lugubres se plongea.

L'étoile maintenant n'était qu'une étincelle.

Il entra plus avant dans l'ombre universelle,
S'enfonça, se jeta, se rua dans la nuit,
Gravit les monts fangeux dont le front mouillé luit,
Et dont la base au fond des cloaques chancelle,
Et, triste, regarda devant lui.

L'étincelle
N'était plus qu'un point rouge au fond du gouffre obscur.

VI

Comme entre deux créneaux se penche sur le mur
L'archer qu'en son donjon le crépuscule gagne,
Farouche, il se pencha du haut de la montagne,
Et sur l'astre, espérant le faire étinceler,
Comme sur une braise il se mit à souffler,
Et l'angoisse gonfla sa féroce narine.
Le souffle qui sortit alors de sa poitrine
Est aujourd'hui sur terre et s'appelle ouragan.
A ce souffle, un grand bruit troubla l'ombre, océan
Qu'aucun être n'habite et qu'aucuns feux n'éclairent,
Les monts qui se trouvaient près de là s'envolèrent,
Le chaos monstrueux plein d'effroi se leva
Et se mit à hurler: Jéhova! Jéhova!
L'infini s'entr'ouvrit, fendu comme une toile,

He ran, he flew, he cried out:—Golden star!
Brother! Wait for me! I am coming! Do not die out yet!
Do not leave me alone!—

Thus did the monster
Clear the first lakes of this dead vastness,
This ancient, empty chaos, already stagnating,
And plunge into the dismal depths.

The star was now but a spark.

He entered further into the all-embracing darkness,
Was thrust, thrown, hurled into the night,
Scaled the miry mountain whose moist crest glistened,
And whose base swayed in the depths of cesspools,
And looked before him, mournful.

The spark
Was no more than a red speck at the bottom of the dark gulf.

VI

Just as twilight overtakes the archer in his turret,
Stooped over the wall between two battlements,
So does Satan bend over from the height of the mountain,
And begin to savagely blow on the star,
As on embers, hoping to make it gleam,
His fierce nostrils flaring with the agonized effort.
The breath which came from his lungs
Dwells on Earth today and is called Hurricane.
At this gust of wind, a great uproar disturbed the darkness,
That ocean which no Being inhabits and which no fire illuminates;
The nearby mountains fled,
And monstrous, fearful Chaos rose up
And began to howl: Jehovah! Jehovah!
The infinite half-opened, rent like a fabric,

Mais rien ne remua dans la lugubre étoile;
Et le damné criant:—Ne t'éteins pas! j'irai!
J'arriverai!—reprit son vol désespéré.

Et les glaciers mêlés aux nuits qui leur ressemblent
Se renversaient ainsi que des bêtes qui tremblent,
Et les noirs tourbillons et les gouffres hideux
Se courbaient éperdus pendant qu'au-dessus d'eux,
Volant vers l'astre ainsi qu'une flèche à la cible,
Passait, fauve et hagard, ce suppliant terrible.
Et depuis qu'il a vu ce passage effrayant,
L'âpre abîme, effaré comme un homme fuyant,
Garde à jamais un air d'horreur et de démence,
Tant ce fut monstrueux de voir, dans l'ombre immense,
Voler, ouvrant son aile affreuse loin du ciel,
Cette chauve-souris du cachot éternel!

VII

Il vola dix mille ans. Pendant dix mille années,
Tendant son cou livide et ses mains forcenées,
Il vola sans trouver un faîte où se poser.
L'astre parfois semblait s'éteindre et s'éclipser,
Et l'horreur du tombeau faisait frissonner l'ange;
Puis une clarté, pâle, obscure, vague, étrange,
Reparaissait: et lui, joyeux, disait: Allons.
Autour de lui planaient les oiseaux aquilons.
Il volait. L'infini sans cesse recommence.
Son vol dans cette mer faisait un cercle immense.
La nuit regardait fuir ses horribles talons.
Comme un nuage sent tomber ses tourbillons,
Il sentait s'écrouler ses forces dans le gouffre.
L'hiver murmurait: tremble! et l'ombre disait: souffre!
Enfin il aperçut au loin un noir sommet
Que dans l'ombre un reflet formidable enflammait.
Satan, comme un nageur fait un effort suprême,

But nothing stirred in the mournful star;
And the accursed one, crying:—Do not go out! I am coming!
I shall arrive!—resumed his desperate flight.

And the glaciers, mingling with the nights that resemble them,
Turned belly-up like frightened beasts,
And the dark whirlwinds and the hideous chasms
Recoiled in terror, while above them,
Flying towards the star as an arrow towards its target,
Passed, rageful and gaunt, this terrible supplicant.
And ever since it saw this frightful flight,
This bitter, unfathomable gulf, frightened like a fleeing man,
Keeps forever an air of horror and madness,
So dreadful was it to see fly, in the immense darkness,
Opening its hideous wings far from the sky,
This bat of the eternal dungeon!

VII

He flew for ten thousand years. For ten thousand years,
Straining his ghastly neck and his frenzied hands,
He flew without finding a height on which to rest.
At times the star appeared to die out and be eclipsed,
And the horror of the tomb would make the angel shudder;
Then a pale, dark light would reappear, vague and obscure,
And, joyous, he would say: I must hurry!
Around him soared the birds of the north wind.
With hardly a pause, the infinite one renewed his efforts afresh.
His flight into this sea described an immense circle.
The night watched flee his horrible talons; and
As a cloud feels its eddies subside,
He felt his strength desert him in the abyss.
Winter murmured: Tremble! and the darkness said: Suffer!
Finally he saw, in the distance, a black summit
Casting a great light into the darkness.
Satan, like a swimmer making a supreme effort,

Tendit son aile onglée et chauve, et, spectre blême,
Haletant, brisé, las, et, de sueur fumant,
Il s'abattit au bord de l'âpre escarpement.

VIII

Le soleil était là qui mourait dans l'abîme.

L'astre, au fond du brouillard, sans vent qui le ranime,
Se refroidissait, morne et lentement détruit.
On voyait sa rondeur sinistre dans la nuit;
Et l'on voyait décroître, en ce silence sombre,
Ses ulcères de feu sous une lèpre d'ombre.
Charbon d'un monde éteint! flambeau soufflé par Dieu!
Ses crevasses montraient encore un peu de feu
Comme si par les trous du crâne on eût vu l'âme.
Au centre palpitait et rampait une flamme
Qui par instants léchait les bords extérieurs,
Et de chaque cratère il sortait des lueurs
Qui frissonnaient ainsi que de flamboyants glaives,
Et s'évanouissaient sans bruit comme des rêves.
L'astre était presque noir. L'archange était si las
Qu'il n'avait plus de voix et plus de souffle, hélas!
Et l'astre agonisait sous ses regards farouches.
Il mourait, il luttait. Avec ses sombres bouches
Dans l'obscurité froide il lançait par moments
Des flots ardents, des blocs rougis, des monts fumants,
Des rocs tout écumants de sa clarté première:
Comme si ce géant de vie et de lumière,
Englouti par la brume où tout s'évanouit,
N'eût pas voulu mourir sans insulter la nuit
Et sans cracher sa lave à la face de l'ombre.
Autour de lui le temps et l'espace et le nombre
Et la forme et le bruit expiraient, en créant
L'unité formidable et noire du néant.
Le spectre Rien levait sa tête hors du gouffre.

Stretched his bare, taloned wings, and, pale ghost,
Breathless, broken, spent, and, steaming sweat,
Fell to the edge of the rugged scarp.

VIII

The sun that was dying in the abyss was there.

Without a wind to revive it, the star in the depths of the mist
Slowly cooled and faded, becoming dull.
Its sinister roundness was visible in the night;
And in this dark silence, one could see
Its ulcers of fire decreasing under a leprosy of shadows.
The coal of an extinct world, a torch blown out by God,
Its fissures still showed a little fire as if,
Through holes in the skull, one could see the soul.
In the center flickered and crawled a flame
Which at times licked the outer edges,
And from each crater issued forth some rays of light
Which trembled like flaming swords,
And then soundlessly vanished, as do dreams.
The star was nearly black. The archangel was so weary
That he had neither voice nor breath, alas!
But the star was perishing under his fierce gaze.
It was dying. It fought. At times, from the dark orifices
In this cold darkness it launched scorching floods,
Reddened masses, smoking mountains,
And rocks all frothing with primeval light,
As if this giant of life and light,
Absorbed by the mist where everything vanishes,
Did not wish to die without insulting the night,
Without spitting its lava in the face of the darkness.
Around it time and space, number
And form, and sound expired, creating
A formidable, black nothingness.
The barren void raised its head out of the pit.

Soudain, du cœur de l'astre, un âpre jet de soufre,
Pareil à la clameur du mourant éperdu,
Sortit, brusque, éclatant, splendide, inattendu,
Et, découpant au loin mille formes funèbres,
Enorme, illumina, jusqu'au fond des ténèbres,
Les porches monstrueux de l'infini profond.
Les angles que la nuit et l'immensité font
Apparurent. Satan, égaré, sans haleine,
La prunelle éblouie et de cet éclaire pleine,
Battit de l'aile, ouvrit les mains, puis tressaillit
Et cria:—Désespoir! le voilà qui pâlit!—

Et l'archange comprit, pareil au mât qui sombre,
Qu'il était le noyé du déluge de l'ombre;
Il reploya son aile aux ongles de granit,
Et se tordit les bras, et l'astre s'éteignit.

IX

Or, près des cieux, au bord du gouffre où rien ne change,
Une plume échappée à l'aile de l'archange
Était restée, et pure et blanche, frissonnait.
L'ange au front de qui l'aube éblouissante naît
La vit, la prit, et dit, l'œil sur le ciel sublime:
—Seigneur, faut-il qu'elle aille, elle aussi, dans l'abîme?
Dieu se tourna, par l'être et la vie absorbé,
Et dit:—Ne jetez pas ce qui n'est pas tombé.

*

Antres noirs du passé, porches de la durée
Sans dates, sans rayons, sombre et démesurée,
Cycles antérieurs à l'homme, chaos, cieux,
Monde terrible et plein d'êtres mystérieux,
O brume épouvantable où les préadamites
Apparaissent, debout dans l'ombre sans limites,

Suddenly, from the heart of the star, a fierce jet of sulfur,
Like the frantic outcry of the dying,
Shot out, startling, radiant, splendid, unexpected, enormous,
Revealing in the distance a thousand funereal forms,
Illuminating, in the far reaches of darkness,
The monstrous portals of the infinite deep.
The spectacles which night and vast space create
Appeared. Satan, bewildered, breathless,
His eye dazzled and full of this lightning,
Beat his wings, opened his hands, then trembled,
And cried:—Despair! Everything is growing dim!—

And the archangel understood that, like a sinking ship's mast,
He was drowning in a flood of darkness;
He folded his wings with their talons of stone,
Wrung his hands, and the star died out.

IX

Now, near the heavens, at the edge of the pit where nothing
Changes, a pure, white feather, which had escaped from the
Wings of the archangel, sat fluttering, precariously.
The angel before whom a dazzling dawn was breaking,
Saw it, gathered it up, and said, his eyes resting on the sublime sky:
—Lord, should this feather also go into the abyss?—
God, absorbed in Being and in Life, turned,
And said:—Do not cast down that which has not fallen.

*

Dark caves of the past, portals from a time without dates,
Without light, dark and immeasurable,
Eons prior to man, chaos, heavens,
A world, terrible and full of mysterious Beings,
O dreadful fog where the preadamites
Appeared, dwelling in the limitless gloom,

Qui pourrait vous sonder, gouffres, temps inconnus!
Le penseur qui, pareil aux pauvres, va pieds nus
Par respect pour Celui qu'on ne voit pas, le mage,
Fouille la profondeur et l'origine et l'âge,
Creuse et cherche au-delà des colosses, plus loin
Que les faits dont le ciel d'à présent est témoin,
Arrive en pâlissant aux choses soupçonnées,
Et trouve, en soulevant des ténèbres d'années
Et des couches de jours, de mondes, de néants,
Les siècles monstres morts sous les siècles géants.
Et c'est ainsi que songe au fond des nuits le sage
Dont un reflet d'abîme éclaire le visage.

Who can sound you, chasms, times unknown!
The thinker, the magus, who, like the poor, goes barefoot
Out of respect for the One we can not imagine,
Mines the depths and the origins and the epochs,
Explores and seeks beyond the Colossi,
Further than what the heavens now witness,
Turns pale as he reaches things long suspected,
And, by uncovering the darkness of the years,
And the layers of days, worlds and emptinesses,
Discovers monstrous dead ages under these immense centuries.
And so it is that the Sage dreams in the depths of night, the Sage
Whose face is lit by a reflection from the abyss.

La première page

I

L'ENTRÉE DANS L'OMBRE

I

Noë rêvait. Le ciel était plein de nuées.
On entendait au loin les chants et les huées
Des hommes malheureux qu'un souffle allait courber.
Un nuage muet soudain laissa tomber
Une goutte de pluie au front du patriarche.
Alors Noë, suivi des siens, entra dans l'arche,
Et Dieu pensif poussa du dehors le verrou.

Le mal avait filtré dans les hommes. Par où?
Par l'idole; par l'âpre ouverture que creuse
Un culte affreux dans l'âme humaine ténébreuse.
Ces temps noirs adoraient le spectre Isis-Lilith,

The first page

I

THE ENTRY INTO DARKNESS

I

Noah was brooding, the sky full of thick clouds,
And one could hear the far-off songs and jeers of
Ill-fated men whom a gust of wind was soon to ruin.
A silent cloud suddenly let fall
A drop of rain upon the brow of the patriarch.
And Noah, with family, entered the ark.
God, deep in thought, thrust closed the bolt from without.

Evil had infected humankind. But how?
Through the worship of idols; through a bitter opening in the
Lightless human soul where would burrow a hideous cult.
These ominous times worshipped the specter Isis-Lilith,

La fille du démon, que l'Homme eut dans son lit
Avant qu'Ève apparût sous les astres sans nombre,
Monstre et femme que fit Satan avec de l'ombre
Afin qu'Adam goutât le fiel avant le miel,
Et le baiser du gouffre avant celui du ciel.
Ève était nue. Isis-Lilith était voilée.
Les corbeaux l'entouraient de leur fauve volée;
Les hommes la nommaient Sort, Fortune, Anankè;
Son temple était muré, son prêtre était masqué;
Elle buvait du sang dans le bois solitaire;
Elle avait des autels effrayants. Et la terre
Subissait cette abjecte et double obscurité:
En bas Idolâtrie, en haut Fatalité.

Aussi depuis longtemps tout était deuil et crainte.
Le juste—un seul restait—attendait la mort sainte
Comme un captif attend qu'on lève son écrou.

Le tigre en sa caverne et la taupe en son trou
Disaient depuis longtemps: l'homme commet des crimes.
Une noire vapeur montait aux cieux sublimes,
Fumée aux flots épais des sombres actions.
Depuis longtemps l'azur perdait ses purs rayons,
Et par instants semblait plein de hideuses toiles
Où l'araignée humaine avait pris les étoiles.
Car dans ces temps lointains, de ténèbres voilés,
Où la nature et l'homme étaient encor mêlés,
Les forfaits dans l'éther rayonnaient en désastres,
Et les vices allaient éteindre au ciel les astres.
Le mal sortait de l'homme et montait jusqu'à Dieu.
Le char du crime avait du sang jusqu'à l'essieu;
Le meurtre, l'attentat, les luxures livides
Riaient, buvaient, chantaient, régnaient; les fils avides
Soufflaient sur les parents comme sur un flambeau;
Ce que la mort assise au seuil noir du tombeau
Voyait d'horreurs, faisait parler cette muette.

Daughter of the devil, monster whom Satan
Created out of darkness, whom Man took to his bed
Before Eve appeared beneath the countless stars,
That Adam might taste the gall before the honey,
The kiss of Hell before that of Heaven.
Eve was naked, Isis-Lilith was veiled
And encircled by a fierce flight of ravens.
She was named Fate, Fortune, Anagke,
Her temple was walled; her priest masked,
She drank blood in the solitary wood;
She had frightful altars. And the earth
Was subjected to this abject, two-fold darkness:
Down below, Idolatry, on high, Fate.

Thus, for a long time everything had been grief and fearfulness.
The just man—one alone remained—awaited a pious
Death, as a prisoner awaits his release.

The tiger in its cave and the mole in its hole
For ages had said: Man is criminal;
And a black vapor, thick billows of somber deeds,
Ascended to the sublime heavens.
For a long time the azure had been losing its pure light,
And at times seemed full of hideous cobwebs
Where the human spider had ensnared the stars.
For in these distant times of veiled darkness,
Where Nature and Man were still one,
Heinous crimes manifested as disasters in the firmament,
And the vices rose to extinguish the heavenly stars.
Evil issued from Man and rose up unto God,
And Crime's chariot became mired in blood to its axles;
Murder, outrage, and ghastly lusts
Laughed, drank, sang, and held sway; gluttonous sons
Blew out their parents' lives like candles;
What death, seated at the black threshold of the grave,
Saw of horrors, made even this silent creature speak.

La nuit du cœur humain effrayait la chouette;
L'ignorance indignait l'âne; les guets-apens,
Les dols, les trahisons faisaient honte aux serpens;
Si bien que l'homme ayant rempli son âme immonde
D'abîmes, Dieu put dire au gouffre: Emplis le monde.

L'urne du gouffre alors se pencha. Le jour fuit;
Et tout ce qui vivait et marchait devint nuit.
Ève morte frémit dans sa tombe profonde.

II

Tout avait disparu. L'onde montait sur l'onde.
Dieu lisait dans son livre et tout était détruit.
Dans le ciel par moments on entendait le bruit
Que font en se tournant les pages d'un registre.
L'abîme seul savait, dans sa brume sinistre,
Ce qu'étaient devenus l'homme, les voix, les monts.
Les cèdres se mêlaient sous l'onde aux goémons;
La vague fouillait l'antre où la bête se vautre.
Les oiseaux fatigués tombaient l'un après l'autre.
Sous cette mer roulant sur tous les horizons
On avait quelque temps distingué des maisons,
Des villes, des palais difformes, des fantômes
De temples dont les flots faisaient trembler les dômes;
Puis l'angle des frontons et la blancheur des fûts
S'étaient mêlés au fond de l'onde en plis confus;
Tout s'était effacé dans l'horreur de l'eau sombre.
Le gouffre d'eau montait sous une voûte d'ombre;
Par moments, sous la grêle, au loin, on pouvait voir
Sur le blême horizon passer un coffre noir;
On eût dit qu'un cercueil flottait dans cette tombe.
Les tourbillons hurlants roulaient l'écume en trombe.
Des lueurs frissonnaient sur la rondeur des flots.
Ce n'était ni le jour ni la nuit. Des sanglots,
Et l'ombre. L'orient ne faisait rien éclore.

This dark night of the human heart frightened the owl;
Man's ignorance made the donkey indignant; treacheries,
Deceptions, treasonous acts shamed the serpents;
And since Man had filled his squalid soul
With abysses, God could say to the abyss: Fill the world.

The urn of the abyss tilted, day fled;
And all that lived and walked became night,
While lifeless Eve trembled in her deep grave.

II

All the world had disappeared. Wave mounted upon wave.
God read from his register and all was destroyed.
In the sky one could hear, at times,
The sound of his pages turning,
And the abyss alone knew, in its sinister mist,
What had become of Man, the voices, the mountains.
Cedars mingled with seaweed beneath the watery waste
That sought out the cavern, that haunt of the beast.
The exhausted birds fell one by one.
Beneath this sea which rolled o'er every horizon
One could sometimes glimpse houses,
Cities, shapeless palaces, ghosts of temples whose
Domes were shaken by the high seas; then the corners
Of the pediments and the whiteness of the columns
Got intertwined with indistinct forms under the billowing waves,
And everything vanished in the horror of the somber waters.
The vast deep rose under a vault of darkness;
From time to time, under a hail, one could see pass
On the pale, distant horizon, a black chest;
It looked to be a coffin floating in this tomb.
The howling whirlwinds turned spume into waterspouts,
And lights quivered upon the rise of the waves.
It was neither day, nor night. Only sobs,
And darkness. Nothing appeared in the east,

Il semblait que l'abîme eût englouti l'aurore.
Dans les cieux, transformés en gouffres inouïs,
La lune et le soleil s'étaient évanouis;
L'affreuse immensité n'était plus qu'une bouche
Noire et soufflant la pluie avec un bruit farouche.
La nuée et le vent passaient en se tordant.
On eût dit qu'au milieu de ce gouffre grondant
On entendait les cris de l'horreur éternelle.
Soudain le bruit cessa. Le vent ploya son aile.
Sur le plus haut sommet où l'on pouvait monter
La vague énorme enfin venait de s'arrêter,
Car l'élément connaît son mystère et sa règle.
Le dernier flot avait noyé le dernier aigle.
—Plus rien.—On ne vit plus, dans l'univers puni,
Que l'eau qui se taisait dans l'ombre, ayant fini.
Le silence emplissait la lugubre étendue.
La terre, sphère d'eau dans le ciel suspendue,
Sans cri, sans mouvement, sans voix, sans jour, sans bruit,
N'était plus qu'une larme immense dans la nuit.

III

Dans ce moment-là, tout étant dans l'insondable,
Un fantôme apparut sur l'onde formidable.
Ce géant était trombe, ouragan et torrent.
Des hydres se tordaient dans son œil transparent;
Il semblait encor plein de la tempête enfuie;
Sa face d'eau tremblait sous ses cheveux de pluie;
Et voici ce que l'ombre effarée entendit:

Le géant se tourna vers le gouffre maudit,
Fit trois pas, et cria:—Chaos, reprends ce monde!

Une tête sortit de la brume profonde;
Aveugle, énorme, horrible, à l'autre bout des cieux;
Ayant deux gouffres noirs à la place des yeux;
Se dressa, pâle, et dit:—Je ne veux pas, déluge!

For it seemed that the abyss had engulfed the dawn;
And in the heavens, transformed into incredible chasms,
The moon and the sun had vanished;
The hideous vastness was no more than a black
Mouth blowing the rain with a fierce roar.
The thick cloud and the wind both passed by, writhing,
And it seemed that in the midst of this rumbling chasm
One could hear the cries of eternal horror.
Suddenly the noise ceased. The wind lowered his wing.
On the highest peak that one could climb,
The enormous wave had at last stopped, because
It understood the mystery, and the law that ruled it.
The last wave had drowned the last eagle.
—Nothing more.—Nothing left living in the punished Universe,
But the water, which lay quietly in the darkness,
Its task done. Silence filled the gloomy expanse.
The earth, a sphere of water suspended skyward,
Without a cry, motionless, speechless, without day, soundless,
Was no more than an immense teardrop in the night.

III

At that very moment, everything being fathomless,
A phantom appeared upon the fearsome waters.
This giant was whirlwind, hurricane and torrent.
Hydras writhed in its transparent eye;
And it seemed still full of the departed storm.
Its watery countenance trembled under its hair of rain;
And here is what the frightened darkness heard:

The giant turned towards the accursed abyss,
Took three steps, and shouted:—Chaos, take back this world!

A head emerged from the deep mist at the other end
Of the heavens, blind, enormous, horrible,
And having two black chasms for eyes.
Of pale visage, it drew itself up, and said:—I do not want to, Deluge!

IV

LE DÉLUGE

Reprends-le.

LE CHAOS

Non.

LE DÉLUGE

Il est rejeté.

LE CHAOS

Par quel juge?

LE DÉLUGE

Par Lui.

LE CHAOS

Pourquoi?

LE DÉLUGE

Le ver s'est glissé dans le fruit.
Le condamné d'en bas a soufflé dans la nuit
Le mal au cœur de l'homme à travers la nature;
L'homme, ouvert à l'erreur, au piège, à l'imposture,
Jusqu'au crime de vice en vice descendu,
Est devenu vipère, et sa bouche a mordu;
Le talon du Seigneur a senti la piqûre;

IV

THE FLOOD

Take it back!

CHAOS

No.

THE FLOOD

It has been rejected.

CHAOS

By what judge?

THE FLOOD

By Him.

CHAOS

Why?

THE FLOOD

Because the worm has crept into the fruit.
In the night, the Condemned One from below has breathed
Evil into the heart of Man, through nature,
And Man, vulnerable to delusion, deception, imposture,
Descended from vice to vice unto crime,
Became a viper, and bit;
The heel of the Lord has felt the sting;

Et voilà ce qu'a fait, du fond de l'ombre obscure,
L'être qui vit sous terre au Dieu qui vit au ciel.
Ce monde étant mauvais et noir, l'être éternel
Le laisse tomber, monstre, et tu peux le reprendre.

LE CHAOS

Pourquoi me l'a-t-il pris, si c'est pour me le rendre?

LE DÉLUGE

J'ai roulé sur les monts le flot sombre et tonnant.
Tout est mort. J'ai fini; c'est à toi maintenant.
Reçois ce monde au fond de l'abîme où nous sommes.

LE CHAOS

J'ai déjà les dragons, je ne veux pas des hommes.

V

L'éclair cria:—Silence aux pieds d'Adonaï!—
Et le chaos se tut dans le gouffre ébloui.

Et l'archange qui veille entre deux pilastres
Du seuil mystérieux plein d'yeux qui sont des astres,
Se courba sous l'azur sans oser faire un pas
Et dit au Dieu vivant: Le chaos n'en veut pas.
Et Dieu dit: Je consens que ce monde revive.

And that is what, from the depths of darkness,
The Being who lives below, did to God who lives in Heaven.
This world being wicked and dark, the eternal Being
Has rejected it, monster, and you can have it back.

CHAOS

Why take it from me, only to return it?

THE FLOOD

Because I rolled across the mountains the dark and thunderous
Flood. Everything is dead. I have finished; it belongs to you now.
Receive this world at the heart of the abyss where we are.

CHAOS

I already have dragons, I have no wish for men.

V

Lightning cried:—Silence, at the feet of Adonaï!—
And Chaos became silent in the dazzled abyss.

And the archangel who keeps watch between the two pilasters
Of the mysterious threshold sown with eyes which are stars,
Fearing to take a step, bowed beneath the azure, and
Said to the living God:—Chaos does not want any of this.
And God said: I thus grant that this world shall live again.

II

LA SORTIE DE L'OMBRE

I

L'eau baissa, comme un flux qui s'en va d'une rive,
Et les flots monstrueux, décroissant par degrés,
Descendirent du haut des monts démesurés.
Au-dessus de la terre une voix dit: clémence!
Le crâne décharné de la noyée immense
Apparut, et l'horreur éclaira sous les cieux
Ce cadavre sans souffle et sans forme et sans yeux,
Les rochers, les vallons, et les forêts mouillées
Qui pendaient à son front de marbre, échevelées.
L'antre, où les noirs arrêts dans l'ombre étaient écrits,
Semblait la bouche ouverte encor pleine de cris;
Les monts sortaient de l'eau comme une épaule nue.
Comme l'onde qui bout dans l'airain diminue,
L'océan s'en allait, laissant des lacs amers.
Ces quelques flaques d'eau sont aujourd'hui nos mers.
Tout ce que le flot perd, la nature le gagne.
L'île s'élargissant se changeait en montagne;
Les archipels grandis devenaient continents.
De son dos monstrueux poussant leurs gonds tournants,
Le déluge fermait ses invisibles portes.
Les ténèbres dormaient sur les profondeurs mortes,
Et laissaient distinguer à peine l'ossement
Du monde que les eaux découvraient lentement.
Soudain, réverbérée au vague front des cimes,
Une lueur de sang glissa sur les abîmes;
On vit à l'horizon lugubrement vermeil
Poindre une lune rouge, et c'était le soleil.

Pendant quarante jours et quarante nuits sombres,
La mer, laissant à nu d'effroyables décombres,

II

THE EMERGENCE FROM DARKNESS

I

The waters abated, like a flood receding from a riverbank,
And the monstrous seas, slowly diminished,
Descended from the height of the measureless mountains.
Above the Earth a voice said: Mercy!
The fleshless skull of the immense drowned being
Appeared, and the horror under the heavens illuminated
This corpse without eyes, without shape, without breath,
The rocks, the vales, and the sodden forests
Hanging, disheveled, from its marble brow.
The cave, where dark judgments were written in the shadows,
Seemed an open mouth still full of screams;
Mountains arose from the water like naked shoulders.
Just as water boils away in a brass pot,
So the ocean was diminished, leaving bitter lakes.
And these few puddles are now our seas.
All that the flood loses, nature gains, and
The widening islands became mountains,
And the increased archipelagoes, continents.
With his monstrous back, the Flood
Closed on its hinges his invisible gates.
Darkness slept upon the dead depths,
And let barely be seen the bones of the
World that the waters slowly exposed.
Suddenly, reflected upon the vague brow of the summit,
A glimmer of blood slid down the abyss;
And one could see a red moon appear on the ominous,
Rosy horizon; it was the sun.

For forty days and forty dark nights,
The sea, revealing frightful ruins,

Recula, posant l'arche aux monts près d'Henocha,
Puis ce lion, rentré dans l'antre, se coucha.

II

Dieu permit au soleil de jeter l'étincelle.
Alors un bruit sortit de l'ombre universelle,
Le jour se leva, prit son flambeau qui blêmit,
Et vint; le vent, clairon de l'aube, se remit
A souffler; un frisson courut de plaine en plaine;
L'immensité frémit de sentir une haleine,
La montagne sourit, le désert s'éveilla,
Et le brin d'herbe au bord des eaux dit: me voilà!

Mais tout était hagard, morne et sinistre encore,
Et c'est dans un tombeau que se levait l'aurore.

III

Derrière ces grands monts où plus tard l'aube a lui
Et que nous appelons les Alpes aujourd'hui,
Un marais descendait vers l'océan sans borne.
Dans cette plaine vaste, impénétrable et morne,
Comme un serpent hésite à travers les roseaux,
Un fleuve, né d'hier, traînait ses pâles eaux,
Et découpait une île au pied d'un coteau sombre,
Sans savoir qu'en ces joncs, pleins de souffles sans nombre,
Germait, fœtus géant, la plus grande des Tyrs.
Le coteau, qui plus tard fut le mont des martyrs,
Lugubre, se dressait sur l'île et sur le fleuve.
L'oiseau, l'être qui va, la bête qui s'abreuve,
Étaient absents; l'espace était vide et muet,
Et le vent dans les cieux lentement remuait
Les sombres profondeurs par les rayons trouées.
Dans la fange expiraient des hydres échouées.

Receded, setting the ark down upon the mountains near Enoch;
Then this lion, gone back into its lair, lay down.

II

God allowed the sun to cast scant gleams of light.
Then was heard a sound from the collective gloom,
Day arose, took his pale torch,
And came forth; the wind, the clarion of dawn,
Began to blow anew; a shiver ran from plain to plain;
The immensity trembled at feeling this breeze,
The mountain smiled, the desert awakened,
And the blade of grass at the edge of the water, said: Behold me!

Yet everything was haggard, mournful and sinister still,
And it was as within a tomb that the dawn arose.

III

Behind these great mountains where later glowed the dawn,
And which we today call the Alps,
A swamp stretched down to the limitless sea.
Through this vast, impenetrable and forlorn plain,
A river, born yesterday, trailed its pale waters,
Like a serpent snaking through the reeds,
And carved out an island at the foot of a forbidding hillside,
Without knowing that in these rushes, full of numberless winds,
Grew a giant fetus, the largest of the Tyrs.
The mournful hill, which later became Montmartre,
Reared up upon this island above this river.
The birds, the creatures that move about, the beasts that drink,
All were absent; the land was empty and mute,
And the wind in the heavens slowly stirred
The somber deep, pierced by rays of light.
The hydras, stranded in the mire, died.

C'est dans cet endroit-là, tout étant mort, pendant
Que les nuages gris croulaient sur l'occident
Comme de lourds vaisseaux qui dans la nuit chavirent,
C'est là que les forêts et les collines virent
Soudain, tout se taisant dans l'univers détruit,
Un voile blanc marcher droit dans l'ombre et sans bruit;
Et l'ombre eut peur; et l'arbre, et la vague, et l'étoile,
Et les joncs, frissonnaient de voir passer ce voile.

Il allait, comme si quelqu'un était dessous.
Les êtres du passé, dans la vase dissous,
Semblaient, cherchant encore à tordre leurs vertèbres,
Rouvrir quand il passait leurs yeux pleins de ténèbres.
Le ciel qui s'entr'ouvrait referma son azur.
Tout à coup une voix sortit du voile obscur;
Le flot, qui sous le vent redevenait sonore,
Se tut, et quatre fois cette voix vers l'aurore,
Vers le sud, vers le triste occident, vers le nord,
Cria: Je suis Isis, l'âme du monde mort!

IV

Un long frisson émut le cadavre; la fange,
Pleine de monstres morts, fit une plainte étrange;
Et le spectre se mit à parler dans les vents:
—Il a pu noyer l'homme et les êtres vivants,
Mais il n'a pu tuer l'airain, le bois, la pierre.
Or, nature qui viens de fermer ta paupière,
Écoute, écoutez-moi, flots, rochers, vents du ciel,
Car, ô témoins pensifs du deuil universel,
Il faut que vous sachiez ces sombres aventures:
Lorsque Caïn, l'aïeul des noires créatures,
Eut terrassé son frère, Abel au front serein,
Il le frappa d'abord avec un clou d'airain,
Puis avec un bâton, puis avec une pierre;
Puis il cacha ses trois complices sous la terre

It is in this place, where everything hung, lifeless,
That the grey clouds collapsed upon the west,
Like massive vessels capsizing in the night.
It is here that the forests and hills suddenly
Saw, while all lay silent in the ruined universe,
A white veil move soundlessly straight into the darkness;
And the darkness was afraid; and the tree, the wave, the star,
And the rushes shuddered, to see this veil passing.

It moved as if some Being resided below.
As it passed, the creatures of yesterday tried
Again to free themselves from the mire,
To reopen their eyes full of darkness, and
The sky which had half-opened, closed its azure once more.
Suddenly a voice rang out from amidst the dark veil;
The flood, which could now be heard beneath the wind,
Went silent, and four times this voice cried, towards the
Dawn, towards the south, towards the melancholy west, and towards
The north: I am Isis, soul of the dead world!

IV

A long shudder shook the world; the mire,
Full of morient monsters, made a strange lamentation;
And the specter began to speak in the winds:
—He was able to drown Man and all living creatures,
But he could not kill bronze, wood, or stone.
Nature, you who have just closed your eyes,
Listen, listen to me, tides, rocks, winds of the sky,
For, O pensive witnesses to the universal bereavement,
You must learn of these somber events:
When Cain, ancestor of the dark creatures,
Felled his brother, Abel, he of the serene brow,
He struck him first with a bronze spike,
Followed by a stick, and then a stone;
He then hid these three accomplices beneath the earth

Où ma main qui s'ouvrait dans l'ombre les a pris.
Je les ai. Sachez donc ceci, vents, flots, esprits:
Tant qu'il me restera dans les mains ces trois armes,
Je vaincrai Dieu; matin, tu verseras des larmes!
L'être qui vit sous terre et moi, nous lutterons.
Si Dieu veut sous les eaux engloutir les affronts,
Les haines, les forfaits, le meurtre, la démence,
Les fureurs, il faudra toujours qu'il recommence.
Et les déluges noirs, pareils aux chiens grondants
Qui veulent qu'on les lâche et qui montrent les dents,
Tant que le vieux Caïn vivra sous ces trois formes,
Pourront à l'horizon gonfler leurs flots énormes.

V

Le voile en s'écartant laissa voir dans deux mains
Un bâton, une pierre arrachée aux chemins,
Puis un long clou, semblable au verrou d'une porte;
Et si, dans ce tombeau de la nature morte,
Quelque œil vivant eût pu rester dans l'ombre ouvert,
Sur le clou, sur le bois noueux et jadis vert,
Et sur l'affreux caillou pareil aux crânes vides,
Cet œil eût distingué trois souillures livides;
Et le spectre montra ces trois taches au ciel,
Et cria: Cieux profonds! voici du sang d'Abel!

Alors une lueur sortit, sinistre et sombre,
De ces trois noirs témoins des temps qui sont dans l'ombre;
L'être toujours voilé, blanc et marchant sans bruit,
Se pencha vers la terre et cria dans la nuit,
Et comme s'il parlait à quelqu'un sous l'abîme:
—O père! j'ai sauvé les trois germes du crime!

Sous la terre profonde un bruit sourd répondit.

Where my hand, which opened in the darkness, found them.
I have them now. Therefore know this, winds, tides, spirits,
As long as I have these three weapons in hand,
I shall overcome God; at dawn, you shall shed tears!
I and the Being who lives below shall do battle.
If God merely wishes to engulf, under the waters,
These outrages, these hatreds, crimes, murders, madnesses,
Passions, he shall always have to begin anew.
And just like growling dogs who wish to be released,
And bare their fangs, as long as ancient
Cain lives under these three aspects, these dark floods
Shall extend their enormous tides to the horizon.

V

The veil opened, revealing two hands holding
A stick, a stone from the road, and
Then a long spike, like the bolt to a door;
And if in this, nature's grave,
Some living eye could have remained open in the darkness,
Upon the nail, upon the gnarled and once green wood,
And upon the hideous cobblestone resembling an empty skull,
This eye would have spied three pale stains;
And the specter brandished these three stains, and to all
Creation, cried: boundless heavens! Behold the blood of Abel!

Then a light was cast, sinister and pale,
From these three black witnesses of the times shrouded
In darkness; this Being, still veiled, white, moving soundlessly,
Stooped down towards the earth and cried into the night,
As if speaking to someone beneath the abyss:
—O father! I have saved the three seeds of crime!

Below the deep earth a muffled voice replied.

Il reprit:—Clou d'airain qui servis au bandit,
Tu t'appelleras Glaive et tu seras la guerre;
Toi, bois hideux, ton nom sera Gibet; toi, pierre,
Vis, creuse-toi, grandis, monte sur l'horizon,
Et le pâle avenir te nommera Prison.

She continued:—Spike of bronze, used by Cain,
You shall be called Sword, and become War;
You, hideous wood, your name shall be Gibbet; you, stone,
Live, become hollow, grow tall, rise upon the horizon,
And the dim future shall name you Prison.

Livre premier *Le Glaive*

.:.:.:.:.:.:.:.:.:.:.

STROPHE TROISIÈME

SELON ORPHÉE ET SELON MELCHISÉDECH

I

Dans son désœuvrement Nemrod, d'ombre chargé,
Ravagea de nouveau le monde ravagé,
Recommença, brûla deux fois les mêmes villes,
Rougit la vaste mer du flamboiement des îles,
Brûla Ségor, brûla Gergesus, brûla Tyr.
Puis, ayant tout détruit, il se mit à bâtir.
Il construisit Achad, il créa Babylone,
Il bâtit Gour dans l'ombre où le vent tourbillonne,

First Book *The Sword*

.:.:.:.:.:.:.:.:.:.:.

THIRD STROPHE

ACCORDING TO ORPHEUS AND ACCORDING TO MELCHISEDECH

I

In his idleness Nimrod, full of darkness,
Ravaged again the already ravaged world,
Returned and burned the same cities twice,
Reddened the vast sea, setting islands ablaze,
Burned Segor, burned Girgash, and Tyre;
And then, having destroyed all, began to build.
He built Achad, he built Babylon,
He built Ghor in the shadow of the whirlwind,

Resen dans les palmiers, Chalanné sur les monts;
Lieux qu'on ne nommait pas comme nous les nommons.
Il fit, pour abriter Pytiunte et Dioscure,
Un mur énorme au fond de la Tauride obscure;
Il habilla d'acier ses soldats triomphants;
Il fit trembler des tours au dos des éléphants;
Il troua le Caucase ébranlé sur son axe;
Il versa dans la mer le Cyrus et l'Araxe;
Mais rien n'emplit son âme; il disait:—J'ai vécu.
Que faire?—et, chaque jour, plus las et plus vaincu,
Morne, il sentait monter dans son cœur solitaire
L'immense ennui d'avoir conquis toute la terre.

II

L'an deux mille, Nemrod, passant les flots émus,
Vint jusqu'à Dodanim que nous nommons l'Hémus.
Là, dans un noir désert dont le lion est l'hôte,
Il entendit quelqu'un qui parlait à voix haute.
C'était Orphée. Orphée au front calme, écouté
Par la sombre nature émue à sa clarté,
Homme à qui se frottait le dos des bêtes fauves,
Racontait aux forêts, aux vents, aux vieux monts chauves,
La bataille où les dieux vainquirent les typhons.
Voici ce que disait Orphée aux bois profonds:

« Les géants n'avaient plus de montagnes. Leur fuite
Commençait; l'Hémonie était presque détruite.
Ils avaient entassé Pinde, Ossa, Pélion,
Rhodope, et ces monts noirs d'où fuyait le lion,
Nus, renversés, fumaient d'éclairs et de brûlures,
Et leurs torrents pendaient comme des chevelures.
Et les géants couraient vers les mers où fut Tyr.
Ils voyaient les dieux vaincre, et Neptune engloutir
Oromédon sous Cos, Polybe sous Nisyre.
Thryx embrasé fondait comme un flambeau de cire.

Resen amongst the palm trees, Calneh in amongst the
Mountains, places not named as we have named them.
To shelter Pitiunt and Dioscurias, he raised up
An enormous bulwark at the base of dark Tauris;
He dressed in steel his triumphant soldiers;
He made towers sway on the backs of elephants;
He pierced the Caucasus, shaken upon its axis;
He poured into the sea the Araxes and the river Cyrus;
But nothing satisfied his soul; he said:—I have lived my life through.
What more is to be done?—And, every day, more weary,
Dispirited, and sad, he felt rising in his lonely heart
An immense ennui from having conquered the entire world.

II

In the year two thousand, Nimrod, crossing the restless tides,
Came as far as Dodanim, which we name Hæmus.
There, in a black desert where the lion reigns,
He heard someone declaiming in a loud voice:
It was Orpheus of the calm visage, heard by dark nature,
Which was moved by his radiance, and by Man, against
Whose back the wild beasts rub: Orpheus, who spoke to
The forests, the winds, and to the old, bare mountains,
Of the battle in which the gods conquered the Typhons.
Here is what Orpheus said to the deep woods:

"The giants had only the mountains left.
Their flight began, and Aemonia was nearly destroyed.
They had piled high Pindus, Ossa, Pelion, and Rhodope,
And then the place whence the lion had fled, those barren,
Black mountains, upcast and smoking, scorched by
Lightning strikes, their torrents hanging like tresses.
The Giants fled toward the seas, toward Tyre, and there,
As well, they saw the gods victorious, Neptune engulfed,
Oromedon under Kos, Polybotes under Nisyros,
Thryx, ablaze, melting like a waxen torch.

Porphyrion, levant ses mains vides, criait
A la terre, rôdant au loin, spectre inquiet:
Mais apporte-nous donc une montagne, mere!
Crès, par la foudre étreint, lui jetait l'onde amère.
Andès, frère d'Astrée et père de Thallo,
S'en allait à grands pas au plus profond de l'eau,
Et jusqu'à la ceinture avait la mer Egée;
Zéus Jupiter vint, la main d'éclairs chargée,
Et lui cria: Sois pierre, ô monstre! Et le géant
Vit Zéus, devint roche et s'arrêta béant.
Et Titan dit: Merci! tu nous donnes des armes!
Et, pendant que tremblait la terre, aïeule en larmes,
Il courut, et, prenant Andès par le milieu,
Il jeta le géant à la tête du dieu. »

Et Nemrod s'écria:—Titan est mon ancêtre.

Il revint vers les monts où l'on voit l'aube naître;
Il rentra dans Assur que la splendeur revêt.
Son glaive, d'où la guerre était sortie, avait
Une tache inconnue, empreinte indélébile,
Que Nemrod par moments contemplait immobile.

Un soir, dans un lieu sombre où marchait ce bandit,
Une voix qui parlait dans un rocher, lui dit:
—Passe, Dieu reste.—Et lui, cria:—J'ai pour royaume
Le monde; toi, qu'es-tu?—La voix reprit:— Fantôme,
Je suis Melchisédech, je vivrai dans mille ans.—
Nemrod dit:—Qu'as-tu vu depuis que dans ses flancs
Ce roc t'enferme?—Et l'être enfoui sous la pierre
Dit: « Je suis âme, et l'âme est un œil sans paupière.
Le monde a commencé par être horrible. Avant
Que le front se dressât plein de l'esprit vivant,
Avant que, dominant l'animal et la plante,
La pensée habitât la prunelle parlante,
Et qu'Adam, par la main tenant Ève, apparût,

Roaming afar, Porphyrion, that inquiet phantom,
Raised his empty hands and shouted at the Earth:
Mother, at least bring us one mountain!
Cres, gripped by the lightning, cast upon him the briny wave;
Andes, brother of Astraios, father of Talos,
Who departed by great strides for the the deepest waters,
Was soon waist-deep in the Aegean Sea;
Zeus Jupiter came, his hand teeming with lightning bolts,
And cried to him: Become stone, O monster! And the giant,
Seeing Zeus, became stone, and stopped, gaping.
And Titan said: Thank you! You give us weapons!
And, whilst the earth trembled, grandmother in tears,
He ran, and, grasping Andes about the waist,
Cast the giant at the head of the god."

And Nimrod exclaimed:—Titan is my ancestor.

He returned to the mountains where one sees the Dawn
Born, and reentered Assyria, magnificently arrayed.
His sword, the source of War, had a strange
Indelible stain imprinted on it, which Nimrod at
Times contemplated as he sat alone, motionless.

One evening, in a dark place where this marauder walked,
A voice speaking in a rock, said to him:
—Pass on, God alone dwells here.—And he shouted:—I have
The world for a kingdom; who are you?—The voice resumed:—Phantom,
I am Melchisedech, and I shall live in a thousand years.—
Nimrod said:—What have you seen since confined
Within this rock?—And the Being buried within the stone
Said: "I am soul, and the soul is a lidless eye.
In the beginning, the world was a frightening place.
Before the brow of Man arose, a full and living spirit,
Before thought resided in the expressive eye, dominating
The animals and plants, and before Adam appeared, leading
Eve by the hand, before all this, the first primordial beginnings

L'ébauche fourmillait dans la nature en rut,
Le poulpe aux bras touffus, la torpille étoilée,
D'immenses vers volants, dont l'aile était onglée,
De hauts mammons velus, nés dans les noirs limons,
Troublaient l'onde, ou levaient leurs trompes sur les monts.
Sous l'enchevêtrement des forêts inondées
Glissaient des mille-pieds long de cinq cent coudées;
Et de grands vibrions, des volvoces géants
Se tordaient à travers les glauques océans.
L'être était effrayant. La vie était difforme.
Partout rampait l'impur, l'affreux, l'obscur, l'énorme.
La vermine habitait le globe chevelu.
Et l'homme était absent; Dieu n'ayant pas voulu
Donner ce noir spectacle à voir à l'âme humaine.
Satan, dans ce lugubre et féroce domaine,
Passait, comme un chasseur qui souffle dans son cor;
Mais, avant ces temps-là, c'était plus sombre encor.
Tout l'univers n'était qu'une morne fumée.
Ainsi que des oiseaux dans une main fermée,
L'horreur tenait captifs le germe et l'élément.
Un tout, qui n'était rien, vivait confusément.
Des apparitions flottaient sur l'insondable.
Au fond de cette brume étrange et formidable,
Comme si, quoique rien ne fût encor puni,
Le gouffre eût essayé d'engloutir l'infini,
On voyait, aux lueur des visions funèbres,
S'ouvrir et se fermer la gueule des ténèbres.
Partout apparaissait, à l'œil épouvanté,
La face du néant, faite d'obscurité.
A chaque instant, le fond redevenait la cime;
Et, comme une nuée au-dessus d'un abîme,
Dans cette ombre où rampaient les larves des fléaux,
Le monstre Nuit planait sur la bête Chaos.
C'était ainsi quand Dieu se levant dit à l'ombre:

Of nature were swarming everywhere, in heat:
Thick-tentacled octopi, starry torpedos,
Immense flying worms with talonned wings,
Tall, shaggy mammoths, born of the black slime,
Disturbing the waves or lifting their trunks upon the
Mountains. Under the tangle of flooded forests
Slithered centipedes five hundred cubits long,
And immense vibrios, giant volvox,
Writhed across the sea-green oceans.
Existence was dreadful. Life was deformed.
Everywhere crawled the impure, the hideous, the dark,
The enormous. Vermin infested the scalp of the globe.
And Man was absent, God not wishing
To reveal this black spectacle to the human soul.
Satan passed through this mournful, savage domain,
A hunter blowing upon his horn.
But, before those times, it was darker yet.
The entire universe was in a gloomy mist.
Like birds in a closed hand,
The horror held captive the seed and the element.
It was a vaporous whole, living in turmoil.
Apparitions floated on the fathomless.
Although nothing was as yet punished,
At the bottom of this strange and formidable fog,
As if the abyss had tried to engulf infinity,
One could see, in the light of these funereal visions,
The maw of darkness open and close.
To the terrified eye, everywhere seemed
The face of nothingness, composed of gloom.
At every moment, the bottom again became the top;
And, like a thick cloud above an abyss,
In this shade where crawled the larvae of plagues,
The monster Night hovered over the beast Chaos.—
Thus it was when God, arising, said to the darkness:

Je suis. Ce mot créa les étoiles sans nombre,
Et Satan dit à Dieu: Tu ne seras pas seul. »

Nemrod pensif cria:—Satan est mon aïeul.

III

Il resta trente jours au fond des solitudes,
Rêvant parmi les rocs aux sombres attitudes;
Quand il revint, son œil brillait comme un flambeau.
Son eunuque Zaïm, plus noir que le tombeau,
Se prosternant, lui dit:—Roi, vous avez la terre.
Vous êtes roi d'Assur, dont Tyr est tributaire.
Il a suffi qu'Assur vînt pour qu'il triomphât
Aux sources de Cadès qu'on nomme aussi Misphat.
Dieu règne moins que vous. Votre face est sacrée.
Et vous faites couler, sur la terre qu'il crée,
Des rivières de sang près de ses fleuves d'eau.
L'homme porte Nemrod, et l'âne porte son fardeau.
A qui sont les palmiers d'Édom, l'herbe fleurie
D'Hébron, les trois cents tours qui gardent Samarie?
A vous. A qui les fronts, les yeux et les genoux
Des vieillards, des enfants et des femmes? A vous.
A qui l'Ibère brun qui parle avec emphase?
A vous. Sarapanis, citadelle du Phase?
A vous. Vous avez pris, sous les dattiers lointains,
Sa ville à Phetrusim, père des philistins.
Le Nil est votre chien, Thèbe est votre captive.
Trois chars passent de front sur les murs de Ninive;
Et Ninive est à vous. Gour veut vous obéir.
Sidon, les horréens dans les monts de Seïr,
Ophir, les bijoutiers qui sculptent des ivoires
Dans Cariathaïm, la ville aux portes noires,
Tout est à vous; Sichem, Chanaan, Hazerod.
Il ne reste plus rien.

—Que le ciel, dit Nemrod.

I am. These words created numberless stars;
And Satan said to God: Thou shalt not be alone."

Pensive Nimrod exclaimed:—Satan is my ancestor.

III

He remained thirty days in the depths of solitude,
Dreaming amidst the rocks with somber aspects;
When he returned, his eye shone like a torch.
His eunuch Zaïm, blacker than the tomb,
Prostrating himself, said to him:—Sire, you rule the earth.
You are king of Assyria, on whom Tyre is dependent.
Assur had but to come, for him to triumph
At the sources of Kadesh, which we also call Enmishpat.
God reigns over less than you. Your face is sacred.
And you make flow on the earth, which he created,
Rivers of blood beside his rivers of water.
Man bears Nimrod, as the donkey bears its burden.
To whom belong the palms of Edom, the flowering grass
Of Hebron, the three hundred towers that guard Samaria?
To you. To whom belong the faces, eyes and knees of
The elderly, the women and the children? To you.
Who owns the brown Iberian who speaks with bombast?
You. Sarapanis, citadel of Phasis?
You. You captured, beneath the distant date palms,
His city at Pathrusim, father of the Philistines.
The Nile is your dog, Thebes your captive.
Three chariots pass, abreast, upon the walls of Niniveh
And Niniveh is yours. Ghor wishes to obey you.
Sidon, the Horims in the mountains of Seir,
Ophir, the jewelers who carve ivory
In Cariathaim, the city with the black portals,
All belong to you; Sichem, Canaan, Hazeroth.
Nothing more remains.

—But Heaven, said Nimrod.

. : . : . : . : . : . : . : . : . : .

STROPHE SIXIÈME

LES MAGES ATTENTIFS

Nemrod en s'en allant n'emporta pas la Guerre.
Elle resta, parlant plus haut que le tonnerre;
Son regard au sillon faisait rentrer l'épi;
Et ce spectre, mille ans, sur le monde accroupi,
Lugubre, et comme un chien mâche un os, rongeant l'homme,
Couva l'œuf monstrueux d'où sortit l'aigle Rome.
Et pendant ce temps-là, comme parfois aux yeux
Une vapeur trahit un feu mystérieux,
Il sortait par endroits de la terre où nous sommes
D'affreux brouillards vivants qui devenaient des hommes,
Puis des dieux, qu'on nommait Teutatès, Mars, Baal,
Et qui semblaient avoir en eux l'âme du mal.
L'horreur, le sang, le deuil couvraient la race humaine;
Et les mages, que Dieu dans le désert amène,
Collaient l'oreille au sable, et, de terreur ployés,
Frémissants, sous la terre, au-dessous de leurs pieds,
Ils entendaient quelqu'un dans les nuits éternelles
Qui volait, et heurtait la voûte de ses ailes.

. : . : . : . : . : . : . : . : . : . : .

SIXTH STROPHE

THE MINDFUL MAGI

Nimrod's dying did not end War.
It remained, heard above the thunder;
Its glance at the furrow made the wheat disappear;
And this specter, for a thousand years, crouched upon the world,
Mournful, and as a dog chews a bone, gnawing upon Man,
Hatched the monstrous egg from which emerged the eagle Rome.
And during that time, just as sometimes a smoke betrays
To the eyes a mysterious fire, so war poured forth
Upon the earth, where we reside,
Hideous living fogs which became men,
Then gods, whom we named Teutates, Mars, Baal,
And who seemed to have the soul of evil within.
Horror, bloodshed, grief enveloped the human race;
And the Magi, whom God led into the desert,
Placed their ear to the sands; and, terrified,
Trembling, heard below their feet,
In the endless nights, someone, aflight,
Striking the vault with his wings.

Hors de la terre II

LA PLUME DE SATAN

La plume, seul débris qui restât des deux ailes
De l'archange englouti dans les nuits éternelles,
Était toujours au bord du gouffre ténébreux.
Les morts laissent ainsi quelquefois derrière eux
Quelque chose d'eux-mêmes au seuil de la nuit triste,
Sorte de lueur vague et sombre, qui persiste.

Cette plume avait-elle une âme? qui le sait?
Elle avait un aspect étrange; elle gisait
Et rayonnait; c'était de la clarté tombée.

Les anges la venaient voir à la dérobée.
Elle leur rappelait le grand Porte-Flambeau;
Ils l'admiraient, pensant à cet être si beau
Plus hideux maintenant que l'hydre et le crotale;
Ils songeaient à Satan dont la blancheur fatale,
D'abord ravissement, puis terreur du ciel bleu,

Beyond the Earth II

SATAN'S FEATHER

The feather, the sole remnant of the wings
Of the archangel engulfed in eternal night,
Still lay on the brink of the dark abyss.
The dead thus sometimes leave behind them
Something of themselves at the threshold of mournful night,
Some kind of vague and somber light, which persists.

Had this feather a soul? Who knows?
It had a strange appearance; it lay there
And shone; it was made of fallen light.

The angels furtively came to look, for
It reminded them of the great Torchbearer;
They marveled at it, thinking of that Being once so beautiful,
Now more hideous than the hydra and the rattlesnake;
They thought of Satan whose fatal whiteness, first the delight,
Then the dread of the blue heavens, became

Fut monstrueuse au point de s'égaler à Dieu.
Cette plume faisait revivre l'envergure
De l'Ange, colossale et hautaine figure;
Elle couvrait d'éclairs splendides le rocher;
Parfois les séraphins, effarés d'approcher
De ces bas-fonds où l'âme en dragon se transforme,
Reculaient, aveuglés par sa lumière énorme;
Une flamme semblait flotter dans son duvet;
On sentait, à la voir frissonner, qu'elle avait
Fait partie autrefois d'une aile révoltée;
Le jour, la nuit, la foi tendre, l'audace athée,
La curiosité des gouffres, les essors
Démesurés, bravant les hasards et les sorts,
L'onde et l'air, la sagesse auguste, la démence,
Palpitaient vaguement dans cette plume immense;
Mais dans son ineffable et sourd frémissement,
Au souffle de l'abîme, au vent du firmament,
On sentait plus d'amour encor que de tempête.

Et sans cesse, tandis que sur l'éternel faîte
Celui qui songe à tous pensait dans sa bonté,
La plume du plus grand des anges, rejeté
Hors de la conscience et hors de l'harmonie,
Frissonnait, près du puits de la chute infinie,
Entre l'abîme plein de noirceur et les cieux.

Tout à coup un rayon de l'œil prodigieux
Qui fit le monde avec du jour, tomba sur elle.
Sous ce rayon, lueur douce et surnaturelle,
La plume tressaillit, brilla, vibra, grandit,
Prit une forme et fut vivante, et l'on eût dit
Un éblouissement qui devient une femme.
Avec le glissement mystérieux d'une âme,
Elle se souleva debout et, se dressant,
Éclaira l'infini d'un sourire innocent.
Et les anges tremblants d'amour la regardèrent.

Monstrous to the point of making him the equal of God.
This feather reawakened the breadth
Of that Angel, colossal and haughty;
It covered the rock with magnificent lightning-flashes;
Sometimes the Seraphim, too fearful to approach,
Recoiled before these shallows where the soul is
Transformed into a dragon, blinded by its enormous light;
A flame seemed to float in the down of this feather;
And one sensed, seeing it shiver, that it had once
Been part of a rebellious wing;
Day and night, tender faith, atheist audacity,
Curiosity of the abysses, limitless
Flights, braving all hazards and fates—
The wave and the air, majestic wisdom, madness—
All palpitated faintly in this immense plume;
But in its ineffable and voiceless quivering,
With the breath of the abyss, with the wind of the firmament,
One still sensed more love than tempest.

While the One, who in his goodness ponders all,
Was now deep in thought on the eternal summit,
The feather of the greatest of the angels, rejected
Out of conscience and to preserve peace,
Trembled without cease near the well of the infinite Fall,
Between the abyss full of darkness, and the heavens.

Suddenly a light beam from His prodigious eye,
Which formed the world from daylight, fell upon it.
Under this shaft of soft and supernatural light,
The feather quivered, shone, pulsated, grew,
Took shape, came alive, and seemed
A splendor transformed into a woman.
With the mysterious shifting of a soul,
She arose, and, standing erect,
Lit infinity with her innocent smile.
And the angels, trembling with love, beheld her.

Les chérubins jumeaux qui l'un à l'autre adhèrent,
Les groupes constellés du matin et du soir,
Les Vertus, les Esprits, se penchèrent pour voir
Cette sœur de l'enfer et du paradis naître.
Jamais le ciel sacré n'avait contemplé d'être
Plus sublime parmi les souffles et les voix.
En la voyant si fière et si pure à la fois,
La pensée hésitait entre l'aigle et la vierge;
Sa face, défiant le gouffre qui submerge,
Mêlant l'embrasement et le rayonnement,
Flamboyait, et c'était, sous un sourcil charmant,
Le regard de la foudre avec l'œil de l'aurore.

L'archange du soleil, qu'un feu céleste dore,
Dit:—De quel nom faut-il nommer cet ange, ô Dieu?

Alors, dans l'absolu que l'Être a pour milieu,
On entendit sortir des profondeurs du Verbe
Ce mot qui, sur le front du jeune ange superbe
Encor vague et flottant dans la vaste clarté,
Fit tout à coup éclore un astre:—Liberté.

The twin cherubs clinging one to the other,
The constellations of morning and evening,
The Virtues, the Spirits, leaned forward to see
This sister born of hell and of paradise.
Never had the sacred heavens, amidst murmurs
And whispers, contemplated a being more sublime.
Seeing her both so proud and so pure,
They hesitated between calling her eagle or virgin.
Her face, melding flame with brilliance,
Blazed, defying the engulfing abyss;
It was, under a charming brow,
The glance of lightning with the eye of Dawn.

The archangel of the sun, guilded by a celestial fire,
Said:—O Lord, what shall we call this angel?

Then, in the absolute where this Being dwells,
One heard emerge from the depths of the Logos,
This Word which suddenly made a star blossom
Upon the brow of the magnificent, young angel,
Still half-formed and floating in the vast light:—Liberty.

Victor Hugo, *Le Burg à la croix* (The Town with the Cross), detail, 1850, Musée Maison de Victor Hugo

Livre deuxième *Le Gibet*

I

LA JUDÉE

I

LA TERRE SOUS LE TROISIÈME CÉSAR

En ce temps-là, le monde était dans la terreur;
Caïphe était grand-prêtre et Tibère empereur;
Hérode roi des juifs gouvernait sous Pilate;
Rome était la nuée où le tonnerre éclate;
Jérusalem était l'âne sous le bâton.
Des proconsuls assis le poing sous le menton,
Vêtus de pourpre, ayant le roi pour satellite,
Remplaçaient au-dessus du peuple israélite
Les pharaons à l'œil fixe et mystérieux.
Quelques rares autels fumaient sur les hauts lieux,
Mais c'étaient les autels des guèbres, que tolère

Second Book *The Gibbet*

I

JUDEA

I

THE EARTH UNDER THE THIRD CAESAR

At this time, the world in a perilous state,
With Caiaphas high priest, Tiberius emperor,
Herod ruled as king of the Jews under Pilate;
Rome was the cloud wherein thunder roared;
And Jerusalem the donkey under the stick.
Proconsuls, purple-clad and sitting,
Fists under chins, the king their menial,
Governed the Israelites, replacing the intent,
Mysterious gaze of the Pharaohs.
At times, altars of the Guebres, smoking on the
High grounds, were tolerated by a Rome

Rome ayant trop de dieux pour croire avec colère.

Temps fatals! César roi, tout le reste sujet.
La conquête romaine, immense, submergeait
Les peuples qu'elle avait saisis l'un après l'autre;
Et cette vague épaisse où le soldat se vautre
Grossissait, et, de proche en proche, envahissait
La terre, où les songeurs disaient: qu'est-ce que c'est?
Cette inondation de Rome était lugubre;
L'empire était partout comme une onde insalubre;
Il croissait comme un fleuve épars sous des forêts,
Et changeait lentement l'univers en marais.
Les docteurs méditaient sur ce second déluge.
Ayant leurs livres saints pour cime et pour refuge,
Les prêtres, rattachés aux textes, au-dessus
Des hommes débordés dans un gouffre aperçus,
Laissaient couler sous eux ces mornes avalanches,
Pareils à des serpents enroulés dans des branches.

Un peuple commandait, le monde subissait.
Les jaguars, les lions, les ours pris au lacet,
Le tigre redouté même de sa femelle,
Rugissaient sous les pieds de Rome pêle-mêle
Avec les nations dans le même filet.
Partout la servitude à voix basse parlait.
L'unique grandeur d'âme était l'insouciance.
La force avait le droit. Qu'était la conscience?
De la reptilité sous de l'écrasement.
On regardait l'autel en face et le serment,
Et l'on se parjurait, et l'hymne et la huée
Riaient, et l'âme humaine était diminuée.
L'honnête et le néfaste et le mal et le bien
S'effaçaient dans les cœurs; l'homme ne voyait rien
Qu'une noirceur croissante au-dessus de sa tête;
Une rougeur de torche illuminait le faîte
De l'univers sur qui marchaient les conquérants;

With too many gods, itself, for fervent worship.

A fateful time! Caesar was king, all the rest subjects.
The vast Roman conquest quelled
Nations, defeated, one after the other;
And this thick wave in which the soldier wallows,
Grew, and, bit by bit, flooded
The land where the dreamers said: What is it?
This Roman inundation was heart-rending,
This empire was everywhere like a pestilent wave,
A swollen river spread forest-wide,
The universe transformed to swamp.
Scholars meditated upon this second Flood.
Their sacred books both summit and refuge,
The priests, embracing these texts,
Atop abyss-mired men,
Let flow beneath them this dismal deluge,
As serpents coiled upon the branches of a tree.

A People governed, the world submitted.
Jaguars, lions, bears entrapped,
The tiger, feared even by its mate,
Roared confusion at Rome's feet,
With nations equally ensnared.
Everywhere servitude spoke in a whisper,
Insouciance the soul's highest nobility.
Might ruled. What was the conscience?
A crushed reptile. People looked
The altar and the solemn oath in the face,
And were faithless; the hymn and the hooting
Laughed, and the human soul was diminished.
The honest and the baneful, the evil and the good
Faded from people's hearts; and Man saw
But increasing darkness o'erhead;
Red torchlight illuminated the heights
Of the universe where conquerors trampled,

Les uns étaient petits, les autres étaient grands,
Personne n'était pur, saint, vénérable et juste;
De même que d'Octave avait pu naître Auguste,
De la fange partout sortait l'autorité.
Le destin avait l'air d'un abîme irrité;
L'ombre se résolvait en haine autour de l'âme.
L'or sentait bon. Le sage était celui qui blâme
La vertu, le devoir, la foi, le dévouement;
Le plus voisin du vrai c'était celui qui ment;
La mort régnait avec les licteurs pour ministres;
Le genre humain pendait en deux haillons sinistres,
Comme si Dieu l'avait déchiré de ses mains;
Les hommes d'un côté, de l'autre les romains.

.:.:.:.:.:.:.:.:.:.

III

CELUI QUI EST VENU

Or il était alors question dans les villes
De quelqu'un d'étonnant, d'un homme radieux
Que les anges suivaient de leurs millions d'yeux;
Cet homme, qu'entourait la rumeur grossissante,
Semblait un dieu faisant sur terre une descente;
On eût dit un pasteur rassemblant ses troupeaux;
Les publicains, assis au bureau des impôts,
Se levaient s'il passait, quittant tout pour le suivre;
Cet homme, paraissant hors de ce monde vivre,
Tandis qu'autour de lui la foule remuait,
Avait des visions dont il restait muet;
Il parlait aux cités, fuyait les solitudes,
Et laissait sa clarté dans l'œil des multitudes;
Les paysans le soir, de sa lueur troublés,
Le regardaient de loin marcher le long des blés,

Some diminutive, others mighty, and
No one pure, holy, venerable or just;
Even as Octavian arose Augustus,
So authority emerged everywhere from the mire.
Destiny appeared an angry chasm;
Darkness resolved itself in hatred about the soul.
Gold smelled good. The sage censured
Virtue, duty, faith, devotion;
The one most truthful was the liar;
Death reigned with lictors for ministers;
The human race hung, a sinister rag rent
In twain as if by God's own hands,
Humankind on one side, Romans upon the other.

.:.:.:.:.:.:.:.:.:.:.

III

THE ONE WHO CAME

Now, there was talk in the towns
Of some astonishing, radiant man
Whom angels followed with their countless eyes;
This man, shrouded in ever-increasing rumors,
Seemed a god descended to earth,
A shepherd gathering his flock; and
The publicans, seated at the tax offices,
Arose upon his passing, leaving all, to follow him;
This otherworldly man had visions,
Of which he remained silent,
While the crowd bustled all about him.
Fleeing the wilderness, he spoke in the cities,
Dazzling the eyes of the multitudes;
In the evening, from afar, the peasants, disturbed by
His light, watched him walk along the wheatfields,

Et sa main qui s'ouvrait et devenait immense,
Semblait jeter aux vents de l'ombre une semence.
On racontait sa vie, et qu'il avait été
Par une vierge au fond d'une étable enfanté
Sous une claire étoile et dans la nuit sereine;
L'âne et le bœuf, pensifs, l'ignorance et la peine,
Étaient à sa naissance, et sous le firmament
Se penchaient, ayant l'air d'espérer vaguement;
On contait qu'il avait une raison profonde,
Qu'il était sérieux comme celui qui fonde,
Qu'il montrait l'âme aux sens, le but aux paresseux,
Et qu'il blâmait les grands, les prêtres, et tous ceux
Qui marchent entourés d'hommes armés de piques.
Il avait, disait-on, guéri des hydropiques;
Des impotents, cloués vingt ans sous leurs rideaux,
En le quittant, portaient leur grabat sur leur dos;
Son œil fixe appelait hors du tombeau les vierges;
Les aveugles, les sourds,—ô destin, tu submerges
Ceux-ci dans le silence et ceux-là dans la nuit!—
Le voyaient, l'entendaient; et dans son vil réduit
Il touchait le lépreux, isolé sous des claies;
Ses doigts tenaient les clefs invisibles des plaies,
Et les fermaient; les cœurs vivaient en le suivant;
Il marchait sur l'eau sombre et menaçait le vent;
Il avait arraché sept monstres d'une femme;
Le malade incurable et le pécheur infâme
L'imploraient, et leurs mains tremblantes s'élevaient;
Il sortait des vertus de lui qui les sauvaient;
Un homme demeurait dans les sépulcres; fauve,
Il mordait, comme un loup qui dans les bois se sauve;
Parfois on l'attachait, mais il brisait ses fers
Et fuyait, le démon le poussant aux déserts;
Ce maître, le baisant, lui dit: Paix à toi, frère!
L'homme, en qui cent damnés semblaient rugir et braire,
Cria: Gloire! et, soudain, parlant avec bon sens,
Sourit, ce qui remplit de crainte les passants.

And his hand opening and becoming vast,
Seemed to scatter seeds to the winds of darkness.
People spoke of him, and how, under a
Bright star one serene night, he was
Born of a virgin in the back of a stable;
The wistful donkey and ox, nescience and sorrow,
Were present at his birth, and leaning toward him
Beneath the firmament, appeared quietly hopeful;
It was rumored that he had a grave resolve,
Was serious as he who lays mighty foundations,
That he revealed the soul to the senses, showed purpose to the
Listless, and that he censured the nobles, priests, and all those
Who went about surrounded by guards armed with pikes.
It was said of him that he cured the dropsied;
The infirm, confined for twenty years behind their curtains,
Could leave him, carrying their wretched pallet upon their backs;
His intent gaze called forth virgins from their graves;
The blind and the deaf,—O fate, you bury
The latter in silence and the former in night—
Saw him and heard him; and he touched the leper
In his vile retreat, isolated behind his screens;
His fingers fathomed the invisible clues to his wounds,
And closed them; souls pursuing him came alive;
He walked upon the dark water and threatened the wind;
He had purged seven monsters from out a woman;
The incurably ill and the vile sinner
Implored him, and their trembling hands were raised;
He drew on his virtues to heal them;
A man dwelled in the tombs; wild,
He bit, like a wolf fleeing into the forest;
Sometimes he was chained, but broke free
And stole away, the demon driving him into the deserts;
This master, kissing him, said: Peace unto you, brother!
The man, in whom a hundred damned souls seemed to roar and
Bray, cried: Glory! And, suddenly, speaking with good
Sense, smiled, frightening those near to hand.

Ce prophète honorait les femmes économes;
Il avait à Gessé ressuscité deux hommes
Tués par un bandit appelé Barabbas;
Il osait, pour guérir, violer les sabbats,
Rendait la vie aux nerfs d'une main desséchée;
Et cet homme égalait David et Mardochée.

Un jour ce redresseur, que le peuple louait,
Vit des vendeurs au seuil du temple, et prit un fouet;
Pareils aux rats hideux que les aigles déterrent,
Tous ces marchands, essaims immondes, redoutèrent
Son visage empourpré des célestes rougeurs;
Sévère, il renversa les tables des changeurs
Et l'escabeau de ceux qui vendaient des colombes.
Son geste surhumain ouvrait les catacombes.
L'arbre qu'il regardait changeait ses fleurs en fruits.
Un jour que quelques juifs dans la loi sainte instruits
Lui disaient: «—Dans le ciel que le pied divin foule,
Quel sera le plus grand? » cet homme dans la foule
Prit un petit enfant qu'il mit au milieu d'eux.
Calme, il forçait l'essaim invisible et hideux
Des noirs esprits du mal, rois des ténébreux mondes,
A se précipiter dans les bêtes immondes.
Et ce mage était grand plus qu'Isaïe, et plus
Que tous ces noirs vieillards épars dans les reflux
De la vertigineuse et sombre prophétie;
Et l'homme du désert, Jean, près de ce Messie,
N'était rien qu'un roseau secoué par le vent.
Il n'était pas docteur, mais il était savant;
Il conversait avec les faces inconnues
Que l'homme endormi voit en rêve dans les nues;
Des lumières venaient lui parler sur les monts;
Il lavait les péchés ainsi que des limons,
Et délivrait l'esprit de la fange charnelle;
Satan fuyait devant l'éclair de sa prunelle;
Ses miracles étaient l'expulsion du mal;

This prophet honored prudent woman;
In Goshen he had brought back to life two men
Killed by a bandit named Barabbas;
In order to heal, he dared violate the Sabbath,
And restored life to a withered hand;
He was the equal of David and Mordecai.

One day this rectifier, whom the people praised,
Saw vendors at the threshold to the temple, and took a whip;
All these merchants, a squalid lot,
Like the hideous rats which eagles unearth,
Feared his face flushed with a celestial rouge;
He sternly overturned the tables of the money changers
And the stools of those who sold doves.
His divine gesture opened the catacombs.
The tree he beheld transformed its flowers to fruits.
One day, when some Jews instructed in holy law
Said to him:—"In Heaven where the divine foot treads,
Who shall be the greatest?"—this man placed
Before them a child from the crowd.
He serenely compelled the invisible and hideous swarm
Of black, evil spirits, sovereigns of the dark worlds,
To rush headlong into the midst of filthy beasts.
And this mage was greater than Isaiah, and greater
Than all those downcast old men caught up in the ebb
Of vertiginous, somber prophecy;
And the man from the desert, John, beside this Messiah,
Was but a reed stirred by the wind.
He was not a doctor, but he was learnèd;
He conversed with strange countenances
Seen by men asleep in cloud-enveloped dreams;
Radiances came to speak with him up upon the mountains;
He purged sins as he would silt,
And delivered the spirit from the carnal mire;
Satan fled before the blaze of his eyes;
His miracles expelled evil;

Il calmait l'ouragan, haranguait l'animal,
Et parfois on voyait naître à ses pieds des roses;
Et sa mère en son cœur gardait toutes ces choses.
Des morts blêmes, depuis quatre jours inhumés,
Se dressaient à sa voix; et pour les affamés
Les pains multipliés sortaient de ses mains pures.

Voilà ce que contait la foule; et les murmures,
Les cris du peuple enfant qui réclame un appui,
Environnaient cet homme; on l'adorait; et lui
Était doux.

Tout les mots qui tombaient de sa bouche
Étaient comme une main céleste qui vous touche.
Il disait: —« Les derniers sont les premiers.—La fin,
C'est le commencement.—Ne fais pas au prochain
Ce que tu ne veux pas qu'on te fasse à toi-même.
—On récolte le deuil quand c'est la mort qu'on sème.
—Celui qui se repent est grand deux fois.—L'enfant
Touche à Dieu.—Par le bien, du mal on se défend.
—Que le puits soit profond, mais que l'eau reste claire. »
Il disait: —« Regardez les choses sans colère;
Car si l'œil est mauvais, le corps est ténébreux.
—L'aube est pour les Gentils comme pour les Hébreux.
—Mangez le fruit des bois, buvez l'eau de la source;
N'ayez pas de souliers, pas de sac, pas de bourse,
Entrez dans les maisons et dites: Paix à tous!
—Nul n'est exempt du pli sublime des genoux;
Donc, qui que vous soyez, priez. Courbez vos têtes.
—Dieu, présent à la nuit, n'est pas absent des bêtes;
Dieu vit dans les lions comme dans Daniel.
—Errer étant humain, faillir est véniel.
Absolvez le pécheur en condamnant la faute.
—On ajoute à l'esprit ce qu'à la chair on ôte. »
Il tenait compte en tout des faits accidentels.
Au peuple qui lapide il disait des mots tels

He calmed the storm, harangued the beast,
And sometimes were seen roses abloom at his feet;
And his mother preserved all these things in her heart.
The pale dead, buried for four days, raised
Themselves at the sound of his voice; and for the famished,
He multiplied bread with his pure hands.

The crowd spoke of this; and the murmurs,
The cries of the childlike people craving sustenance,
Embraced this man; they adored him; and were
Gentle towards him.

All the words that fell from his lips
Were like the touch of a celestial hand.
He said:—"The last shall be first.—The end,
Is the beginning.—Do unto others
As you would have them do unto you.
—Those who sow death shall reap mourning.
—He who repents is twice great.—The child
Touches God.—Through good we protect ourselves from evil.
—Let the well be deep, but let the water remain clear."
He said:—"Look at things without anger;
For if the eye is evil, the body is sinister.
—Dawn is for the Gentiles as well as for the Hebrews.
—Eat of the fruit of the forest, drink of the water of the spring;
Have no shoes, no sack, no purse,
Enter abodes and say: Peace be unto all!
—No one is exempt from the sublime kneeling;
So, whoever you may be, pray. Bow your heads.
—God, present at night, is not absent in animals;
God lives within the lions as within Daniel.
—To err being human, failing is easily forgiven.
Absolve the sinner while condemning the sin.
—We add to the spirit what we remove from the flesh."
He took entirely into consideration every accidental act.
To those who stoned he said words such

Que nul n'osait toucher à la première pierre;
Il haïssait la haine, il combattait la guerre.
Il disait: Sois mon frère! à l'esclave qu'on vend;
Et, tranquille, il passait comme un pardon vivant;
Il blanchissait le siècle autour de lui, de sorte
Que les justes, dont l'âme encor n'était pas morte,
Dans ces temps sans pitié, sans pudeur, sans amour,
Pouvaient voir au réveil luire deux points du jour,
L'aurore dans le ciel et sur terre cet homme.
Cet être était trop pur pour être vu par Rome.
Pourtant parmi les juifs, dans leur temple obscurci,
Chez leur roi lâche et triste, on en prenait souci;
Et Caïphe y songeait dans sa chaire d'ivoire;
Et, sans savoir encor ce qu'il en devait croire,
Hérode était allé jusqu'à dire:—Il paraît
Qu'il existe un certain Jésus de Nazareth.

Quelques hommes, de ceux qui ne savent pas lire,
De pauvres pâtres, pris d'on ne sait quel délire
Et du ravissement de l'entendre parler,
Le suivaient, l'aimaient tant qu'il les faisait trembler,
Et le montraient au peuple en disant: c'est le maître.
L'un d'eux, vieillard, semblait près de cet homme naître;
Et le plus jeune, enfant, avait l'air près de lui
D'un sombre aïeul pensif, gravement ébloui.
Humbles, ils lui tendaient leurs cœurs comme des urnes.
Et ces hommes, pareils à des lampes nocturnes
Adorant un soleil dans une vision,
Étaient devant ce maître en contemplation,
Et l'entouraient, ainsi qu'une auréole d'âmes.

That no one dared raise the first stone;
He hated hatred, he battled war;
He said: Be my brother! to the auctioned slave;
And, tranquil, he moved about like embodied forgiveness;
He cleansed the generation around him,
So that the righteous, whose souls were not yet dead,
In these merciless, shameless, loveless times,
Could see shine, upon waking, two daybreaks:
The dawn skyward and this man on earth.
This Being was too pure to be noticed by Rome.
Nevertheless among the Jews, in their darkened temple,
Home of their cowardly, melancholy king, people were concerned;
And Caiaphas, on his ivory throne, was scheming;
And, without yet knowing what to believe,
Herod had even said:—It seems
That there exists a certain Jesus of Nazareth.

Several men, poor, illiterate shepherds,
Possessed of an unaccountable madness,
Who became rapturous upon hearing him speak,
Followed him, loved him such that he made them tremble,
And pointed him out to the people, saying: He is the Master.
One of them, an old man, seemed a newborn when near this man;
And the youngest, the child, when near, had the air
Of a somber, pensive grandfather, gravely moved.
Humble, they tendered him their hearts, like urns.
And these men, like night-lamps
Adoring a sun in a vision,
Gathered about this teacher in contemplation,
Surrounding him, like a halo of souls.

IV

LES TREIZE PORTES DE JÉRUSALEM

Dans les vieux temps, l'archange aux quatre ailes de flammes,
Stellial dit un jour au noir Zorobabel,
Quand ce maçon, porteur d'une échelle du ciel,
Eut entouré Sion de murailles très fortes:
—Pourquoi donc à la ville as-tu fait treize portes?
Et Zorobabel dit:—Ninive aux larges tours
Eut autant de portails que l'année a de jours,
Pour que jamais le temps, qui du ciel même arrive,
Quel qu'il fût, ne restât en dehors de Ninive.
—Eh bien, dit Stellial, l'archange couvert d'yeux,
Le zodiaque ayant douze signes aux cieux,
Douze portes, c'était assez, mage imbécile,
Pour que chacun des mois pût entrer dans la ville.
—Ange, j'ai fait, reprit le maçon magistrat,
Treize portes afin que l'avenir entrât.
Chaque année on verra par les douze premières
Passer les douze mois, portant douze lumières,
Purs, bénis, et menant par la main la saison;
Par la treizième doit passer la trahison.

V

LA JUDÉE

D'innombrables hameaux répandent leurs fumées
D'Arphac à Borcéos dans les six Idumées;
La Judée est dorée et verte sous l'azur;
Elle a des bois, des monts, des lacs; son air est pur;
Le vent du sud le trouble et le vent d'est le calme;
Rome estime ses vins; comme l'huile de palme,
L'huile d'olive abonde à flots sous son pressoir;
L'ombre du Sinaï la couvre vers le soir.

IV

THE THIRTEEN GATES OF JERUSALEM

In ancient times, Stellial, the archangel of the four
Flaming wings, said one day to dark Zerubbabel,
When this mason, porter of the ladder of Heaven,
Had surrounded Zion with quite strong ramparts:
—Why have you made thirteen gates to the city?
And Zerubbabel said:—Nineveh, with her broad towers,
Had as many gates as the year had days,
So that, whenever Time arrived from Heaven itself,
Whatever the day, it never remained outside.
—And yet—said Stellial, the archangel strewn
With eyes—with the zodiac having twelve signs
In the heavens, how is it that twelve gates do not suffice
For each of the months to enter the city?
—Angel—answered the master mason—I have created
Thirteen gates so that the future might enter.
Every year we shall see the twelve months
Pass through the first twelve gates, carrying twelve lights,
Pure, holy, and leading the season by the hand;
Through the thirteenth must pass the betrayal.

V

JUDEA

Innumerable hamlets pour out their smoke
From Arpha to Borceos, within the six Idumeas;
Judea is golden and verdant under the azure, and
Has forests, mountains, and lakes; her air is pure;
The south wind disturbs her and the east wind calms her;
Rome esteems her wines; and like the palm oil,
The olive oil gushes under her press;
Come evening, she is enshrouded by the shadow of the Sinai.

La Judée est la terre où de temps en temps passe
Une lueur de Dieu qui se perd dans l'espace.

L'Égypte est, au couchant, cette plaine des blés
Où, dans les noirs tombeaux, dont les puits sont comblés,
Un miroir d'or massif pend au cou des momies
Pour refléter l'essaim des spectres, les lamies,
Les stryges, et la face errante des démons;
Au midi, les chacals, les rats, les ichneumons,
Remplissent le désert; au Nord, la mer murmure.

La moisson en Judée est deux fois par an mûre;
Le moindre champ y donne un boisseau de maïs.

Ce qui va se passer dans ce fatal pays
Fait un nuage obscur sur l'avenir, et trouble
Abraham enterré dans la caverne double
Dont on voit l'âpre brèche et le seuil délabré
Au champ d'Ephron, voisin des chênes de Mambré.

.:.:.:.:.:.:.:.:.:.:.

VII

CAÏPHE EN CONTEMPLATION

Les deux guetteurs du temple ont aperçu la lune;
Le mois commence.

Aux champs la terre est encor brune;
Il pleut sur le mont Glon et sur le mont Sion;
Mais l'hiver va finir. On fait l'ablution
Du temple, dont on brosse et dérouille les chaînes,
Les gonds et les verrous, pour les fêtes prochaines.

Judea is the land where, from time to time, a glimmer of light from
God passes near, only to vanish to the heavens.

To the west, Egypt is this plain of wheat fields
Where, in the dark tombs whose wells are filled,
Dense mirrors of gold hang from the necks of the mummies,
Reflecting the host of specters, lamiae,
Strigoi, and the wandering faces of demons;
To the south, jackals, rats, ichneumons,
Fill the desert; to the north, the sea murmurs.

The harvest in Judea is ripe twice yearly, and
The slightest field there yields a bushel of corn.

What will occur in this fateful country
Places a dark cloud upon the future, and troubles
Abraham, who is buried in the two-fold cave,
With its bitter breach and ruined threshold,
There, in Ephron's field, near the oaks of Mamre.

.:.:.:.:.:.:.:.:.:.:.

VII

CAIAPHAS CONTEMPLATING

The two watchmen of the temple beheld the moon;
The month begins.

In the fields the earth is dark still,
And it rains upon Mount Glon and Mount Zion;
But winter will soon end. They are purifying
The temple, whose chains, hinges and latches they
Scrub and polish for the approaching festivals.

Seul près du grand autel derrière le rideau,
Tandis que, se courbant sur des vases pleins d'eau,
Et répandant partout le nard et l'hyacinthe,
Les lévites portiers lavent la triple enceinte
Et s'arrêtent parfois pour baiser les pavés,
Le grand-prêtre se tient debout, les bras levés.
On dirait un fantôme avec son blanc suaire.

L'arche est sur une estrade au fond du sanctuaire;
Élohim lui laissa l'empreinte de son doigt;
Un éblouissement l'environne, et l'on voit
Des boîtes de parfum d'aspic sur chaque marche
Du degré qui se perd sous la splendeur de l'arche.

Caïphe est de la chose éternelle occupé.

Un docteur cependant, Rosmophim de Joppé
A soulevé ce voile et marche vers Caïphe
Qui ne dérange pas son geste de pontife
Et n'ouvre qu'à demi son œil vague et fermé.

Le prêtre dit:—Je viens. Je me suis informé,
Hannasci, de celui des douze auquel tu penses.
C'est lui que dans la bande on charge des dépenses;
Quand on voyage, il compte avec les hôteliers;
Les autres semblent fiers de porter leurs colliers;
Lui seul a l'air d'un loup parmi des chiens; sa voie
Est obscure; à Naïm, une fille de joie
Avait, avec du baume et des parfums, lavé
Les pieds du maître, un peu meurtris par le pavé;
Cet homme s'emporta contre elle jusqu'à dire:
—Tu viens de perdre là pour vingt deniers de myrrhe!
Et Caïphe répond:—C'est l'homme qu'il faudrait.
—Oui, repond Rosmophim, il est jaloux, secret,
Triste, oblique, inquiet, solitaire, économe.

While Levitical caretakers, bending o'er water-filled vessels,
And spreading, throughout, spikenard and hyacinth,
Wash the triple enclosure,
Sometimes pausing to kiss the paving stones,
Behind the curtain, near the high altar,
The high priest stands up with arms raised,
Appearing a white-enshrouded ghost.

The ark is on a platform at the heart of the sanctuary;
Elohim left the impression of his finger on it;
A radiance surrounds it, and one can see
Boxes of lavender perfume upon each step of
The stair that gets lost in the splendor of it.

Caiaphas is taken up with eternal matters.

However, a priest, Rosmophim of Joppa,
Has raised the veil and steps toward Caiaphas,
Who does not stay his pious rites
But merely opens, half-way, his closed, vacant eyes.

The priest says:—I came, Hannasci, and
Made inquiry of the one of the twelve that interests you.
He controls the group's monies, and
When they travel, pays the hoteliers;
The others seem proud to wear their collars,
But he, alone, looks a wolf among dogs;
His manner is puzzling; at Naim, a prostitute
Had, with balm and perfumes, washed
The Master's feet bruised by the road;
This man raged against her, saying:
—You have just wasted much valuable myrrh!
And Caiaphas responds:—He is the man we will need.
—Yes, says Rosmophim; he is jealous, secretive,
Melancholy, devious, anxious, solitary, frugal.

Prince, tu désirais savoir comme on le nomme.
Je l'ignorais le jour où tu le demandas.
Je le sais aujourd'hui.—Quel est son nom?—Judas.

VIII

LA SIBYLLE

La sibylle d'Achlab parle dans sa caverne;
Elle est seule; un esprit farouche la gouverne,
La courbe comme un feu sous un vol de démons,
Et de sa bouche obscure et de ses noirs poumons
Fait sortir le hasard des paroles terribles.
Des feuilles, qui plus tard augmenteront les bibles,
S'échappent par moments de son antre, et s'en vont
En vagues flamboiements dans l'espace sans fond.
Elle les suit des yeux, et rit; puis recommence,
L'immensité s'étant mêlée à sa démence,
Et le souffle infini la traversant toujours.
Elle s'adresse à l'ombre, au gouffre, aux rochers sourds.
Spectre par le regard, par la maigreur squelette,
Elle parle une langue étrange où se reflète
L'avenir, à demi visible sur son front,
Et prononce déjà des mots qui ne seront
Dits par le genre humain que dans trois mille années.

Ses mains sur ses seins nus se crispent décharnées;
Son œil lugubre songe, ivre d'obscurité;
Ce spectre balbutie avec autorité;
On dirait qu'elle fait la lecture éperdue
D'un mystérieux livre ouvert dans l'étendue;
Parfois elle s'arrête en disant: Je ne puis.

En ce moment, au fond de sa grotte, affreux puits
Plein de l'effarement des visions occultes,

Prince, you wished to know his name.
I did not know the day you inquired.
Today I know.—What is his name?—Judas.

VIII

THE SIBYL

The Sibyl of Ahlab speaks in her cavern;
She is alone, and a fierce spirit governs her,
Weighing her down like a fire beneath a flight of demons.
Terrible, chance words issue from her
Dark mouth and dark lungs;
Writings, which will later exalt Bibles,
Escape at times from her grotto, and vanish
In vague blazes into fathomless space.
She follows them with her eyes, and laughs, then begins anew,
The vastness mingled with her madness,
And the infinite wind traversing her, forever.
She addresses the shadows, the abyss, the unhearing rocks.
By her glance a specter, spare as a skeleton,
She speaks a strange tongue which shows forth
The future, half visible on her brow,
And even now utters words which shall only be
Spoken by humankind three thousand years hence.

Whilst this phantom murmurs prophetically,
Her wizen hands on her naked breasts move impulsively,
And her mournful eyes dream, inebrious of darkness;
It seems she is passionately reading aloud
From a mysterious book open in the great expanse;
Sometimes she stops, saying: I cannot continue.

At this moment, at the nether reaches of her cave,
That hideous well full of the terror of occult visions,

Ce sont les fondateurs de dogmes et de cultes
Et de religions que son regard poursuit.
Il semble qu'elle parle, à travers l'âpre nuit,
A ceux qui cherchent Dieu pour le montrer aux hommes....

. : . : . : . : . : . : . : . : . : . : .

...Pendant qu'elle parlait, pleine du sphinx caché,
Sur l'antre ténébreux quelqu'un s'était penché;
Le soleil éclairait sur le seuil de la cave
Une figure douce, éblouissante et grave;
Un homme était pieds nus dans l'herbe et les genêts.

—Je ne t'ai jamais vu, mais je te reconnais.
Salut, Nazaréen! dit la femme hagarde.

Et, montrant du doigt l'ombre, elle ajouta: Prends garde.

Alors entre la femme et cet homme, tandis
Que l'aube réchauffait les serpents engourdis
Et que les fleurs ouvraient au soleil leurs corolles,
Il se fit un échange auguste de paroles
Que la terre ignora, personne n'écrivant
Ce dialogue sombre emporté par le vent.

LE NAZARÉEN

O Prophétesse, il faut pourtant sauver les hommes.

LA SIBYLLE

A quoi bon?

Her glance follows the movement of these founders of
Dogmas and cults and religions. It seems that she
Speaks, through the bitter night, to those who
Seek God in order to reveal him to Man....

.:.:.:.:.:.:.:.:.:.:.

...Whilst she spoke, possessed of the mysterious sphinx,
Someone had leaned o'er the dark lair.
At the threshold of the cave the sun shone upon
A gentle face, radiant and grave—
A man stood barefoot in the grass and broom.

—We have not met, but I recognize you.
Greetings, Nazarene!—Said the gaunt woman.

And, pointing to the darkness, she added: Beware!

Then, while the dawning light warmed the drowsy snakes,
And the flowers opened their petals to the sun,
There was, between the woman and this man,
A dark converse carried by the wind,
An august colloquy that the earth
Ignored and no scribe recorded.

THE NAZARENE

O sibyl, still we must save humankind.

THE SIBYL

To what avail?

LE NAZARÉEN

Pour sortir de cette ombre où nous sommes.

LA SIBYLLE

Restes-y.

LE NAZARÉEN

C'est la loi de monter vers le jour,
Qu'après l'iniquité la justice ait son tour,
C'est la loi.

LA SIBYLLE

La justice sur terre est un rêve.

LE NAZARÉEN

Les hommes pleins de haine ont à la main le glaive.
O femme, en les aimant on peut les apaiser.
Que dis-tu de l'amour? Parle.

LA SIBYLLE

Crains le baiser.

THE NAZARENE

To escape this current darkness.

THE SIBYL

Remain there.

THE NAZARENE

But it is the law that one rise towards the daylight,
That after iniquity, justice have its turn,
It is the law.

THE SIBYL

Justice on earth is a dream.

THE NAZARENE

Men full of hate have the sword in hand.
O woman, by loving them one can appease them.
What say you of love? Speak.

THE SIBYL

Fear the kiss.

II

JÉSUS-CHRIST

.:.:.:.:.:.:.:.:.:.:.

III

LE TRIOMPHE

C'est ainsi que chantait, devant le ciel qui brille,
Le jeune homme alternant avec la jeune fille,
Un groupe des enfants du bourg de Bethphagé.
Au delà d'un vallon de brume submergé,
On distinguait des tours, un mur blanc, une porte;
C'était Jérusalem. L'encens que l'aube apporte,
Les souffles purs, les fleurs s'éveillant dans les bois,
Les rayons, se mêlaient à l'ivresse des voix;
Et c'était à côté du chemin de la ville.
Hors du village, et près de la borne du Mille,
Tout en allant aux champs, ils s'étaient rencontrés;
L'herbe était verte, et l'aube éblouissait les prés;
Les hommes avaient dit: Trêve au travail austère!
Et les femmes avaient posé leur cruche à terre,
Et, sereins, ils s'étaient mis à chanter, tandis
Que les oiseaux poussaient des cris du paradis;
Une aïeule riait au seuil d'une masure;
Trois laboureurs hâlés, pour marquer la mesure,
Frappaient la terre avec le manche de leur faulx;
Les vierges, au front pur comme un lys sans défauts,
Songeaient, et, l'œil noyé, la bouche haletante,
Regardaient l'horizon dans une vague attente.

Tout à coup, au moment où les femmes en chœur
Jetaient aux forêts l'hymne enflammé de leur cœur
Que marquait la cadence agreste des faucilles,

II

JESUS CHRIST

. : . : . : . : . : . : . : . : . : . : .

III

THE TRIUMPHAL PROCESSION

Thus sang, before the luminous sky,
The boy and girl, by turns,
Those children from Bethphage.
Beyond the valley immersed in fog,
One could make out towers, a white wall, a gate;
'Twas Jerusalem. The incense-bearing dawn,
The pure winds, the flowers waking in the wood,
The rays of light, mingled with the rapture of the voices:
This, beside the road to the city.
They had met on their way to the fields, well-nigh
A mile outside the village; the grass was luxuriant,
And dawn shed luster upon the meadows;
The men had said: Let us take rest from this hard labor!
And the women had placed their jars upon the earth,
To begin a serene hymn, whilst
Birds uttered cries from paradise;
A grandmother laughed at the threshold of a hut;
And three tanned ploughmen, to mark the beat,
Struck the earth with the handle of their scythes;
The virgins, their brows as pure as a spotless lily,
Mused and, breathless, eyes brimming,
Looked to the horizon with veiled expectation.

Suddenly, at the moment the chorus of women
Cast towards the forests their ardent, heart-felt hymn,
Marked by the rustic cadence of the sickles,

Quelqu'un dit:—Ecoutez! paix!—Et les jeunes filles
S'arrêtèrent, le doigt sur la bouche, entendant
Derrière le coteau brûlé du jour ardent,
D'autres voix qui chantaient, douces comme des âmes:

« Le bien-aimé, celui que vous attendez, femmes,
C'est celui-ci qui passe et que nous amenons.
Le triomphe nous a choisis pour compagnons,
La lumière permet que nous marchions près d'elle,
Et nous menons le maître à son peuple fidèle.
Voici le bien-aimé des âmes! et celui
Sur qui la grande étoile éblouissante a lui!
Toutes les majestés forment son diadème;
Il pourrait foudroyer, il préfère qu'on l'aime;
Il console Rachel, il relève Sara;
Il marche entre la paix et la joie; il sera
Comme un bouquet de myrrhe entre deux seins célestes;
Son sceptre anéantit dans les rayons les restes
Du vieux monde féroce où se tord le serpent;
Son nom divin est comme une huile qu'on répand;
Au-dessus de sa tête, étonnement des anges,
Le ciel est un murmure immense de louanges;
Il est plus glorieux qu'Alexandre, et plus beau
Que Salomon qui tient un lys dans son tombeau;
Il a pour champ la terre, et l'esprit pour domaine;
Il vient ôter la nuit de dessus l'âme humaine;
Il fera reculer l'Hydre qui triomphait;
Il transfigurera le monde stupéfait;
L'abîme le regarde et l'aurore l'approuve;
Le grondement du tigre et le cri de la louve,
La haine, la fureur soulevant un pavé,
La guerre, se tairont devant son doigt levé.
Dans son immensité, Moloch s'écroule et sombre.
Il est sans tache, il est sans borne, il est sans nombre;
Il produit, en fixant au ciel son œil béni,
La disparition du mal dans l'infini.

Someone exclaimed—Hark! be still!—And the women,
Motionless, their fingers to their lips, heard
Beyond the hillside afire from the blazing day,
Other voices singing, sweet as souls:

"The belovèd, he whom you await, women,
It is he who passes, he whom we bring.
The Exultation has chosen us for companions,
Light allows us to walk beside her,
And we lead the Master to his faithful flock.
Behold the belovèd of souls! and the one
Upon whom the great radiant Star casts its light!
All majesties form his crown;
He could hurl thunderbolts, but prefers that we love;
He consoles Rachel, he raises up Sara;
He walks surrounded by peace and delight and shall be
As a bouquet of myrrh between two celestial breasts;
His scepter destroys with its light beams the remnants
Of the fierce old world where the serpent writhes;
His divine name is spreading like an oil;
And above his head, wonder of the angels,
The heavens are a vast murmur of praise;
He is more glorious than Alexander and more noble
Than Solomon, who holds a lily within his tomb;
He has for his field the earth, and for his domain the spirit;
He comes to remove Night from atop the human soul;
He shall make the triumphant Hydra recoil;
He shall transform the astounded world. The abyss
Observes him and the dawn is well-pleased with him;
The roar of the tiger and the howl of the wolf,
Hatred, rage heaving up a bedrock,
War, shall keep silent before his raised finger.
Within his immensity, Moloch collapses and sinks.
He is flawless, boundless, numberless;
Fixing his blessèd eye on Heaven, he causes
The dispersal of evil into the infinite.

Les chars de Pharaon près de lui sont de l'ombre.
Il est plus radieux que Nemrod n'était sombre;
Il brille plus qu'Ammon à qui rien ne manquait,
Et dont le trône était le centre d'un banquet;
Il dépasse Cyrus debout sur son pilastre.
Peuple, toute son âme est une clarté d'astre.
C'est un roi; plus qu'un roi. C'est lui le Conquérant,
C'est lui le pur, c'est lui le vrai, c'est lui le grand!
Gloire à lui! le soleil le voit, l'ombre l'écoute. »

Alors on aperçut, au tournant de la route,
Un homme qui venait monté sur un ânon.

Cet homme, dont chacun se redisait le nom,
Était le même à qui Sadoch, l'autre semaine,
Avait jeté du haut du temple un cri de haine.
Il avait les cheveux partagés sur le front;
Des femmes qui riaient et qui dansaient en rond,
Le suivaient, et de fleurs elles étaient couvertes,
Et des petits enfants portaient des branches vertes;
Et de partout, des champs, des toits, des bois obscurs,
Et de Jérusalem dont on voyait les murs,
Sortait la foule, gaie, heureuse, pêle-mêle;
Des mères lui montraient leur fils à la mamelle,
Et les vieillards criaient: Hosanna! Quelques-uns
Soufflaient sur des réchauds où brûlaient des parfums;
Il s'avançait avec le calme du mystère;
Et ces hommes louaient cet homme, et sur la terre
Étendaient leurs habits pour qu'il passât dessus;
Quelques lambeaux de pourpre à la hâte cousus
Faisaient une bannière en avant du cortège;
Et tous disaient:—Que Dieu le Père le protège!
Voilà celui qui vient pour nous rendre meilleurs!—
Lui, pensif, regarda Jérusalem, les fleurs,
Le soleil au plus haut des cieux comme une fête,
Ces tapis sous ses pieds, ces rameaux sur sa tête,

The chariots of Pharaoh about him seem as if from the shadows.
He is more radiant than Nimrod was dark;
He outshines Ammon who lacked nothing
And whose throne was at the heart of a banquet;
He exceeds Cyrus, atop his pilaster.
People, his soul is starlight. He is king;
More than king, he is conqueror,
He is pure, he is true, he is great! Glory unto him!
The sun beholds him, the darkness harkens to him."

Then they saw at the bend of the road,
A man mounted on a donkey.

This man, his name on every lip,
Was he at whom Sadoc, the other week, hurled
Down from the temple height a cry of hatred.
His hair was spread across his brow;
Women encircled him, laughing
And dancing, bestrewn with flowers,
And small children bore him fresh green branches;
From everywhere, from the fields, the roofs, the dark
Wood, and from near Jerusalem,
Came the happy crowd, abandoned and gay;
Mothers showed him to their suckling sons,
And old men shouted, Hosanna! Others
Blew on their censers of incense;
He approached with the calmness of a mystery;
And these men praised this man, and upon the earth
Spread their coats that he might pass across them;
Some purple rags, hastily sewn,
Formed a banner to head the procession;
And all said:—May God the Father protect him!
Behold the one who comes to make us better!—
He thoughtfully regarded Jerusalem, the flowers,
The sun—a feast atop the heavens—these carpets
Spread beneath his feet, these branches upon his head,

Et les femmes chanter, et le peuple accourir,
Et sourit, en disant: je vais bientôt mourir.

IV

LE DEVOIR

Marie était assise entre Thomas et Jude;
Et le maître debout disait:—La solitude
Est un rayon d'en haut qu'on met dans son esprit;
Mais le sauveur va droit au peuple et s'y meurtrit;
Dieu livre le Messie aux multitudes viles;
La palme ne croît pas aux déserts, mais aux villes;
Malheur à qui se cache et malheur à qui fuit!
Laissons mûrir sur nous la mort ainsi qu'un fruit;
Et ne la troublons pas dans sa lente croissance;
Dieu, quand il juge un homme en sa toute-puissance,
Voit ce qu'il a vécu moins que ce qu'il a fait;
Au soleil de la mort David se réchauffait;
Ce serait mal aimer un frère que lui dire:
Recule! quand vers Dieu le sépulcre l'attire;
Et ce serait haïr et perdre son enfant
Que l'ôter du chemin funeste et triomphant;
Le calice est amer, mais l'exemple est utile;
Et c'est pourquoi je suis venu dans cette ville.

Ainsi parlait le fils et la mère écoutait.

V

DEUX DIFFÉRENTES MANIÈRES D'AIMER

C'est l'heure où le ramier rentre au nid et se tait.

Une femme se hâte en une rue étroite;
Elle regarde à gauche, elle regarde à droite,

The women singing, the people passing,
And smiled, saying: Soon I shall die.

IV

THE DUTY

Mary was seated between Thomas and Jude, and the
Master said, standing before them:—Solitude is a ray of
Light from above that we place in our spirit; but the Savior
Goes straight to the people and gets himself hurt there;
God delivers up the Messiah to the vile multitudes,
For the palm branch does not grow in the deserts, but in the cities;
And woe unto him that hides and woe unto him that flees!
Let death ripen above us like a fruit!
And let us not disturb it in its slow growth;
When God, in his omnipotence, judges a man, he sees less
What that man has endured than what he has brought forth;
In the sunlight of death, David warmed himself;
There would be no comfort in loving a brother who says:
Draw back! when towards God the sepulcher entices him;
And it would be to hate and to lose the child were one
To remove him from the deathly and triumphant path;
The cup is bitter, but the example is necessary;
And that is why I came into this city.

Thus spoke the son, and the mother listened.

V

TWO DIFFERENT WAYS TO LOVE

It is the hour when the dove returns to the nest and is still.

A woman hurries down a narrow street;
She looks left, she looks right,

Et marche. S'il faisait moins sombre au firmament,
On pourrait à ses doigts distinguer vaguement
Le cercle délicat des bagues disparues;
Son pied blanc n'est pas fait pour le pavé des rues;
Elle porte un long voile aux plis égyptiens
Plein de rayons nouveaux et de parfums anciens;
Jeune et blonde, elle est belle entre toutes les femmes;
Elle a dans l'œil des pleurs semblables à des flammes;
C'est Madeleine, sœur de Lazare.

Elle court.
Près de son pas céleste un oiseau serait lourd.
Où va-t-elle?

Il est nuit, et personne ne passe.

Une lumière brille en une maison basse.

Une autre femme, grave, est debout sur le seuil.
Son front est gris; elle est sévère sans orgueil,
Douce comme un enfant et grande comme un sage.
Elle pleure et médite; on voit sur son visage
L'âpre acceptation du sacrifice noir;
On dirait la statue en larmes du devoir;
Le cœur tremblant s'appuie en elle à l'âme forte;
C'est la mère.

Elle a l'air de garder cette porte.

Madeleine l'aborde, et presque avec des cris
Lui parle, et s'épouvante, et tord ses bras meurtris.

—Mère, ouvre-moi. Je viens. Il s'agit de sa vie.
Me voici. J'ai couru de peur d'être suivie.
On creuse l'ombre autour de ton fils. Je te dis

And continues on. If it were less dark in the firmament,
One might vaguely distinguish on her fingers
The delicate circles of missing rings;
Her white foot is not made for the cobbled streets;
She wears a long veil with Egyptian folds
Full of fresh light and ancient perfumes;
Young and fair, she is beautiful amongst women;
She has tears in her eyes like flames;
It is Magdelene, sister of Lazarus.

She is running,
Her heavenly step lighter than a bird in flight.
Where is she going?

It is night, and no one passes.

A light burns in a small house.

Another woman stands on the threshold, grave and
With furrowed brow; she is austere, humble,
Sweet as a child and wise as a sage.
She weeps, is pensive, and we see etched on her face
The resigned acceptance of a dark sacrifice;
She appears the tearful statue of Duty,
Whose trembling heart relies on the strength of her soul.
This is the mother.

And she appears to be guarding this door.

Magdelene approaches her, terrified, wringing her
Distressed hands, and, almost shouting, exclaims:

—Mother, let me enter. I come concerning his life.
I ran, for fear of being followed.
They are shrouding your son in darkness. I tell you

Que je sens fourmiller les serpents enhardis.
J'ai connu les démons, du temps que j'étais belle;
Je sais ce que l'enfer met dans une prunelle;
Je viens de voir passer Judas; cela suffit.
C'est un calculateur de fraude et de profit;
C'est un monstre. Ouvre-moi, que j'entre chez le maître.
Le temps presse. Il sera trop tard demain peut-être.
Il faut que ce soir même il fuie, et que jamais
Il ne revienne! ô mère! et, si tu le permets,
Je vais l'emmener, moi! Ces prêtres sont infâmes!
Manquer sa mission, ne point sauver les âmes,
Que nous importe, à nous les femmes qui l'aimons!
Il sera mieux avec les tigres dans les monts
Que dans Jérusalem avec les prêtres. Mère,
Qu'il renonce au rachat des hommes, sa chimère,
Qu'il fuie! oh! n'est-ce pas? nous baisons ses talons,
Et qu'il vive, voilà tout ce que nous voulons.
Ces juifs l'égorgeront! Demande à ma sœur Marthe
Si c'est vrai, s'il n'est pas nécessaire qu'il parte.
Laisse-moi l'arracher à son affreux devoir!
Oh! te figures-tu cela, mère? le voir
Saisi, lié, tué peut-être à coups de pierre!
O Dieu! le voir saigner, lui, ce corps de lumière!
Ouvre-moi. Je sais bien qu'il est dans ta maison
Puisque je vois sa lampe à travers la cloison.
O mère, laisse-moi l'implorer pour que vite
Il s'en aille et s'échappe et qu'il prenne la fuite!
A quoi songes-tu donc que tu ne réponds rien?
Si tu veux, à nous deux, nous le sauverons bien!
Veux-tu te joindre à moi pour arracher notre ange
Au gouffre monstrueux de ce devoir étrange,
Aux bourreaux, à Judas, son hideux compagnon?

La mère en sanglotant lui fait signe que non.

That I sense the impending arrival of emboldened serpents,
For I have known demons from the time when I was
Beautiful, and I know when an eye has Hell in it.
I have just seen Judas pass by; that is enough.
He is an imposter, and interested only in profit;
He is a monster. Open up, that I may see the master.
Time is pressing. It may be too late tomorrow.
He must flee this very evening, and never
Return! O mother! if you allow it,
I, myself, shall lead him to safety! These priests are infamous!
To miss his calling, to not save souls,
What does it matter to us women who love him!
He will be better off amidst tigers in the mountains
Than in Jerusalem with the priests. Mother,
He must renounce the redemption of men, his dream,
And flee! Oh! Is it not so? We kiss his heels,
And that he may live, that is all we desire.
These Jews will slay him! Ask my sister Martha
If it is not so, if it is not necessary that he leave.
Let me save him from his terrible duty!
Oh! Imagine him, Mother, seized,
Bound, possibly stoned to death!
O God! Imagine him bleeding, him, this body of light!
Open up. I know well that he is in your house,
Because I see his lamp through the partition.
O mother, let me beg him to quickly
Leave, take flight, escape!
Of what are you thinking, that you do not answer me?
If you want, both of us shall surely save him!
Will you not join me in wresting our angel
From the monstrous abyss of his strange duty,
From his executioners, from Judas, his hideous companion?

The mother, weeping, shakes her head "no."

VI

APRÈS LA PÂQUE

On était aux grands jours où le temple flamboie,
Où les petits enfants s'éveillent pleins de joie;
La Pâque était venue. On avait dans les fours
Cuit le pain sans levain qu'on vend aux carrefours.

Or Jésus-Christ était sur la montagne obscure,
Au lieu même où plus tard fut un temple à Mercure
Bâti par Adrien, détruit par Constantin.

C'était le soir; Jésus avait dit le matin
Aux disciples rangés autour de lui: «—Vous, Jacques,
Vous, Pierre, vous, Thomas, voici le jour de Pâques;
Vous irez dans la ville où des gens passeront;
Vous trouverez un homme ayant sa cruche au front;
A l'endroit où cet homme ira, quel qu'il puisse être,
Vous irez à sa suite, et vous direz:—Le Maître
Vient faire ici la Pâque.—Et pour cette raison
Le maître du logis donnera sa maison.
Il sied que Dieu toujours nous mène où bon lui semble.
Et nous célébrerons la Pâque tous ensemble.»

Et cela s'était fait ainsi qu'il l'avait dit.

Ce que la Cène vit et ce qu'elle entendit
Est écrit, dans le livre où pas un mot ne change,
Par les quatre hommes purs près de qui l'on voit l'ange,
Le lion, et le bœuf, et l'aigle, et le ciel bleu;
Cette histoire par eux semble ajoutée à Dieu
Comme s'ils écrivaient en marge de l'abîme;
Tout leur livre ressemble au rayon d'une cime;
Chaque page y frémit sous le frisson sacré;
Et c'est pourquoi la terre a dit: je le lirai!
Les peuples qui n'ont pas ce livre, le mendient,

VI

AFTER PASSOVER

These are the great days when the temple glows,
When the young children awake full of joy;
Passover has come; and they bake
The unleavened bread to sell at the crossroads.

But Jesus Christ was upon the dark mountain,
In the very place where a temple to Mercury
Was later built by Hadrian, and destroyed by Constantine.

It was evening; Jesus had said that morning
To the disciples ranged before him:—"You, James,
You, Peter, you, Thomas, today begins the Passover;
You shall go into the city to where people are out and about,
And you shall find a man bearing a jug upon his head;
Wherever this man goes, whoever he may be,
You shall follow him, and say:—The Master
Comes to celebrate the Passover here.—And for this
Reason, this master of the house shall give of his dwelling.
It is fitting that God always leads us wherever he pleases.
And we shall celebrate the Passover together."

And it was done as he had said.

What the Last Supper saw and what it heard
Is written, in the book where not a word changes,
By four simple men near to whom can be seen the angel,
The lion, the ox, the eagle and the blue firmament above;
This story seems added by them to God,
As if they wrote on the margin of the abyss;
Their entire book resembles a shaft of light from a summit;
Each page thrills there under the sacred shudder;
And that is why the earth said: I shall read it!
The peoples who have not this book, beg for it, and twenty

Et vingt siècles penchés dans l'ombre l'étudient.

Donc c'était le soir même où cet être divin
Venait de partager le gâteau sans levain;
Christ, assis, lui treizième, au centre de la table,
—Et ce noir chiffre Treize est resté redoutable,—
Avait rompu le pain, versé le vin, disant:
« Mangez, voici ma chair; buvez, voici mon sang. »
Puis il avait repris: « Allons où Dieu qui nous mène! »
Et tous étaient allés en sortant de la Cène
Au jardin qui fleurit derrière le Cédron.

Ce torrent, que jamais n'a touché l'aviron,
Coulait hors de la ville au pied d'une colline.
Les pâtres y montraient la cave sibylline
De Lilith, femme spectre, amante du démon;
C'est près de ce coteau que le prêtre Simon
Fit creuser le canal à laver les hosties;
Des sources y versaient, à travers les orties,
Une eau qui de la ville emplissait les viviers;
Et ce lieu s'appelait le Mont des Oliviers.

On venait sur ce mont aux époques de jeûnes.

Une plantation d'oliviers alors jeunes
Le couvrait en effet, jetant aux verts sentiers
Une ombre qui faisait durer les églantiers.
Christ y vint, murmurant tout bas: Que Dieu m'assiste!
Et ce qui s'y passa ce soir-là fut si triste,
Si lâche et si fatal qu'aujourd'hui ce jardin
Est voisin de l'enfer comme du ciel l'Éden.

Voici ce que Jésus disait sur la montagne:
« Ce qu'on perd sur la terre au ciel on le regagne.

Qui regarde en arrière et s'étonne de peu,
Celui-là n'est pas propre au royaume de Dieu.

Centuries, stooped over in the darkness, study it.

So it was that very evening when this divine being
Came to share the unleavened cake;
Christ, the thirteenth, seated at the center of the table,
—And this black number Thirteen has remained forever direful—
Having broken bread, poured the wine, saying:
"Eat, this is my flesh, drink, this is my blood."
Then he continued: "Let us follow God who leads us!"
And they all departed the Last Supper
For the garden that blooms behind the Kedron.

This torrent, untouched by an oar,
Flowed outside the city at the foot of a hill.
There the shepherds pointed out the sibylline cave
Of Lilith, woman specter, mistress of the devil;
It was near this hill that the priest Simon
Dug the canal to wash the offerings for sacrifice;
It was there that springs poured through the nettles
A water that filled the fish-ponds of the city;
And this place was called the Mount of Olives.

People came to this mountain in times of fasting,

And, indeed, a grove of young olive trees
Covered it, casting on the green paths
A shadow that made the wild roses last longer.
Christ came there, whispering: May God help me!
And what occured there that night was so sad,
So shameful and so irrevocable that today this garden
Is as close to Hell as is Eden to Heaven.

Here is what Jesus said on the Mount:
"What you lose on earth you regain in Heaven.

Whoever glances back and wonders at little,
This man is not fit for the kingdom of God.

Dieu se dévoile assez pour que l'homme le voie.

Je suis moins grand que lui, mais c'est lui qui m'envoie.
Quand je parle, c'est lui qui dit ce que je dis.

Si vous vous aimez bien, voilà le paradis.

Soyez bons. Dieu choisit ceux que je lui désigne.

Il est le vigneron, et moi je suis la vigne.
Il viendra, comme il fit pour Job et pour Amos,
Une serpe à la main, émonder mes rameaux,
Et, gardant les féconds, coupera les stériles.

Enseignez tendrement le peuple dans les villes,
Souriez, n'ayez point entre vous de débats.

Quand vous êtes parmi les tombes, parlez bas;
Car au fond du sépulcre une oreille est ouverte;
Ceux qu'on croit endormis sous la grande herbe verte,
Écoutent, et vos voix leur parlent dans les vents,
Et sachez que c'est là la maison des vivants.

Qui maudit doit trembler. Ne faites rien trop vite.
Esdras, voyant l'enfant d'une femme maudite,
Le prit et le jeta tout vivant dans la mer
Par l'effet surprenant d'un zèle trop amer.
Dieu l'a puni.

Marchez dans la route tracée.
Aimez. N'enviez pas à d'autres leur pensée;
Il faut se contenter des lumières qu'on a;
L'un est plus sage et l'autre est plus doux; Dieu donna
Plus de fruit au figuier, plus d'ombre au sycomore.
Croyez. »

God reveals himself enough for Man to behold him.

I am less great than he, but it is he who sent me.
When I speak, he speaks through me.

If you truly love one another, that is paradise.

Be good. God chooses those whom I indicate.

He is the vine grower, and I am the vine.
He will come, as he did for Job and for Amos,
Bill-hook in hand, to prune my branches,
And, retaining the fruitful, shall remove the unfruitful.

Teach the city dwellers with tenderness,
Smile, have no disputes amongst yourselves.

When you are amidst the tombs, converse quietly;
For there is an open ear at the bottom of the grave;
Those we believe asleep under the tall, green grass,
Are listening, and your voices speak to them in the winds;
Know that the house of the living resides here.

He who calls down curses must tremble with fear.
Do nothing hastily. Ezra, seeing the child of an
Accursed woman, took him and cast him, quite alive,
Into the sea, the rash result of a too bitter zeal.
God punished him.

Walk in the suggested manner.
Love. Do not envy others their thought.
Be content with the lights you possess;
Someone may be wiser, and yet another, gentler;
God gave more fruit to the fig tree, more shade to the sycamore.
Believe."

Il ajouta d'autres choses encore;
Puis soudain il dit, pâle et d'un frisson saisi:

—Allons! celui qui doit me vendre est près d'ici.

VII

COMMENCEMENT DE L'ANGOISSE

Alors il s'éloigna de près d'un jet de pierre,
Et se mit à genoux, et fit une prière.

Il resta longtemps seul et comme plein d'effroi.

Il disait:—« Écartez ce calice de moi,
Seigneur! S'il faut mourir pourtant, que la Mort vienne!
Que votre volonté soit faite, et non la mienne. »

Le reste dans le ciel ténébreux se perdit.

Les disciples dormaient. Christ revint, et leur dit:

—Quoi donc! vous n'avez pu même veiller une heure!

Il reprit:

—C'est ainsi qu'il convient que je meure.
Cela doit être, et nul au monde n'y peut rien.
Je suis venu pour être abandonné. C'est bien.
Il faut qu'on me rejette ainsi qu'un misérable.

On distinguait au loin le temple vénérable
Bâti par Salomon sur le mont Moria.

He added more as well;
Then suddenly he exclaimed, pale and seized by a shudder:

—Let us leave! he who must sell me is near.

VII

THE AGONY BEGINS

Then he withdrew nearly a stone's throw,
And knelt and prayed. He remained for a

Long time alone, seemingly full of dread.

He said:—"Take this chalice from me,
Lord! But if I must die, then let Death come!
Thy will be done, not mine."

The rest was lost in the dark sky.

The disciples were sleeping. Christ returned and said:

—What then? you could not even keep watch for an hour!

He continued :

—Thus it is decreed that I must die.
And nothing in the world can change that.
I came, to be forsaken. That's as it should be.
I must be spurned like the wretched.

Far off could be seen the venerable temple
Built by Solomon on Mount Moriah.

—Pardon pour tous! dit Christ. Mais Pierre s'écria:

—Si quelqu'un vous délaisse et vous quitte, ô mon maître,
Ce ne sera pas moi, car je suis votre prêtre.

Que le tombeau pour vous s'ouvre, j'y descendrai.

Jésus lui répondit, calme, tandis qu'André,
Jude et Thomas tournaient vers lui leurs têtes grises:

—Vous m'aurez renié, vous Pierre, à trois reprises,
Que le coq n'aura pas encor chanté trois fois.

VIII

CHRIST VOIT CE QUI ARRIVERA

Il alla de nouveau prier au fond du bois.

Il songeait, et sa voix disait:

                                        —Mon âme est triste
Jusqu'à la mort; et l'homme en moi tremble et résiste;
Je frémis comme Job, je crains comme Judith.

Puis il parla si bas que Dieu seul entendit.

Soudain il s'écria, pâle comme un prophète:

—Deuil, lamentation et douleur sur ta tête,
O Balaath qu'emplit un peuple querelleur!
Malheur, Corozaïm! Bethsaïde, malheur!
Parce que vous avez dédaigné mes oracles,
Parce que si j'avais fait les mêmes miracles,
Crié le même appel et le même pardon
Dans Ninive aux cent tours, dans Tyr et dans Sidon,

—All are forgiven! said Christ. But Peter exclaimed:

—If someone forsakes you and leaves you, O my Master,
It will not be I, for I am your priest.

If the tomb opens for you, I shall enter.

Jesus calmly answered while Andrew,
Thomas and Jude turned their gray heads towards him:

—Even before the cock crows thrice,
You yourself, Peter, will have denied me thrice.

VIII

CHRIST SEES WHAT WILL COME TO PASS

He again went to pray at the heart of the woods.

He meditated, and finally spoke:

—My soul is saddened
Unto death; and the man in me trembles and resists;
I quiver, like Job, I am afraid, like Judith.

Then he spoke so softly that God alone heard.

Suddenly he cried out, pale as a prophet:

—Mourning, lamentation and sorrow upon your head,
O Balaath, filled with a quarrelsome people!
Woe unto you, Chorazin! Bethsaida, woe unto you!
Because you disdained my oracles,
Because if I had performed the same miracles,
Shouted the same appeal, offered the same forgiveness
In Nineveh with the hundred towers, in Tyre and in Sidon,

On aurait vu pleurer Ninive, et Tyr descendre
De son trône, et Sidon vêtir le sac de cendre!
C'est fini. Je vous vois désertes. Vous voilà
Muettes comme un lac dont toute l'eau coula.
Vos jardins ont l'odeur des charniers insalubres.
Tout croule. Vos palais sont devenus lugubres
Sous le passage obscur des châtiments divins;
Ce sont des pans de mur inutiles et vains;
Les mâchoires des morts ne sont pas plus terribles.
Malheur! on ne voit plus le grain sortir des cribles;
Plus de fille de joie assise sur son lit;
On n'entend plus cracher les passants; l'herbe emplit
Les sentiers que suivaient les mulets et les zèbres.
Le plein midi ne fait qu'augmenter vos ténèbres;
On a beau peindre en blanc le sépulcre, il est noir.
Le soleil est présent à votre désespoir;
Vos décombres sont pleins d'antres épouvantables.
O Moïse, ils ont fait une fêlure aux tables,
Ils ont brisé la loi; c'est bien, mourez. Assez!
Vous serez si tremblants, peuples, et si chassés
Que vous ferez sous terre une seconde ville.
Comme sous le pressoir on voit déborder l'huile,
Le sang en longs ruisseaux jaillit sous le talon
Des princes écrasant Ruben et Zabulon;
Issachar et Lévi sont abolis. Partage
Et désert, comme après la chute de Carthage.
On vend un peuple ainsi qu'une bête au marché.
Malheur, Jérusalem! ô maison du péché,
Malheur! tu seras morte entre les cités mortes;
Les rois feront sculpter un pourceau sur tes portes;
Tu seras une ville infâme et sans témoin,
Qu'il sera défendu de regarder de loin.
La femme pleurera d'être grosse ou nourrice.
Qui te verra croira qu'il voit la cicatrice
Des tonnerres au front du monde châtié;
Et tu seras l'endroit où finit la pitié.

We would have seen Nineveh weep, and Tyre descend
From her throne, and Sidon dressed in ash-laden sackcloth.
It is done. I see you deserted. Behold, you are
Mute as a lake whose waters are no more.
Your gardens have the scent of the charnel-house.
Everything is crumbling, your palaces mournful
Under the dark passage of divine punishments;
They are useless and vain pieces of wall;
The jawbones of the dead are no more terrible.
Alas! We no longer see the grain being sifted;
No more the prostitute atop her bed;
No more the sound of the passers-by spitting.
Grass fills the paths mules and zebras once trod.
In broad daylight your darkness only increases;
Try as one may to paint the sepulcher white, it is black.
The sun is present in your despair;
Your ruins are full of dreadful caverns.
O Moses, they have made a crack in the Tables,
And they have shattered the law. It is well, die. Enough!
You shall be so fearful and so persecuted
That you shall create a second city underground.
Just as one sees the olive oil brimming o'er the press,
So shall blood flow in long streams under the heel
Of the princes crushing Reuben and Zebulun;
Issachar and Levi are done away with. Diaspora
And wilderness, as after the fall of Carthage.
People are sold like beasts in the market place.
Woe unto you, Jerusalem! O house of sin,
Woe unto you! You shall be dead among the dead cities;
Kings will sculpt a pig above your gates,
You shall become an infamous city, without witness,
And it shall be forbidden to look upon you from afar.
Women shall weep to be with child or nursing.
Whosoever sees you shall believe he sees the scars
Of thunderbolts on the brow of the chastised world;
And you shall be the place where pity ends.

Quand il eut ainsi fait des reproches aux villes,
Il s'approcha des siens et dit:

—Soyez tranquilles;
Ce n'est pas à présent votre jour, c'est le mien.
Tout est bon si ma mort délivre, tout est bien
Si dans la vérité l'homme se désaltère.
Or je m'élèverai de dessus cette terre
Et j'attirerai tout à moi du haut du ciel.
Christ finit le combat commencé par Michel.

Son œil devint étrange et semblait voir des choses
Au fond de son esprit confusément écloses.

—Les trois femmes en deuil dans la tombe entreront,
Marchant l'une après l'autre, humbles, courbant le front
A cause du lieu bas et de l'entrée étroite,
Et verront un jeune homme assis dans l'angle à droite
Qui leur dira, serein comme un soleil levant:
« Pourquoi parmi les morts cherchez-vous le vivant? »

La vision d'un être inouï qui se lève
Dans un sépulcre avec la lumière du rêve,
Fera fuir les soldats pleins d'un effroi sacré.

Trois jours après ma mort je ressusciterai;
Mais quand j'apparaîtrai blanc près de la fontaine,
Vous me verrez ainsi qu'une forme incertaine;
Madeleine croira que c'est le jardinier;
Thomas commencera par douter et nier,
Mais les trous de mes pieds le forceront à croire;
Et quand il aura mis dans ma blessure noire
Son doigt qu'il ôtera tiède et mouillé de sang,
Il s'en ira songer dans l'ombre en frémissant.

Priez. Ne livrez point ma doctrine aux querelles.

When he had thus rebuked the cities,
He approached his disciples and said:

—Be at peace;
This is not your day now, it is mine.
All is well if my death sets humankind free;
All is well if truth quenches Man's thirst.
Now I shall rise above this earth
And I shall draw all things to me from heaven.
Christ shall end the battle begun by Michael.

His eye became strange and seemed to see
Things dimly dawning in the depths of his spirit.

—Three women in mourning shall enter the tomb,
Following one after the other, humble, stooping
Through the low, narrow entryway, and they
Shall see a young man seated in the right-hand corner,
Who shall say to them, serene as a sunrise:
"Why amongst the dead do you seek the living?"

The vision of an incredible being who arises
In a tomb, suffused with the light of the dream,
Shall make the soldiers flee, full of holy terror.

Three days after my death I shall rise again;
But when I appear attired in white near the fountain,
You will not recognize me;
Magdelene will believe that it is the gardener;
Thomas will begin by doubting and denying,
But the wounds in my feet will force him to believe;
And when he will have placed in my black wound
His finger which he will remove warm and wet with blood,
He will leave to ponder in the shadows, trembling.

Pray. Never make of my teachings a matter of debate.

Est-ce que les épis sont pour les sauterelles?
Quand je serai parti, vous répandrez ma loi.
Beaucoup se tromperont, l'erreur naîtra de moi.
L'ombre est noire toujours même tombant des cygnes.

Quand je ne serai plus vous verrez de grands signes.
Les ténèbres croîtront sur le front d'Israël;
On entendra parler une voix dans le ciel,
Et tous regarderont l'ombre extraordinaire;
Luc dira: c'est un ange; et Jean, c'est le tonnerre.

Je porterai les cœurs ainsi que des fardeaux.
Des laboureurs feront des sillons sur mon dos;
Ces laboureurs, c'est vous; et votre œuvre est austère.
L'homme n'a rien, ni sac plein d'or, ni coin de terre,
Qu'il puisse regarder ici-bas comme sien.
Allez sans hésiter dire au pharisien:
« Prends garde à cette fange immonde où tu te vautres! »
Soyez doux. Aimez-vous toujours les uns les autres.

En cet instant Jésus tressaillit, se parla
A lui-même, et, fermant les yeux, dit: le voilà.

Judas parut suivi d'hommes armés d'épées.

IX

JUDAS

Et Judas s'approchant, blême et les mains crispées,
Baisa Christ.

Et le ciel sacré fut obscurci.
—Mon ami, dit Jésus, que viens-tu faire ici ?

Puis il reprit, tourné vers Dieu:

Are sheaves of wheat for the locusts?
When I shall have left, you will spread my law abroad.
Many will go astray; false teaching will arise from me.
The shadow is always dark, even when cast by swans.

When I am no more, you shall see great signs.
Darkness will spread across the brow of Israel;
You shall hear a voice speaking from Heaven,
And all will behold the extraordinary darkness:
Luke will exclaim: It is an angel; and John: It is the thunderbolt.

I shall carry hearts as well as burdens.
Ploughmen shall make furrows upon my back;
These ploughmen, they are you; and your work is arduous.
Down here, Man has nothing, no bag of gold,
No piece of land that he can call his own.
Without hesitation go tell the Pharisee:
"Beware of this filthy mire wherein you wallow!"
Be gentle. Always love one another.

At this moment Jesus gave a start, and, speaking
To himself, closed his eyes, murmuring: He is here.

Judas had just appeared, followed by men armed with swords.

IX

JUDAS

And pale Judas approached, and with his trembling hands clenched,
Kissed Christ.

And the sacred sky became dark.
—My friend, said Jesus, what have you come to do here?

Then he continued, turned towards God:

—Tu m'abandonnes;
Mais je ne perds aucun de ceux que tu me donnes,
Seigneur. Ma mort suffit, et seul je la subis.
Le pasteur doit périr en sauvant les brebis.

Et, désignant du doigt ses disciples, le maître
Dit aux soldats:

—Le Christ est facile à connaître.
Je suis celui qu'on cherche et dont on a souci.
Me voici. Prenez-moi. Laissez aller ceux-ci.

Or Simon surnommé Pierre avait une épée.
Il cria:
—Dieu par qui Jézabel fut frappée,
Viens défendre ton Christ, ô Dieu qui châtias
Hérode pour avoir fait mourir Mathias!
Et, levant son épée, il vint droit à la troupe,
Et blessa le premier qui s'offrit dans le groupe,
Un nommé Malchus, aide et garde du bourreau.
— Remettez, dit Jésus, votre épée au fourreau.
Qui frappe avec le glaive est frappé par le glaive.
Il reprit:—Puisqu'on a commencé, qu'on achève.—
Et se mit de lui-même au milieu des soldats.
Il ne regardait rien, pour épargner Judas.
Quelqu'un du temple dit:—Marchons. L'heure s'écoule.
—Vous pouviez me saisir tous les jours dans la foule,
Dit Jésus, en offrant aux cordes ses poignets;
Quand j'allais dans le temple et lorsque j'enseignais,
J'étais sous votre main. Vous n'aviez qu'à l'étendre;
Et c'est par trahison que vous venez me prendre!
Et vous venez la nuit comme pour un voleur!
Je pourrais dire à Dieu: Père, apparaissez-leur!
Et vous entendriez accourir les tempêtes,
Et vous verriez, tremblants, au-dessus de vos têtes,
S'ouvrir et flamboyer l'ombre, et des millions

—You abandon me;
But I shall not lose any of these others you gave to me,
Lord. My death is enough, and only I need suffer.
The shepherd must perish saving his flock.

And, pointing out his disciples, the Master
Said to the soldiers:

—The Christ is easy to recognize.
I am the one you seek, the one that troubles you.
Here I am. Take me. Let the others go.

But Simon, renamed Peter, had a sword,
And shouted:
—God, who struck down Jezebel, O God
Who punishes Herod for having Mathias put to death!
Come defend your Christ!
Then, raising his sword, he came straight at the troop,
Wounding the first one to step forward,
One named Malchus, aide and guard to the executioner.
—Resheath your sword, said Jesus;
He who strikes with the sword shall be struck down by the sword.
He continued:—Since we have begun, let us finish it.—
And he placed himself amidst the soldiers.
He looked at no one, in order to spare Judas.
Someone from the temple said:—Let us go; time is passing.
—You could have seized me from the crowd at any time,
Jesus said, offering his wrists for binding.
When I was in the temple or when I was teaching,
I was within your grasp, you had only to reach out;
Yet it is through treachery that you come to take me!
And you come at night like a thief!
I could say to God: Father, appear before them!
And you would hear rushing tempests,
And you would see, trembling, above your heads,
Darkness opening, in flame, and a myriad

D'anges, et tout l'abîme avec tous ses lions!
Et si j'ajoutais: Viens toi-même! vos prunelles
Verraient soudain, parmi les foudres éternelles,
Sortir de la nuée un front prodigieux!
Mais il ne convient pas que j'appelle les cieux;
Faites; car c'est ici votre heure, et la puissance
Des ténèbres, et Dieu vous livre l'innocence;
Et tout doit s'accomplir ainsi qu'il est écrit.

Alors on acheva de lier Jésus-Christ;
Et le chef dit:—Il faut l'emmener. Ce qu'ils firent.
Et tous ceux que cet homme avait aimés, s'enfuirent.

X

LILITH-ISIS

O Jean, visionnaire effaré de Pathmos,
Comme tu te cachais derrière les rameaux,
Avec Saint Marc, alors jeune et l'un des lévites,
En vous penchant parmi les arbres noirs, vous vîtes
Sur la colline un être étrange, vague, seul,
Debout dans le frisson livide d'un linceul;
C'était de l'ombre ayant la forme d'une femme;
Cet être épiait Christ dans cette troupe infâme,
Comme s'il était là pour une mission;
Or la bande aperçut, en rentrant dans Sion,
Cette femme fixant sur eux dans les ténèbres
Ses deux yeux qui semblaient deux étoiles funèbres;
Un d'eux, que le Toldos appelle Eddon-Azir,
Courut vers elle, et comme il allait la saisir,
L'être, pareil aux feux fuyant dans l'ossuaire,
Disparut, lui laissant dans les mains le suaire.

Et plus tard les soldats, contant après l'arrêt
Comment ils avaient pris Jésus de Nazareth,

Of angels, and the entire abyss with all its lions!
And if I added: Come Yourself! your eye
Would suddenly see emerge from the thick cloud,
Amidst the eternal wraths, a mighty brow!
But it is not fitting that I call upon Heaven;
Be done; for this is your hour, and the power
Of darkness, and God, deliver up innocence to you;
And all must be fulfilled as it is written.

Then they finished binding Jesus Christ; and the leader said:
—We must away with him. Which they did.
And all those that this man had loved, fled.

X

LILITH-ISIS

O John, bewildered visionary of Patmos,
As you hid behind the boughs with Saint Mark,
Then young and one of the Levites,
Crouched amidst the black trees, you saw
A strange, shadowy, lone figure standing on the hill,
In the ghastly horror of a shroud;
It was Gloom in the shape of a woman;
As if there on a mission, this being
Spied upon Christ amidst this infamous troop.
While returning into Zion, the troop saw
This woman fixing on them, in the darkness,
Her two eyes that seemed two funereal stars;
One of them, whom the Toldos calls Eddon-Azir,
Ran towards her, and as he was about to seize her,
This being, as fires fleeing in the ossuary,
Disappeared, leaving behind her shroud in his hands.

And later the soldiers, after the arrest, telling of
How they had captured Jesus of Nazareth,

Dirent qu'ils avaient vu sur la montagne sombre
La fille de Satan, la grande femme d'ombre,
Cette Lilith qu'on nomme Isis au bord du Nil.

. : . : . : . : . : . : . : . : . : . : .

XIV

LA FIDÉLITÉ DU MEILLEUR

Une servante vint dans la cour et vit Pierre
Qui se chauffait, ouvrant ses mains devant le feu:

—Vous étiez, lui dit-elle, un des gens de ce dieu,
De ce Jésus, car c'est le nom dont on le nomme.

Et Pierre répondit:—Femme, quel est cet homme?
Je ne le connais point.

Alors le coq chanta.

Cependant les bourreaux, au haut du Golgotha,
Creusaient la terre afin d'y planter la potence.

Dans la cour du grand prêtre et parmi l'assistance,
Pierre pensait.
Quelqu'un tout à coup l'appela
Et cria:—Vous suiviez ce Nazaréen-là.

Pierre dit:—Je ne sais ce que vous voulez dire.

Une femme, un moment après, se prit à rire,
Disant:—Vous connaissez l'homme qu'on juge ici.
Car vous êtes venu de Galilée aussi.

Said that they had seen on the dark mountain
The daughter of Satan, the great woman of darkness,
This Lilith, who is called Isis alongside the river Nile.

.:.:.:.:.:.:.:.:.:.

XIV

THE LOYALTY OF THE BEST

A servant came into the courtyard and saw Peter
Warming himself, opening his hands before the fire:

—You were, she said to him, one of the followers of this God,
Of this Jesus, for it is thus that he is called.

And Peter answered:—Woman, who is this man?
I know him not.

Then the cock crowed.

But the executioners atop Golgotha
Were digging the earth to plant the cross there.

In the courtyard of the high priest and amidst the onlookers,
Peter was meditating.
Suddenly someone called out to him,
Shouting:—You followed that Nazarene.

Peter said:—I know not what you mean.

A woman, a moment later, laughed,
Saying:—You used to know the man who was tried here.
For you, also, came from Galilee.

Alors Pierre jura d'une exécrable sorte:
Non! je n'ai jamais vu cet homme!
Et sur la porte
Le coq chanta.

La nuit couvrait les noirs chemins.

Pierre, se souvenant, prit son front dans ses mains
Et se mit à pleurer amèrement dans l'ombre.

.:.:.:.:.:.:.:.:.:.:.

XVI

ROSMOPHIM

Les fossoyeurs de croix piochent sur le Calvaire.
Le brouillard, ce manteau de deuil du ciel sévère,
Couvre le mont, où, seuls, ces hommes, loin du bruit,
Dans l'ombre, ont travaillé presque toute la nuit.
On entend le Cédron mugir; ses eaux sont grosses.
Ils s'arrêtent après avoir creusé deux fosses.
Et l'un d'eux, le plus vieux, dit aux autres:—Je crois
Que c'est tout; nous n'avons d'ordres que pour deux croix,
Pour deux larrons qu'on doit mettre à mort dans les fêtes;
Dismas et Gestas; or, les deux fosses sont faites.

Un prêtre, en ce moment, Rosmophim de Joppé,
Qui vient de survenir, d'ombres enveloppé,
Sort de la brume ainsi qu'un tigre sort de l'antre,
Et leur dit:

—Creusez-en une troisième au centre.

.:.:.:.:.:.:.:.:.:.:.

But Peter vowed in a shameful manner:
No! I have never seen this man!
And beyond the gate
The cock crowed.

Night enveloped the black pathways.

And Peter, remembering, placed his brow in his hands
And wept, bitterly, in the dark.

.:.:.:.:.:.:.:.:.:.

XVI

ROSMOPHIM

The diggers of crosses labor upon Calvary.
The fog, austere Heaven's cloak of mourning,
Covers the mount, where, alone, these men, far from the din,
Have worked almost the entire night in the dark.
One can hear the Kedron roar with its high waters of springtide.
They stop, following the excavation of two holes.
And the eldest of them says to the others—I think
That is all; we have orders for only two crosses,
For two thieves, Dismas and Gestas, to be executed during
The festivities; now, both pits are dug.

At this moment, a priest, Rosmophim of Joppa,
Who had just arrived unexpectedly, emerges from the fog
Like a tiger from his lair, veiled in shadows,
And says to them:

—Dig a third one in the middle.

.:.:.:.:.:.:.:.:.:.

XX

LA MARCHE AU SUPPLICE

La première heure allait finir quand de la geôle
Jésus sortit, portant une croix sur l'épaule;
On avait délié les cordes du poignet;
Ayant été battu de verges, il saignait;
On le huait; la loi frappe, le peuple accable;
La croix, démesurée, écrasante, implacable,
Dont la cognée à peine avait taillé les nœuds,
Était faite d'un bois féroce et vénéneux
Et qui semblait avoir déjà commis des crimes.

La foule, allant, courant, mangeant les pains azymes,
Chantant, montrait les poings à Christ des deux côtés
De la route où marchaient ses pas ensanglantés;
Des vierges, reflétant l'aube sur leur visage,
L'insultaient, et battaient des mains sur son passage,
Et riaient des cailloux déchirant ses talons;
Et Christ marchait, voyant des têtes d'enfants blonds
Aux portes des maisons, pour la fête fleuries.

Quelques disciples, fronts baissés, les trois Maries,
Sa mère, le suivaient de loin dans le trajet.

L'œil sinistre de Jean dans le ciel noir plongeait.
Le jour, blême, fuyait. L'attente était profonde.

Quatre anges se tenaient aux quatre coins du monde;
Ces anges arrêtaient au vol les quatre vents,
Pour qu'aucun vent ne pût souffler sur les vivants,
Ni troubler le sommet des montagnes de marbre,
Ni soulever un flot, ni remuer un arbre.

XX

THE WALK TO THE EXECUTION

The first hour was coming to an end when, from the gaol,
Jesus emerged, bearing a cross upon his shoulder;
They had loosened the cords about his wrists;
Having been scourged, he was bleeding;
The mob jeered at him; the law strikes, but the people crush;
The cross, enormous, overwhelming, pitiless,
Whose knots the ax had barely cut,
Was made of a fierce and venomous wood,
And seemed to have already committed crimes.

The crowd, restless, hurrying, eating unleavened bread,
Singing, shook their fists at Christ from both sides
Of the road where were traced his bloody steps;
Some Virgins, reflecting the dawn upon their faces,
Insulted him, applauded his passing,
And laughed at the stones tearing his heels;
And Christ proceeded, seeing in the doorways of the houses
The heads of fair children festooned with flowers for the feast.

Some disciples, heads bowed, the three Marys,
His mother, followed from a distance.

The sinister eye of John plunged into the dark sky.
Pale Day fled. The waiting was profound.

Four angels stood at the four corners of the world;
These angels stopped the four winds in their flight,
That no breeze might blow upon the living,
Nor disturb the summit of the marble mountains,
Nor raise a flood, nor stir a tree.

. : . : . : . : . : . : . : . : . : .

III

LE CRUCIFIX

Depuis ce jour, pareille à celui qui rend compte,
La morne humanité, sur qui pèse la honte
Des justes condamnés et des méchants absous,
Est comme renversée en arrière au-dessous
D'une vision triste, éternelle et terrible.
Un Calvaire apparaît dans la nuée horrible
Que tout le genre humain regarde fixement;
Une lividité de crâne et d'ossement
Couvre ce mont difforme où monte un homme pâle;
L'homme porte une croix, et l'on entend son râle,
Ses pieds dans les cailloux saignent, ses yeux noyés
Pleurent, pleins de crachats qu'on n'a pas essuyés;
Le sang colle et noircit ses cheveux sur sa tempe;
Et l'homme, que la croix accable, tombe, rampe,
Se traîne, et sur ses mains retombe, et par moment
Ne peut plus que lever son front lugubrement.

Et l'œil du genre humain frémissant continue
De regarder monter cet homme dans la nue.

Une tourbe le suit; il arrive au plateau;
D'infâmes poings crispés arrachent son manteau;
Cris féroces; Va donc! pas de miséricorde!
Il va, montrant son dos rouge de coups de corde,
Hué par l'aboiement et mordu par les crocs
D'on ne sait quel vil peuple, envieux des bourreaux;
Au milieu des affronts il est comme une cible.
On étend l'homme, nu comme un Adam terrible,
Sur le gibet qu'il a traîné dans le chemin;
On enfonce des clous dans ses mains; chaque main

.:.:.:.:.:.:.:.:.:.

III

THE CRUCIFIX

Since this day, despondent humanity,
Like one who must be held accountable, and upon
Whom weighs the shame of condemning the just and
Absolving the wicked, is as though staggered
Beneath a sad, terrible and eternal vision.
A Calvary appears in the horrible, thick cloud,
Which the entire human race looks at fixedly;
A lividity of skull and bone covers this deformed
Mount where ascends a pale man dragging a cross.
His feet are made bloody by the stones, and one can hear
His groan. Tears flow from his eyes covered with
Spittle that no one will wipe away,
While blood darkens the hair stuck to his temple;
Overwhelmed by the weight of the cross, the man falls,
Crawls, drags himself up, falls again upon his hands,
And at times can do no more than lift his head mournfully.

And the eye of quivering Mankind continues
To watch this man ascending into the clouds.

A rabble follows him; he attains the plateau;
Vicious, twitching hands tear away his mantle,
As they shout savagely: Go thus! We show no mercy!
He goes on, his back bloody from the lashings,
Jeered by the barking and bitten by the fangs
Of this vile people who envy the executioners;
In the midst of these insults he is like a target.
Naked as a terrible Adam, they stretch this man
Upon the cross that he had dragged along the road;
They drive nails into his hands; each hand

Jette un long flot de sang à celui qui la cloue,
Et le bourreau blasphème en essuyant sa joue;
La foule rit. On cloue, après les mains, les pieds;
Le marteau maladroit meurtrit ses doigts broyés;
On appuie à son front la couronne d'épines;
Puis, entre deux bandits expiant leurs rapines,
On élève la croix en jurant, en frappant,
En secouant le corps qui se disloque et pend;
Le sang le long du bois en ruisseaux vermeils coule;
Et la mère est en bas qui pleure et cette foule
Rit:—Voyons, dieu Jésus, descends de cette croix!—
Une éponge de fiel se dresse.—As-tu soif? bois!—
Le peuple horrible a l'air du loup dans le repaire;
Et le grand patient dit: —Pardonnez-leur, Père,
Car ces infortunés ne savent ce qu'ils font.

Et voici que la terre avec le ciel se fond.
Nuit! ô nuit! tout frémit, même le prêtre louche.
Et soudain, à ce cri qui sort de cette bouche:
—Élohim! Élohim! lamma sabacthani!—
On voit un tremblement au fond de l'infini,
Et comme un blême éclair qui tressaille et qui sombre
Dans l'immobilité formidable de l'ombre.

*

Et pendant que les cœurs, les mains jointes, les yeux,
Sont éperdus devant ce gibet monstrueux,
Pendant que, sous la brume épouvantable où tremble
Ce crime qui contient tous les crimes ensemble,
Brume où Judas recule, où chancelle la croix,
Où le centurion s'étonne et dit: je crois!
Pendant que, sous le poids de l'action maudite,
Sous Dieu saignant, l'effroi du genre humain médite,
Des voix parlent, on voit des songeurs bégayants,
La pitié se déchire en lugubres récits.

Casts a long stream of blood upon the one who nails it
And the executioner curses, wiping his cheek;
The crowd laughs. After the hands, they nail his feet;
The clumsy hammer bruises his crushed toes;
They place on his brow the crown of thorns;
Then, between two thieves crucified for their crimes,
They raise the cross, swearing, striking
And shaking the body which then collapses;
Blood flows in ruby streams along the wood;
Below is the mother, weeping, and the crowd
Laughs:—Let's see god Jesus come down from this cross!—
A sponge of gall is raised.—Are you thirsty?
Drink!—The people are like the wolf in its lair;
And the great patient one says: Forgive them, Father;
For these unfortunates know not what they do.

At this, the earth merged with the sky.
Night! O night! All tremble, even the deceitful priest.
And suddenly, with this cry which emerges from his mouth:
—Eli, Eli, lama sabachthani!—
A trembling is seen in the depths of the infinite,
Like a pale lightning flash that quivers and sinks
Into the formidable stillness of the darkness.

*

And while hearts, clasped hands, eyes,
Are aghast before this monstrous cross,
While, under the dreadful mist where trembles
This crime which contains all crimes as one,
This mist where Judas recoils, where the cross reels,
Where the astonished centurion exclaims: I believe!
While, under the weight of the cursed act,
Under the bleeding God, the fear of humankind broods,
Voices speak, one sees dreamers falter,
And pity is rent into mournful narratives.

La tradition, fable errante qu'on recueille,
Entrecoupée ainsi que le vent dans la feuille,
Apparaît, disparaît, revient, s'évanouit,
Et, tournoyant sur l'homme en cette étrange nuit,
La légende sinistre, éparse dans les bouches,
Passe, et dans le ciel noir vole en haillons farouches;
Si bien que cette foule humaine a la stupeur
Du fait toujours présent là-haut dans la vapeur,
Vrai, réel, et pourtant traversé par des rêves.

*

....

« Comme il montait, suant et piqué par les glaives,
Une femme eut pitié, le voyant prêt à choir,
Et l'essuya, posant sur son front un mouchoir;
Et, quand elle rentra chez elle, cette femme
Vit sur le mouchoir sombre une face de flamme. »

....

« Comme il continuait de monter, tout en sang,
Il s'arrêta, livide, épuisé, fléchissant
Sous la croix exécrée et l'infâme anathème.
Un homme lui cria: Marche!—Marche toi-même,
Dit Jésus-Christ. Et l'homme est errant à jamais. »

....

« Un des larrons lui dit:—Faux dieu! tu blasphémais!
Es-tu dieu? Sauve-nous et sauve-toi toi-même!
L'autre larron cria:—Jésus! je crois! je t'aime!
Souviens-toi qu'un mourant s'est à toi confié!
Alors, levant ses yeux vers ce crucifié,
Jésus agonisant parvint à lui sourire:

The tradition, the wandering fable which we collect,
Separated like wind in the leaves,
Appears, disappears, returns, vanishes,
And, swirling about Man in this strange night,
The sinister legend, passed from mouth to mouth,
Is transmitted, flying in grim tatters in the darkened sky;
So that this human mob has the bewildering
Fact always present above in the mist,
True, real, and yet mixed with dreams.

*

....

"As he ascended, sweating and prodded by swords,
A woman took pity, seeing him about to fall,
And wiped his brow with a cloth;
And, when she returned home, this woman
Saw upon this somber cloth a face of flame."

....

"As he continued to climb, bathed in blood,
Stopping, pale, exhausted, and yielding
Under the hated cross and the vile anathema,
A man shouted at him: Walk!—Walk, thyself,
Said Jesus Christ. And the man has been wandering ever since."

....

"One of the thieves said to him:—False god! You blasphemed!
Are thou not God? Save us and save yourself;
The other thief shouted:—Jesus! I believe! I love you!
Remember that a dying man confided in you!
Then, raising his eyes towards this crucified man,
Dying Jesus managed to smile at him:

—Homme, pour avoir dit ce que tu viens de dire,
O voleur sur la croix misérable expirant,
Tu vas entrer aux cieux, et tu seras plus grand
Qu'un empereur portant la couronne et le globe. »

....

« Ils se sont partagé le manteau, mais la robe
N'ayant pas de couture, ils l'ont jouée aux dés. »

....

« De six à neuf, les monts furent d'ombre inondés;
Toute la terre fut couverte de ténèbres;
Comme si quelque main eût ployé ses vertèbres,
Il baissa tout à coup la tête, et dans ses yeux
Lugubres apparut la profondeur des cieux;
Et, poussant un grand cri, Jésus expira. L'ombre
Monta, fumée infâme, aux étoiles sans nombre;
Dans le temple, les bœufs d'airain firent un pas,
Le voile se fendit en deux, du haut en bas.
Hors des murs, il se fit un gouffre où se dressèrent
D'affreux êtres sur qui les rochers se resserrent
Et que la vaste fange inconnue enfouit;
Et tout devint si noir que tout s'évanouit;
Les sépulcres, s'ouvrant subitement, restèrent
Béants, montrant leur cave où les taupes déterrent
Les squelettes couchés dans des draps en lambeaux;
Des morts blêmes, étant sortis de leurs tombeaux,
Furent vus par plusieurs personnes dans la ville. »

*

—Man, for having spoken those words,
O thief, perishing on your miserable cross,
You shall enter Heaven, and you shall be greater
Than an emperor carrying his crown and orb."

....

"They divided his mantle amongst themselves, but his robe,
Having no seam, they played for with dice."

....

"From the sixth to the ninth hour, the mountains were flooded
In shadow. The whole earth was covered with darkness,
And as if some hand had pushed from behind,
Jesus suddenly lowered his head, and in his sad
Eyes were revealed the depths of the heavens;
Then, giving forth a great cry, he breathed his last.
Darkness, vile smoke, rose to the numberless stars;
In the temple, the brazen oxen moved,
And the veil was rent in twain, from top to bottom.
Outside these walls, there formed a gulf where arose
Some frightful Beings enclosed by the rocks
And buried in the vast, unknown mire;
And it became so black that everything vanished;
Tombs, suddenly opened wide,
Revealed their caverns where the moles dug up
Fragments of skeletons lying in shrouds;
The ghastly dead, having emerged from their graves,
Were seen by several of those who dwelled in the city."

*

. . . .

Ainsi sur ce troupeau frémissant, immobile,
Lugubre et stupéfait, qu'on nomme Humanité,
Tombent, du fond de l'ombre et de l'éternité,
On ne sait quels lambeaux de chimère et d'histoire
Et de songe, où l'enfer mêle sa lueur noire.
Et l'homme a peur du ciel qui saigne à l'orient.
Et l'ouragan est plein de spectres s'écriant:
O nations! le meurtre éternel se consomme!
Et, parmi tous les mots que peut prononcer l'homme,
Pas un, si frissonnant qu'il fût, ne suffirait
A peindre cette horreur de tombe et de forêt,
Le sourd chuchotement des quatre evangelists,
Et l'agitation des grandes ailes tristes
Qu'en ce gouffre de deuil et de rébellion
Dressent l'aigle, le bœuf, l'archange et le lion.

*

Dix-huit cents ans ont pu s'écouler sans que l'homme,
Autour duquel mouraient Byzance, Athène et Rome,
Et passait Charlemagne et montait Mahomet,
Ait quitté du regard cette croix, ce sommet,
Cette blancheur sanglante, et ces lueurs divines
Sous l'entrelacement monstrueux des épines;
Et sans qu'il ait cessé d'entendre un seul moment
L'immense cri jeté dans le noir firmament,
Et lisible à jamais sur ce sombre registre,
Et le déchirement du grand voile sinistre,
Et dans l'obscurité consciente, au-dessus
De ce gibet où pend l'être appelé Jésus,
Au-dessus des songeurs étudiant les bibles,
Le sanglot effrayant des bouches invisibles.

. . . .

So, we know not what shreds of fancy and history
And dream, mingled with the melancholy light of Hell,
Have fallen from the heart of the eternal
Darkness on this trembling, motionless herd,
Gloomy and stunned, that we call humanity.
And Man fears the sky that bleeds from the east.
The hurricane is full of specters exclaiming:
O nations! Eternal murder is committed!
And, among all the words that Man can pronounce,
Not one, however expressive of horror, would suffice
To paint this repugnance of tomb and forest,
The muffled murmur of four evangelists,
And the agitation of the great, mournful wings
That in this abyss of grief and rebellion
The eagle, the ox, the archangel and the lion raise up.

*

Eighteen hundred years have passed, and humankind,
Around whom Byzantium, Athens and Rome have perished,
And Charlemagne passed, and Mohammed arisen,
Has never averted its glance from this cross, this summit,
This blood-stained purity, and these divine lights
Under the monstrous interlacing of thorns,
And has never ceased hearing for a single moment
The great cry cast into the black firmament,
Legible forever on this somber register,
And the tearing of the great sinister veil,
And in the conscious darkness, above
This cross where hangs the being called Jesus,
Above the dreamers studying their Bibles,
The frightening sob of invisible mouths.

*

Quand donc pourra-t-on dire: Hommes, le mal n'est plus!
Quand verra-t-on finir le flux et le reflux?

O nuit! ce qui sortit de Jésus, c'est Caïphe.

Le tigre, ayant encor de ce sang à la griffe,
Remonta sur l'autel et dit: Je suis l'agneau.
Christ, ce libérateur, ne brisa qu'un anneau
De la chaîne du mal, du meurtre et de la guerre;
Lui mort, son dogme, hélas! servit à la refaire;
La tiare s'accrut de son gibet. Jésus,
Dans les cieux au delà du sépulcre aperçus,
S'en alla, comme Abel, comme Job, comme Élie;
Quand il eut disparu, l'œuvre étant accomplie,
En même temps qu'au loin se répandait sa loi:
«—Vivez! aimez! marchez! délivrez! ayez foi!—»
Le serpent relevait son front dans les décombres,
Et l'on vit, ô terreur! ô deuil! des prêtres sombres
Aiguiser des poignards à ses préceptes saints,
Et de l'assassiné naître des assassins!
Ghisleri, Borgia, Caraffa, Dominique!...—
Faites donc que jamais l'homme ne soit inique,
Et que jamais le prêtre, impie et solennel,
N'emploie à quelque usage infâme l'Éternel!

*

La flagellation du Christ n'est pas finie.
Tout ce qu'il a souffert dans sa lente agonie,
Au mont des oliviers et dans les carrefours,
Sous la croix, sur la croix, il le souffre toujours.
Après le Golgotha, Jésus, ouvrant son aile,
A beau s'être envolé dans l'aurore éternelle;

*

So, when can it be said: Men, evil is no more!
When will there be an end to this ebb and flow?

O night! What emerges from Jesus, is Caiaphas.

The tiger, still with blood-drenched claw,
Climbs back upon the altar and says: I am the lamb.
Christ, this liberator, broke a mere link
Of the chain of evil, murder and war;
When he died, his teachings, alas! served only to mend it;
The tiara grew from his cross. Jesus
Went away to Heaven perceived beyond the
Sepulcher, as did Abel, Job, and Elijah;
When he had disappeared, his work
Accomplished, his law spreading far and wide:
"Live! Love! Go forth! Deliver! Have faith!," at the same time
The serpent again raised his brow from out of the rubble,
And, O terror! O grief! somber priests were seen
Sharpening their daggers with his holy rules,
And murderers born from the murdered:
Ghisleri, Borgia, Carafa, Dominic!...
So, ensure that Man is never unjust,
And that the godless and solemn priest never
Puts to some vile use the Eternal!

*

The flagellation of Christ has not ended.
All that he suffered in his slow agony,
Upon the Mount of Olives and at the crossroads,
Under the cross, upon the cross, he suffers still.
After Golgotha, Jesus spread his wings
And soared to the eternal dawn in vain;

Il a beau resplendir, superbe et gracieux,
Dans la tranquillité sidérale des cieux,
Dans la gloire, parmi les archanges solaires,
Au-dessus des douleurs, au-dessus des colères,
Au-dessus du nuage âpre et confus des jours;
Chaque fois que sur terre et dans nos temples sourds
Et dans nos vils palais, des docteurs et des scribes
Versent sur l'innocent leurs lâches diatribes,
Chaque fois que celui qui doit enseigner, ment,
Chaque fois que d'un traître il jaillit un serment,
Chaque fois que le juge, après une prière,
Jette au peuple ce mot: Justice! et, par derrière,
Tend une main hideuse à l'or mystérieux,
Chaque fois que le prêtre, époussetant ses dieux,
Chante au crime hosanna, bat des mains aux désastres,
Et dit: gloire à César! là-haut, parmi les astres,
Dans l'azur qu'aucun souffle orageux ne corrompt,
Christ frémissant essuie un crachat sur son front.

—Torquemada, j'entends le bruit de ta cognée.
Tes bras sont nus, ta face est de sueur baignée;
A quoi travailles-tu seul dans ton noir sentier?—
Torquemada répond:—Je suis le charpentier.
Et j'ai la hache au poing dans ce monde où nous sommes.
—Qu'est-ce donc que tu fais?—Un bûcher pour les hommes.
—Avec quel bois?—Avec la croix de Jésus-Christ.

*

Après avoir courbé sous la loi qui flétrit
Et sous la loi qui tue, hélas! cet être auguste,
Après avoir cloué sur le gibet ce juste
D'où ruisselle le sang et d'où le pardon sort,
Devant l'obscurité des sentences de mort,
Devant l'affreux pouvoir d'ôter la vie, et d'être
Celui qui fait mourir, mais qui ne fait pas naître,

In vain did he glitter, stately and graceful,
In the sidereal tranquility of the heavens,
In glory, amidst the solar archangels,
Above pain, above anger,
Above the cloud of confused and bitter days;
Every time on earth, in our furtive temples
And in our vile palaces, teachers and scribes
Pour on the innocent their shameful diatribes,
Every time the one who must teach, lies,
Every time from a traitor springs a promise,
Every time the judge, following prayer,
Casts down to the people this word: Justice! And, behind
His back, holds out a hideous hand for mysterious gold,
Every time the priest, dusting off his gods,
Sings Hosanna to crime, claps his hands at disaster,
And exclaims: glory to Caesar! in Heaven above, among the
Celestial bodies, in the azure that no turbulent wind
Impairs, shuddering Christ suffers a spit on his brow.

—Torquemada, I hear the sound of your ax.
Your arms are bare, your face is bathed in sweat;
What are you working at there, alone, on your dark path?—
Torquemada answers:—I am a carpenter.
And I have the axe in hand, in this world where we live.
—What is it that you are making there?—A stake for humankind.
—With what wood?—With the cross of Jesus Christ.

*

After having subjected this august Being
To the law that scourges and kills, alas! and
After having nailed this righteous man to the cross, this man
From whom blood streams and yet whence forgiveness
Flows, does Man recoil before the darkness of
Death sentences, before the hideous power to
End Life, to be the one causing death

Devant le tribunal, devant le cabanon,
Devant le glaive, l'homme a-t-il reculé? Non.
Sous cette croix que charge une horreur inconnue,
Ce qu'on nomme ici-bas Justice, continue.
Ce spectre aveugle et sourd, dont l'ombre est le manteau,
A peine se souvient d'avoir à ce poteau
Attaché cette immense innocence étoilée.

En présence du bien, du mal, dans la mêlée
Des fautes, des erreurs, où le juste périt,
Pas un juge n'a peur de ce mot: Jésus-Christ!
Le Calvaire n'a point découragé la Grève;
Montfaucon à côté du Golgotha s'éleve;
Et le Messie a pu mourir sans éclairer.
L'homme n'a pas cessé de se dénaturer
Dans le tragique orgueil de condamner son frère.
L'ouverture hideuse, infâme, téméraire,
Du sépulcre au milieu des lois, c'est là le port;
Et le noir genre humain s'abrite dans la mort.

Tristes juges! de quoi leur âme est-elle faite?
Le grand spectre qui porte au-dessus de sa tête
L'écriteau ténébreux et flamboyant: INRI,
Pâle, éploré, sanglant, fouetté, percé, meurtri,
Pend devant eux au bois de la croix douloureuse,
Tandis que chaque mot prononcé par eux, creuse
Une fosse dans l'ombre et dresse un échafaud:
—A mort cet homme! à mort cette femme! il le faut!
A mort le fils du peuple! à mort l'enfant du chaume!
—Vous ne voyez donc pas mes clous! dit le fantôme.

*

Et que de justes morts! Que de bons condamnés!
Que de saints, d'un arrêt infâme couronnés!
O martyre! escalade horrible du supplice!

Without restoring life, before the tribunal,
Before the dark cell, before the sword? No.
Under this cross burdened with a strange horror,
That which is called Justice here on earth, continues.
This blind and deaf specter, with its mantle of darkness,
Hardly remembers having nailed
To this post this immense star-studded Innocence.

In the presence of goodness, of evil, in this melange
Of faults and errors where the righteous perish,
Not one judge fears these words: Jesus Christ!
Calvary never discouraged the Grève;
The Montfaucon gallows rises up beside Golgotha;
And the Messiah died without enlightening us.
Humankind has not stopped perverting itself
In that tragic arrogance of condemning his brother.
The hideous, vile, rash opening
Of the tomb in the midst of the Law, is Man's refuge:
Dark humankind takes shelter in death.

Despicable judges! Of what does their soul consist?
The great specter who carries above his head
The dark and blazing sign: INRI,
Palid, tearful, bloody, flogged, pierced, bruised,
Hangs before them on the wood of the sorrowful cross,
While every word uttered by them digs
A grave in the darkness, and raises up a scaffold:
—Death to this man! Death to this woman! It is necessary!
Death to the son of the people! Death to the child of the thatch!
—So, do you not see my nails! says the phantom.

*

And how many just ones have died! How many
Condemned ones. How many saints, rewarded an infamous
Sentence! O martyr! horrible escalade of agony!

Le meurtre fier, sacré, public; la loi complice!
Flots du sang innocent! Si, sur quelque sommet,
L'homme des anciens jours, Jacob, se rendormait,
Il reverrait encore une ascension d'anges,
Pensifs, purs, tout baignés de lumières étranges,
Montant l'un après l'autre, ayant de l'orient
Et de l'immensité sur leur front souriant,
Ceux-ci levant leurs mains, ceux-là dressant leur aile,
Calmes, éblouissants, sereins, et cette échelle,
Sœur de celle que l'ombre à ses yeux dérobait,
Hélas, n'aboutit pas au ciel, mais au gibet.

*

Oh! puisque c'est ainsi que les choses sont faites,
Puisque toujours la terre égorge ses prophètes,
Qu'est-ce qu'on doit penser et croire, ô vastes cieux!
Contre la vérité le prêtre est factieux;
Tous les cultes, soufflant l'enfer de leurs narines,
Mâchent des ossements mêlés à leurs doctrines;
Tous se sont proclamés vrais sous peine de mort;
Pas un autel sur terre, hélas, n'est sans remord.
Les faux dieux ont partout laissé leur cicatrice
A la nature, sainte et suprême matrice;
Partout l'homme est méchant, cœur vil sous un œil fier,
Et mérite la chute immense de l'éclair;
Toute divinité dans ses mains dégénère
En idole, et devient digne aussi du tonnerre.
Qui donc a tort? qui donc a raison? qu'affirmer?
Dieu semble chaque jour plus avant s'abîmer
Dans la profondeur sourde et fatale du vide;
Le Zend est ténébreux; le Talmud est livide;
Nul ne sait ce qu'un temple, et le dieu qu'on y sent,
Aime mieux voir fumer, de l'encens, ou du sang?
Toute église a le meurtre infiltré dans ses dalles;
Les chaires font en bas d'inutiles scandales,

The proud, sacred, public murder; the law an accomplice!
Rivers of innocent blood! If, on some mountain peak,
Jacob, from olden times, fell back asleep,
He would again witness an ascent of angels,
Pensive, pure, entirely bathed in strange light,
Rising one after the other, with the East
And the Vastness on their smiling faces,
Raising their hands here, raising their wings there,
Quiet, stunning, serene; and this ladder,
Sister to that which the darkness had concealed from his sight,
Alas, does not lead to Heaven, but to the gallows.

*

Oh! Since this is the way things are to be,
Because the world always slays her prophets,
What are we to think and believe, O vast Heaven?
The priest is factious towards the truth;
All cults, blowing out Hell from their nostrils,
Chew bones infused with their doctrines;
All have proclaimed themselves true on pain of death;
No altar on earth, alas, is guiltless.
Everywhere false gods have left their scars
On nature, the supreme and holy womb;
Everywhere Man is wicked, mean-hearted and proud-eyed,
And deserves mighty strikes of lightning;
In his hands every deity degenerates
Into an idol, and becomes also deserving of thunderbolts.
So, who is wrong? Who is right? Who knows the answer?
Every day God seems to be further engulfed
In the soundless and fatal depths of empty space;
The Zend is dark; the Talmud pale;
One wonders what the temples, and the gods sensed there,
Prefer to see smoking: incense, or blood?
In every church murder has seeped into its flagstones;
Pulpits create needless scandals down below, and

Les foudres font en haut d'inutiles éclats;
Ce qu'on doit faire avec ce qu'on doit croire, hélas!
Lutte presque toujours et rarement s'accorde.
L'abîme profond s'ouvre; un dogme est une corde
Qui pend dans l'ombre énorme et se perd dans le puits.

*

Ainsi mourut Jésus; et les peuples depuis,
Atterrés, ont senti que l'Inconnu lui-même
Leur était apparu dans cet Homme Suprême,
Et que son évangile était pareil au ciel.
Le Golgotha, funeste et pestilentiel,
Leur semble la tumeur difforme de l'abîme;
Fauve, il se dresse au fond mystérieux du crime;
Et le plus blême éclair du gouffre est sur ce lieu
Où la religion, sinistre, tua Dieu.

Thunderbolts cast needless lightning up above;
How one must act and what one must believe, alas!
Are almost always in conflict and rarely in accord.
The deep chasm opens; a dogma is a rope hanging in
The vast shadow, and vanishing into the pit.

*

Thus did Jesus die; and the people, dismayed,
Have since felt that the Unknown, itself,
Had appeared before them embodied in this Supreme Being,
And that his gospel was as Heaven.
Golgotha, sinister and pestilential,
Seems to them the deformed tumor of the abyss;
Wild beast, it arises from the unutterable bosom of corruption;
And the abyss casts its palest lightning on this place
Where sinister religion murdered God.

Victor Hugo, *Coucher de soleil au bord de la mer* (Sunset by the Sea), detail, ca. 1850, Musée Victor Hugo-Maison Vacquerie

Hors de la terre III

I

SATAN DANS LA NUIT

I

Je l'aime!—Nuit, cachot sépulcral, mort vivante,
Ombre que mon sanglot ténébreux épouvante,
Solitudes du mal où fuit le grand puni,
Glaciers démesurés de l'hiver infini,
O flots du noir chaos qui m'avez vu proscrire,
Désespoir dont j'entends le lâche éclat de rire,
Vide où s'évanouit l'être, le temps, le lieu,
Gouffres profonds, enfers, abîmes! j'aime Dieu.
Je l'aime. C'est fini.—Lumière! fiancée
De tout esprit; soleil! feu de toute pensée;
Vie! où donc êtes-vous? Je vous cherche. O tourment!
La création vit dans l'éblouissement;

Beyond the Earth III

I

SATAN IN THE NIGHT

I

I love him!—Night, sepulchral cell, living death,
Darkness that my sombrous sob frightens,
Solitudes of evil where flees the great punished one,
Measureless glaciers of infinite winter,
O torrents of dark chaos which saw me banished,
Despair whose cowardly peal of laughter I hear,
Void where Being, Time, Place, vanish,
Deep chasms, hells, abysses! I love God.
I love him. That is all.—Light! Betrothed
Of all spirits; Sun! Fire of all thought;
Life! Where art thou? I seek thee. O agony!
Creation lives in a state of resplendence;

O regard innocent de l'aube idolâtrée,
Chaleur dont la nature est toute pénétrée!
Les fleuves sont joyeux dans l'herbe; l'horizon
Resplendit; le vent court; des fleurs plein le gazon,
Des oiseaux, des oiseaux, et des oiseaux, encore;
Tout cela chante, rit, aime, inondé d'aurore;
Le tigre dit: Et moi! je veux ma part du ciel!
L'aube dore le tigre et l'offre à l'Éternel.

Moi seul, je reste affreux! Hélas! rien n'est immonde.
Moi seul, je suis la honte et la tache du monde.
Ma laideur, vague effroi des astres soucieux,
Perce à travers ma nuit et va salir les cieux.
Je ne vois rien, étant maudit; mais dans l'espace
J'entends, j'entends dans l'eau qui fuit, dans l'air qui passe,
J'entends dans l'univers ce murmure: Va-t'en!
Le porc dit au fumier: je méprise Satan.
Je sens la nuit penser que je la déshonore.
Le tourbillonnement du grand souffle sonore,
Le vent du matin, libre et lâché dans le ciel,
Évite mon front morne et pestilentiel.

Jadis, ce jour levant, cette lueur candide,
C'était moi.—Moi!—J'étais l'archange au front splendide,
La prunelle de feu de l'azur rayonnant,
Dorant le ciel, la vie et l'homme; maintenant
Je suis l'astre hideux qui blanchit l'ossuaire.
Je portais le flambeau, je traîne le suaire;
J'arrive avec la nuit dans ma main; et partout
Où je vais, surgissant derrière moi, debout,
L'hydre immense de l'ombre ouvre ses ailes noires.

Les profonds infinis croisent leurs promontoires.
Tout devant moi, vers qui jadis l'amour vola,
Recule et fuit.

O innocent glance of worshipped dawn,
Warmth with which nature is entirely imbued!
Rivers are joyful amidst the grass; the horizon is
Aglow; the wind wanders; flowers fill the greensward,
Birds, birds, and more birds still;
They all sing, laugh, love, flooded by the dawn;
The tiger says: What about me! I want my share of Heaven!
And so the dawn gilds the tiger and offers him to the Eternal.

I, alone, remain hideous! Alas! Nothing else is unclean.
I, alone, am the shame and the stain of the world.
My ugliness, vague terror of the anxious stars,
Pierces my night and so stains the heavens.
I see nothing, being cursed; but beyond,
I hear, I hear in the water that flees, in the air that passes,
I hear in the universe this murmur: Go away!
The pig says to the dung-heap: I despise Satan.
I sense the night thinking that I dishonor her.
The whirling of the great sonorous breath,
The morning wind, free and released into the sky,
Avoids my sad and pestilential brow.

Formerly, this daybreak, this innocent light,
Was I.—Me!—I was the archangel with the
Splendid brow, the fiery eye of the radiant azure,
Gilding the sky, life and Man; now
I am the hideous star that bleaches the heap of bones.
I once bore the torch, but I now drag the shroud;
I arrive with night in hand; and everywhere I go,
Rearing up behind me, fully erect, is the immense Hydra
Of darkness, opening its black wings.

The boundless deeps retreat across their headlands.
Everything before me, towards whom love once flew,
Recoils and flees.

Je fus envieux. Ce fut là
Mon crime. Tout fut dit, et la bouche sublime
Cria: Mauvais! Et Dieu me cracha dans l'abîme.

Oh! je l'aime! C'est là l'horreur, c'est là le feu!
Que vais-je devenir, abîmes? J'aime Dieu!
Je suis damné!

II

L'enfer, c'est l'absence éternelle.
C'est d'aimer. C'est de dire: hélas! où donc est-elle,
Ma lumière? Où donc est ma vie et ma clarté?
Elle livre aux regards éperdus sa beauté.
Elle sourit là-haut à d'autres; d'autres baisent
Ses yeux, et dans ses sein s'enivrent et s'apaisent;
D'autres l'ont. Désespoir!

Oh! quand je fus jeté
Du haut de la splendeur dans cette cécité,
Après l'écroulement de l'ombre sur ma tête,
Après la chute, nu, précipité du faîte
A jamais, à la tombe inexorable uni,
Quand je me trouvai seul au bas de l'infini,
J'eus un moment si noir que je me mis à rire;
La vaste obscurité m'emplit de son délire,
Je sentis dans mon cœur, où mourait Dieu détruit,
La plénitude étrange et fauve de la nuit,
Et je criai, joyeux, triomphant, implacable:
—« Guerre à ces firmaments dont la lumière accable!
Guerre à ce ciel où Dieu met tant de faux attraits!
Il a cru m'en chasser, c'est moi qui m'y soustrais.
Il me croit prisonnier, je suis libre. Je plane.
Et le démon, c'est l'aigle, et le monde, c'est l'âne.
Et je ris. Je suis fier et content. J'ai quitté
Les anges vains, abjects, vils, et toi, la clarté,

I was envious. That was my
Crime. All was said, and the sublime mouth
Cried: Evil! And God spat me into the abyss.

Oh! I love him! That is the horror, that is the fire!
What will become of me, abysses? I love God!
I am damned!

II

Hell is eternal absence.
Hell is loving. It is saying: Alas! So, where is she,
My light? Where is my life and luminosity?
She shows to bewildered glances her beauty.
She smiles up there at others; others kiss
Her eyes, and upon her breast become inebriated
And grow quiet; others possess her. Despair!

Oh! when I was cast
Down from the height of splendor into this blindness,
After the collapse of darkness upon my head,
After the fall, naked, hurled from the summit,
Forever, joined to the inexorable tomb,
When I found myself alone at the bottom of infinity,
I had a moment so dire that I began to laugh;
The vast darkness filled me with its ecstasy,
God was dying to me, and I felt in my heart
The strange and wild plenitude of night.
I shouted, joyful, triumphant, relentless:
—"I declare war on these firmaments whose light is overwhelming,
War on this heaven where God places so many false charms!
He thought to chase me here, but it is I who escaped here.
He believes me prisoner, but I am free. I soar.
It is the Devil that is the eagle, and the world, the donkey.
And I laugh. I am proud and happy. I left
The vain, despicable, mean angels, and you, the Light

Qui les corromps, et toi, l'amour, qui les subornes!
Quel bonheur que la haine alors qu'elle est sans bornes!
Ce Dieu, ce cœur de Tout, ce père lumineux
Que l'ange, l'astre, l'homme, et la bête, ont en eux,
Ce centre autour duquel le troupeau se resserre,
Cet être, seul vivant, seul vrai, seul nécessaire,
Je vais m'en passer, moi le colosse puni!
C'est bien. Comme je vais maudire ce béni,
Et faire contre lui, tandis qu'Adam l'encense,
De la révolte avec mon ancienne puissance
Et de la flamme avec les rayons que j'avais!
Comme je vais rugir sur lui! Comme je vais,
Moi, l'affreux, face à face avec lui le suprême,
Le haïr, l'exécrer et l'abhorrer! »—Je l'aime!

DANS L'AIR

CHANSON DES OISEAUX

Vie! ô bonheur! bois profonds,
　　Nous vivons.
L'essor sans fin nous réclame;
Planons sur l'air et les eaux!
　　Les oiseaux
Sont de la poussière d'âme.

Accourez, planez! volons
　　Aux vallons,
A l'antre, à l'ombre, à l'asile!
Perdons-nous dans cette mer
　　De l'éther
Où la nuée est une île!

Du fond des rocs et des joncs,
　　Des donjons,
Des monts que le jour embrase,

Who corrupts them, and you, Love, who suborns them!
What a delight, this hatred, when it is boundless!
This God, this heart of Everything, this radiant Father
That the angel, the star, Man, and beast have in them,
This heart around which the flock gathers,
This Being, alone vital, alone true, alone necessary,
That I am going to do without, me the punished colossus!
It is good. How I shall curse this blessèd one!
Whereas Adam praises him to the sky, I shall oppose him
With insurrection, using my old power,
And with flame, using the light rays I once possessed!
How I shall roar at him! With what fervor I,
The hideous one, shall confront, hate, execrate
And loathe him, the supreme one."—and yet I love him!

IN THE AIR

SONG OF THE BIRDS

Life! O joy! Deep woods,
    We are alive.
Endless flight entreats us;
Let us float upon the air, o'er the waters!
    Birds
Are made of soul-dust.

Come soar! Fly
    To the vales,
To the grottos, the shade, the places of respite!
Let us lose ourselves in this
    Ethereal sea
Where the cloud is an island!

From the heart of the rocks and rushes,
    From turrets,
From mounts which the day sets ablaze,

Volons, et, frémissants, fous,
Plongeons-nous
Dans l'inexprimable extase!

Oiseaux, volez aux clochers,
Aux rochers,
Au précipice, à la cime,
Aux glaciers, aux lacs, aux prés;
Savourez
La liberté de l'abîme!

Vie! azur! rayons! frissons!
Traversons
La vaste gaieté sereine,
Pendant que sur les vivants,
Dans les vents,
L'ombre des nuages traîne!

Avril ouvre à deux battants
Le printemps;
L'été le suit, et déploie
Sur la terre un beau tapis
Fait d'épis,
D'herbe, de fleurs, et de joie.

Buvons, mangeons; becquetons
Les festons
De la ronce et de la vigne;
Le banquet dans la forêt
Est tout prêt;
Chaque branche nous fait signe.

Les pivoines sont en feu;
Le ciel bleu
Allume cent fleurs écloses;
Le printemps est pour nos yeux

Let us fly, and, quivering, mad,
    Plunge
Into the indescribable ecstasy!

Fly, birds, to the bell-towers,
    To the promontories,
To the cliffs, the mountain peaks,
To the glaciers, lakes, and meadows;
    Savor
Your freedom from the abyss!

Life! azure! rays of light! thrills!
    Let us traverse
The vast, serene merriment,
While high above the living,
    In the winds,
The shadow of the clouds trails close behind!

April flings wide open the gates
    Of spring;
Summer follows, and unfurls
Upon the earth a beautiful carpet
    Of wheat,
Of grasses, of flowers, of joy.

Let us drink, and eat; let us pick
    Festoons
From the bramble and vine;
The banquet in the forest
    Is ready;
Each branch is beckoning.

The peonies are on fire;
    The blue sky
Inflames a hundred blooming flowers;
The spring is, for our quite

Tout joyeux
Une fournaise de roses.

Tu nous dores aussi tous,
Feu si doux
Qui du haut des cieux ruisselles;
Les aigles sont dans les airs
Des éclairs,
Les moineaux des étincelles.

Nous rentrons dans les rayons;
Nous fuyons
Dans la clarté notre mère;
L'oiseau sort de la forêt
Et paraît
S'évanouir en lumière.

Parfois on rampe accablé
Dans le blé,
Mais juillet a pour ressource
L'ombre, où, loin des chauds sillons,
Nous mouillons
Nos pieds roses dans la source.

Depuis qu'ils sont sous les cieux,
Soucieux
Du bonheur de la prairie,
L'herbe et l'arbre chevelu
Ont voulu
Dans leur tender rêverie

Qu'à jamais le fruit, le grain,
L'air serein,
L'amourette, la nichée,
L'aube, la chanson, l'appât,
Occupât
Notre joie effarouchée.

Delighted eyes,
A fiery furnace of roses.

You also gild us all,
Fire so sweet that
Streams down from the heavens;
The eagles in flight are
Flashes of lightning,
The sparrows, sparks.

We return to the light-beams;
We flee
To our mother limpidity;
The bird flies beyond the forest
And appears
To vanish in the light.

Sometimes we move about the wheat,
Overwhelmed;
But July has for resource
The shade, where, far from the warm furrows,
We moisten
Our pink feet in the spring.

Since they lie beneath the heavens,
Caring for
The happiness of the mead,
The grass and the hairy-tree
Wished
In their tender reverie

That the fruits, the grain,
The tranquil air,
The love-affair, the nest,
The dawn, the song, the allure,
Should engage
Forever our timorous joy.

Vivons! chantons! Tout est pur
Dans l'azur;
Tout est beau dans la lumière!
Tout vers son but, jour et nuit,
Est conduit;
Sans se tromper, le fleuve erre.

Toute la campagne rit;
Un esprit
Palpite sous chaque feuille;
—Aimons! murmure une voix
Dans les bois;
Et la fleur veut qu'on la cueille.

Quand l'iris a diapré
Tout le pré,
Quand le jour, plus tiède, augmente,
Quand le soir luit dans l'étang
Éclatant,
Quand la verdure est charmante,

Que dit l'essaim ébloui?
Oui! oui! oui!
Les collines, les fontaines,
Les bourgeons verts, les fruits mûrs,
Les azurs
Pleins de visions lointaines,

Le champ, le lac, le marais,
L'antre frais,
Composent, sans pleurs ni peine,
Et font monter vers le ciel
Éternel
L'affirmation sereine.

Let us live! Let us sing! Everything is pure
        In the blue;
Everything is beautiful in the light!
Everything towards its purpose, day and night,
        Is led;
Unerringly, the river meanders.

The whole countryside laughs;
        A spirit
Beats beneath each leaf;
—Let us love! whispers a voice
        In the woods;
And the flower wishes to be plucked.

When the iris has adorned
        The entire meadow,
When the warmer days increase,
When the evening glows in the
        Glittering pond,
When the greenery is lovely,

What says the dazzled gathering?
        Yes! yes! yes!
The hills, the fountains,
The green buds, the ripe fruit,
        The azures
Full of distant visions,

The field, the lake, the marsh,
        The cool cave,
Compose and, with neither tears nor sorrow,
Raise towards the eternal
        Heavens,
This serene affirmation.

L'aube et l'éblouissement
Vont semant
Partout des perles de flamme;
L'oiseau n'est pas orphelin;
Tout est plein
De la mystérieuse âme!

Quelqu'un que l'on ne voit pas
Est là-bas
Dans la maison qu'on ignore;
Et cet inconnu bénit
Notre nid,
Et sa fenêtre est l'aurore.

Et c'est à cause de lui
Que l'appui
Jamais ne manque à nos ailes,
Et que les colombes vont
Sur le mont
Boire où boivent les gazelles.

Grâce à ce doux inconnu,
Adam nu
Nous souriait sous les branches;
Le cygne sous le bouleau
A de l'eau
Pour laver ses plumes blanches.

Grâce à lui, le piquebois
Vit sans lois,
Chéri des pins vénérables,
Et délivrant des fourmis
Ses amis
Les cèdres et les érables.

The dawn and the dazzlement
Go on their way, sowing
Everywhere pearls of flame;
The bird is not an orphan;
Everything is filled
With the mysterious soul!

Someone unseen
Is far away
In the unknown house;
And this stranger blesses
Our nest,
And his window is the dawn.

And it is thanks to him
That our wings
Never lack for support,
And that the doves go
Onto the mountain
To drink where the gazelles drink.

Through this gentle unknown,
Naked Adam
Smiled at us beneath the boughs;
The swan under the birch
Finds water
To wash his white feathers.

Thanks to him, the woodpecker
Lives free,
Darling of the venerable pines,
Delivering of ants
His friends,
The cedars and maples.

Grâce à lui, le passereau
        Du sureau
S'envole, et monte au grand orme;
C'est lui qui fait le buisson
        De façon
Qu'on y chante et qu'on y dorme.

Il nous met tous à l'abri,
        Colibri,
Chardonneret, hochequeue,
Tout l'essaim que l'air ravit
        Et qui vit
Dans la grande lueur bleue.

A cause de lui, les airs
        Et les mers,
Les bois d'aulnes et d'yeuses,
La sauge en fleur, le matin,
        Et le thym,
Sont des fêtes radieuses;

Les blés sont dorés, les cieux
        Spacieux,
L'eau joyeuse et l'herbe douce;
Mais il se fâche souvent
        Quand le vent
Nous vole nos brins de mousse.

Il dit au vent:—Paix, autan!
        Et va-t'en!
Laisse mes oiseaux tranquilles.
Arrache, si tu le veux,
        Leurs cheveux,
De fumée aux sombres villes!—

Thanks to him, the sparrow
From the elderberry
Flies up to the lofty elm;
It is he who creates the bush
Wherein
We may sing and sleep.

He shelters us all,
Hummingbird,
Goldfinch, wagtail,
The entire multitude delighted by the air
And living
In the majestic blue glow.

Because of him, the breezes
And the seas,
The stands of alders and holm-oaks,
The morning, the sage in flower,
And the thyme,
Are radiant fêtes;

The wheat is golden, the skies
Spacious,
The water joyful and the grass soft;
But he often gets angry
When the wind
Steals from us our strands of moss.

He says to the wind:—Peace, south wind!
And go!
Leave my birds alone.
Tear, if you will,
The tresses
Of smoke from the dark cities!

Celui sous qui nous planons
 Sait nos noms.
Nous chantons. Que nous importe?
Notre humble essor ignorant
 Est si grand!
Notre faiblesse est si forte!

La tempête au vol tonnant,
 Déchaînant
Les trombes, les bruits, les grêles,
Fouettant, malgré leurs sanglots,
 Les grands flots,
S'émousse à nos plumes frêles.

Il veut les petits contents,
 Le beau temps,
Et l'innocence sauvée;
Il abaisse, calme et doux,
 Comme nous,
Ses ailes sur sa couvée.

Grâce à lui, sous le hallier
 Familier
A notre aile coutumière,
Sur les mousses de velours,
 Nos amours
Coulent dans de la lumière.

Il est bon; et sa bonté
 C'est l'été;
C'est le charmant sorbier rouge;
C'est que rien ne vienne à nous
 Dans nos trous
Sans que le feuillage bouge.

The one beneath whom we soar
    Knows our names.
We sing. We are free of care.
Our humble, unwitting flight
    Is so great,
Our weakness so strong!

The storm, in thunderous flight,
    Unleashing
Waterspouts, hail, tumult,
Lashing, despite their tears,
    The large waves,
Are dulled by our frail feathers.

He wants the small creatures happy,
    The weather fine,
And innocence saved;
He lowers, calm and gentle,
    As do we,
His wings o'er his brood.

Thanks to him, in the familiar
    Thicket, to which
Our wing is accustomed,
On velvet moss,
    Our loves
Are shed in the light.

He is good; and his goodness
    Is the summer;
It is the charming red rowen;
It causes nothing to befall us
    In our hollows
Without that the leaves stir.

Sa bonté, c'est Tout; c'est l'air,
    Le feu clair,
Le bois où, dans la nuit brune,
Ta chanson, qui prend son vol,
    Rossignol,
Semble un rêve de la lune.

C'est ce qu'au gré des saisons
    Nous faisons;
C'est le rocher que l'eau creuse;
C'est l'oiseau, des vents bercé,
    Composé
D'une inquiétude heureuse.

Il est puissant, étoilé,
    Et voilé.
Le soir, avec les murmures
Des troupeaux qu'on reconduit
    Et le bruit
Des abeilles sous les mûres,

Avec l'ombre sur les toits,
    Sur les bois,
Sur les montagnes prochaines,
C'est sa grandeur qui descend,
    Et qu'on sent
Dans le tremblement des chênes.

Il n'eut qu'à vouloir un jour,
    Et l'amour
Devint l'harmonie immense;
Tous les êtres étaient là;
    Il mêla
Sa sagesse à leur démence.

His goodness is Everything; it is the air,
    The clear flame,
The woods where, at evening dusk,
Your song, which takes flight,
    Nightingale,
Seems a dream of the moon.

It is what according to the seasons
    We do;
It is the rock which the water hollows;
It is the bird, lulled by the winds,
    Formed of
A happy inquietude.

He is powerful, star-studded,
    And veiled.
In the evening, with the murmurs
Of the flocks being escorted home,
    And the sound
Of bees under the blackberries,

With the darkness upon the roofs,
    Upon the forest,
Upon the near mountains,
It is his grandeur which descends,
    And which we feel
In the trembling of the oaks.

He had only to wish, one day,
    And love
Became the immense harmony;
All Beings were there;
    He mixed
His wisdom with their madness.

Il voulut que tout fût un;
Le parfum
Eut pour sœur l'aurore pure;
Et les choses, se touchant
Dans un chant,
Furent la sainte nature.

Il mit sur les flots profonds
Les typhons;
Il mit la fleur sur la tige;
Il apparut fulgurant
Dans le grand;
Le petit fut son prodige.

Avec la même beauté
Sa clarté
Créa l'aimable et l'énorme;
Il fit sortir l'alcyon
Du rayon
Qui baise la mer difforme.

L'effrayant devint charmant;
L'élément,
Monstre, colosse, fantôme,
Par Lui, qui le veut ainsi,
Radouci,
Vint s'accoupler à l'atome.

On vit alors dans Ophir
L'humble asfir
Vert comme l'hydre farouche;
Le flamboiement de l'Etna
Rayonna
Sur l'aile de l'oiseau-mouche.

He wished that all be one;
    Perfume
Had for a sister the pure dawn;
And things, touching
    In a song,
Acquired a saintly nature.

He placed upon the deep waters
    Typhoons;
He set the flower upon its stem;
In large form he appeared
    Fulgurant;
The small was his miracle.

With the same beauty
    His lucidity
Created both the pleasing and the enormous;
He caused to emerge from the light-beam
    The halcyon,
Which kisses the colossal sea.

The terrible became charming;
    The element,
Monster, giant, ghost,
Created by Him who wished
    It so,
Came to pair with the atom.

Then we saw in Ophir
    The humble asfir,
Green as the ferocious hydra;
And the blaze of Etna
    Shone
Upon the wing of the hummingbird.

Vie est le mot souverain,
Et serein,
Sans fin, sans forme, sans nombre,
Tendre, inépuisable, ardent,
Débordant
De toute la terre sombre.

L'aube se marie au soir;
Le bec noir
Au bec flamboyant se mêle;
L'éclair, mâle affreux, poursuit
Dans la nuit
La mer, sa rauque femelle.

Volons, volons, et volons!
Les sillons
Sont rayés, et l'onde est verte.
La vie est là sous nos yeux,
Dans les cieux,
Claire et toute grande ouverte.

Hirondelle, fais ton nid.
Le granit
T'offre son ombre et ses lierres;
Aux palais pour tes amours
Prends des tours,
Et de la paille aux chaumières.

Le nid que l'oiseau bâtit
Si petit,
Est une chose profonde;
L'œuf ôté de la forêt
Manquerait
A l'équilibre du monde.

Life is the sovereign and
　　Serene word,
Without end, without form, without number,
Gentle, inexhaustible, ardent,
　　Overflowing
The entire dark earth.

Dawn marries dusk,
　　The black beak
Mates with the flaming beak;
The flash of lightning, hideous male, pursues
　　At night
The sea, his raucous female.

Let us fly, fly, and fly!
　　The furrows
Are plowed, and the wave is green.
Life is there before our eyes,
　　In heaven,
Bright and fully revealed.

Swallow, make your nest.
　　The granite
Offers you his shade and his ivy;
For your love, take turrets
　　From the palace,
And straw from the humble cottage.

The nest which the bird builds
　　So small
Is a profound thing;
The egg removed from the forest
　　Would
Unbalance the world.

III

Si je ne l'aimais point, je ne souffrirais pas.
Laissez-moi remonter, gouffres!...—Non! pas à pas
Je descends, je m'enfonce, à chaque effort je glisse
Plus avant. Le malheur de la nuit, son supplice,
C'est d'adorer le jour et de rester la nuit.
Cet amour est sinistre, et le mal est son fruit.
O ma lumière, où donc es-tu? Satan t'implore.
M'entends-tu, dis? reviens, aurore, aurore, aurore!
Ne leur dis pas: toujours; ne me dis pas: jamais!
Je souffre!—Oh! tout est noir, je ne vois pas, je hais!

Je hais!—Oui, je vous hais, tas humain, foule blême,
Parce que vous l'aimez, parce que Dieu vous aime,
Parce que sa clarté brille à travers vos os,
Parce que vous plongez vos urnes aux ruisseaux,
Parce que vous passez vivants dans la nature,
Parce que vous avez, pendant que la torture
Me tenaille et que j'ai mon âme pour vautour,
Dans vos yeux l'espérance et dans vos cœurs l'amour!

Hommes, larves, néants, ombres, faces rapides,
Vous n'êtes pas contents! ô favoris stupides,
Vous vous plaignez d'aller chaque jour vieillissant,
De passer, de sentir refroidir votre sang,
Et vous accusez Dieu! Quel rêve est donc le vôtre!
J'ai perdu plus que vous, moi! j'ai, l'un après l'autre,
Vu tomber mes rayons, comme vous vos cheveux!

IV

Ne pouvoir remonter, même quand je le veux!

Quoi! les morts repentants s'envolent de leurs tombes
Radieux, les hiboux se changent en colombes,

III

If I did not love him, I would not suffer.
Let me reascend, abysses!...—But no! bit by bit
I fall, I sink, at each effort I slip further.
The curse of the night, his means of torture,
Is to worship daylight but to remain in the dark.
This love is sinister, and evil is its fruit.
O my light, where art thou? Satan implores you.
Do you hear me? Speak. Return, dawn, dawn, dawn!
Do not tell them: forever; and me: never!
I suffer!—Oh! everything is black, I do not see, I hate!

I hate!—Yes, I hate you, human heap, bloodless crowd,
Because you love him, because God loves you,
Because his light sparkles through your bones,
Because you immerse your urns in his streams,
Because you pass, living, into nature,
Because, while torture torments me,
And I have, for vulture, my own soul, you have
Hope in your eyes and love in your hearts!

Men, larvae, nothingnesses, shadows, harried faces,
You are unhappy! O foolish chosen ones,
You complain of aging every day,
Of fading away, of sensing your blood growing cold,
And you accuse God! How fanciful you are!
I have lost more than you! I have seen fall, one after
The other, my beams of light, and you, merely your hair!

IV

Unable to rise up, even when I desire it!

What! repentant souls fly up from their tombs,
Radiant; owls become doves;

Les démons pardonnés rentrent au firmament,
Et moi, le spectre noir, je les vois lentement
Blanchir dans la nuit sombre et redevenir anges!
Des astres, fleurs du gouffre, éclosent dans les fanges!
Quoi! César est parti! Torquemada s'en va!
Busiris, dans la cave où le tient Jéhovah,
Distingue une lueur et commence à sourire!
Nemrod attend; je viens d'entendre Judas dire,
Dans la geôle où, son crime et moi, nous le lions:
—Je n'ai plus maintenant que quatre millions
De siècles à rester à la chaîne dans l'ombre.—
Que Judas est heureux! il peut compter un nombre.
Pour tous, pour tous, pour tous, le jour reparaîtra.
Caïn, le vieux Caïn, lui-même sortira!
Moi seul, je resterai dans les déserts funèbres.
Horreur sans fond! je suis l'éternel des ténèbres.

Je suis le misérable à perpétuité.

V

Mais je me vengerai sur son humanité,
Sur l'homme qu'il créa, sur Adam et sur Eve,
Sur l'âme qui sourit, sur le jour qui se lève,
Sur toi, l'astre! sur toi, l'aile! sur toi, la fleur!
Sur la vierge, et la mère, et sur l'enfant! Malheur!
Je défigurerai la face universelle.
Serpent, je secouerai dans l'ombre ma crécelle.
J'inventerai des dieux, Moloch, Vishnou, Baal.
Je prendrai le réel pour briser l'idéal,
Les pierres des édens pour bâtir les sodomes.
A travers les rameaux de la forêt des hommes
On verra mes yeux luire, et l'on dira: c'est lui.
Plus effaré du mal que du bien ébloui,
Le sage doutera de Dieu. Je mordrai l'âme.
J'enlaidirai l'amour dans le cœur de la femme.

Demons, forgiven, return to the firmament;
And I, abject specter, seeing them slowly turning
White in the dismal night, again becoming angels!
Stars, those flowers of the abyss, bloom in the mires!
What! Caesar has departed! Torquemada gone away!
Busiris, in the cavern where Jehovah holds him,
Discerns a light and begins to smile!
Nimrod is waiting; I have just heard Judas say,
In the gaol where his crime and I bind him:
—I now have no more than four million
Centuries left, chained in the darkness.—
How happy Judas is! he can count.
For all, for everyone, daylight will reappear.
Cain, even agèd Cain himself, will depart!
Whereas I, alone, shall remain in the mournful deserts.
Bottomless horror! I am lord of the shades.

I shall remain wretched, forever.

V

But I shall take revenge upon his humanity,
Upon Man whom he created, upon Adam and Eve,
Upon the smiling soul, upon the breaking day,
Upon you, star! upon you, wing! you, flower!
Upon the virgin, and the mother, and upon the child!
Woe unto you! I shall deform the universal countenance.
Being serpent, I shall shake my rattle in the darkness.
I shall invent gods, Moloch, Vishnu, Baal.
I shall use the real to crush the ideal,
Stones of edens to build sodoms.
Through the branches of the forest of men will be
Seen my gleaming eyes, and it shall be said: It is he.
More afraid of evil than inspired by good,
The wise shall doubt God. I shall bite the soul.
I shall make love unseemly in the hearts of women.

Je mêlerai ma cendre à ces charbons éteints.
Et, mauvais, je rirai, rayant tous leurs instincts
Et toutes leurs vertus de l'ongle de mes ailes.
Je serai si hideux que toutes les prunelles
Auront je ne sais quoi de sombre; et les méchants
Et les pervers croîtront comme l'herbe des champs.
Le fils, devant le juge aux lèvres indignées,
Apparaîtra, tenant dans ses mains des poignées
De cheveux blancs du père égorgé. Je dirai
Au pauvre: vole; au riche: opprime. Je ferai
Jeter le nouveau-né par la mère aux latrines.
Tremble, ô Dieu! J'ouvrirai de mes mains leurs poitrines,
J'arracherai, fumant, et je tordrai leur cœur,
Et j'en exprimerai tous les crimes, l'horreur,
La trahison, le meurtre, Achab, Tibère, Atrée,
Sur ta création rayonnante et sacrée!
Tu seras Providence et moi Fatalité.
J'ai fait mieux que la Haine; ô vide! ô cécité!
J'ai fait l'Envie. En vain ce Dieu bon multiplie
Ces colosses dont l'âme est de rayons remplie,
Le génie et l'amour et l'héroïsme; moi
Par la négation je fais ronger la foi;
Je suis Zoïle; autour des Socrates j'excite
Anitus, et je mets sur Achille Thersite,
Et tout pleure; et j'égale, à force de venins,
A l'éclat des géants le gonflement des nains.
La matière a mon signe au front. Je la querelle.
J'effare l'eau sans fond sous des gouffres de grêle.
Je contrains l'océan, que Dieu tient sous sa loi,
Et la terre, à créer du chaos avec moi,
Je fais de la laideur énorme avec leur force,
Un monstre avec l'écume, un monstre avec l'écorce,
Sur terre Béhémoth, Léviathan sur mer.
Je complète partout le chaos par l'enfer,
La bête par l'idole, et les rats, les belettes,
La torpille, l'hyène acharnée aux squelettes,

I shall mix my cinders with these dying coals.
And, evil, I shall laugh, scratching out all their instincts
And all their virtues with the talon of my wings.
I shall be so hideous that all eyes shall possess
Some indefinable darkness; and the evil
And the perverse shall grow like field grass.
The son, before the indignant judge,
Shall appear, holding handfuls of white
Hair from his butchered father. I shall say
To the poor: Steal; to the rich: Oppress. I shall
Make the mother cast her newborn into the latrines.
Tremble, O God! I shall open their breasts with my hands,
I shall tear away their steaming hearts and wring
From them all crime, horror, betrayal,
Murder, Achab, Tiberius, Atreus,
Onto your radiant and sacred creation!
You shall be Providence and I, Fate.
Better than creating Hatred, O emptiness! O blindness!
I have created Envy. In vain does benevolent God
Propagate these giants whose soul is full of
Light beams, genius, love and heroism;
Through denial, I eat away at faith;
I am Zoilus; around Socrates, I call forth
Anytus, and place Thersites in the presence of Achilles;
And all weep; and I make equal, by means of poisons,
The bloating of dwarfs and the splendor of Titans.
Matter has my sign upon her brow. I quarrel with her.
I frighten fathomless water beneath abysses of hail.
I compel the ocean and earth, which God keeps
Under his rule, to create chaos with me;
I fashion enormous deformity with their powers,
A monster out of spume, a monster out of crust,
Leviathan upon the sea, Behemoth upon the earth.
Everywhere do I complete chaos through Hell,
The beast through the idol, and rats, weasels,
The torpedo, the hyena tearing at skeletons,

La bave du crapaud, la dent du caïman,
Par le bonze, l'obi, le fakir et l'iman.
Dieu passe dans le cœur des hommes, j'y séjourne.
Sa roue avec un bruit sidéral roule et tourne,
Mais c'est mon grain lugubre et sanglant qu'elle moud;
Jéhovah reculant sent aujourd'hui partout
Une création de Satan sous la sienne;
Son feu ne peut briller sans que mon souffle vienne.
Il est le char; je suis l'ornière. Nous croisons
Nos forces; et j'emploie aux pestes, aux poisons,
Aux monstres, aux déserts, son pur soleil candide;
C'est Dieu qui fait le front, moi qui creuse la ride;
Il est dans le prophète et moi dans les devins.
Guerre et deuil! je lui prends tous ses glaives divins,
Le glaive d'air, le vent, le glaive d'eau, la pluie,
L'épée éclair, stupeur de la terre éblouie,
Et je m'en sers, terrible; et la nature a peur.
A mon haleine une hydre éclôt dans la vapeur,
Et la goutte d'eau s'enfle en déluge agrandie;
Avec le clair foyer qui chauffe, j'incendie;
Je fais du miel le fiel, je fais l'écueil du port;
Dieu bénit le meilleur, je sacre le plus fort;
Dieu fait les radieux, je fais les sanguinaires.
Oui, pour broyer ses fils je prendrai ses tonnerres!
Oui, je me dresserai de toute ma hauteur!
Je veux dans ce qu'il fait tuer ce créateur,
Je veux le torturer dans son œuvre, et l'entendre
Râler dans la justice et la pudeur à vendre,
Dans les champs que la guerre accable de ses bonds,
Dans les peuples livrés aux tyrans, dans les bons
Et dans les saints, dans l'âme humaine tout entière!
Je veux qu'il se débatte, esprit, sous la matière;
Qu'il saigne dans le juste assassiné; je veux
Qu'il se torde, couvert de prêtres monstrueux,
Qu'il pleure, bâillonné par les idolâtries;
Je veux que des lys morts et des roses flétries,

The slaver of the toad, the tooth of the crocodile,
Through the bonze, the obi, the fakir, and the imam.
God passes through the heart of men, but I remain there.
His wheel rolls and turns with a sidereal sound,
But it is my dismal and bloody grain that it grinds;
A recoiling Jehovah now senses, everywhere,
A creation of Satan beneath his own;
His fire cannot flame without that my breath appear;
He is the chariot, and I the rut. Our forces
Overlap; and I use his pure, innocent sun
To create plagues, poisons, monsters, deserts;
It is God who creates the brow, and I the care engraved upon it;
He is in the prophet and I, in the soothsayers.
War and grief! I take from him all his divine swords,
The sword of air: wind, the sword of water: rain,
Lightning's sword, the bewilderment of the dazzled earth,
And I make terrible use of them; and nature is afraid.
From my breath, a hydra hatches in the vapor,
And the drop of water swells into a mighty torrent;
With the bright hearth that warms, I set ablaze;
I make from honey, gall, I make the reef from the harbor;
God blesses the best, I anoint the strongest;
God creates the radiant, and I the bloodthirsty.
Yes, to crush his children I shall take his thunderbolts!
Yes, I shall draw myself up to my full height!
I wish to slay this creator in all that he creates.
I wish to torture him in his work, and to hear his
Death rattle amidst justice and decency corrupted,
In the fields that war crushes with its bounding,
In the peoples delivered up to tyrants, in good folk
And in saints, in the entire human soul!
I want that he struggle, spirit beneath matter;
That he bleed in the murdered, just man; I want
That he writhe, covered with monstrous priests,
That he weep, gagged by idolatries;
I want that lilies die and roses wither,

Du cygne sous le bec des vautours frémissant,
Des beautés, des vertus, de toutes parts, son sang,
Son propre sang divin sur lui coule et l'inonde.
Voyez, regardez, Cieux! L'échafaud, c'est le monde,
Je suis le bourreau sombre, et j'exécute Dieu.
Dieu mourra. Grâce à moi, les chars sous leur essieu,
Les rois sous leur pouvoir, les aigles sous leurs griffes,
Les dogmes ténébreux et noirs, sous leurs pontifes,
Tout ce qui sur la terre à cette heure est debout,
Même les innocents sous leurs pieds, ont partout
Quelque chose de Dieu que dans l'ombre ils écrasent.
Mes flamboiements rampant sous l'univers l'embrasent.
Je suis le mal; je suis la nuit; je suis l'effroi.

VI

Grâce! pardonne-moi! rappelle-moi! prends-moi!
Grâce! Ne sens-tu pas qu'il faut que toute chaîne
Se rompe, et que le mal finisse, et que la haine
S'éteigne, évanouie en ta sérénité?
Quoi! le bien infini, le mal illimité!
Toi le bien, moi le mal! est-ce que c'est possible?
Le monde gouverné par un double invisible!
Y songez-vous, Seigneur? un partage entre nous!
Non, vous êtes la face, et je suis les genoux.
Laissez-moi me plier et tomber, maître immense,
Sur ce pavé des cieux qu'on nomme la clémence!
Grâce, ô Dieu! L'univers, les terres et les eaux,
L'azur sans bornes, plein d'invisibles oiseaux,
Les glauques océans qui font rugir leurs ondes,
L'énormité vivante où rayonnent les mondes,
Quoi! c'est une balance où nous pesons tous deux!
Qu'en dites-vous, soleils? Lui charmant, moi hideux!
Quoi! lui dans un plateau, soleils, et moi dans l'autre!
La chair est ma servante et l'âme est son apôtre.
Je lutte. Nous tenons chacun notre côté.

That from the swan quivering under the beak of vultures,
From the beauties, the virtues, from everywhere, his blood,
His own divine blood, flow on him and drown him.
Behold, look, heavens! The scaffold is the world.
I am the dark executioner, and I execute God.
God shall die. Thanks to me, the chariots underneath their axles,
Kings with their power, the eagles with their claws,
Sinister, obscure dogmas from pontiffs,
All that stand upon earth at this time,
Even the innocent, will have something of God
That they will crush beneath their feet in the darkness.
My flames creeping beneath the universe, shall set him ablaze.
I am evil; I am night; I am terror.

VI

Have mercy! forgive me! summon me back! make away with me!
Have mercy! Should not all chains
Be broken, all evil end, and all hatred
Be extinguished, disappearing amidst your serenity?
What! the good is infinite, evil is without limit!
You the good, I the evil! Is it possible?
The world governed by an invisible pair!
Of what are you thinking, Lord? a sharing between us!
No, you are the countenance, and I the knees.
Let me bend and drop, immense master,
Onto this bedrock of Heaven called Clemency!
Have mercy, O God! The universe, the lands and waters,
The boundless azure, full of invisible birds,
The glaucous oceans which roar out their waves,
The living enormity whence shine the worlds,
What! it is a balance on which we both bear weight!
What say you, suns? He charming, I hideous!
What! he on one scale, suns, and I on the other!
The flesh is my handmaid and the soul is his apostle.
I struggle. We each take sides.

Avoir l'infini, c'est avoir l'égalité.
Ton paradis ne fait qu'équilibre à mon bagne.
Ah! la création ainsi qu'une montagne
Pèse sur moi; je lève à travers les chaos
Mon front d'où mes douleurs retombent en fléaux;
Je me tords sans repas, sans fin, sans espérance.
C'est une majesté qu'une telle souffrance.
Oui, c'est l'énigme, ô nuit, de tes millions d'yeux:
Le grand souffrant fait face au grand mystérieux.
Grâce, ô Dieu! pour toi-même il faut que je l'obtienne.
Ma perpétuité fait ombre sur la tienne.
Devant ton œil flambeau rien ne doit demeurer,
Tout doit changer, vieillir et se transfigurer.
Toi seul es. Devant toi tout doit avoir un âge.
Et c'est pour ta splendeur un importun nuage
Qu'on voie un spectre assis au fond de ton ciel bleu,
Et l'éternel Satan devant l'éternel Dieu!

VII

Ils sont là-haut! Ils sont dans l'hymne et dans la joie;
L'éther des paradis devant eux se déploie;
Ils planent satisfaits, bienveillants, sérieux,
Dans le rayonnement du ciel mystérieux;
Leurs robes dans l'azur font des plis de lumière;
Ils ont leur innocence et leur blancheur première.
Ils vont d'un monde à l'autre ainsi que des oiseaux.
L'amour les courbe ainsi que le vent les roseaux,
Et les redresse ainsi que le foyer ses flammes.
Ils s'abîment en Dieu tout en restant des âmes,
Et contemplent, heureux, la face de clarté.
Ils s'accouplent, noyés dans la félicité.
Ils le regardent être, il les regarde vivre.
Ils montent à jamais vers lui. Lui les enivre
Du sourire inouï de son immensité.

To be infinite, is to be equal.
Your paradise simply balances my prison.
Ah! Creation presses down on me
Like a mountain; I raise my brow through the
Chaos whence my pains fall again as plagues;
I writhe without respite, without end, without hope.
It is a majesty, such suffering.
Yes, it is the enigma, O night, of your millions of eyes:
The great sufferer faces the great mysterious one.
Have mercy, O God! for you, yourself, I must obtain it.
My eternity casts darkness on yours.
Before your eye-torch nothing must remain,
Everything must change, grow old, and be transformed.
You alone exist. Before you all must have an age.
And, for your grandeur, it is an unwelcome cloud,
This specter that one can see seated at the heart of your
Azure heaven, eternal Satan sitting before eternal God!

VII

They are up there, on high! They are amidst the hymn and
The jubilation. The æther of paradise unfolds before them.
They soar happy, caring, earnest,
In the brilliance of mysterious heaven.
Their robes in the azure make folds of light;
They are in their first innocent and pure state.
They go from one world to the other as do the birds.
Love bends them as the wind does the reeds,
And again uplifts them as the hearth lifts its flames.
They are engulfed in God while remaining souls,
And contemplate, happy, the face of illumination.
They mate, flooded in bliss.
They watch him be, he watches them live.
They rise forever towards him. He intoxicates them
With the unheard-of smile of his vastness.

Il les voit; Il leur parle; il est Grâce et Beauté;
L'impénétrable est doux, le formidable est tendre...—
Oh! je voudrais saisir, arracher, tenir, prendre,
Oh! je voudrais broyer l'étoile du matin!

Le boiteux, le lépreux, et l'aveugle incertain,
Ceux qui marchent pieds nus et ceux qui n'ont pas même
Un toit l'hiver, ce sont des riches. Dieu les aime.
Ils ont pour vêtement ton regard de bonté.
Dieu! n'être pas aimé, c'est là la nudité!
Être maudit, c'est là le bitume et le soufre.

VIII

J'ai mis sous une pierre et scellé dans un gouffre
La justice, le bien, le pur, le vrai, le beau,
Tout ce qui peut servir à l'homme de flambeau,
La vertu, la raison, penser, espérer, croire,
Ce qu'on nomme sagesse et ce qu'on nomme gloire,
Et je rêve accoudé sur ce tombeau profond.
Je suis grand. Et sous moi les ténèbres défont
Ce qu'a fait la lumière, et dans les noirs abîmes,
Pensif, j'entends tomber goutte à goutte les crimes.
Le chaos me contemple, et j'ai le pied dessus.
Hélas! hélas! mieux vaut l'étable où naît Jésus
Que Babel et Ninive et Tyr et Babylone,
Et Job sur son fumier que Satan sur son trône!

Oh! si j'étais heureux, je serais bon! pitié!
Je ne maudirais pas! L'onagre a-t-il crié,
Le bœuf a-t-il mugi quand ils ont eu de l'herbe?
L'amour, l'azur, les lys, la lumière superbe,
Les grands rayons dorés qui vont s'élargissant,
Les vierges, les enfants joyeux, l'ange innocent,
La frange d'or de l'aube au rebord des ravines,
Oh! je crie éperdu vers ces choses divines

He sees them. He speaks to them; He is Grace and Beauty;
The impenetrable is gentle, the formidable is tender...—
Oh! I should like to seize, to tear away, to hold, to capture,
Oh! I should like to crush the morning star!

The lame, the leprous, and the hesitant blind,
Those who walk unshod and those who have no
Shelter in the cold, they are rich. God loves them.
They have for raiment your kind-hearted gaze.
God! To be unloved, that is nakedness!
To be accursed is pitch and brimstone.

VIII

I placed under a stone and sealed in a chasm
Justice, goodness, purity, truth, beauty;
All that could serve Man as a torch:
Virtue, reason, thought, hope, belief,
That which is called wisdom, and that which is called glory;
And I dream as I lean upon this deep tomb.
I am immense. And beneath me the darkness uncreates
What the light has created, and in the black abysses,
Brooding, I hear crimes accruing drop by drop.
Chaos contemplates me, and I tread on him.
Alas! Alas! better the stable where Jesus was born
Than Babel and Nineveh and Tyre and Babylon,
And better Job on his dunghill than Satan on his throne!

Oh! If I were happy, I would be good! Pity!
I would not invoke malediction! Did the wild ass bray,
Did the ox bellow while grazing happily in their fields?
Love, the azure, the lilies, the magnificent light,
The great golden rays that lengthen as they pass,
The virgins, the joyful children, the innocent angel,
The golden fringe of dawn at the edges of the ravines,
Oh; I shout desperately toward these divine things

Que je ne vois plus!—Dieu!—Dieu!—Les splendeurs
Ajoutent de la nuit, hélas, à mon cachot. [d'en haut
Il me tombe de tous les concerts des huées.
Torture! Je voudrais attendrir les nuées,
Je tends les mains aux fleurs, je crie aux aquilons:
Grâce! Ayant tous les maux du monde pour haillons,
Je pleure, je demande à la ronce, à la gerbe,
Au nuage, à la tombe, à l'étoile, au brin d'herbe,
Aux bêtes reculant devant le front humain,
Aux cailloux qu'un forçat casse au bord du chemin,
A tout, au jour qui naît, au vent qui recommence,
De la pitié! Je suis le mendiant immense.

IX

Encor si je pouvais dormir! Si seulement
Une heure, une minute, un instant, un moment,
Le temps qu'une onde passe au fond du lac sonore,
Fût-ce pour m'éveiller plus lamentable encore,
Sur n'importe quels durs et funèbres chevets,
Si je pouvais poser mon front! si je pouvais,
Nu, sur un bloc de bronze ou sur un tas de pierres,
L'une de l'autre, hélas! rapprocher mes paupières,
Et m'étendre, et sentir quelque chose de frais,
De doux et de serein, comme si je mourais!
Si je pouvais me perdre un moment dans un songe,
Apaiser dans mon flanc ce qui remue et ronge,
Aspirer un fluide étrange, aérien,
Impalpable, et flotter, et n'entendre plus rien,
Ni mon aile frémir, ni battre mon artère,
Ni ces cris dont je suis la cause sur la terre:
—Tuons! Frappons! Damnons! J'ai peur! J'ai froid! J'ai faim!
Sentir ma misérable oreille sourde enfin!
Oh! me coucher, rentrer mes griffes sous ma tête,
Dire: « C'est bien! je dors, tout comme une autre bête,
Comme un léopard, comme un chacal, comme un loup!

That I can no longer see!—God! God!—The splendors
Of heaven, alas, add more of night to my prison.
Howls fall on me from all the harmonies.
Torture! I wish to touch the thick clouds,
I reach out to the flowers, I shout to the north winds:
Forgive me! Having all the ills of the world for rags and tatters,
I weep, I ask the bramble, the wheat,
The cloud, the tomb, the star, the blade of grass,
The animals recoiling before the human countenance,
The stones which the convict breaks beside the road,
Everything, the day which dawns, the wind which blows anew,
From them all, I ask for pity! I am the immense beggar.

IX

Still, if I could sleep! If only for
An hour, a minute, an instant, one moment,
The time that a wave spends on a sonorous lakebed,
Could I but lay my brow on some hard and
Funerial bedside, even to wake up
More lamentable! If I could, naked,
On a block of bronze or on a pile of stones,
One or the other, alas! but close my eyes,
And stretch out, and feel something fresh,
Soft and serene, as if I died!
If I could but lose myself for a moment in a dream,
Soothe in my side what is restless and wearing,
Inhale a strange, ærial, impalpable
Fluid, and float, hearing nothing,
Neither my flapping wing, nor my beating heart,
Nor these shouts on earth of which I am the cause:
—Kill! Strike! Damn! I am scared! I am cold! I am hungry!
Sensing my miserable ear deaf at last!
Oh! to lie down, to pull my talons in under my head,
To say: "It is good! I sleep, just like any other beast,
Like a leopard, a jackal, a wolf!

Une nuée auguste et calme me dissout! »
Mais non! jamais! Je traîne à jamais l'insomnie
Dans une immensité sinistre d'agonie.
Ne pas mourir, ne pas dormir. Voilà mon sort.
En songe on ne sort pas, mais on croit que l'on sort;
C'est assez. Je n'ai point cette trêve. Ma peine
C'est d'être là, toujours debout; d'être une haîne
Éternelle, veillant dans l'ombre affreusement,
Et c'est de regarder sans cesse fixement
Les escarpements noirs du mystère insondable.
Voir toujours fuir, ainsi qu'une île inabordable,
Le sommeil et le rêve, obscurs paradis bleus
Où sourit on ne sait quel azur nébuleux!
O condamnation!

Je suis sous cette voûte.
Je regarde l'horreur profonde, et je l'écoute.
Pas un être ne peut souffrir sans que j'en sois.
Je suis l'affreux milieu des douleurs. Je perçois
Chaque pulsation de la fièvre du monde.
Mon ouïe est le centre où se répète et gronde
Tout le bruit ténébreux dans l'étendue épars;
J'entends l'ombre. O tourment! le mal de toutes parts
M'apporte en mon cachot sa triste joie aiguë;
J'entends glisser l'aspic et croître la ciguë;
Le mal pèse sur moi du zénith au nadir;
La mer a beau hurler, l'avalanche bondir,
L'orage entre-heurter les foudres qu'il secoue,
L'éclatant zodiaque a beau tourner sa roue
De constellations, sombre meule des cieux,
A travers le fracas vaste et prodigieux
Des astres dont parfois le groupe énorme penche,
A travers l'océan, la foudre et l'avalanche
Roulant du haut des monts parmi les sapins verts,
J'entends le pas d'un crime au bout de l'univers.
La parole qu'on dit tout bas, qui n'est pas vraie,

An august, calm cloud dissolves me!"
But no! never! I drag insomnia along, forever,
In a sinister vastness of agony.
To not die, to not sleep. This is my fate.
In a dream, one does not vanish, though one believes so,
That is enough. I have no such respite. My punishment
Is to be here, still standing; to be an eternal
Hatred, watching fearfully in the dark,
My eye evermore fixed on the
Black cliffs of unfathomable mystery.
To see always fleeing, as an unattainable isle,
Sleep and Dream, the vague, blue paradises
Where smiles some indescribable misty azure!
O condemnation!

I remain under this vault.
I regard profound horror, and harken to it.
No being can suffer without that I am there.
I am the hideous sphere of sorrows, and feel
Each pulsation of the world's fever.
My hearing is the point of confluence where is repeated
And muttered all the sinister sounds in the sparse expanse;
I hear the darkness. O torment! Evil from far and near
Brings to my prison its mournful, bitter joy;
I hear the asp slither and the hemlock grow;
Evil from the zenith to the nadir presses down on me;
The sea may well squall, the avalanche rumble,
The storm appear—to hurl down thunderbolts—
The brilliant zodiac may well turn its wheel
Of constellations, dark millstone of the heavens,
Through the enormous and prodigious roar
Of the stars whose vast cluster sometimes cants,
Through the ocean, the lightning, and the avalanche
Rolling from the mountain heights amidst the green pines,
I still hear the tread of a lone crime at the far end of the universe.
I discern everything: the whispered word, which is false,

L'obscur tressaillement du blé qu'étreint l'ivraie,
La gangrène qui vient mordre la plaie à vif,
Le chuchotement sourd des flots noyant l'esquif,
Le silence du chien près du nid de la grive,
J'entends tout, je n'échappe à rien, et tout m'arrive
A la fois dans ce bagne où je suis submergé;
Tous les fléaux en moi retentissent; et j'ai
Le contre-coup de tous les monstres; et je songe,
Écoutant la fureur, la chute, le mensonge
De toute cette race immonde de Japhet;
Je distingue le bruit mystérieux que fait
Dans une conscience un forfait qu'on décide;
O nuit! j'entends Néron devenir parricide.

Sommeil, lieu sombre, espace ineffable, où l'on est
Doux comme l'aube et pur comme l'enfant qui naît,
Dormir, ô guérison, détachement, rosée,
Stupeur épanouie, immense ombre apaisée,
Repos sacré, douceur muette, bercement
Qui trempe dans les cieux les cœurs, noir et charmant,
Oh! ce bain des remords, ce baume des ulcères,
La paix qui fait lâcher ce qu'on a dans les serres,
N'avoir jamais cela! jamais! n'avoir jamais
Cet assoupissement sur les vagues sommets,
Ce sommeil, devant qui les âmes sont pareilles,
Qui change l'antre en nid, et permet aux abeilles
De voler dans la gueule ouverte des lions!
Oh! cette voix qui dit: calmons et délions!
Ne l'entendre jamais dans mes nuits convulsives!
La flamme à la prunelle et la bave aux gencives,
Veiller, veiller, veiller, grincer des dents, voilà
Dans quelles profondeurs ma faute me scella!
Sort hideux! m'enfermer dans la nuit, et m'exclure
Du sommeil! me livrer à cette âcre brûlure,
La veille sans repos, le regard toujours noir,
Toujours ouvert! O nuit sans pitié! ne pouvoir

The dark thrill of the wheat that embraces the tares,
The gangrene that comes to bite the open wound,
The voiceless murmur of the waves flooding the skiff,
The silence of the dog near the thrush's nest,
I can escape nothing, and everything befalls me,
At once, in this prison where I am submerged;
All plagues resound within me; and I feel
The consequence of every monster; and I dream,
Listening to the fury, the fall, the lie
Of this entire squalid race of Japheth;
I even distinguish the mysterious sound made by a
Heinous crime planned within a conscience;
O night! I hear Nero becoming a parricide.

Sleep, darksome abode, ineffable space, where one is
Soft as the dawn and pure as the newborn child!
To sleep, O healing, detachment, dew,
Stupor in full bloom, immense, soothèd shadow,
Sacred repose, silent tenderness, a lulling, dark and
Charming, which steeps the hearts in the heavens,
Oh! this bath for remorse, this balm for ulcers,
The peace which is releasing what was caught in the claw,
To never have that! Never! never to have
This slumber on hazy summits,
This sleep, before whom souls are the same,
Which transforms the lair into a nest, and permits bees
To fly in the open mouths of lions!
Oh! This voice: let us become calm and unfettered!
To never hear it in my convulsive nights!
The enflamed eyes and the slavering gums,
To stay awake, awake, to gnash one's teeth,
Those are the depths to which my fault has sealed me!
Hideous fate! to lock me in Night, and deprive me
Of sleep! to deliver me unto this pungent burning,
Vigil without repose, the regard always dire,
Always open! O pitiless night! to be unable

Lui prendre un peu de calme, et l'avoir sur moi toute!
Englouti dans l'oubli, n'en pas boire une goutte!

Toujours être aux aguets! toujours être en éveil!

O vous tous, êtres! fils de l'ombre ou du soleil,
Qui que vous soyez, morts, vivants, oiseaux des grèves,
Esprits de l'air, esprits du jour, larves des rêves,
Faces de l'invisible, anges, spectres, venez,
Vous trouverez Satan les yeux ouverts. Planez,
Rampez, allez-vous-en, revenez; Satan veille
Les yeux ouverts. C'est l'ombre ou c'est l'aube vermeille,
Il a les yeux ouverts. Hier, demain, toujours!
Laissez s'enfuir les pas du temps, tardifs ou courts,
Après des millions de jours, de mois, d'années,
De siècles, de saisons écloses ou fanées,
De flux et de reflux, de printemps et d'hivers,
Venez, vous trouverez Satan les yeux ouverts.
Deux yeux fixes, voilà le fond de l'épouvante.

L'obscurité spectrale, informe, décevante,
Chimérique, me tient dans ces gouffres, béant
Et ployé sous le poids monstrueux du néant.
Je souffre. Oh! seulement un instant, que je dorme!

X

Je l'aime d'être beau, moi qui suis le difforme.
Que j'oublie un instant!—ô souvenir!—Je vois
Les anges lui parler dans l'ombre à demi-voix.
Que leur dit-il? Je suis jaloux! Je me rappelle
Qu'il me parlait aussi, que la lumière est belle.
Je l'aime d'être bon, moi qui suis le mauvais.
Oh! le temps d'un éclair, hélas! si je pouvais
Au fond de mon chaos voir son ombre apparaître!
Je l'adore, ce Dieu, plus que Jephté son prêtre,

To take from it a little peace, and have it entirely enwrap me!
Sunk in oblivion, to not taste a drop of it!

To always be watchful! always on the alert!

O all you Beings! sons of darkness or of sunlight,
Whoever you may be, dead, living, birds of the Grèves,
Ærial spirits, spirits of the day, embryos of dreams,
Faces of the invisible, angels, ghosts, come,
You shall find Satan with eyes open.
Soar, crawl, depart, return: Satan watches
With eyes open. Be it darkness or rosy dawn,
His eyes are open. Yesterday, tomorrow, forever!
Let flee the treads of time, be they sluggish or brief,
After millions of days, months, years,
Centuries, seasons born or fading,
Ebbs and flows, springs and winters,
Come, you shall find Satan with eyes open!
Two fixed eyes, that is the very nadir of terror.

The ghostly, unformed, deceitful, chimerical,
Darkness keeps me in these chasms, gaping
And burdened by the monstrous weight of Nothingness.
I suffer. Oh! Would that I could sleep, if but for an instant!

X

I love him for being beautiful, I, who am so deformed.
For one moment, let me forget!—O memory!—I see
The angels whisper to him in the dark.
What does he say to them? I am jealous! I remember that
He once spoke with me, that the light was beautiful.
I love him for being good, I who am evil.
Oh! If, for the length of a lightning flash, alas! I could but
See his shadow appear, here at the bottom of my chaos!
I adore him, this God, more than Jephthah his priest,

Plus qu'Amos son prophète et David son chanteur.
Je l'aime d'être vrai, moi qui suis le menteur.
Le sang brûle mes yeux, l'écume emplit ma bouche,
Et, chien de l'infini, chassé du ciel, farouche,
Hagard, pleurant mon maître, à la porte du jour,
Mâchant le genre humain, je hurle mon amour!
Oui, chien!

En lui parlant ma voix devient horrible.
Parfois, pensif, courbé sous mon plafond terrible,
J'entends les séraphins le chanter dans les cieux,
Et, quand ils ont fini, l'écho chante après eux;
Alors je dis:—Eh bien, moi comme eux, moi de même,
Dieu, je veux te chanter! ô lumière, je t'aime!
Je veux d'un chant d'enfer ravir l'écho du ciel.
Satan est une lyre ainsi que Gabriel.
Dieu! c'est à toi, vrai jour, c'est à toi, seul refuge,
Dieu! c'est à toi, pasteur, roi, père, maître et juge,
Que la création songe éternellement!—
Et fou, vieux cœur de fer attiré par l'aimant,
Je dis: gloire! et ma strophe éclate en diadème,
Et je leur chante un hymne ineffable et suprême,
Hymne aux versets charmants d'ombre et d'extase emplis,
Et qui pourrait sortir de la bouche d'un lys,
Puis j'écoute; et l'écho qui me répond aboie!

XI

Les plus mornes cachots ont une claire-voie;
Au fond de l'oubliette, au fond du cabanon,
Quelque chose encor semble exister; ici, non.

Satan vers Jéhovah se tourne, las d'abîme.
Oh! l'unique assassin et l'unique victime,
C'est moi. J'ai pour tourment le mal que mes mains font.
Les autres êtres sont, puis ne sont plus, ils vont

More than Amos his prophet and David his singer.
I love him for being honest, I who am a liar.
Blood burns my eyes, foam fills my mouth,
And, dog of infinity, driven from Heaven, fierce,
Wild, crying for my master at the threshold of day,
Chewing upon the human race, I howl out my love!
Yes, dog!

While speaking of him, my voice becomes hideous.
Sometimes, feeling pensive, stooped under my terrible vault,
I hear the seraphim singing of him in the heavens,
And, when they are through, the echo sings after them;
Then I say:—Well, I also, like they,
God, wish to sing of you; O light, I love thee!
I wish, with an infernal song, to delight the echo of Heaven.
Satan is a lyre as well as Gabriel.
God! it is of you, true day, it is of you, sole refuge,
God! it is of you, shepherd, king, father, teacher, judge,
That creation dreams eternally!—
And foolish, old heart of iron attracted by the magnet,
I say: glory! And my strophe bursts out into a crown,
And I sing them an ineffable and supreme hymn,
A hymn of charming verses filled with darkness and ecstasy,
And which could have come from the mouth of a lily…
Then I listen; and the echo that answers me barks!

XI

Even the gloomiest prisons have a clerestory;
At the bottom of the dungeon, at the bottom of the hutch,
Something still seems to exist; here, nothing.

Satan turns towards Jehovah, weary of the abyss.
Oh! The sole murderer and the sole victim,
Is I. I have for torment only the evil which my own hands create.
Other beings exist, and then are no more; they move,

Puis s'arrêtent, un bruit, puis rien; je les envie.
Les autres sont morts;—moi, je suis veuf de la vie.
L'effroyable vivant du sépulcre, c'est moi.

Oui, le supplicié râle et rugit; la loi
Le tient dans ses poignets de bronze qu'on redoute,
Le tue à petit feu, l'égorge goutte à goutte,
Et s'interrompt parfois pour qu'il meure longtemps;
Ses pieds fument, sa chair pétille, et par instants
Flambe, et l'on voit sortir du ventre ses entrailles;
Il hurle; l'huile bout dans la cuve; tenailles,
Plomb fondu, roue, horreur! par degrés cependant,
Malgré le vil bourreau de plus en plus ardent,
Sur l'homme évanoui la torture s'émousse;
La sinistre agonie arrive, affreuse et douce;
Le tourment vaincu semble à la surface errer;
Le misérable sent, au moment d'expirer,
Comme un éloignement ténébreux du supplice.
Entre ses cils brûlés un rayon pâle glisse,
C'est la mort, c'est le ciel, c'est l'infini profond;
Il y tombe, il y flotte, il lui semble qu'il fond;
Ses yeux tout grands ouverts se fixent sur du vide;
Il est mort.—Oh! cela, gouffres, j'en suis avide,
Je l'implore, et je crie: A mon secours, bourreaux!
La roue aux mille dents, les chevalets, les crocs,
L'attention du juge affreux, lent et barbare,
Les pinces, les crampons rougis, les coups de barre,
L'huile ardente rongeant la cuve de granit,
Le fer, le feu, c'est bon, c'est doux, cela finit.

XII

Ayez de la pitié, gouffres, prison, géhenne,
Sépulcre, chaos, nuit, désolation, haine,
Ayez de la pitié, si le ciel n'en a pas!
Sur Satan, de si haut précipité si bas,

Then stop; a sound, then nothing; I envy them.
They are dead, whereas I am widowed of Life.
I am the frightful living being of the tomb.

Yes, the tortured one howls and emits the death rattle;
The law holds him in dreadful irons,
Kills him slowly, butchers him bit by bit,
And sometimes pauses, that the dying might be prolonged;
His feet smoke, his flesh crackles, and at times
Flames, and we see the entrails from his belly;
He screams; the oil boils in the vat; tongs,
Molten lead, the wheel, horror! By degrees, however,
Despite the vile and increasingly ardent torturer,
The torture is wasted on an unconscious man;
Grim agony arrives, dreadful, gentle;
Vanquished torment seems to wander about the surface;
And the sufferer, at the time of dying, feels
A mysterious estrangement from the torture;
From between his burnt lashes a dim light slips away.
It is death, it is heaven, it is deep infinity;
He sinks there, he drifts there, he feels himself dissolving:
His open eyes become fixed on the void;
He is dead!—Oh! that, abysses, is what I so desire.
I crave it, and I shout: Help me, executioners!
The wheel with the thousand teeth, the rack, the hooks,
The attentions of the frightful, deliberate and barbaric judge,
Pincers, red hot clamps, blows with iron bars,
The burning oil eating away at the granite vat,
The iron, the fire, it is good, it is gentle, it bestows an end.

XII

Have pity, abysses, prison, Gehenna,
Tomb, chaos, night, desolation, hatred,
Have pity, if Heaven will not!
On Satan, fallen so low from such heights,

O voûtes de l'enfer, laissez tomber des larmes!
Non, c'est Dieu, c'est le ciel, c'est l'azur plein de charmes,
L'aurore se livrant toute nue à mes yeux,
C'est le baiser du jour, c'est l'amour que je veux!
Rien; le deuil. Rien! l'hiver. Rien! l'âpre solitude.
Le vil chaos, toujours dans la même attitude!
Les blocs mystérieux de l'expiation!
Je ne puis même, hélas! voir une vision,
Un reflet, comme on voit du jour aux trous d'un crible.
J'écoute du néant le monologue horrible.
L'immensité pour moi ne contient qu'un affront.
Jamais Dieu!—Tout est noir.—Quand ma main sur mon front
Cherche les deux rayons de l'archange, elle y trouve
Les deux cornes du bouc; je ne sais quelle louve
Qui tient l'être en sa gueule et l'emporte et le mord,
Vient me lécher dans l'ombre, et dit: Je suis la mort.
Quoi! j'ai le désespoir à jamais pour demeure!
Horreur! je t'aime, ô Dieu! Grâce, ô mon Dieu!

Bien, pleure;
Sanglote, implore, écume, aime! et sois rebuté!
Recommence toujours la même lâcheté!
Chien Satan, vautre-toi toujours dans ta bassesse!—
Oh! je monte et descends et remonte sans cesse,
De la création fouillant le souterrain;
Le bas est de l'acier, le haut est de l'airain,
A jamais, à jamais, à jamais! Je frissonne,
Et je cherche et je crie et j'appelle. Personne!
Et furieux, tremblant, désespéré, banni,
Frappant des pieds, des mains et du front l'infini,
Ainsi qu'un moucheron heurte une vitre sombre,
A l'immensité morne arrachant des pans d'ombre,
Seul, sans trouver d'issue et sans voir de clarté,
Je tâte dans la nuit ce mur, l'éternité.

O vaults of Hell, let your tears flow!
No, it is God, it is Heaven, it is the azure full of charms,
The dawn surrendering herself fully revealed to my eyes,
It is the kiss of day, it is love that I desire! But I have
Nothing, only mourning. Nothing but winter! Nothing but bitter
Solitude! Vile chaos, always in the same posture!
Mysterious masses of expiation!
I may not even, alas! see a vision, or
The subdued light one can see in the daytime through a sieve.
I hear the monstrous monologue of nothingness,
And the unlimitedness for me contains only insult.
Never God!—Everything is black.—When my hand seeks,
On my brow, the two light beams of the archangel, it only finds there
The two horns of the billy goat; I do not know what she-wolf
Holds existence in her mouth, carries it off and bites it,
And comes to lick me in the darkness, saying: I am death.
What! Must despair be my eternal dwelling!
Horror! I love thee, O God! Forgive me, O my God!

Indeed, do weep;
Sob, beseech, foam with rage, love! and be rebuffed!
Always repeat the same baseness!
Dog Satan, wallow eternally in your lowliness!—
Oh; I rise up and descend and rise again unceasingly,
Searching the cavern of creation;
The base is steel, the ceiling, bronze,
Forever, and ever, and ever! I shudder,
And I seek, I shout, and I call. No one!
And furious, trembling, desperate, banished,
Striking the infinite with my feet, hands, and brow,
As a gnat strikes a dark windowpane,
Tearing patches of shadow from the mournful vastness,
Alone, finding no exit, sightless,
In the night, I grope along this wall: Eternity.

II

L'ANGE LIBERTÉ

I

De la lumière. Et puis de la lumière encore.
Chaos de firmaments dans des gouffres d'aurore.

L'ange Liberté plane en l'azur spacieux.
On dirait que son œil cherche une issue aux cieux.
Elle voit une étoile. Elle s'approche:—Écoute,
Étoile; conduis-moi sous la fatale voûte;
Dieu permet que je parle à celui qui fut grand.
—Je ne puis, répond l'astre. Et Liberté reprend:
—Du moins, dis-moi la route et comment y descendre.
—Parle à l'Éclair, dit l'astre. Il peut seul te l'apprendre.
Cet ange est dans le ciel le seul qui sait tomber.

D'une aile que le vent même ne peut courber,
L'ange Liberté part et franchit l'éther sombre.

Elle vola longtemps;—l'homme n'a pas de nombre
Pour compter ce temps-là;—son vol fier était sûr.

Tout à coup, dans un angle informe de l'azur,
Elle vit l'écurie énorme des nuées.
On entendait sonner des chaînes dénouées,
Et rouler on ne sait quels effrayants essieux;
L'ange Éclair travaillait dans cet antre des cieux;
Il en faisait sortir tous les chars du tonnerre;
Quelques-uns n'étaient faits que de flamme ordinaire;
D'autres semblaient forgés dans l'enfer par les nuits;
Et des ruissellements de foudres inouïs
Ébauchaient vaguement leur forme épouvantable;
Les écueils dans la mer, les taureaux dans l'étable

II

THE ANGEL LIBERTY

I

Light. And then more light still.
Chaos of constellations in the abysses of dawn.

The angel Liberty soars in the spacious azure.
It seems that she is seeking a way out of Heaven.
She sees a star, and approaches:—Listen,
Star; lead me beneath the fatal vault;
God permits me to talk to him who was once great.
—I cannot, answers the celestial body. And Liberty continues:
—At least tell me where, and how I may descend.
—Speak to the Lightning, says the star. He alone can tell you.
He, alone, of Heaven's angels, knows how to fall.

And the angel Liberty, on wings over which even the
Wind has no say, left, and crossed the dark æther.

Her flight was eterne—Man has no number with
Which to measure the time—and was proud and sure.

Suddenly, in a formless corner of the azure,
She spied the huge stable of thick clouds.
One could hear the sound of loose chains,
And of we know not what terrible axles rolling;
The angel Lightning, at work in this, one of the Heavenly
Caverns, was releasing all the chariots of thunder,
Some composed of common flame,
Others as if forged in Hell by the nights;
And incredible streamings of lightning
Traced vaguely their dreadful shapes;
The reefs in the sea, the bulls in the stable,

Sont des roucoulements près des monstrueux bruits
De tous ces chars avec de l'abîme construits.

Liberté s'avança vers l'Éclair. L'immortelle
Sourit:—Ange, tu dois connaître, lui dit-elle,
L'éclatant Lucifer tombé dans le trépas.
—C'est moi qui l'ai frappé, je ne le connais pas,
Dit l'Éclair.—Mais le gouffre où tu jetas cette âme,
Tu peux me le montrer?—Non, dit l'esprit de flamme.
Va trouver le vieil ange Hiver. Il est le seul
Qui connaisse les plis ténébreux du linceul.
Moi, je ne me souviens de rien. Je brise, et passe.

Puis, il montra du doigt un point noir dans l'espace.
C'était la terre.

—Va, dit-il. Le triste enfer
Touche à ce monde, et là tu trouveras l'hiver.

Et l'ange Liberté, telle qu'un jet de fronde,
Partit, et vit grandir la sphère obscure et ronde,
Et, superbe, et bravant la bise et le mistral,
S'abattit sur la terre à l'endroit sépulcral.

Dans ce cercle effrayant que les glaciers enserrent,
Au fond du désert blême où jamais ne passèrent
Les Colomb, les Gama, ces lumineux sondeurs,
Dans ces obscurités et dans ces profondeurs
Sur la création par le néant conquises,
Au delà des spitzbergs, des flots et des banquises,
Au centre de la brume où tout rayon finit,
Loin du jour, dans l'eau marbre et dans la mer granit,
Le sombre archange Hiver se dresse sur le pôle;
La trompette à la bouche et l'ombre sur l'épaule,
Il est là, sans qu'il sorte, au milieu de ce deuil,
De son clairon un souffle, un éclair de son œil;

Make mere cooings beside the monstrous din
Of all these chariots forged in the abyss.

Liberty advanced toward the angel Lightning. She,
The Immortal one, smiled, and spoke:—Angel,
You must know brilliant Lucifer, fallen to his doom.
—It is I who struck him down, yet I know him not,
Says Lightning.—But to the abyss where you cast this soul,
Can you guide me?—No, says the spirit of flame.
Go seek out the old angel Winter. He, alone,
Knows the dark folds of the shroud.
I, however, remember nothing. I merely strike, and pass on.

Then he pointed to a black speck in space.
It was the earth.

—Go, he says. Sad Hell
Borders on this world, and there you shall find Winter.

And the angel Liberty, taking wing like a catapult shot,
Watched the dark, round sphere growing near, and,
Magnificent, braving the north wind and the mistral,
Landed on the earth in the sepulchral place.

In this frightful circle enclosed by glaciers,
At the bottom of the ghastly desert where never passed
Columbuses, or da Gamas, those luminous probers,
In this darkness and in these depths
Conquered by Nothingness upon their creation,
Beyond the Spitzbergs, the floods and ice floes,
In the center of the mist where light beams end,
Far from day, in the marble water, in the granite sea,
The somber archangel, Winter, draws himself up upon the Pole;
The trumpet at his mouth and the shadow upon his shoulder,
Forever there, in the midst of this bereavement,
From his clarion a breath, a lightning flash from his eye;

Il ne rêve pas même, étant un bloc de neige;
Les vents ailés, pareils à l'oiseau pris au piège,
Sont dans sa main, captifs du silence éternel;
Son œil éteint regarde affreusement le ciel;
Le givre est dans ses os, le givre est sur sa tête;
L'horreur pétrifiée autour de lui s'arrête;
Sa sinistre attitude effare l'infini;
Dur, morne, il est glacé, c'est-à-dire banni;
La terre sous ses pieds, de ténèbres vêtue,
Se tait; il est la blanche et muette statue
Debout sur ce tombeau dans l'éternelle nuit;
Jamais une lueur, un mouvement, un bruit,
N'effleurent le géant, seul sous de sombres voiles.
Mais quand, à ces cadrans qu'on nomme les étoiles,
L'heure du dernier jour sans terme et sans milieu
Sonnera, le rayon de la face de Dieu
Dégèlera le spectre, et tout à coup sa bouche
Se gonflera d'un pli formidable et farouche,
Et les mondes, esquifs roulant sans aviron,
Entendront l'ouragan sortir de son clairon.
Jamais le séraphin constellé d'yeux n'approche
Cette âme du silence et du deuil, faite roche,
Geôlière des cieux morts et des firmaments noirs;
Ce brouillard gris, pareil à la chute des soirs,
Fait peur aux chérubins extasiés et tendres;
Les neiges, cette forme effroyable des cendres,
Font de cet horizon, dont l'aube hait le seuil,
Quelque chose qui semble un dedans de cercueil.

L'ange-vierge, à travers les glaciers, blancs décombres,
Vola droit au géant, seul dans ces déserts sombres
Dont le jour ne veut pas et qu'il n'a pas reçus.
D'abord elle plana radieuse au-dessus
Du lourd colosse, avec les grands cercles de l'aigle;
Puis, s'approchant, lui dit: —Celui qui juge et règle,
Celui qui fait tout vivre et qui fait tout trembler,

Never does he even dream, being composed of snow;
The wingèd winds, resembling trapped birds,
Are enclosed within his hand, captives of the eternal silence;
His blear eye looks hideously at the sky,
The hoarfrost in his bones, the hoarfrost upon his head;
Petrified horror comes to rest about him; and
His sinister bearing frightens the Infinite;
Hard, dismal, he is ice-bound, that is to say, banished;
The earth under his feet, clad in darkness,
Keeps silent; he is the white and mute statue
Standing upon this tomb in the eternal night;
Nary a light, a movement, a sound,
Touch this giant, alone as he is under somber veils.
But when, on these dials that we call stars,
The hour of the last day without end and without middle
Chimes, the light shining from God's countenance
Shall thaw this specter, of a sudden his mouth
Shall swell with a formidable, fierce fold,
And the worlds, those aimless, oarless skiffs,
Shall hear the hurricane burst forth from his clarion.
Never does the seraph spangled with stars approach
This soul of silence and mourning, turned to stone,
Gaoler of the dead heavens and the black firmaments;
This grey fog, like eventide,
Frightens the rapturous and tender cherubs;
The snows, that horrifying body of ash,
Make of this horizon whose verge is scorned by Dawn,
Something like the inside of a crypt.

The Angel-virgin, across the glaciers, those white ruins,
Flew straight towards the giant, alone in these dark deserts
That Day desires not, nor does it recognize.
At first she glided, radiant, above
The menacing colossus, with the great circlings of the eagle.
Then, upon approaching, she spoke:—The One who judges
And rules, the One who makes everything live and who makes

M'a permis de venir ici; je veux parler
A quelqu'un d'effrayant dont seul tu connais l'antre;
Ô géant, ouvre-moi le gouffre, pour que j'entre.

Le vieillard de la Nuit resta sourd et muet;
Pas un pli du brouillard pesant ne remuait
Dans cette immensité d'ombre et de solitude;
Seulement, sans que rien troublât son attitude,
Et sans qu'un mouvement fît voir qu'il entendît,
La glace sous ses pieds lentement se fendit.
Une crevasse étrange apparut; ouverture
D'on ne sait quelle horreur qui n'est plus la nature,
Bouche d'un puits livide et morne, escarpement
D'un abîme qui va plus loin que l'élément,
Vision du néant formidable, enfermée
Entre deux murs sans forme où rampe une fumée;
Deuil, brume; obscurité sans fond et sans contour.

La vierge Liberté, blanche et faite de jour,
Sentit le froid du lieu funeste où rien n'existe.
La désolation de ce gouffre était triste
Et profonde; et c'était l'infini de la nuit.

Elle ouvrit sa grande aile où l'azur des cieux luit,
Et, calme, descendit dans cette ombre terrible.

II

Or, en ce même instant, l'horreur indivisible,
Sans palpitation, sans souffle et sans échos,
La lugubre unité de tombe et de chaos
Qu'on nomme Enfer, voyait une chose inouïe.

Une forme, parfois soudain évanouie,
Puis renaissant, flottant au loin, puis s'abîmant,

Everything tremble, allowed me to come; I wish to speak
To a frightening Being whose cave only you know.
O giant, open the abyss for me, so that I may enter.

The Old Man of the Night remained deaf and mute;
Hardly a fold of the heavy fog did stir
In this immensity of darkness and solitude;
Yet, with nothing appearing to disturb him,
And with no movement showing he had heard,
The ice under his feet slowly began to crack.
A strange fissure appeared, opening
Onto an unknown and no longer natural horror,
The mouth of a pale and gloomy well, a steep slope
Of a chasm leading towards the beyond,
A vision of a formidable nothingness enclosed
Within two walls without form whence smoke was rising,
Mourning, mist, fathomless darkness without contour.

The virgin Liberty, pure and composed of daylight,
Felt the cold from this deadly place where nothing exists.
The desolation of this abyss was mournful
And profound; and it was endless night.

She opened her great wings where the blue of the Heavens
Shines, and calmly descended into this terrible darkness.

II

Now, at this very moment, the inseparable horror,
Without palpitation, breathless and echoless,
The sorrowful union of tomb and chaos
That we call Hell, saw something extraordinary.

A form, sometimes suddenly vanishing,
Then reappearing, floating far off, then engulfed,

Sorte de voile ayant un vague mouvement,
Glissait sous ce plafond qu'on prendrait pour un rêve.

Cette figure était la même que la grève
Du fleuve Seine avait vue errer autrefois,
Et jeter dans les vents sa redoutable voix.

Elle allait, comme l'algue erre...—A travers le voile
La fixité des yeux flamboyait, et la toile
Dont ce voile était fait semblait avoir été
Tissée avec du rêve et de l'obscurité.
Elle sondait l'enfer qui sans fin se prolonge;
Dans la stagnation des ténèbres, qui songe,
Et qui, farouche, a l'air d'un crime qui se tait,
Elle passait, tournait, descendait, remontait,
Prenant on ne sait quels plis informes pour guides,
Blême aux endroits obscurs, noire aux endroits livides.
Ainsi vole à travers les branches l'émouchet.
Parfois, comme quelqu'un qui cherche, elle touchait
Le mur prodigieux de la cave du monde.
Elle serpentait, lente et souple comme une onde,
Dans l'abîme où l'esprit lit ce mot triste: Absent.
Souvent elle laissait derrière elle en passant
Le bleuissement pâle et fugitif du soufre.

Soudain, comme sentant sous elle plus de gouffre,
Elle hésita, pencha ce qui semblait son front,
Et regarda.

La nuit qu'aucun jour n'interrompt
Gisait dans l'étendue effroyable et sublime.
Ce précipice était de la mort, faite abîme.
On y sentait flotter du sépulcre dissous.
On voyait de la nuit sous la nuit; au-dessous
De l'ombre, dans un vide étrange, on voyait l'ombre.

A kind of veil stirring uncertainly,
Dropped under this ceiling which we would take for a dream.

This figure was like that which the bank
Of the river Seine had seen wandering in days of old,
Casting into the winds its formidable voice.

She wandered, as seaweed wanders...—Through the veil
The fixedness of her eyes blazed, and the cloth
Of which this veil was composed seemed to have been
Woven of dream and darkness.
She sounded the hell that stretches on forever.
In this stagnation of mystery, which muses,
And has the fierce air of a voiceless crime,
She made a pass, turned, descended, reascended,
Taking who knows what formless folds for guides,
Here pale in dark places, there dark in pale places.
Thus does the kestrel fly amidst the branches of trees.
Sometimes, as someone searching, she touched
The prodigious wall of the vault of the world.
She meandered, slow and supple as a wave,
In the abyss where the spirit reads this mournful word: Absent;
And she often left behind, in passing,
The fleeting, pale blue stain of sulphur.

But suddenly sensing more abyss beneath her,
She paused, tilted her head,
And looked.

The night no day interrupts
Lay in that terrible and sublime expanse.
This precipice was a chasm composed of Death,
And one sensed the dissolved sepulcher floating there.
One could see night beneath night; below the darkness,
In that strange space, could be seen more darkness.

Tout au fond remuait une apparence sombre;
Un fantôme entrevu, submergé, trouble, enfui,
Errant, rampant; c'était le Damné; c'était Lui.

On distinguait un front, des ailes, des vertèbres.

C'était l'archange larve, âme des lieux funèbres,
Mêlant en lui de l'astre avec de l'animal;
C'était l'être sinistre en qui pense le mal;
C'était le criminel que le crime exécute;
C'était plus qu'un esprit tombé; c'était la Chute.

Le chaos se roulait sur l'ange en se gonflant;
Par intervalle, un ongle, un large crâne, un flanc
Rayé comme les lynx, les guêpes et les zèbres,
Se dressait dans le spasme horrible des ténèbres.
Ses écailles semblaient de fumée et de jais.
On croyait voir quelqu'un de ces vagues objets
Tortueux et flottants, dont on craint la piqûre.
Offrant tous les aspects dans une ébauche obscure,
Céleste, bestial, humain, vertigineux,
Laissant voir une face au milieu de ses nœuds,
Enflant des plis confus dans l'ombre où rien ne brille,
C'était par instants l'hydre et parfois la chenille.
Il se traînait, visqueux, blême, éclipsé, terni,
Reptile colossal du cloaque infini.

La caverne d'en bas de Tout; voilà ce gouffre.

C'était du vide en pleurs et du miasme qui souffre.
D'affreux rocs ébauchaient de noirs décharnements;
On croyait, dans la brume épaisse, par moments,
Entrevoir le cadavre effrayant de la Cause;
Tout était mort; Satan rôdait dans quelque chose
D'informe et de hideux qui paraissait détruit;
De sorte qu'au milieu de la fétide nuit,

Right at the very bottom moved a dark shape;
This glimpsed ghost, immersed, troubled, fleeing,
Wandering, crawling, was He, the Accursed.

One could see his brow, his wings, his spine.

It was the archangel specter, soul of the funereal places,
Mixing celestial body with beast;
It was the sinister Being in whom Evil thinks;
It was the criminal executed by Crime;
It was more than a fallen soul; it was the Fall.

Chaos turned over on the angel, and swelled up inside him;
At times a talon, a wide skull, a flank crossed
With lines like lynxes, wasps and zebras,
Rose up in the horrible spasm of darkness.
Its scales looking jet black and made of smoke,
It seemed like one of those vague, meandering,
Floating things whose sting we fear.
Offering all of its aspects in a lurid sketch,
Celestial, bestial, human, vertiginous,
Letting show one face in the midst of its coils,
Swelling with confused folds in the gloom where nothing shines,
It was at times the hydra and sometimes the larva.
It dragged itself along, viscous, pallid, eclipsed, soiled,
Colossal reptile of the infinite cesspool.

The nethermost cavern of Everything—that was this abyss.

It was space in tears, and miasma that suffers.
Hideous rocks prefigured black emaciations;
At times one believed that one glimpsed,
In the thick mist, the terrible corpse of Cause;
Everything was dead; Satan was prowling about in some
Formless and hideous place which seemed destroyed;
So that in the midst of fetid night,

Tout étant noirceur, peste, épouvante, misère,
Lividité, ruine, il semblait nécessaire
Qu'au fond de cette tombe on vît ramper ce ver.

Si quelque ange, égaré dans l'éternel hiver,
Fouillant la profondeur du deuil impénétrable,
Hélas! fût arrivé jusqu'à ce misérable,
Il n'eût rien retrouvé dans ce roi de l'enfer
Du géant éclaireur qu'on nommait Lucifer.
L'abîme avait fini par entrer dans sa forme.
La condamnation, lourde, lépreuse, énorme,
S'était, sur cet archange à jamais rejeté,
Lentement déposée en monstruosité.
L'impur typhus sortait de son haleine amère.
Parfois, dans ce puits sombre et rempli de chimère,
Que la vision seule aperçoit et connaît,
Quelque ruissellement de lueur dessinait
Son dos ou la membrane immonde de son aile.
La rondeur de sa rouge et luisante prunelle
Semblait, dans la terreur de ces lieux inouïs,
Une goutte de flamme au fond du puits des nuits.
Sa face était le masque effaré du vertige.
A de certains moments, phases du noir prodige,
Un flamboiement, sortant de lui, glissait sur lui;
L'abîme aveugle était brusquement ébloui;
Alors, vision noire! à travers l'insondable,
A travers l'inconnu qui n'est pas regardable,
Dans l'étrange épaisseur du gouffre devenu
Glauque autour du colosse inexprimable et nu,
Satan apparaissait dans toute sa souffrance;
Le démon fulgurant, dans cette transparence,
Horrible, se tordait comme un éclair noyé.
Puis la nuit revenait, glacée et sans pitié;
La vaste cécité refluait sous la voûte
De l'éternel silence et l'engloutissait toute;
Et l'enfer, un instant montré, se refermant,
Lugubre, s'emplissait d'évanouissement.

Everything being blackness, plague, terror, suffering,
Lividity, ruin, it seemed destined that,
In the depths of this grave, this crawling worm would be seen.

If some angel, wandering in the eternal winter,
Searching the depths of impenetrable bereavement,
Alas, happened upon this wretch,
He would find nothing, in this king of Hell,
Of the enlightened giant once called Lucifer.
The abyss had finally absorbed him.
The condemnation—heavy, leprous, enormous—
Had, on this forever rejected archangel,
Slowly been deposited as monstrosity.
Impure typhoid was on his bitter breath.
Sometimes, in this dark well filled with chimeras
That the imagination alone sees and understands,
Some streaming of light traced
His back or the foul membrane of his wing.
The roundness of his red, glistening eye
Seemed, in the terror of these incredible places,
A drop of flame deep in the wells of night.
His face was the frightened mask of vertigo.
At certain times, phases of this prodigous gloom,
A blazing fire escaped from him, engulfing him;
The blind abyss was suddenly luminous;
Then, dark vision! through the fathomless,
Through the unknown that is not watchable,
In the strange depths of the chasm become
Sea-green around the unspeakable and naked giant,
Satan appeared in all his suffering;
The fulgurant devil, frightful in this translucence,
Writhed like drowned lightning.
Then came back the night, icy and merciless;
The vast cecity flowed back under the vault
Of eternal silence and swallowed him whole;
And Hell, revealed for but a moment, closed again,
Mournful, fading away into blackness.

.:.:.:.:.:.:.:.:.:.

VII

Tout fit silence au fond du gouffre sans reflux,
Et rien ne troubla plus l'immobilité morte.

Pareil au goëmon que le flot berce et porte,
Satan dormait toujours.

Dans la nappe de nuit
Où s'enfonçait son corps de chimère construit,
Ce qu'on entrevoyait, c'était sa forme humaine.

Semblable au flocon blanc qu'un vent d'hiver amène,
L'ange arrêta sur lui ses ailes qui flottaient,
Et pleura.

L'on eût dit que ses larmes étaient
De la lumière en pleurs coulant de deux étoiles.
Comme la tarentule au centre de ses toiles,
Le vaste malheureux et le vaste méchant
Palpitait; et la vierge immortelle, penchant
L'escarboucle allumée au sommet de sa tète,
Tendit les bras vers l'ange englouti dans la bête,
Et lui parla, planant et pourtant à genoux;
Et l'accent de sa voix divine était plus doux
Que l'incarnation vague et sombre des sphères.

« O toi; je viens. Je pleure. Ici, dans les misères,
Dans le deuil, dans l'enfer où l'astre se perdit,
Je viens te demander une grâce, ô maudit!
Ici, je ne suis plus qu'une larme qui brille.
Ce qui survit de toi c'est moi. Je suis ta fille.
Sens-tu que je suis là? Me reconnais-tu, dis?

.:.:.:.:.:.:.:.:.:.:.

VII

Everything was silent at the bottom of the ebbless gulf,
And dead immobility was disturbed no more.

Like seaweed that the waters support and lull,
Satan still slept.

Under the cover of night
Where sank his body built of fancy,
What one glimpsed was his human form.

Like the white snowflake carried by a winter wind,
The angel stopped on her floating wings,
And wept.

Her tears seemed
Tears of light flowing from two stars.
Like the tarantula amidst its silken webbing,
The great wretched and wicked one
Was palpitating; and the immortal virgin, tilting
The lit carbuncle atop her head,
Stretched her arms towards the angel engulfed within the beast,
And spoke, hovering, and yet still upon her knees;
And the tone of her divine voice was softer
Than the faint, dark incarnation of the spheres.

"O Thou; I come. I weep. Here, in the miseries,
In mourning, in the Hell where starlight has disappeared,
I come to beseech you, O cursed one!
Here, I am no more than a glistening tear.
What survives of you is me. I am your daughter.
Do you sense my presence? Tell me, do you recognize me?

M'entends-tu? C'est du fond des divins paradis,
C'est de la profondeur lumineuse et sacrée,
C'est de ce grand ciel clair où vit celui qui crée,
Que je viens, éperdue, à toi, l'ange enfoui!
J'ai crié vers Dieu; Dieu formidable a dit: Oui.
Il me laisse descendre au fond des nuits difformes,
Et, pour que je te parle, il permet que tu dormes.
Car, Père, pour tes yeux, hélas, le firmament
Ne peut plus s'entr'ouvrir qu'en songe seulement!
Oh! toute cette nuit, c'est affreux! Père, Père!
Quoi! toi dans ce cachot! Quoi! toi dans ce repaire!
Toi puni! toi mauvais! toi, l'aîné des élus!
Te voilà donc si bas que Dieu ne te voit plus!
L'enfer! l'océan Nuit! pas de flot, pas d'écume,
Pas de souffle. Partout le Noir. C'est, dans la brume,
Ta respiration lugubre que j'entends.
La longueur de ton deuil dépassera le temps;
Le chiffre de tes maux dépassera le nombre.
Les soleils me disaient: prends garde, il est dans l'ombre!
Et moi j'ai dit: je veux voir le désespéré.
Hélas, l'astre du ciel te hait, la fleur du pré
Te craint, autour de toi tous les êtres ensemble
Frémissent, les clartés frissonnent, l'azur tremble,
L'infini te redoute et t'abhorre; eh bien, moi,
Je t'apporte en amour tout cet immense effroi!

« Je viens te prier, toi qu'on proscrit. Toi qu'on souille,
Je viens avec des pleurs te laver. J'agenouille
La lumière devant ton horreur, et l'espoir
Devant les coups de foudre empreints sur ton front noir!
Entends-moi dans ton rêve à travers l'anathème.
Ne te courrouce point, père, puisque je t'aime!
Le blessé ne hait pas la main qui le soutient;
L'affamé n'a jamais maudit celui qui vient
Disant: Voici du pain et de l'eau; bois et mange.
Oh! quand j'étais mêlée à tes ailes, quel ange

Do you hear me? It is from the depths of the divine paradises,
It is from the bright and sacred deep,
It is from this great, lucent heaven where lives the One who creates,
That I come, desperate, to you, the angel buried!
I cried out to God; and formidable God said: Yes.
He lets me descend to the bottom of the deformed nights,
And, so that I may speak to you, he lets you sleep.
Because, Father, for your eyes, alas!
The firmament can half-open only in dream!
Oh! All this darkness is hideous! Father, Father!
What! You in this dungeon! What! You in this lair!
You punished, you evil, you, the eldest son of the elect!
You here, thus, so low that God no longer sees you!
Hell! ocean of Night! no wave, no spume,
No wind. Everywhere Blackness. It is, in the mist,
Your sorrowful breath that I hear.
The length of your mourning shall exceed Time;
The amount of your troubles shall exceed Number.
The Suns said to me: take care, he is in the darkness!
But I said: I must see this desperate being.
Alas, the star in the sky abhors you, the flower in the meadow
Fears you, around you all the beings together
Shudder, brightness quivers, the azure trembles,
Infinity dreads you and loathes you; well,
I nonetheless, bring you, with love, all this immense dismay!

"I come to beseech you in your exile. In your tarnished state,
I come to bathe you in tears. I make the Light kneel
Down before your horror, and I make Hope kneel down
Before the lightning strikes imprinted on your black brow!
Hear me in your dream through the anathema.
Be not angry, father, because I love you!
The wounded person does not hate the hand that supports him;
The starving man has never cursed the one who arrives
Saying: here is some bread and here, some water; drink and eat.
Oh! When I was still amongst your feathers, what an angel

Que Satan, dans l'aurore et dans l'immensité!
Dieu se nommant Bonté, tu t'appelais Beauté.
Ta chevelure était blonde et surnaturelle,
Et frissonnait splendide, et laissait derrière elle
Une inondation de rayons dans la nuit!
L'abîme était par toi comme par Dieu conduit.
Un jour les éléments te prirent pour Lui-même;
Comme tu te dressais avec ton diadème
Sur le ciel, de ton lustre effrayant envahi,
L'air dit: Emmanuel! et l'onde: Adonaï!
Ton char faisait jaillir des mondes sous sa roue.
Près de toi Raphaël, Gabriel, qui secoue
Un météore épars en flammes sur son front,
Michel, dont la clarté jamais ne s'interrompt,
Ithuriel, qui mêle aux rayons les dictames,
Stellial, Azraël, porte-flambeau des âmes,
N'étaient plus que l'essaim confus de la forêt;
Un resplendissement de blancheur t'entourait;
Et l'aube en te voyant s'écriait: Je suis noire!
Tu passais au milieu d'un ouragan de gloire;
Les éthers t'attendaient pour devenir azurs;
Les univers naissaient, prodigieux et purs,
Avec des millions de fleurs et d'étincelles,
Dans un rythme marqué par tes battements d'ailes;
Tu faisais, en fixant sur eux ton œil charmant,
Reculer les soleils dans l'éblouissement;
Tu flamboyais, candeur et force; un lys archange!
Comme après le héros s'avance la phalange,
A ta suite marchaient les constellations;
L'ombre pleurait d'amour quand nous la traversions;
La nuit, tu te levais dans un triomphe d'astres;
Et les dômes divins et les sacrés pilastres,
Et les éternels cieux et l'éden nouveau né,
T'adoraient dans ta joie immense, infortuné!

Satan was, in the dawn and in the immensity!
God naming himself Goodness, you were named Beauty.
Your hair was fair and preternatural,
It quivered magnificently, and left behind it
A flood of light rays in the night!
The abyss was governed by you as well as by God.
One day, the elements took you for him;
As you raised yourself up with your diadem
Into the heavens flooded by your frightening sheen,
The breeze said: Emmanuel! and the wave: Adonai!
Your chariot made worlds spring up under its wheels.
Next to you, Raphael, Gabriel, whose brow
Sheds a meteor scattered in flames,
Michael, whose light never ceases,
Ithuriel, who combines light beams with solaces,
Stellial, Azrael, torchbearer of souls,
Were no more than the confused creatures inhabiting the forest;
A brilliance of whiteness surrounded you;
And the dawn upon seeing you exclaimed: I am dark!
You passed by in a storm of glory;
The æthers awaited you, that they might become azures;
Universes were born, prodigious and pure,
With millions of flowers and fulgurations,
In a rhythm marked by the beating of your wings;
You made, by fixing upon them your charming eye,
The suns draw back in resplendence;
You glowed, innocence and strength; a lily archangel!
Just as, behind the hero, marches the phalanx,
So, in your retinue, walked the constellations;
The darkness wept with love when we traversed her;
At night, you rose up in a triumphal procession of stars;
And the divine vaults and the sacred pilasters,
And the eternal heavens and the newborn Eden,
Adored you in your immense joy, unfortunate one!

« Hélas, dès qu'en ce bagne, où nul regard ne plonge,
Tu fus précipité, Satan, tu fis ce songe
De te venger, démon géant, sur l'infini!
Prés de l'ange proscrit tu mis l'homme banni;
Tu fis tomber Adam et tu fis déchoir Ève;
Tu voulus frapper Dieu dans le germe et la sève,
Dans l'enfant, dans le nid des bois, dans l'alcyon;
Seul, à jamais muré sous la création,
Tu devins, dans l'horreur, le grand rêveur funeste;
Dans les vierges forêts tu fis sortir la peste
De l'épaisseur charmante et terrible des fleurs;
Avec les voluptés tu forgeas les douleurs;
Tu te mêlas à l'être auguste qui gouverne;
L'espace alors s'emplit d'un esprit de caverne;
Tu dis à l'Éternel: à nous deux maintenant!
Tu souillas l'infini rien qu'en l'espionnant.
A travers l'océan tu soufflas le naufrage;
Captif, tu pénétras la terre de ta rage;
Le dessous ténébreux de la vie appartint
A ta vengeance, et fut par ton haleine atteint;
Tu mordis les tombeaux; tu mordis les racines;
Tu mêlas aux parfums les herbes assassines;
Tu mis partout le monstre à côté de la loi;
Une émanation de nuit sortit de toi,
Et tu déshonoras l'univers magnanime.
Dieu rayonnait le bien, tu rayonnas le crime.
Tu fis d'en bas, avec tes miasmes, des démons;
Tu pris les instincts vils et les impurs limons
Et tu créas avec cette fange les traîtres,
Les lâches, les cruels; et tu fis dieux et maîtres
Des êtres de l'abîme et des esprits forçats;
Tu poussas les Nemrods aux guerres, tu dressas
Les Caïphes sanglants contre les Christs sublimes;
Et souvent là-haut, nous, les anges, nous pâlîmes
D'entendre dans le deuil les prêtres et les rois
Rire, et de voir grandir le glaive énorme en croix.

"Alas, as soon as you were cast down into this prison,
Where no glance enters, you created this dream,
In order to avenge yourself, giant demon, on Infinity!
Near the exiled angel you placed banished Man;
You brought down Adam and you made Eve fall;
You wished to strike God in the bud and the sap,
In the child, in the nest amongst the trees, in the halcyon;
Alone, walled up forever under Creation,
You became, in horror, the great disastrous dreamer;
In the virgin forests you made the plague emerge
From the delightful and astonishing wealth of flowers;
With the pleasures you forged pains;
You took on the role of the august Being who governs;
Space was then filled with a spirit of the cavern;
You said to the Eternal: There are two of us now!
You soiled Infinity by merely spying on it.
Across the Ocean you blew shipwreck;
Captive, you pierced the earth with your fury;
The melancholy underside of life belonged
To your vengeance, and was tainted by your breath;
You gnawed on tombs; you gnawed on roots;
You mixed perfumes with dead weeds;
You placed everywhere the monster beside the law;
A night emanation issued from you,
And you dishonored the noble universe.
God shone the good, you shone crime. You
Created in the nether regions, with your miasmas, demons;
You took vile instincts and impure mud and
Created, from this clay, the traitorous, the cowardly,
The malevolent; and you made gods and masters
From creatures of the abyss and convict spirits;
You impelled Nimrods to war, you pitted the
Bloody Caiaphases against the sublime Christs; and often
Above, we, the angels, turned pale, hearing, during our
Bereavement, the priests and kings laughing, and seeing,
Growing ever larger, the enormous sword in the shape of a cross.

« A quoi cela t'a-t-il servi? plus de misère;
Voilà tout. Ton éclair ronge et brûle ta serre;
Ton empoisonnement du monde a commencé
Par toi-même, ô géant d'un combat insensé.
Le mal ne fait pas peur à Dieu; Dieu se courrouce,
Et frappe. Tu croyais que la vengeance est douce;
Elle est amère. Hélas! le crime est châtiment.
La croissance du mal augmente ton tourment;
Le mal qu'on fait souffrir s'ajoute au mal qu'on souffre;
Ta lave au fond des nuits sur toi retombe en soufre;
Et toi-même on t'entend par moments l'avouer.
Le supplice de Tout sur toi vient échouer.
Tu fais tout chanceler, tout trembler sur sa base,
Tout crouler, et c'est toi que ton effort écrase;
Toute la terre étant sous ton joug à présent,
Te voilà, toi, sous plus d'épouvante gisant!
Te voilà plus difforme, et ton cœur d'airain saigne!

« Mais, Satan, il faut bien qu'à la fin on te plaigne,
Tu dois avoir besoin de voir quelqu'un pleurer,
Je viens à toi!

« Je viens gémir, luire, éclairer,
T'ôter du moins le poids de la terrestre chaîne,
Et guérir à ton flanc la sombre plaie humaine.
Mon père, écoute-moi. Pour baume et pour calmant,
Pour mêler quelque joie à ton accablement,
Tu n'as jusqu'à cette heure, en ton âpre géhenne,
Essayé que la nuit, la vengeance et la haine,
O Titan misérable, essaie enfin le jour!
Laisse planer le cygne à ta place, ô vautour!
Laisse un ange sorti de tes ailes répandre
Sur les fléaux un souffle irrésistible et tendre.
Faisons lever Caïn accroupi sur Abel.
Assez d'ombre et de crime! Empêchons que Babel

"What purpose has it served? More suffering;
That is all. Your flash of lightning eats away and burns
Your talons; your poisoning of the world began
With yourself, O giant of senseless combat.
Evil does not frighten God; God gets angry,
And strikes. You believed that vengeance is sweet;
It is bitter. Alas! Crime is punishment.
The growth of evil increases your own agony;
The evil you inflict adds to the evil you suffer;
Your lava in the depth of the nights falls back on you again as
Brimstone; and you yourself have at times been heard to confess it.
Your torture of Everything is going to revert to you.
You make everything falter, everything tremble at its base,
Everything collapse, and it is you whom your effort crushes;
All the Earth, at present, being under your yoke,
See! you, yourself, are weighed down by more dread!
See! you, yourself, are more deformed, and your brazen heart bleeds!

"But, Satan, we must surely in the end pity you.
You must see someone weeping,
And so I come to you!

"I come to lament, but also to illumine,
To enlighten, to at least remove the weight of the terrestrial
Chain, and cure the somber human wound in your side.
My father, listen to me. For balm and for anodyne,
To mix some joy with your dejection,
You have till this hour, in your bitter Gehenna,
Tried only night, vengeance and hatred,
O wretched Titan, try, at last, daylight!
Let the swan soar instead of you, O vulture!
Let an angel taken from your wings waft
Onto the plagues an irresistible and tender breath.
Let us raise Cain, who cowers atop Abel.
Enough darkness and crime! Let us prevent Babel

Élève encor plus haut ses hideuses spirales.
Oh! laisse-moi rouvrir les portes sépulcrales
Que, du fond de l'enfer, sur l'âme tu fermais!
Laisse-moi mettre l'homme en liberté. Permets
Que je tende la main à l'univers qui sombre.
Laisse-moi renverser la montagne de l'ombre;
Laisse-moi jeter bas l'infâme tour du mal!

« Permets que, grâce à moi, dans l'azur baptismal
Le monde rentre, afin que l'Éden reparaisse!
Hélas! sens-tu mon cœur tremblant qui te caresse?
M'entends-tu sangloter dans ton cachot? consens
Que je sauve les bons, les purs, les innocents;
Laisse s'envoler l'âme et finir la souffrance.
Dieu me fit Liberté; toi, fais-moi Délivrance!
Oh! ne me défends pas de jeter dans les cieux
Et les enfers, le cri de l'amour factieux;
Laisse-moi prodiguer à la terrestre sphère
L'air vaste, le ciel bleu, l'espoir sans borne, et faire
Sortir du front de l'homme un rayon d'infini.
Laisse-moi sauver tout, moi ton côté béni!
Consens! Oh! moi qui viens de toi, permets que j'aille
Chez ces vivants, afin d'achever la bataille
Entre leur ignorance, hélas, et leur raison,
Pour mettre une rougeur sacrée à l'horizon,
Pour que l'affreux passé dans les ténèbres roule,
Pour que la terre tremble et que la prison croule,
Pour que l'éruption se fasse, et pour qu'enfin
L'homme voie, au-dessus des douleurs, de la faim,
De la guerre, des rois, des dieux, de la démence,
Le volcan de la joie enfler sa lave immense! »

VIII

Tandis que cette vierge adorable parlait,
Pareille au sein versant goutte à goutte le lait

Raising even higher its hideous spirals.
Oh! Let me reopen the sepulchral gates
That, in the depths of Hell, you closed on the soul!
Let me release man into Freedom.
Let me reach out to the sinking universe.
Let me knock down the mountain of shadows;
Let me pull down the vile tower of evil!

"Allow, through me, the world to return
To the baptismal azure, so that Eden may reappear!
Alas! Do you feel my trembling heart that cherishes you?
Do you hear me sobbing in your dungeon? Allow
Me to save the good, the pure, the innocent;
Let the soul take flight and suffering end.
God made me Liberty; you, make me Deliverance!
Oh! Do not forbid me to cast into the Heavens
And Hells, the factious cry of love;
Let me lavish on the terrestrial sphere
The vast air, blue sky, boundless hope, and cause to
Emerge from the brow of Man an immeasurable beam of light.
Let me save everything, I, your blessèd side!
Consent! Oh! I who emanate from you, allow me to go
Amongst the living, to complete this battle
Between their ignorance, alas! and their reason,
To place a sacred crimson at the horizon,
So that the hideous past may vanish into the darkness,
So that the earth may tremble and the prison collapse,
So that the eruption may take place, and so that finally
Man may see, beyond the pain, hunger,
War, kings, gods, insanity,
The volcano of joy casting up its copious lava!"

VIII

While this lovely virgin was speaking,
Like the breast giving milk drop by drop

A l'enfant nouveau né qui dort, la bouche ouverte,
Satan, toujours flottant comme une herbe en l'eau verte,
Remuait dans le gouffre, et semblait par moment
A travers son sommeil frémir éperdument;
Ainsi qu'en un brouillard l'aube éclôt, puis s'efface,
Le démon s'éclairait, puis pâlissait; sa face
Était comme le champ d'un combat ténébreux;
Le bien, le mal, luttaient sur son visage entre eux
Avec tous les reflux de deux sombres armées;
Ses lèvres se crispaient, sinistrement fermées;
Ses poings s'entre-heurtaient, monstrueux et noircis;
Il n'ouvrait pas les yeux, mais sous ses lourds sourcils
On voyait les lueurs de cette âme inconnue;
Tel le tonnerre fait des pourpres sous la nue;
L'ange le regardait, les mains jointes; enfin
Une clarté, qu'eût pu jeter un séraphin,
Sortit de ce grand front tout brûlé par les fièvres;
Ainsi que deux rochers qui se fendent, ses lèvres
S'écartèrent, un souffle orageux souleva
Son flanc terrible, et l'ange entendit ce mot: Va!

To the newborn child who sleeps with opened mouth,
Satan, still floating like a leaf of grass in emerald water,
Stirred in the abyss, and seemed at times
To tremble desperately in his sleep;
Thus, as dawn breaks, then fades in a fog,
So the devil got brighter, then turned pale; his face
Was like a battlefield of darkness;
The struggle between good and evil was revealed upon it,
An ebb and flow of two dark armies;
His sinister, closed lips twitched; his fists beat
One against the other, becoming dark and monstrous;
His eyes did not open, but under his heavy lids
Could be seen the glow of this strange soul,
Just as the thunderbolt turns the sky magenta under a cloud.
The angel watched him, her hands clasped; finally
A light that a seraph might have cast,
Radiated from this great, feverish brow.
Like two rocks cleaving asunder, his lips
Parted, a thunderous breath lifted his dreadful
Flank, and the angel heard this word: Go!

Victor Hugo, *Phare des Casquets* (The Casquets Lighthouse), 1866, Musée Maison de Victor Hugo

Livre troisième *La Prison*

LES SQUELETTES

[—Les quatre squelettes se réveillent dans le cachot de la Bastille, et se parlent....—]

. . .

La tour est âpre et noire, et, du haut jusqu'en bas,
Elle est un instrument de supplice; un étage
Fait agoniser moins ou souffrir davantage;
Changer de cabanon, c'est changer de tourment;
Le captif, dans la cave, expire lentement;
Sous le toit, dans un trou qu'on nomme la calotte,
Il étouffe en juillet, en décembre il grelotte;
Sous plus ou moins d'horreur l'homme se sent plier
A mesure qu'il monte ou descend l'escalier;
Nulle part le repos, l'air frais, la clarté pure;
Chaque chambre a la forme utile à la torture;
Ici l'on gèle; ici l'on brûle; ici l'on meurt.

. . .

Third Book The Prison

THE SKELETONS

[—The four skeletons awaken in the dungeon of the Bastille, and speak....—]

...

The tower is bitter and black, and, from top to bottom,
It is an instrument of torture; each floor
Created to cause more or less suffering;
To change the dark cell is to change merely the torment;
The captive, in his cave, dies slowly;
Under the roof, in a hole called the Skullcap,
He stifles in July, and shivers in December;
The man feels himself wilt under greater or lesser horror,
Depending on whether he climbs or descends the steps;
No rest, no fresh air, no pure light;
Every chamber has the shape that befits its torture;
Here one freezes; here one burns; here one dies.

...

Dans ce lieu morne,
La minute est bourreau, l'heure est épouvantail.
Une horloge apparaît au-dessus du portail.
Autour du cadran triste, une chaîne est sculptée,
Cercle affreux, chaîne énorme à lier Prométhée;
Elle entoure le temps, et, monstrueuse à voir,
Saisit par ses deux bouts, au bas du fronton noir,
Une statue étrange et morne, prisonnière
Qui grince et fait effort pour sortir de la pierre;
La statue a deux fronts, l'un jeane et l'autre vieux;
Sur le cadran, rouillé par l'hiver pluvieux,
L'aiguille, résumant dans une heure une vie,
Par la chaîne toujours à tous ses pas suivie,
Part du jeune homme et vient aboutir au vieillard.
Lugubre, elle paraît marcher sous un brouillard;
On croit voir l'affreux doigt de la bastille sombre
Montrant ce qu'elle fait du prisonnier dans l'ombre,
Et disant—c'est ici que les pas sont tremblants,
Et que les cheveux noirs deviennent cheveux blancs.

Effroyable prison qui n'a point de mémoire!
La geôle, au dehors noire est aveugle au dedans;
Elle prend, sans les voir, des hommes dans ses dents
Et, sans s'informer d'eux, les mâche et les dévore.

En entrant dans ces murs terribles, où, pour eux,
Les heures maintenant, hélas, seront si lentes,
Les captifs sont inscrits sur des feuilles volantes;
Pas de livre d'écrou. Tous est fait de façon
Que rien ne laisse trace en cette âpre prison,
Et que le nom s'y perde en même temps que l'homme.
Quel est ce prisonnier, et comment on le nomme,
Après dix ou vingt ans, personne ne le sait;
Pas même lui. La dalle ignore ce que c'est,
Le carcan le saisit au cou sans le connaître,
Et le ver, qui déjà goûte à sa chair peut-être,

In this melancholy place,
The minute is a tormentor, the hour a terror.
A clock appears above the gate; and
Around its forlorn dial, a chain is carved in a
Hideous circle, an enormous chain to bind Prometheus;
It surrounds time, enclosing within its links
A strange and mournful statue, monstrous to see,
At the foot of the black pediment—a prisoner,
Clawing away, desperate to escape the stone.
The statue has two faces, one young and the other agèd;
And on the dial, made rusty by the winter rain,
The hand, attending the chain at every step,
Traces a life in an hour, beginning at
Youth and ending at old age.
Gloomy, it appears to be moving in a fog;
We believe we see the Bastille's hideous, forbidding finger,
Revealing what it does with the prisoner in the dark,
And saying:—it is here that men's steps tremble,
Here that their dark hair turns white.

Appalling prison with no memory!
The gaol, outside black, inside blind,
Takes men in its sightless teeth, and,
Without inquiring their name, chews up and devours them.

Upon entering these terrible walls,
Where the hours shall, alas! pass so slowly,
Recordings on mere scraps of paper suffice,
That there be no registry, that there
Be no trace left in this harsh place,
That the name be lost along with the man.
Who this prisoner, and what his name,
In ten or twenty years becomes unknown,
To even him. The flagstone knows it not;
The shackles seize him by the neck without knowing it,
And the worm, which, perhaps, already tastes his flesh,

Ne peut dire son nom au rat qui glisse et fuit.
Hier, aujourd'hui, demain, ne font qu'un. Plus un bruit.
L'homme qui maintenant va mourir goutte à goutte,
Une fois qu'il a mis le pied sous cette voûte,
Sent au-dessus de lui son propre effacement.
Sa vie est à jamais mêlée à ce ciment.
Le fil qui nous rattache au monde dont nous sommes,
Et lie à travers l'ombre un homme aux autres hommes,
Se brise ici. Sans air, sans jour, sans point d'appui,
L'homme le sent flotter rompu derrière lui.
Un vivant n'est plus là qu'un rêve dans un gouffre.
Entrer là, c'est entrer dans de l'oubli. L'on souffre,
On rampe, on saigne, on râle, on crie; on ne sait pas.
Le captif va, vient, tremble; il fait de vagues pas,
Sent à son pied sa chaîne et s'arrête farouche,
Boit à sa cruche, mord à son pain noir, se couche,
Se lève, se rendort, tressaille, et, réveillé,
Dit—où suis-je? que suis-je? et tâte un mur mouillé.
Il ne sait plus qu'il souffre, il ne sent plus qu'il pleure;
Il semble à ce damné qu'il s'enfonce à chaque heure
Plus bas dans la prison, et que, dans lui vivant,
La prison chaque jour pénètre plus avant;
La Bastille le tient; hagard, il s'incorpore
A cet épouvantable et hideux madrépore;
Morne, il constate, au froid toujours croissant du fer,
La transformation de son bagne en enfer;
Il croit que l'heure est morte au-dessus de sa tête,
Et que l'éternité dans son cachot s'arrête.
Est-ce que son œil voit? est-ce que son cœur bat?
Il s'accoude des mois entiers sur son grabat,
Écoutant dans un coin filer quelque araignée.
Son âme se détache et lui semble éloignée;
Il croit heurter sa bière en touchant à son lit;
L'évanouissement par degré le remplit;
Il ne peut plus fixer un temps, compter un nombre;
La pierre devient nuit, lui-même il devient ombre,

Can not recount it to the rat which scurries and flees.
Yesterday, today, tomorrow, are one. Not a sound.
Once setting foot beneath this vault,
This man, who will slowly begin to die,
Senses his own disappearance looming o'er him.
His life is merged forever with this concrete.
The thread which connects us to our world
And binds us across the darkness, one to the other,
Is broken here. Without air, without light, without support,
He feels it floating, broken, behind him.
A living soul, there, is but an abyss-bound dream.
Entering, there, is to enter oblivion. One suffers, one crawls,
One bleeds, groans, and cries out; but one comprehends not.
The prisoner comes and goes, trembling; he takes hesitant steps,
Feels his chain upon his foot and comes grimly to a halt.
He drinks from his jar, bites into his black bread, lies down,
Gets up, falls asleep again, quivers, and, awake,
Says:—where am I? what am I? and feels a damp wall.
He no longer knows that he suffers, no longer senses that he
Weeps; it seems to this damned soul that he sinks lower by
The hour in this prison, and that, into his being,
The prison every day penetrates further still;
The Bastille holds him; haggard, he becomes part of
This dreadful and hideous madrepore;
Mournful, he notices, in the ever increasing cold of the iron,
The transformation of his prison into hell;
He believes that time has died overhead,
And that eternity remains behind in his cell.
Does he see? does his heart beat?
For months on his mean bed, he rests upon his elbow,
Listening to some spider spinning in a corner.
His soul detaches itself and seems remote from him;
He imagines he strikes his coffin when touching his bed,
And little by little he fades away;
He can no longer tell time, or count numbers;
The stone becomes night, he himself becomes darkness,

Et sent croître, à travers la stupeur de l'ennui,
Autour de lui la tombe et le fantôme en lui.
. . .
O triste genre humain! Sur tous les échafauds
Tant de sang fut versé dans les deux hémisphères
Que du fer qu'on en eût tiré l'on eût pu faire,
Hélas! tous les barreaux de toutes les prisons!
. . .
... le cabanon prépare à l'échafaud.
Le patient commence au captif; les supplices
Ont pour aide la geôle obscure, et pour complices
La cruche d'eau, l'ennui, la paille, le barreau;
Qu'est-ce que les verrous? des valets du bourreau.
. . .
L'énorme tour a douze étages de cachots,
Noirs, hideux, et selon la saison, froids ou chauds;
Des fournaises en juin, en janvier des glacières;
Chaque cellule est basse, et l'on voit des poussières
Qui jadis ont vécu, dans l'ombre des piliers;
Des squelettes, dans l'angle obscur des escaliers,
Sont adossés au mur, ayant au cou des chaînes;
On entend le vent fuir dans les forêts prochaines,
Et les captifs au fond du donjon sont pensifs;
Les portes sont de fer, les verrous sont massifs,
Et le trousseau de clefs fait la charge d'un homme.
Le roi, qui des deniers du peuple est économe,
A quinze ou vingt palais à meubler, de façon
Qu'il n'a pas de quoi mettre un lit dans la prison;
Aussi les prisonniers couchent-ils sur la pierre.
Cent-vingt archers de guet, à la longue rapière,
Graves, muets, portant la jaquette à longs plis
Sous le hoqueton bleu semé de fleurs de lys,
Veillent du haut en bas, six devant chaque porte.
. . .
Oh! qu'elle avait commis de crimes, la géante!

And through the stupor of ennui, feels growing
Around him, the grave, and within him, the ghost.

...

O sad human race! On all the scaffolds
So much blood was shed in both hemispheres
That from all the iron we drew, we could have made,
Alas! all the bars of all the prisons!

...

...The dark cell prepares one for the scaffold.
The tortured sufferer begins a captive; the tortures
Have for help the dark gaol, and for accomplices
The jug of water, the boredom, the straw, the bars;
What are the bolts? Servants of the executioner.

...

The enormous tower has twelve floors of cells,
Black, hideous, and according to the season, cold or hot;
Furnaces in June, in January iceboxes;
Every cell is low, and we see the remains of those
Who formerly lived, in the shadow of the pillars;
Skeletons, in the dark corners of the staircases,
Are set, their backs against the wall, chains about their necks;
We hear the wind fleeing in the nearby forest,
And the captives at the bottom of the keep are brooding;
The gates are iron, the bolts are massive,
And the ring of keys a great burden.
The King, thrifty with the public funds,
Must furnish fifteen or twenty palaces,
And so cannot furnish the prison with beds;
Thus do the prisoners sleep on stone.
The long-rapiered watch, one hundred and twenty strong,
Grave, mute, wearing the long-folded jacket
Beneath the blue hoqueton strewn with fleur-de-lis,
Stand from bottom to top, six before each door.

...

Oh! What crimes it has committed, this giant!

Hors de la terre IV

SATAN PARDONNÉ

. . .
Le sanglot de Satan dans l'ombre continue.

I

—Ici la tombe, là le chaos; sur ma tête
La noirceur, sous mes pieds, la chute; où je m'arrête,
La profondeur s'écroule, et tout est vide; eh bien,
Tous ces gouffres mêlés sur moi ne seraient rien
Si je pouvais donner le change à ma pensée,
Moi-même m'enivrer de ma fureur versée,
Et me persuader que je hais! Ce n'est pas
De la crypte stupide et sourde du trépas,
Ce n'est pas du cachot, du puits, de la géhenne,
Ce n'est pas du verrou, ce n'est pas de la chaîne,

Beyond the Earth IV

SATAN FORGIVEN

. . .
In the darkness Satan's sobbing continues.

I

—Here is the tomb, and there, chaos; overhead,
Blackness, beneath my feet, the Fall; where I stop,
The deep collapses on itself, and everything is empty;
Well, all these abysses mingled above me would be nothing
Were I, myself, to alter my thought,
Were I able to revel in my pent-up fury,
And persuade myself that I hate! It is not
The stupefied, voiceless crypt of doom,
It is not the prison, the pit, the Gehenna,
It is neither the lock, nor the chain,

C'est de son propre cœur qu'on est le prisonnier.
Haïr délivre.

II

Hélas, à force de nier,
Et d'enfoncer dans tout mon sarcasme, âpre lame;
A force de railler le grand épithalame,
Et de crier d'en bas aux crimes: je suis là!
Et de continuer Nemrod dans Attila,
Et de recommencer dans Borgia Caïphe,
A force d'ajouter à toute aile une griffe,
A force d'inspirer les basses actions,
A force de jeter mon cloaque aux rayons,
A force d'être l'ange infâme que sature
Tout le crime possible en la sombre nature,
A force de m'emplir de ténèbres, j'ai froid.

III

Oh! l'essence de Dieu, c'est d'aimer. L'homme croit
Que Dieu n'est, comme lui, qu'une âme, et qu'il s'isole
De l'univers, poussière immense qui s'envole;
Mais moi, l'ennemi triste et l'éternel moqueur,
Je le sais, Dieu n'est pas une âme, c'est un cœur.
Dieu, centre aimant du monde, à ses fibres divines
Rattache tous les fils de toutes les racines,
Et sa tendresse égale un ver au séraphin;
Et c'est l'étonnement des espaces sans fin
Que ce cœur effrayant, blasphémé par les prêtres,
Ait autant de rayons que l'univers a d'êtres.
Pour lui, créer, penser, méditer, animer,
Semer, détruire, faire, être, voir, c'est aimer.
Splendide, il aime, et c'est par reflux qu'on l'adore;
Tout en lui roule; il tient à la nuit par l'aurore,
Aux esprits par l'idée, aux fleurs par le parfum;

It is one's own heart that holds one captive.
To hate brings deliverance.

II

Alas, through too much abnegation,
And by sinking my bitter blade, derision, into everything;
By mocking the great nuptial poems,
And shouting in the depths at the crimes: I am with you!
And by perpetuating Nimrod in Attila,
And Caiaphas in Borgia,
By dint of adding to every wing a claw,
By inspiring the lowliest deeds and
Casting my cesspool into the beams of light,
By being the infamous angel steeped in
Every crime possible in dark nature, and
By saturating myself with darkness, I am cold.

III

Oh! God's essence is to love. Man believes
That God is, like him, merely a soul, and that he absents himself
From the universe, an immense cloud of dust taking wing;
But I, sad enemy and eternal mocker,
I know this: God is not a soul, but is a heart.
God, loving center of the world, to his divine fibers
Attaches all the rootlets of all the roots,
And his tenderness is the same for the worm as for the seraph.
The endless expanses are astonished that this
Appalling heart, blasphemed by the priests,
Has as many light beams as the universe has beings.
For him, to create, think, meditate, bring to life,
To sow, to destroy, to make, to be, to see—is but to love. Magnificent,
He loves, and in natural response his creatures worship him;
Everything permeates him; he prizes the night through the dawn,
The spirits through the idea, flowers through their scent;

Et ce cœur dans son gouffre a l'infini, moins un.
Moins Satan, à jamais rejeté, damné, morne.
Dieu m'excepte. Il finit à moi. Je suis sa borne.
Dieu serait infini si je n'existais pas.

Je lui dis: Tu fis bien, Dieu, quand tu me frappas!
Je ne l'accuse point, non! mais je désespère!
O sombre éternité, je suis le fils sans père.
Du côté de Satan il est, mais n'est plus Dieu.

IV

Cent fois, cent fois, cent fois, j'en répète l'aveu,
J'aime! Et Dieu me torture, et voici mon blasphème,
Voici ma frénésie et mon hurlement: j'aime!
J'aime, à faire trembler les cieux!—quoi! c'est en vain!
Oh! c'est là l'inouï, l'horrible, le divin,
De se dresser, d'ouvrir des ailes insensées,
De s'attacher, sanglant, à toutes les pensées
Qu'on peut saisir, avec des cris, avec des pleurs,
De sonder les terreurs, de sonder les douleurs,
Toutes, celles qu'on souffre et celles qu'on invente,
De parcourir le cercle entier de l'épouvante,
Pour retomber toujours au même désespoir!
Dieu veut que l'homme las s'endorme, il fait le soir;
Il creuse pour la taupe une chambre sous terre;
Il donne au singe, à l'ours, au lynx, à la panthère,
L'âpre hospitalité des antres et des monts;
Aux baleines les mers, aux crapauds les limons,
Les roseaux aux serpents secouant leurs sonnettes;
Il fait tourner autour des soleils les planètes
Et dans la blanche main des vierges les fuseaux;
Il entre dans les nids, touche aux petits oiseaux,
Et dit: La bise vient, j'épaissirai leurs plumes;
Il laisse l'étincelle échapper aux enclumes,
Et lui permet de fuir, joyeuse, les marteaux;

And this heart in its abyss has everything,—except one.
Except Satan, forever rejected, damned, mournful.
God excludes me. He ends with me. I am God's outermost limit,
And he would be infinite were I not to exist.

I say to him: you did well, God, when you struck me down!
I by no means accuse him, no! But I despair!
O somber eternity, I am the son without a father.
In regard to Satan, he exists, but is no longer God.

IV

A hundred times, a hundred times over, I repeat the confession:
I love! And God tortures me; and here is my blasphemy,
Here my frenzy and my howling: I love!
I love, enough to make the heavens tremble!—but! it is in vain!
Oh! What is incredible, what is horrible, what is divine,
Is to rise up, opening senseless wings,
Clinging, blood-stained, to every thought
That one can seize, with cries, with tears,
Sounding the terrors, probing the pains,
All those that one suffers and all those that one invents,
Traversing the entire range of dismay,
Only to fall again into the same despair!
God wants that the tired man sleep, so he creates the evening;
He digs for the mole a burrow;
He grants the monkey, the bear, the lynx, the panther,
The harsh haven of caverns and mountains;
To the whales he provides the seas, to the toads, the silt,
And to the serpents shaking their rattles, he proffers reeds;
He causes planets to revolve about their suns
And spindles to revolve in the pure hands of virgins;
He enters nests, touches the fledglings,
And says: the north wind is coming, I shall thicken their feathers;
He lets the spark fly off from the anvils,
And allows it to escape the hammers, joyful;

Il montre son grand ciel aux lions de l'Athos;
Il étale dans l'aube, ainsi que des corbeilles,
Sous des flots de rayons, les printemps pleins d'abeilles;
Sa grandeur pour le monde en bonté se résout.
Une vaste lueur ardente embrase tout,
De l'archange à la brute et de l'astre à la pierre,
Croise en forêt de feu ses rameaux de lumière,
Va, vient, monte, descend, féconde, enflamme, emplit,
Combat l'hiver liant les fleuves dans leur lit,
Et lui fait lâcher prise, et rit dans toute chose,
Luit mollement derrière une feuille de rose,
Chauffe l'énormité sidérale des cieux,
Brille, et, de mon côté, prodige monstrueux,
Ce flamboiement se dresse en muraille de glace!
Oui, la création heureuse s'entrelace
Tout entière, clartés et brume, esprits et corps,
Dans le Dieu bon, avec d'ineffables accords;
L'être le plus souillé retrouve l'innocence
Dans toute sa tendresse et sa toute puissance;
Moi seul, moi le maudit, l'incurable apostat,
Je m'approche de Dieu sans autre résultat
Que de faire gronder vaguement le tonnerre!
Dieu veut que cet essaim d'atomes le vénère,
Il leur demande à tous leur cœur, leur chant, leur fruit,
Leur parfum, leur prière; à moi rien, de la nuit.
O misère sans fond! Écoutez ceci, sphères,
Étoiles, firmaments, ô vieux soleils, mes frères,
Vers qui monte en pleurant mon douloureux souhait,
Cieux, azurs, profondeurs, splendeurs,—l'amour me hait!

DÉNOUEMENT

Satan sous sa voûte—

Je me dresse, marqué par l'effroyable trait:
(Dernier degré de l'horreur!)—L'amour me hait.

He shows his grand heavens to the lions of Athos;
He displays, in the dawn, the springs full of bees,
As well as flowerbeds under floods of light beams;
His pride in the world is transformed into kindness.
A vast burning light sets everything ablaze,
From the archangel to the brute and from the star to the stone.
It intersects in the forest of fire its branches of light,
Goes, comes, falls, fecundates, inflames, fills,
Fights the Winter who binds rivers to their beds,
And makes Winter let them go, and laughs in all matters,
Gleaming softly behind a rose leaf,
Warming the sidereal enormity of the heavens,
And glitters; but, for me, monstrous prodigy,
This blaze rears up in a wall of ice!
Yes, happy creation completely intertwines
Light and mist, spirit and body,
Within this good Lord, forming unutterable harmony.
The most defiled being again finds innocence
In his very tenderness and omnipotence;
I alone, I the cursed, the incurable apostate,
I approach God with no result other
Than to cause faint, rumbling thunder!
God wishes that this swarm of atoms venerate him.
He demands of them their heart, their song, their fruit,
Their perfume, their prayer; from me, nothing, night.
O bottomless misery! Hear this, spheres,
Stars, firmaments, O ancient suns, my brothers,
Towards whom my dolorous desire rises, weeping,
O heavens, azures, depths, splendors—Love hates me!

DENOUEMENT

Satan under his vault—

I draw myself up, marked by the appalling feature:
(The last stage of the horror!)—Love hates me.

Voix à travers l'infini

Non, je ne te hais pas

......

Un ange est entre nous; ce qu'elle a fait te compte.
L'homme, enchaîné par toi, par elle est délivré.
O Satan, tu peux dire à présent: je vivrai!
Viens, la prison détruite abolit la géhenne!
Viens, l'ange Liberté c'est ta fille et la mienne.
Cette paternité sublime nous unit.
L'archange ressuscite et le démon finit,
Et j'efface la nuit sinistre, et rien n'en reste.
Satan est mort, renais, ô Lucifer céleste,
Viens, monte hors de l'ombre avec l'aurore au front!

A Voice across the Infinite

No, I do not hate you

… …

We are related through an angel; what she did affects you.
Man, enchained by you, by her is freed.
O Satan, you need only say: I shall live!
Come, the destroyed prison abolishes Hell!
Come, the angel Liberty is both your daughter and mine.
This sublime fatherhood unites us.
The archangel again lives, and the devil is no more;
I efface the sinister night, and nothing of it remains.
Satan is dead, be reborn, O celestial Lucifer,
Come, arise out of the darkness with the dawn on your brow!

Épilogue

I

LE POINT DU JOUR

Le vent passe en semant des notes sibyllines;
Le matin apparaît au sommet des collines,
Splendide vision;
Le nid s'émeut; la fleur s'ouvre, de pleurs trempée,
L'aube pâle commence à chanter l'épopée
De la création.

II

O mondes du dehors, Dieu rayonne pour tous,
Vos mystères profonds ne regardent que vous.

Epilogue

I

DAYBREAK

The wind passes by, scattering sibylline notes;
Morning appears on the hilltops,
        A radiant sight;
The nest is moved; the flower opens, bathed in tears,
And pale dawn begins to sing the epic
        Of Creation.

II

O worlds from the beyond, God shines for all,
Your profound mysteries regard only you.

III

LES GRANDS MORTS

Au loin sous une brume aux épaisseurs profondes,
L'œil, dans l'obscurité, plus bas que tous les mondes,
Voit vaguement des fronts énormes s'agiter.
Tâchant encor d'aider l'homme et de l'assister,
Ils sont tous là, pensifs, sur de ténébreux trônes,
Les guides des Sions, des Tyrs, des Babylones,
Tous ceux que la nature et l'art ont pour docteurs,
Tous les contemplateurs et tous les rédempteurs
Qui bravèrent du sphinx la figure camuse,
Tous ceux qui, par l'esprit, la vision, la muse,
Fouillant l'énigme monde et l'énigme destin,
De quelque âge nocturne ont été le matin.
Les plongeurs du chaos, les sondeurs du désastre,
Moïse, Orphée, Hermès, Socrate, Zoroastre,
Michel-Ange, Gama, le chercheur hasardeux,
Milton, Newton, Jean Huss, Tell, Shakspeare; et près d'eux,
Tous les autres pasteurs des humanités sombres
Que d'autres sphères vont promenant dans les ombres,
Tous les puissants Colombs et tous les Christs divins,
Tous les Dantes, les Jobs, les Luthers, les Calvins,
Et tous les Mahomets de tous les autres globes,
Géants ayant du jour dans les plis de leurs robes,
Sont là; les Spinosas comme les Aarons;
Formes d'une autre vie et que nous ignorons;
Ils ne se parlent pas; et, d'un geste farouche,
Ils écoutent, penchés et le doigt sur la bouche;
Leur âme en leurs yeux brille; ils écoutent le bruit.

Ce concile de l'ombre est assis dans la nuit.
L'esprit monte, descend et plane l'aile haute,
Sur cette formidable et sombre Pentecôte;
Ils lisent à la fois hier, aujourd'hui, demain;

III

THE GREAT DEAD

Far off in the distance under a thick mist,
In the darkness, lower than all the worlds,
The eye sees barely stirring immense brows.
Trying yet again to help Man, to assist him,
They are all there, brooding, atop their dark thrones,
The guides of the Zions, Tyres, and Babylons,
All those whom nature and art have for teachers,
All the contemplators and all the redeemers
Who braved the flat face of the Sphinx,
All those who, through their spirit, their vision, their muses,
Searching the enigmatic world and questioning enigmatic fate,
For some benighted age, became Morning.
The plungers into chaos, the sounders of disaster,
Moses, Orpheus, Hermes, Socrates, Zoroaster,
Michelangelo, da Gama, that daring explorer,
Milton, Newton, John Huss, Tell, Shakespeare; and beside them
All the other shepherds of somber humanities
That other spheres have walking in the shadows,
All the powerful Colombuses and all the divine Christs,
All the Dantes, the Jobs, the Luthers, the Calvins.
And all the Muhammeds of all the other worlds
Are there, giants bearing Day in the folds of
Their robes; Spinozas as well as Aarons;
Forms of other lives of which we are unaware;
They do not speak; and, with a fierce gesture,
They listen, stooped over with their finger to their lips, whilst
Their souls blaze in their eyes; they harken to a stirring.

This council of darkness gathers at night.
Their spirits arise, and descend, soaring on lofty wing,
This day of fearsome, somber Pentecost;
They read at once the past, the present, the future;

Leur crâne est transparent pour leur œil surhumain;
Et chacun d'eux s'adosse à quelque grand pilastre.
Sur leur tête l'idée éclôt et devient astre,
Et luit comme Vénus qui brille au fond des soirs
A l'heure où le bœuf roux descend aux abreuvoirs,
Où l'on entend hennir sur les monts les cavales.
Ces comètes qu'on voit passer par intervalles
Avec un flamboiement immense dans les cieux,
S'allongeant à travers l'éther silencieux,
Formidables, à l'ombre éternelle mêlées,
Sont des langues de feu de leurs fronts envolées.

Their skull is translucent to their preterhuman eye;
And each of them leans back against some giant pilaster.
From their minds burst forth their thoughts which become
Stars gleaming like Venus shining in the depths of night,
At the hour when the russet ox descends to the drinking-troughs,
When we hear the mares neighing upon the mountains.
These comets are those we sometimes see passing
Through the heavens with an immense brilliance,
Stretching across the silent æther,
Formidable, amidst the eternal shadow,
Tongues of fire from off their crowns taking wing.

Fragments

ET NOX FACTA EST.

Ce bandit, comme s'il grandissait sous l'affront,
Seul dans ces profondeurs que le chaos encombre,
Regarda fixement la caverne de l'ombre.
La nuit vaste y croissait lentement, la clarté
Flottait, mourante et vague, et dans l'immensité,
Les caps de l'infini prolongeaient leurs vertèbres.
Cachant et méprisant son aile de ténèbres,
Il était là, pensif, debout comme un tour.
Le gouffre offrait à l'œil un farouche contour;
A la voûte pendaient de pâles stalactites;
De loin elles semblaient confuses et petites;
De près, c'étaient des blocs dont le moindre eût comble
L'espace de la terre au zénith étoilé.
L'antre en s'élargissant ouvrait une envergure
Immense, où l'on voyait vaguement la figure
De quelques monts affreux, ruines du néant.
L'opaque obscurité formait le ciel béant.

Fragments

AND THEN THERE WAS NIGHT.

This bandit, as if growing under the insult,
Alone in these depths congested by chaos,
Looked fixedly at the cavern of darkness.
There, vast night slowly spread, the light
Drifted, tenuous and dying, and into this immensity
The capes of the infinite stretched out their vertebrae.
Concealing and scorning his wings of darkness,
He stood there like a tower, pensive,
The abyss offering to his gaze a grim relief;
From the vault hung pale stalactites which
From afar seemed dim and small, yet
Near, were blocks, the least of which would have filled
The gap between the earth and the star-studded zenith.
The broadening cavern became a vast
Expanse, where were vaguely discerned
Some frightful mountains, ruins of Nothingness.
The gaping sky was formed of lurid darkness.

CHUTE DE L'ANGE.

Alors ce fut horrible,
Et l'obscurité vint et la clarté décrut;
L'éclatant Lucifer plein d'astres disparut,
Et Satan fut. L'enfer fut créé de la sorte.
Et poussant devant lui la nuit comme on pousse une porte,
Horreur de l'azur vierge et du ciel innocent,
Ce monde noir sortit de l'ombre en rugissant.

Planant les bras ouverts et les talons aux cieux,
L'ange sombre volait comme un aigle sublime;
Le jour derrière lui se levait sur l'abîme,
Et les spectres, fuyant au fond des visions,
S'épouvantaient devant les immenses rayons
Qui passaient par-dessus ses ailes étendues.

LE CANTIQUE DE BETHPHAGÉ.

Elle m'aime! Je suis vainqueur.
Venez voir quelqu'un de superbe.
Tous les rayons sont dans mon cœur
Comme tous les parfums dans l'herbe.

Je ne sais ce que je ferai
Pour mériter cette conquête.
Venez tous voir le préféré,
Celui dont l'âme est une fête,

L'archange qui sort du limon:
Le Memnon vainqueur des colosses
Venez voir le roi Salomon
Avec sa couronne de noces!

FALL OF THE ANGEL.

Then it was horrible,
And the darkness came and the light decreased;
Brilliant Lucifer, teeming with stars, disappeared,
And, lo! there appeared Satan. Thus was Hell created.
And pushing night before it, as one opens a door,
Horror of the virgin azure and the innocent sky,
This black world emerged from the darkness, howling.

Soaring, his arms outstretched and his heels heavenward,
The dark angel flew like a sublime eagle;
The day broke behind him above the abyss,
And specters, fleeing to the furthermost part of the visions,
Were terrified before the immense rays of light
Passing o'er his outspread wings.

THE CANTICLE OF BETHPHAGE.

She loves me! I am victorious.
Come see some proud being.
All the rays of light are in my heart
As are all the perfumes in the grass.

I know not what I did
To deserve this victory.
Come, all, to see the favored one,
The one whose soul is a festival,

The archangel who emerges from the silt:
Memnon, vanquisher of giants,
Come see King Solomon
With his marital crown!

Vous êtes beau dans l'abe et charmant dans la nuit,
Votre front parmi toue et s'épanouit
Comme un bleuet parmi seigles...

*

Voici le lit de Sésostris
Environné de soixante hommes;
J'aime mieux les gazons fleuris
Et l'ombre où tout bas tu me nommes.

Viens, ô miracle de beauté!
Blanche comme l'aube éternelle!
Les petits oiseaux de l'été
S'éblouissent de ta prunelle.

J'ai vu cette fille de Seth;
Elle chantait dans le bois sombre
Une chanson qui suffisait
A la joie obscure de l'ombre.

Pour l'écouter, dans les roseaux,
Tout se taisait, êtres et choses;
Et des roses sortaient des eaux,
Et des esprits sortaient des roses.

Je t'aime; ton chant est joyeux;
Et j'attends que tu te dévoiles;
La nuit, je te cherche des yeux
Dans le prodige des étoiles.

Le soleil luit, je t'aime, viens!
Les fleurs veulent que tu paraisses:
O femme, il n'est pas d'autres biens
Que les rayons et des caresses!

You are beautiful in the dawn and charming at night,
Your brow shines and blooms amidst everything
Like a cornflower amidst the rye...

*

Here is the bed of Sesostris
Surrounded by sixty men;
I prefer the flowery sward and
The dark where softly you name me.

Come, o miracle of beauty!
Fair as the eternal dawn!
The small summer birds
Draw dazzlement from your eye.

I spied this daughter of Seth;
She sang in the somber wood
A song which sufficed
To give the shadow a dark joy.

That she might be heard in the reeds,
All things and all beings remained silent;
And roses emerged from the waters,
And spirits from out the roses.

I love you; your song is joyful;
And I wait for you to reveal yourself;
At night, I seek you with my eyes
Amongst the miracle of stars.

The sun gleams, I love you, come!
Flowers want that you appear:
O woman, there are no blessings
Save light beams and caresses!

J. C.

Dans quelque tremblement des divines demeures,
Dans quelque écroulement d'âmes supérieures,
Il tomba sur la terre, ange, esprit, du ciel bleu;
Et, blanche vision, plus qu'homme, presque Dieu,
Fantôme éblouissant et pâle, créature
Faite d'une autre argile et d'une aube plus pure,
Aperçu des romains, des grecs et des hébreux,
Il parut au-dessus des hommes ténébreux,
Comme dans le chaos des monts, sur une foule
De noirs blocs de granit, un bloc d'albâtre roule.

SATAN (L'ARCHANGE).

… Israël! Israël!
L'idole est dans ton cœur, et tu te prostitues.
Les faux dieux ont partout dans tes champs leurs statues,
Moloch au mont d'Hinnom, Milcom près du Cédron.
La Sibylle, à côté de son hideux chaudron,
Parle bas à la goule, effroyable comme elle,
Prie à la fois Baal et Sabaoth, et mêle
L'affreux nom de Chamos au nom de Jéhovah.

Pendant que Balthazar et qu'Héliogabale
Ont le feston de pourpre où sonne la cymbale,

. . . .

Pendant que les Nérons, le front étoilé d'or,
Se bâtissent des tours de marbre dans les nues,
Que Tibère, ivre et Dieu, parmi des femmes nues,

J. C.

In some trembling of the divine residences,
In some collapse of more exalted souls,
He—angel, spirit—fell to the earth from the blue firmament;
And, pure vision, greater than Man, nearly God,
Lucent, pale ghost, creature
Made of a different clay and a purer dawn,
Barely glimpsed by the Romans, Greeks and Hebrews,
He appeared above somber men,
As a block of alabaster atop a congestion
Of black granite in some mountainous deray.

SATAN (THE ARCHANGEL).

... Israel! Israel!
The idol imbues your heart, and you prostitute yourself.
The statues of false gods are strewn throughout your fields,
Moloch on mount Hinnom, Milcom near the Kedron.
The Sibyl, beside her frightful cauldron,
Speaks softly to the ghoul, as appalling as she,
Beseeching at one and the same time Baal and Sabaoth, and
Confusing the hideous name Chemosh with that of Jehovah.

While Belshazzar and while Heliogabalus
Are festooned in purple where the cymbal sounds,

. . . .

While the Neros, brows spangled with gold,
Raise marble towers to the high clouds,
While Tiberius, drunkard and god, amidst naked women,

Rit sur les lits soyeux que Milet a tissus,
Le fumier saisit Job, le gibet prend Jésus!

Et, comme on voit parfois une obscure fumée
Qui sur un noir taillis de branches tremble et fuit,
Ce sombre essaim sortit ténébreux de la nuit.

Alors on vit tomber dans un chaos d'éclairs
Des astres enchaînés au fond des nuits profondes,
Et quelque chose comme une grappe de mondes.

Laughs atop the silken beds that Milet has weaved,
The dunghill seizes Job, the cross takes Jesus!

And, as we sometimes see a dark smoke
Above a black copse of branches tremble and flee,
This somber, forbidding swarm emerged from the night.

Then we saw fall into a chaos of lightning flashes
Celestial bodies chained to the heart of the deep nights,
And something like a grape-cluster of worlds

GLOSSARY

Aaron: Brother of Moses, became the first High Priest of Israel, and, due to his eloquence, was for a time the spokesman for Moses and the Israelites for the release from Egyptian bondage (Exodus).

Abdera: Ancient town on the coast of Thrace, founded 654 B.C.E., and named for Heracles' fallen friend Abderus. A wealthy town, it was sacked often. Home of Democritus and Protagoras.

Abel: The second son of Adam and Eve, killed by Cain, his older brother (Gen. 4:8).

Abraham: Considered a prophet and father of the people of Israel, by Jews and Christians, through his son Isaac, and the founder and prophet of the Arabs, by the Muslims, through his son Ishmael.

Achab: (Ahab) Old Testament King of Israel ca. 900 B.C.E. Misled by his wife, Jezebel, into committing grave injustices (1 Kings 21:25).

Achad: (Accad) A town that Old Testament King Nimrod built and ruled in the land of Shinar, or in Babylonia. It was perhaps located beside the Argade river in Babylonia (Gen. 10:10).

Achilles: In Homer's *Iliad*, he was the great heroic warrior of the Trojan war. He died of a wound to his heal, his one vulnerable spot.

Adam: In Genesis, the first human being created by God.

Adonai: A Hebrew word for God. It is plural, and literally means "My Lords."

Aemonia: (Haemonia) The ancient name of Thessaly in northern Greece, named after Haemon, son of Pelasgus and Thessalus.

Aesop: A freed slave most likely from Samos, and a famous writer of fables. He lived in the mid-600's B.C.E.

Aglauros: The daughter of Cecrops, the first king of Athens. She threw herself from the Acropolis to fulfill an oracle favorable to the Athenians in battle. A temple was built there in her honor.

Ahlab: A Phoenician town in the territory of the Israelite tribe of Asher, within unconquered Phoenicia (Judges 1:31).

Albunea: A prophetic sibyl in Tibur (now Tivoli), a naiad who lived in a nearby spring, near ancient Rome. Her name (from *albinos*-white) came from the whiteness of the sulfur in the water.

Alexander: Alexander the Great, became king of Macedonia in 336 B.C.E. and by the time of his death in 323 had created an empire that stretched from the Adriatic Sea to the Indus River.

Alhambra: A sprawling 13th century Moorish palace-citadel, with its labyrinth of courtyards, overlooking the city of Granada, Spain.

Allah: In Arabic, means "the God" and is, in a sense, a title. However, it also is the name of the Muslim God, whom Muhammad said was the same God as that of the Christians and Jews.

alveoli: Tiny air sacs or flaps in the lungs that exchange oxygen for carbon dioxide with the red blood cells.

Ammon: In the Old Testament, an ancient nation east of the Dead Sea, in present-day Jordan. The ancient Semitic god Moloch was worshipped there.

Amos: Considered one of the twelve minor prophets in Hebrew tradition, and the eponym of the Book of Amos in the Old Testament. Called by God to travel from Judah to Israel ca. 750 B.C.E., to preach to the rich and remind them to be just.

Anagke: (Ananke) In Greek mythology the goddess of Fate and Destiny, mother of the Three Fates.

Anchiale: A young Titan goddess.

Ancyra: Ancient Hittite city, now modern-day Ankara, capital of Turkey. King Midas ruled it later as a Phrygian power.

Andes: One of the elder Titan sons of Uranus and Gaia, also known as Hyperion.

Andrew: One of the apostles of Jesus.

Anytus: A member of a prominent Athenian family who spoke out against Socrates, and who was one of the accusers leading to his prosecution.

Apollonius: A neo-Pythagorean philosopher and teacher from Tyana in the Roman provinces born ca. 3 B.C.E., of Greek descent. Claimed to be a visionary with miraculous powers. Considered by some less than credulous.

Apteros: Greek for *wingless*. Usually applied to Nike ("Victory") Apteros or Athena Nike Apteros, the statue of Athena on the Acropolis. The Greek goddess of wisdom and courage, it was thought that she was made wingless so that she would not fly away. This name is in contrast to the Winged Victory of Samothrace, or the Nike of Samothrace. The Roman goddess Minerva is identified with Athena, hence Hugo's "Minerva Apteros."

Araxes: One of the longest rivers of the Caucasus. Also called the Aras.

Aristophanes: Born most likely in Athens ca. 444 B.C.E., and a famous writer of Greek Comedies in which he inveighed against such subjects as the Peloponnesian War, Sophism, and Socrates.

Aristotle: Along with Socrates and Plato, one of the most famous Greek philosophers, born in Macedonia in 384 B.C.E., and teacher of Alexander the Great. A student of Plato who systematized logic, and wrote on almost every subject of human knowledge, his work was incorporated into the Scholastic philosophy of the Middle Ages by the Church.

Arpha: According to Roman-Jewish historian Flavius Josephus, an ancient village in Judea at the edge of the kingdom of Agrippa.

asfir: A variant of *asfur*, Arabic for sparrow in particular, or any small perching bird.

Assur: A city of ancient Mesopotamia, situated on the Tigris. Also, the patron deity of the city, and the Assyrian people.

Astraios: (Astraeus) A second generation Titan, and father of the stars and winds.

Athos: One of the Giants of Greek mythology. A mountain that he threw at Zeus became Mount Athos in Macedonia.

Atmeidan: The ancient hippodrome in Constantinople.

Atreus: In Greek mythology, he was a king of Mycenae, father of Agamemnon. He and his twin brother were exiled by their father for fratricide in a power-stuggle over the Olympian throne.

Attila: Attila the Hun, a great military leader and ruler of the Hunnic Empire 434–453, was a fierce enemy of the Roman Empire. Called the "Scourge of God."

Azrael: The angel of death in Islamic and other traditions. He separated the soul from the body upon death. His name means "Help of God."

Baal: Also Ba'al. Similar to Bel, a Semitic title meaning "Lord" or "Master" applied to more than one god. For example, a Baal was worshipped in Samaria (1 Kings 16:31–34), as well as in Phoenicia and Canaan.

Babel: (Gen. 11:1–9) A Babylonian city (now thought to be Babylon) where a tower meant to reach Heaven was constructed.

Babylon: (Gen. 10:8–12) In Old Testament times, an ancient Mesopotamian city located in present-day Iraq, and known for its hanging gardens, one of the Seven Wonders of the Ancient World.

Bacon, Francis: English philosopher and essayist, born 1561 C.E. Advocate of the scientific revolution and proselytizer of science's inductive methodology versus scholasticism's *apriori* method.

Bacon, Roger: English Scholastic philosopher, scientist, and Franciscan monk, ca. 1214 C.E. He was interested in natural science and controlled experiments as well as accurate observation, well in advance of his time. Considered a sorcerer by some.

Balaath: (Also Baalath) A town on the border of the Israeli Tribe of Dan (Joshua 19:44); also the store city of Solomon (I Kings 9:18; II Chron. 8:6). The spelling "Balaath" was used only in the Catholic Douay-Rheims Bible. The alternate spelling, "Baalath," is found in most other editions of the Bible.

Bastille: A fortress built to defend one side of Paris, turned into a prison ca. 1453. Used for religious and political prisoners, amongst others, it was known for its secrecy surrounding those imprisoned. The Bastille was successfully stormed during the French Revolution, to get to the arms that were stored there.

Behemoth: A monstrous beast of the land (Job 40:15–24), and, along with the sea-monster Leviathon, meant as a lesson from God to Job.

Bel: Signifying "Lord" or "Master," it is a title rather than a genuine name, applied to various gods in Babylonian religion, and was especially used for the god Marduk.

Belshazzar: Biblical King of Babylon and son of Nebuchadnezzar (Daniel 5).

Benares: One of the holiest cities in India along the Ganges near where the Buddha once preached and where there were once one hundred temples. There were steps along the banks of the river down which pilgrims walked to bathe in the sacred waters.

Bethphage: A New Testament village on the eastern slope of the Mount of Olives where Jesus began his triumphal entry into Jerusalem (Matt. 21:1; Mark 11:1; Luke 19:29).

Bethsaida: A city, near the Sea of Galilee, where Jesus performed miracles but which remained unrepentant (Luke 10:13).

Bhagavan: In Hinduism, Buddhism, and Jainism, a title of veneration meaning "Lord."

binomial: An equation with two terms joined by either a plus or a minus sign.

Bonzes: Buddhist monks of the Mahayana school.

Borceos: In Book III of *The Wars of the Jews or History of the Destruction of Jerusalem*, first century B.C.E. Roman-Jewish historian Flavius Josephus states that the village of Anuath, also named Borceos, marks the northern border of Judea, separating it from Samaria.

Borgia: He was Pope Alexander VI, 1492–1503, and one of the most controversial of the Renaissance popes. Many different crimes, including adultery, simony, theft, rape, bribery, incest, and murder have been attributed to him.

Brahma: The Hindu god of creation.

Brahmans: Members of the highest, priestly caste in Hinduism.

Bridge of Saint-Cloud: A footbridge over the river Seine six miles from the center of Paris. It was built of wood in 842 C.E., much later of stone, and now has a metal casing. A superstition forbade French Kings using it for fear of dying. Netting was also strung from it to catch the bodies of suicides from further upriver.

Bruno: Italian philosopher and martyr, born 1548 C.E. After fleeing the Dominican Order and the Church, became a wanderer. He was opposed to dogma, and for freedom of the human mind. Later found guilty during the Inquisition, he was burned at the stake.

Also Saint Bruno of Cologne (ca. 1030–1101), founder of the Carthusian order.

Caiaphas: The Jewish high priest who was behind the plot to kill Jesus, found in the New Testament Gospels of John, Luke, and Matthew.

Calabria: The peninsula in southern Italy that forms the toe of the Italian boot, and is separated from Sicily by the Strait of Messina, wherein lies the Scyla rock.

Caligula: One of Rome's most infamous Emperors, 37–41 C.E.

Calneh: One of the first cities built by King Nimrod, along with Achad and Babylon (Gen. 10:10).

Calvary: (Golgotha) The hill on which Christ was crucified.

Calvin: French Protestant theologian and religious reformer, born 1509 C.E., who stressed the utter sovereignty of God's will, and is said, perhaps erroneously, to have celebrated the Last Supper in a cave.

Canaan: The territory otherwise known as Palestine, the Promised Land of the Israelites.

Cape Canistro: At the southern tip of ancient Macedonia, and advancing into the Archipelago between the Gulf of Salonichi and the Gulf of Ajomama.

Capricon: The tenth astrological sign in the Zodiac, symbolized by a goat.

Carafa: Pope Paul IV, was pope from 23 May, 1555 until his death in 1559. The strengthening of the Inquisition continued under him, and few were safe from his drive to reform, even his own cardinals.

Cariathaim: A city founded in Israel by the tribe of Reuben, son of Jacob, following the exodus from Egypt. Thought, erroneously, to be impregnable by its inhabitants (Jer. 48:1).

Carthage: Leader of the Phoenician colonies in the Mediterranean that formed a powerful empire in antiquity, in constant struggle with Greece and then Rome. Destroyed by Rome in the third Punic war.

Caucasus: A region in Eurasia lying between the Black Sea and the Caspian Sea.

cedars of Solomon: Lebanese cedars were famous for their medicinal use, mythological associations, and for building the superstructure of palaces and temples such as the ancient Temple of Solomon in Jerusalem.

Cenobites: Monks living in a community-based, or cenobitic setting, as opposed to the earliest monks, who lived a solitary, eremitic lifestyle.

Cervantes: Spanish novelist and dramatist born in 1547 C.E., author of *Don Quixote*.

Ceylon: The island nation in the Indian Ocean now named Sri Lanka. Long a center of Buddhist culture and religion, it is renowned for its many pagodas, or towering shrines.

Chaos: The void before creation in ancient Greek cosmology, from which came Eros, Tartarus, and Gaia, followed by the other gods and all of creation.

Charlemagne: Charles the Great, a conqueror who revitalized culture and reunited western Europe as Emperor of Rome, 800–814. As Charles I, he was the founder of both the German and the French monarchies.

Chemosh: The idol or god of the Moabites and Ammonites (1 Kings 11:7; 2 Kings 23:13).

Cherubim: Besides being a form of angel, Ezekiel (Ezekiel 1) describes them as four-winged creatures, with faces of an ox, eagle, lion, and man, and with human hands and feet of a calf. They are also found in Revelations, called Living Creatures, and are not angels, but frightening creatures with six wings. Before being seen as angels, Cherubim were also thought of as symbolic animals of the Zodiac.

Chorazin: A New Testament city beside the Sea of Galilee whose citizens rejected the teachings of Jesus despite witnessing many of his miracles (Luke 10:13).

Chronos: The ancient Greek god of Time who was believed to have created Chaos as well as the ordered universe.

Cimmerian: A mythical people in Homer's *Odyssey* who lived in a land of unremitting gloom and darkness.

cippus: In Roman times a low pedestal used for milestones etc.

Circumcellions: Extreme branch of Africa's fourth century Christian Donatist sect, which created much public nuisance while moving about amongst the peasants

—*circum* (around), *cellas* (rooms or hut), and *iens* (going)—and which practiced suicide, thinking it the highest form of martyrdom.

circus: In ancient Rome, a building or large arena for horse, chariot, simulated battle, or acrobatic exhibitions.

Circus of Arle: The Roman Circus at Arles, France, the largest Roman building in the city, built in 149 C.E.

cirque: A hollow landform found among mountains as a result of alpine glaciers. Eventually, the hollow may become a large bowl-shape in the side of the mountain. In French, it means "cirque" as well as "circus" or "arena."

clarion: A medieval trumpet with a high-pitched, piercing sound.

Constantine: The Great, Roman Emperor 306–337, founder of the Eastern Roman Empire. He was the first Roman emperor to convert to Christianity.

Cres: The hero and king who founded Crete, to which he gave his name. He was son of Zeus and the nymph Ida.

cromlech: A massive prehistoric stone structure consisting of upright monoliths surrounding a mound, or with a capstone.

Cronus: In Greek mythology, a Titan, father of Zeus.

croups: Mountain ridges.

cruach: Scottish-Gaelic word for "hill" or "mountain," tending to be steep. In Irish-Gaelic, the word used would be "croagh," e.g. Croagh Patrick, the famous pilgrimage site on the west coast of Ireland.

Cumæ: An ancient Greek colony, near Naples, where a famous sibyl resided, known in Rome as the Sibylla Cumana.

Cyclops: A member of the Greek mythological race of one-eyed Giants.

Cyrselus: Hugo is most likely referring to Cypselus, first tyrant of Corinth, born 655 B.C.E., into the ruling family. His mother hid him in a chest ("cypselus") to prevent their murdering him. It had been prophesized that he would banish them when he grew up, which he did. It is said that he met with the Seven Sages of Greece, one of whom was his son, Periander.

Cyrus: A river in the Caucasus, rising in Iberia and falling into the Caspian Sea, named after the Persian conqueror Cyrus the Great. Now known as the Kur or the Kura.

Dagon: A Semitic god, originally a fertility god.

Dante: Italian poet, born 1265 C.E., and author of the *Divine Comedy*.

Daphne: A nymph in Greek mythology.

David: In the Old Testament, slayer of the giant Goliath, and later King of the Israelites. Born ca. 1037 B.C.E., he was King Solomon's father.

Dædalus: In Greek mythology, an artisan who built the labyrinth on Crete, and wings with which to fly.

Delphi: Site of the temple of Apollo beside Mt. Parnassus, where the Delphic Oracle would answer questions posed.

Delphica: The most ancient of the sibyls, who lived before the Trojan war, and was named by the Romans the Sibylla Delphica.

Democritus: Greek philosopher born in Thrace ca. 460 B.C.E., who traveled widely in pursuit of knowledge, and developed the atomic theory.

Demogorgon: Mentioned as early as the 4th century C.E. as well as in many 16th–19th century texts including *Paradise Lost*, *The Faerie Queene* and *Prometheus Unbound*, as a Christian demonic figure. Although thought to be of Greek origin, it is not known in classical mythology, and yet has been imagined as being of primordial genesis through the centuries.

Demos: A term having several senses. Used to represent the population of democracies in ancient Greek states, having decision-making powers, and for which it is the root. It also referred to the common people as opposed to the rich. In Aristophanes, he a character representing the foibles and weaknesses of the Athenian people.

Diderot: French *philosophe* and man of letters born 1713 C.E., whose chief contribution to the Enlightenment was his *Encyclopédie*, a project of twenty years. A harsh critic of the Church, he later became a great writer of fiction.

Diogenes: The name of three Ionic, Stoic and Cynic Greek philosophers.

Dioscurias: An important ancient seaport at the eastern end of the Black Sea, near the river Phasis. Said to be founded by the *Dioscures*, Castor and Pollux, of Greek and Roman myth.

Dismas: Saint Dismas, one of two thieves crucified alongside Jesus, to his right. Called the good thief, the penitent thief, for having asked Jesus for mercy.

Djinn: Also jinn. In Arabian legend, demons or genies, supernatural creatures who could assume an animal or human shape, and who could have an evil or benevolent influence.

Dodanim: In the Talmud, called Dardania, a neighbor and ally of Troy.

Dodona: The site of the ancient oracle in Epirus, in northern Greece. The oldest oracle in Greece, dedicated to Zeus. It is said that the oracle spoke through the wind rustling the branches of the tall oak or beech trees.

Dominic: The Spanish Saint (1170–1221) who founded the Dominican order, and is associated with the Albigensian Crusade in which there was much death and devastation. Reputed, perhaps erroneously, to be greatly responsible for the resulting, early Medieval Inquisition, in which many Dominicans were involved.

Echmiadzin: City in Armenia with the oldest cathedral in the world, the stone dome of which rests on four massive stone pillars containing bell towers.

Eddon-Azir: According to Claudius Grillet in his 1910 book, *La Bible dans Victor Hugo*, this is a borrowing from the Talmud.

Eden: The location of the Garden of Eden, where Adam and Eve lived after being created by God (Gen. 2:8).

Edom: Spoken of throughout the Old Testament. Edom was an ancient kingdom in southern Jordan founded by Jacob's twin brother Esau in the first millennium B.C.E.

Elijah: A prominent Old Testament prophet of the ninth century B.C.E., who traveled much, in search for answers, and on missions of God (1 Kings 17–19).

Elis: The capital of the ancient Greek region of Elide, the Peloponnesian province where the Olympic games were first organized, and where they were played in a stadium.

Ellora: Site of monumental cave temples carved out of the cliffs by Buddhist, Hindu, and Jain monks over a five century period. Located near Maharashtra, India. Sometimes seven thousand laborers worked the site together.

Elohim: The Hebrew word for "God."

Eli, Eli, lama sabachthani!: "My God, my God, why have you forsaken me?," spoken by Jesus on the cross (Matt. 27:46).

Emmanuel: (Immanuel) From the Old Testament, it means "God is with us" (Isaiah 7:14). In Christian tradition the name refers to Jesus, the coming Messiah.

Empedocles: Pre-Socratic philosopher, ca. 495–432. His treatises on nature and morals first posit the elements fire, air, earth, and water.

Endor: A Canaanite village near Mt. Tabor where lived the Witch or Medium of Endor, consulted by King Saul (1 Sam. 28:7).

Enmishpat: Also En-mishpat (Gen. 14:7). An ancient city in what is now western Syria, south of the original, ancient Kingdoms of Israel and Judah, and also called Cades or Kadesh. Enmishpat means "Fount of Justice," as there was a famous spring there, from which Moses made water run by knocking on a rock, the spring's source.

Enoch: The first city founded by Cain after he was forced by God to wander the earth for killing Abel. Named after his son (Gen. 4:17). According to tradition, Enoch lay east of Eden, in the land of Nod, and was destroyed in the Flood.

Entinopus: A 4th century B.C.E. architect of Candia (Crete), who founded Venice while fleeing the Visigoths.

Ephesus: Chief Ionian city where the temple of Artemis was built, one of the Seven Ancient Wonders of the World.

Ephron: The son of Zohar the Hittite, who sold Abraham a cave near a field in Hebron where Abraham and his wife, Sarah, were buried.

epistyle: An architrave, the lower part of the entablature, a beam resting immediately on top of a column.

Epopt: An initiate, or priest in the Eleusinian Mysteries in ancient Greece.

Erasmus: Great Dutch Humanist and Catholic priest, born ca. 1466. He opposed Luther, but believed in the Reformation and in learning over superstition in general. His satire on the monastic life, *The Praise of Folly*, showed his lighter side as well.

Eritrea: A country in north east Africa, on the North Sea. A source of war elephants for the ancient Egyptians.

Ethan: (1 Kings 4:31) An Old Testament figure, considered one of the wisest men of his time. Also (1 Chron. 16, 25), appears to be conflated with Jeduthun (Idithun in the Douay-Rheims Bible) as musician and one of David's three temple music masters. They are thought of as the same person by some scholars.

Eubages: Druid priests.

Eve: According to the Bible, the first woman, created from Adam's rib (Gen. 2–4).

Ezra: A Hebrew priest and scribe, and the eponym of the Old Testament Book of Ezra, who, in the fifth century B.C.E, led nearly 5000 Jews back to Palestine from captivity in Babylon.

Fakirs: Sufi or Hindu ascetics and mendicants.

Flanders: An area in the low country now lying within Belgian and French territory. In the Middle ages known for its hops, the female flower of the hop plant used to stabilize and flavor beer. Initially outlawed elsewhere, but eventually replaced Roman gruit for flavoring.

Francis of Assisi: Italian monk and Saint, born ca. 1182, was founder of the Franciscans, and a patron saint of animals.

Gabriel: An archangel known as a messenger of God.

Gama, Vasco da: A Portuguese explorer (1469–1524) who was the first to reach India by sea.

Ganges: Sacred river in northern India.

Gavarnie: The Cirque de Gavarnie is at the head of the Gavarnie-Gedre valley in the heart of the French Pyrenees, and is a natural semi-circle of rock carved out by ancient glaciers.

gavial: A large reptile related to the crocodile, living in southern Asia.

Gehenna: A valley south of Jerusalem where children were sacrificed to the god Moloch, and criminals were executed. Originally meant "valley of the son of Hinnom," but came to mean a destination of the wicked, or Hell, especially in the New Testament.

Gestas: Called the impenitent thief, first appearing in the Gospel of Nicodemus. He was on the cross to the left of Jesus, and taunted him for not saving himself.

Ghisleri: Pope Pius V, 1566–1572. Under him, the Inquisition again flourished. He waged war against Islam, and against Protestants throughout the rest of Europe, while intellectual darkness descended once again. He was later canonized a saint.

Ghor: A mountainous region of ancient Persia, in the area of Pakistan and Afghanistan.

Girgash: In biblical times, a city named after the fifth son of Canaan, great-grandson of Noah, and located near the sea of Tiberias (another name for the Sea of Galilee). At some point it was destroyed by the Hebrews. It is mentioned by Flavius Josephus as "Gergesus" in Book I, chapter 6, of his *The Antiquities of the Jews*. The Old Testament speaks of the Girgashites (Gen. 10:16, 15:21; 1 Chron. 1:14, as well as in Deut., Joshua, and Neh.).

gneisse: A metamorphic rock with alternating dark and light banding due to segregation of different mineral types.

Golgotha: (Calvary) The hill on which Christ was crucified.

Goshen: "Gessen" in the Douay-Rheims Bible. Also rendered as "Gesan." Spoken of in the Old Testament as a special land for crops and livestock in Egypt's eastern Delta (Gen. 45–47; Ex. 8:22, 9:26). The Israelites began their exodus from Pithom and Succoth in this area.

Grève: The *Place de Grève* was located beside the river Seine and was a place where most of the public executions took place in early Paris. Hugo called it "the symbol of medieval and ancient regime justice: brutal, corrupt, and inadequate."

Griffin: A mythical creature with the head and wings of an eagle, and the body of a lion. Considered a majestic and powerful presence.

Guebre: The old name for the people or priests who practiced Zoroastrianism in ancient Persia. Persian word for "fire-worshipper."

Hadrian: Roman Emperor, 117–138. He is best known for building Hadrian's Wall.

Hæmus: Mountain in ancient Thrace, the classical prison of the birds, and named after a Thracian tyrant.

Ham: The second son of Noah. According to extra-biblical traditions, rather than taking up the ways of Adam's good son, Seth, as did Ham's brother Shem and his son Enosh and their descendents, he and his son Canaan took up the ways of Cain. Their descendents were the Egyptians, Canaanites, Philistines, Assyrians, and Babylonians.

Hannasci: The Hebrew word for "Prince."

Hazeroth: A place north of Mount Sinai that the Israelites visited during their forty years of wandering in the wilderness, mentioned in the Old Testament (Num. 11, 12, 33; Deut. 1).

Hebron: A sacred city to Moslems and Jews situated south of Jerusalem, mentioned throughout the Old Testament. At an early date it was the capital of the Kingdom of Israel before it was moved to Jerusalem. Isaac and Ishmael buried their father, Abraham, alongside Abraham's wife, Sarah, Isaac's mother, in a cave near a field in Hebron (Gen. 23:19–20).

Hecuba: In Greek mythology, the wife of King Priam of Troy, mother of Hector. She avenged her children's deaths. Ovid's *Metamorphosis* has her turned into a dog, forever mournful.

Heliogabalus: (Elagabalus) Syrian priest installed Emperor of Rome, Marcus Aurelius Antoninus, at age 14, until his assassination four years later in 222 C.E. He placed the Syrian god El-Gabel at the head of the Roman pantheon, moved the sacred Roman vessels to his court, and purportedly led a life of debauchery that led to his demise.

Hellespont: A narrow strait connecting the Aegean Sea to the Sea of Marmara, and on which Troy was located.

Hermes: Hermes Trismegistus (Thrice-Great), a mythic Egyptian who purportedly authored a body of esoteric writings that are attributed more recently to a number of anonymous authors writing ca. 250 C.E. In Classical mythology, Hermes is the messenger of the gods, as well as the god of science and invention.

Herod: Tetrarch, or governor of the Galilee area, and participant in the execution of Christ.

Hinnom: The valley of the son of Hinnom, from which Gehenna derived its name, a valley near Jerusalem where children were sacrificed to Molloch.

Hippodrome: A Greek stadium for horse and chariot racing.

hoqueton: A padded doublet or cloak, impervious to small arrows, that in 1370 was adopted as a replacement of chainmail.

Horace: Roman poet born in 65 B.C.E, son of a freedman, and a favorite of Augustus. He is famous for his *Odes, Satires, Epodes,* and in particular his *Epistles.*

Horeb: Mount Horeb, where Moses struck a rock and obtained water for the Israelites after crossing the Red Sea (Ex. 17:6).

Horims: A people inhabiting areas around Mount Seir in southern Canaan. Their ancestor was Seir (Gen. 14:6, 36:21, 29; Deut. 2:12, 22). This people merged with the Edomites.

Huss, John: (Jan Hus) A Czech priest and Church reformer who inspired Martin Luther, and was burned at the stake in 1415.

Hydra: A seven-headed serpent in Greek legend, whose heads would grow back twofold if cut off. Killed by Hercules as one of his twelve labors meant to expiate the crime of killing his own children.

Iblis: Also called Eblis. This is the Islamic version of Satan, a genie (djinni or jinni) who is the primary devil and ruler of the fallen angels, and who, in the Koran (Suad 38.74, 75 and Ta Ha 20.116), refused to obey Allah's command to worship Adam.

ichneumon: Called "Pharaoh's rat." A cat-sized mongoose worshipped by the ancient Egyptians in part because they killed troublesome crocodiles and asps.

Idithun: (see "Ethan") Also "Jeduthun" in most editions of the Bible, appearing in Psalms, Nehemiah, and Chronicles. Biblical pseudonym for principal master of the temple music, or choir-master. A manuscript in the British Museum shows Idithun, in the company of King David, playing an instrument almost identical to our modern violin.

Idumea: A later, Roman name for Edom, part of the greater kingdom of Judea.

Imam: An Islamic religious leader, in the Mosque and the community.

Imbrasus: The river goddess Hera's temple was located near the Imbrasus River, in Samos, a Greek island in the Aegean, where the legendary goddess annually bathed to renew her virginity.

impost: The topmost part of a column.

infusorian: Any microscopic, unicellular organism found in water.

Irmensul: A sacred, stone pillar, an idol of the ancient Saxons.

Isaac: In Gen. 21, 22, the only son of Abraham and Sarah. One of the three patriarchs of the Jewish people, he was to be sacrificed to God by Abraham until stopped by an angel of God.

Isis: A Mother goddess in ancient Egypt whose influence spread to Greece and Rome.

Issachar: One of the Israelite tribes allocated land in Canaan.

Ithuriel: In Milton's *Paradise Lost,* an angel sent by Gabriel to seek out Satan.

Ixion: King of the Lapithae, he was punished for ingratitude by Zeus. Hermes tied his hands and feet to a wheel that rolled perpetually in the air.

Jacob: In the Old Testament, the son of Isaac and Rebbeca, and considered the father of the Twelve Tribes of Israel.

James: One of the apostles of Jesus.

Janus: In Roman mythology, the god of beginnings, endings, and Time, who is depicted as having two heads, facing the past and the future.

Japheth: One of three sons of Noah (Gen. 5:32, 9:18). The Japhethic race refers to the descendents of Japheth (considered by some to be the Indo-European, or Aryan race), as the Semitic race refers to the descendents of Noah's son Shem.

jaquemart: An automated statue in a bell tower that strikes the hours with a hammer.

Jephthah: He was a regent in Israel as well as a military leader, who sacrificed his daughter to God, that he might defeat the Ammonites in battle (Judges 11,12).

Jeremiah: The "broken-hearted prophet" of the Old Testament, traditionally the author of the Book of Jeremiah and Lamentations, whose prophecies were largely ignored.

Jerome: Saint Jerome, born ca. 347 C.E., and iconographically represented as writing or studying. He is the patron saint of theological learning.

Jerusalem: The holy city of Jews, Moslems and Christians, located in the Middle East between the Mediterranean Sea and the Dead Sea, in the Judean Mountains. It is one of the most fought-over cities in history.

Job: A patriarch in the Book of Job whose piety is tested by God.

John: Author of the Book of Revelation, which was revealed to him in a cave on Patmos, a small Greek island in the Aegean Sea.

John: An Evangelist who wrote the Gospel of John.

Joppa: Also Jaffa. An old city on the Mediterranean, the original port of Jerusalem, but mentioned as early as the 15th century B.C.E. in Egyptian annals. Found throughout the Old and New Testaments (Jonah 1:3; Acts 9:36; 2 Chron. 2:16).

Judas: One of the Apostles of Jesus. Portrayed in the Gospels as having betrayed Jesus, leading to the Crucifixion.

Jude: One of the Apostles of Jesus.

Judea: The Greek form of "Judah," an Israelite tribe, and later the ancient Kingdom of Judah. Created when the kingdom of Israel united by David split, with ten of the twelve Tribes of Israel rejecting Solomon's son Rehoboam as their king. The Tribes of Judah and Benjamin remained loyal to Rehoboam, and formed the southern Kingdom of Judah, while the others formed the northern Kingdom of Israel.

Judith: In the non-canonical Book of Judith, a widow from the Tribe of Reuben, the beautiful heroine who seduced and slayed the Assyrian general, Holofernes, allowing Israel to counter-attack the leaderless Assyrians, and be saved.

Jupiter: In Roman mythology, Jupiter was the god of sky and thunder, the equivalent of Zeus.

Kadesh: An ancient city in what is now western Syria, also called Cades or Enmishpat, where there was a famous "Fount of Judgment." Moses made water spring from it by knocking on the rock. (see Enmishpat)

Kedron: (Cedron or Kidron) The ravine between the Mount of Olives and Mount Moriah, where flowed a river of the same name (1 Kings 15:13; John 18:1). The upper part of it is called the Valley of Jehoshaphat, traditionally identified in Christianity, Islam, and Judaism as the Valley of Decision, the place of final judgment (Joel 3:2, 12, 14).

kestrel: A small falcon which hovers over fields while hunting.

Kos: (Cos) A mountainous Greek island off the coast of Turkey, with an active commercial center in the ancient world, that participated in the Trojan War. Hippocrates was born there.

Lamiae: Monsters in folklore, similar to vampires, traced back to Lamia, a beautiful Libyan queen in Greek myth.

Legion: Hugo's name for "The Human Spirit," it may have been an allusion to the name of a demon in the New Testament: "And he asked him, What is thy name? And he answered, saying, My name is Legion: for we are many" (Mark 5:9), and "And Jesus asked him, saying, What is thy name? And he said, Legion: because many devils were entered into him" (Luke 8:30).

Levi: The one Israelite tribe in the Old Testament not allocated land in Canaan. God was their inheritance. Instead, for religious and political duties performed, they were paid a tithe by the other tribes. Moses was a Levite.

Leviathan: A sea-monster (Job 41), and, along with Behemoth, a monstrous beast of the land, meant as a lesson from God to Job.

lictors: Roman civil servants who served as bodyguards for Roman Magistrates.

Lilith: In Jewish tradition, related to a class of female demons. In the Talmud she is Adam's first wife, who refused to submit to his authority. In the Kabbala she is the daughter of Satan.

Locke: English philosopher, born 1632 C.E. He was the first British empiricist, and wrote the famous *Essay Concerning Human Understanding*.

Louis XI: King of France, 1461–1483. He inherited a country in chaos, and established order and an absolute Monarchy by every means possible.

Lucian: The greatest of second-century Roman Sophists and rhetoricians, born ca. 125 C.E. in Assyria. He was a writer in Greek of many works including *Dialogues*.

Luke: An Evangelist who wrote the Gospel of Luke.

Luther: A German monk and theologian born in 1483 C.E., who influenced the Protestant Reformation. While hiding out in exile at Wartburg Castle, he wrote, translated the New Testament from Greek to German, and called his stay his "Patmos," referring to John's stay in a cave on Patmos where he received his Book of Revelation.

madrepore: A variety of coral including those in the tropical seas.

Magdalene: Mary Magdalene (Madeleine in French), disciple and companion to Jesus, considered a Saint by the orthodox Christian churches. She was present at the Crucifixion, and the first to see Jesus after the Resurrection, according to some of the Gospels.

Malchus: The servant of the High Priest wounded by Peter when the soldiers came with Judas to arrest Jesus (John 18:10).

Mamre: Named after an Amorite in alliance with Abraham, it was the site of a shrine built by the latter. Near the grove stood the "Oak of Mamre" or the "Oak of Abraham" marking a famous event in Abraham's life (Gen. 13:18).

Mars: The Roman god of War.

Martha: Martha and Mary from Bethany were sisters, and friends of Jesus, who raised their brother Lazarus from the dead (John 11, 12). Some believe that Hugo conflates Mary Magdalene and Mary from Bethany. Another school of thought maintains that they are one in the same.

Mary: The mother of Jesus in the New Testament, called the Virgin Mary.

Matthias: The Jewish historian Josephus tells, in his history *Antiquities* (Ant. 17.149–67), of the teacher Matthias and others being put to death by Herod for having removed a great golden eagle from atop the great Gate of the Temple.

Mecca: The capital of Saudi Arabia, the birthplace of Mohammed, and the holiest city in Islam.

Medina: A sacred city of Islam in Saudi Arabia, and site of Mohammed's tomb.

Melchizedek: King of Salem (identified with Jerusalem: "City of Peace" in Hebrew). His name means "King of righteousness." As high priest, he blessed Abraham upon his return from his pursuit of the confederacy of Kings (Heb. 7; Gen. 14).

Mercury: The Roman equivalent of the Greek god Hermes, the messenger god.

Merlin: The story "Childe Rowland" evolved through the centuries from ballad to

English fairy tale, influenced along the way by Arthurian legend and "Chansons Roland." It features Merlin the magician as well as an immense, spinning, blood-red carbuncle, lighting up a great hall, and presumably the source of Hugo's reference.

Messiah: Literally means "anointed" in Hebrew, and generally means "the redeemer." Applied to Jesus in Christianity.

Michael: An archangel seen as the commander of the Army of God.

Milcom: (Melchom or Malcham) A principal Ammonite diety worshipped on the Mount of Olives, usually regarded as the same as Moloch, although in a different location and without child sacrifice (1 Kings 11:5; 2 Kings 23:13).

Milton: An English poet, 1608–1674, best known for his long epic poem, *Paradise Lost.*

Minerva: Roman goddess of wisdom and patroness of the arts and trades. Identified with the Greek goddess Athena, hence Hugo's use of the epithet "Apteros" or "Wingless," usually applied to Athena's large statue on the Acropolis, perhaps the "Colossus" to which Hugo refers.

mistral: Name for the north-east wind in the South of France.

Mohammed: (ca. 571–632) Founded Islam, and is considered a prophet of God.

Moloch: (Molech) Ancient Semitic god of the Ammonites associated with child-sacrifice (Acts 7:43; 1 Kings 11:7; Lev. 20).

Montfaucon: The gallows of Montfaucon was located in the north-east part of Paris and was the principal gallows of the kings of France up until Louis XIII.

Montmartre: A hill in Paris, so named because Saint Denis was executed there ca. 250 C.E.

Mordecai: A noble character in the Old Testament, who raised his cousin Esther as his own daughter (Esther 2–10), and helped avert a massacre of the Jews. He and Esther were considered prophets in the Talmud.

Moses: Prophet and liberator of the Jewish people, he led them out of bondage from Egypt, and received the Ten Commandments on Mount Sinai (Ex. 34; Deut. 5).

Mount Athos: The Holy Mountain, center of Eastern Christian Orthodox monasticism, and home of twenty monasteries.

Mount Glon: Perhaps a reference to Mount Glonn, overlooking the Loire near Nante, France, where 5th century monk Saint Florent retired to a cave as a hermit, after driving out the resident snakes with prayer.

Mount Meru: A sacred mountain in Hindu mythology.

Mount Moriah: (2 Chron. 3:1) On which Solomon built his famous Temple in Jerusalem.

Mount of Olives: A ridge of hills east of Jerusalem, at the base of which was the Garden of Gethsemane where Jesus prayed before his betrayal and crucifixion.

Mount Zion: Also Mount Sion. (Rev. 14:1; Psalms 48:2, 11–12) A hill that changed location several times in the Bible over the centuries. The earliest site accepted by most scholars is the south-eastern hill or ridge south of Jerusalem that was David's citadel. It next becomes the Temple Mount in Jerusalem, and finally the south-western hill south of Jerusalem.

Naim: Also Nain (Luke 7:11–17). A New Testament city in Galilee, identified with present-day Nein, where Jesus had awakened from the dead the sole remaining son of a widow.

Nazarene: An inhabitant of Nazareth, the childhood home of Jesus.

Nebo: Mount Nebo, in a mountain range east of Jordan and the Red Sea, from which Moses viewed the Promised Land, and where he died.

Neptune: The Roman god of the Sea, equivalent to the Greek god Poseidon.

Nimes: An important city during the Roman Empire in present-day France, where there was an immense arena for bullfights and other public events.

Nimrod: (Gen. 10:8–12; 1 Chron. 1:10) A King of great power, and a great-grandson of Noah. Extra-biblical traditions portray him as the first to rebel against God following the Flood, as tyrannical conqueror who forced the people to turn against God, thus creating the first pagan religion. Nimrod is said to have built the Tower of Babel in order to reach God and kill Him for killing his ancestors in the flood. The primary source for Hugo's "Nimrod" narrative, according to E.M. and A.H. Blackmore, is the *Tarikh al-Rusul wa al-Muluk* (*History of the Prophets and Kings*), by the 10th century scholar and historian, al-Tabari.

Nineveh: Capital of the Assyrian Empire, a center of worship of Ishtar, and built most likely by Nimrod (Gen. 10:11), if "Asshur" in that verse stands for "Assyria," and not the son of Shem.

Niobe: The daughter of Tantalus in Greek myth. For having claimed a fertility superior to Ledo's, the gods killed her fourteen children, and then turned her to stone. In this state, she wept perennially for their loss.

Nisyros: A mountainous, volcanic Greek island in the Aegean Sea.

Nubian: From Nubia, an ancient kingdom in the Nile Valley.

Obi: The title of a leader or chief in Nigeria.

Octavian: (63 B.C.E.–14 C.E.) Founder of imperial Rome, and considered its first emperor. Adopted the title "Augustus" upon acquiring supreme power. Rome's greatest Emperor, his reign initiated a two hundred year period of relative peace.

Ombos: Ancient Egyptian city on the Nile with a temple dedicated to the worship of the crocodile and the falcon. The first surgical instruments were found there.

Ophir: A wealthy, ancient land mentioned in the Old Testament, and associated with Jehoshaphat and Solomon (1 Kings 10:11; Job 22:24).

Oromedon: One of the Giants who waged war against the gods, and was buried under the mountainous island of Kos.

Orpheus: A legendary figure in Greek mythology worshipped as chief among poets and musicians, inspiring the Orphic cults.

Ossa: A mountain in northern Greece, between Mt. Pelion and Mt. Olympus.

Pantheon: A temple in Rome dedicated to all the Roman gods.

Parthenon: A temple in ancient Athens dedicated to the Greek goddess Athena.

Pathrusim: Ancestors, in part, of the Philistines, from the country of Pathros, in ancient times the name of Upper Egypt. (Gen. 10:14; 1 Chron. 1:12).

Patmos: A small Greek island in the Aegean Sea. John envisioned his Book of Revelation in a cave there.

Pelion: A mountain in Thessaly near Mt. Olympus.

Pentecost: In Judaism, the Feast of Pentecost commemorates receiving the Law on Mt. Sinai fifty days after departing Egypt, by celebrating their annual harvest of wheat (Deut. 16:9, 10; Exodus 34:22). It is also a Christian festival the seventh Sunday after Easter, celebrating the birth of the Christian Church when the Holy Ghost descended upon the Apostles (Acts 2:1–3).

Peter: Originally named Simon, he was one of the Apostles of Jesus. Following the death of Jesus, Peter denied knowing him three times. Known for his New Testament *Epistles*, although authorship is attributed by some to Paul.

peulven: A name given to a menhir, or large, upright-standing stone, less than 9 feet in height.

Phalaris: A tyrant from Sicily, ca. 570–554 B.C.E.

Phasis: What the ancient Greeks called the current-day Rion River, in western Georgia, running from the Caucasus mountains to the Black Sea. It was the river of the Argonautic expedition to plunder the golden fleece.

Phidias: A Greek sculptor, painter and architect ca. 480–430 B.C.E, commonly regarded as one of the greatest of all sculptors of Classical Greece.

Philippe II: King of France, (1180–1223), consolidated royal power at the expense of the nobility, and doubled the royal domain.

Philistines: A people inhabiting southern Canaan on the Mediterranean coast. In the

Bible they were in a constant state of war against the Israelites.

Phrygia: An ancient kingdom in Anatolia, now modern-day Turkey.

Pindus: A mountain range between Thessaly, Macedonia and Epirus, home of the Muses.

Piranesi: An Italian architect and engraver, (1756–1810), known for his grandiose and extravagant etchings of imaginary, labyrinthine, melancholy, gothic prison interiors.

Pitiunt: Present-day Pitsunda, near the Black Sea, it was the first community of Christianity in the Caucacus, in the 4th century.

Plato: (ca. 427–347 B.C.E.) Greek philosopher who laid the foundation for Western Philosophy. Wrote many dialogues on a variety of subjects, with Socrates as protagonist.

Plautus: Roman comic playwright, born ca. 254 B.C.E. Twenty-one of his comedies are extant, and were extremely popular.

Pliny the Elder: Born 23 C.E. in northern Italy. Writer of the thirty-seven volume *Natural History*.

Pœstum: (Pæstum) Roman city south of Naples, famous for its rose-trees. Originally called Poseidonia.

Polybotes: A Giant who was crushed beneath the mountainous island of Nisyros by Poseidon.

Porphyrion: A Giant, one of the sons of Uranus and Gaia in Greek mythology.

porphyry: A royal-purple stone highly valued in Imperial Rome for its use in buildings and monuments.

Prometheus: In Greek mythology, a Titan who stole fire from Zeus to give to humankind, and whose punishment was to be bound to a rock in the Caucasus and have his constantly rejuvenating liver eaten, daily, by an eagle.

Psamtik I: Long-lived King of the XXVIth dynasty who united all of ancient Egypt, and to whom was attributed, at one time, what is now known to be the remarkable mortuary temple of Seti I in the Valley of the Kings. He died in 609 B.C.E.

Pundits: In India, learned persons or scholars, also called pandits.

pylon: A monumental temple gateway consisting of two towers with a smaller entrance in between.

Pyrrho: Greek philosopher, born ca. 360 B.C.E, and founder of the Skeptical school of philosophy. Originally a painter.

Pythoness: Another name for the priestess who served as the oracle at Delphi, in Greece. Apollo was the prophetic god at Delphi, whose full name there was Pythian Apollo. The dragon or serpent Python was a soothsaying spirit who was killed, and his powers appropriated, by Apollo, son of Zeus, and Greek god of the sun, healing, poetry, music, and truth.

Rabelais: French humanist, born ca. 1494 C.E., who abandoned monastic life to study medicine, later becoming a famous and influential storyteller and satirist.

Rachel: The favorite wife of Jacob, son of Isaac. When Rachel died, Jacob set up a stone pillar over her grave (Gen. 35:19, 20).

Ramesseum: In Luxor, Egypt, the mortuary temple of the ancient Egyptian Pharaoh Rameses II, built in the 13th century B.C.E.

Raphael: An archangel known for his healing.

Resen: A city in ancient Assyria near Nineveh founded by Nimrod, as some scholars think, or by Ashur, son of Shem, grand-son of Noah (Gen. 10:12).

Reuben: The tribe of Reuben, one of the Twelve Tribes of Israel. Reuben was the eldest son of Jacob.

Rhipsime: Virgin Saint and Christian martyr, who was born in Rome and who died ca. 290 C.E. She fled to Armenia from Rome to avoid royal attentions, only to be killed there attempting to avoid similar advances.

Rhodope: A mountain range stretching from Bulgaria to Greece.

rose apple tree: In the Antilles, bearing a fruit with the odor of the rose. Besides *jamrose,* the French also call it *jambosier.*

Rosmophim: As pointed out by Abraham A. Arni, this word combines two names that follow one another in the Old Testament, "Rosh" and "Muppim" (Gen. 46:21).

Rousseau: Swiss writer and tormented genius who contributed to Diderot's *Encyclopédie*, advocated a return to nature, and wrote the famous *Emile*, *The Social Contract*, and *Confessions.*

Sabaoth: (Romans 9:29; James 5:4) Greek form of Hebrew *tseba'oth* (hosts, armies), translated and found most frequently in the phrase "Jehovah God of Hosts."

Sabine: The Sabines, or Sabini, were a powerful ancient nomadic tribe in central Italy later forming part of the Roman people.

Sadoc: (Latin Sadoch) Also Zadok. An ancestor of Ezra (Ezra 7:2; 1 Chr. 6:8, 24:3; 2 Sam. 8:17; 1 Esdras 8:2). Also an ancestor of Jesus (Matthew 1:14). In this instance, most likely a Talmudic borrowing, according to Claudius Grillet.

Sagittarius: A constellation of the Zodiac, meaning "archer."

Saint Gregory: "The Illuminator," the first Armenian to convert to Christianity. Thrown into a pit of snakes for fourteen years, he was later allowed to convert all of Armenia. Saint Gregory built the Etchmiadzin Cathedral as a vaulted basilica in 301–303, from the dome of which hangs a giant chandelier.

Saint Theresa: (1515–1582) A Spanish mystic and Carmelite nun.

Samaria: The earliest Jewish sect, and capital city of the Kingdom of Israel (consisting of the ten tribes) ca. 884 B.C.E. Situated as it was on a hill, it was unconquerable for a time.

Samaritan: The name of a pump house built on the Pont Neuf in 1605 to primarily supply water to the Louvre, and in use until 1813. It also designates an inhabitant of Samaria.

Sara: The Old Testament Sara, or Sarah, was the wife of the patriarch Abraham, mother of Isaac.

Sarapanis: An ancient fortified town of the Laz people in the Caucasus, near the Black Sea, on the left bank of the Phasis river.

Sardica: A Thracian settlement.

satrap: A provincial governor in ancient Persia.

saxifrage: Small flowering plant growing in mild climates.

Scopas: An ancient Greek sculptor and architect ca. 395–350 B.C.E, born on the island of Paros.

Scotus: John Dun Scotus, Scottish theologian and Scholastic philosopher, born ca. 1266 C.E., known as the "subtle doctor" because of the subtle nuances of his thinking. He was a Franciscan.

Scylla: A monster living in a cave in a rock formation off the southern-most tip of Italy, which barked like a dog, had twelve canine legs, six long necks, and heads, each containing three rows of sharp teeth.

Segor: (Also Zoar, in most editions of the Old Testament) Located south-east of the Dead Sea, it was one of five cities including Sodom and Gomorrah destined to be destroyed by God. It was saved through the intervention of Lot (Gen. 19:22).

Seir: A mountain and a land in southern Canaan near the Dead Sea, occupied by the Horites and then the Edomites, named after Seir, the Horite, with whose people Esau's descendants intermarried upon their arrival there (Gen. 36; Deut. 2).

Sejanus: Commander of the Praetorian Guard under Tiberius, turning it into a political force that made him, at one time, the most feared person in Rome.

Selenites: Inhabitants of the moon, associated with Selene, the moon goddess of Greek mythology.

Seth: In the Old Testament, the third son of Adam, born after Cain slew Abel. According to extra-biblical traditions, unlike Cain's cursed descendents, Seth's descendents follow the "Way of Life," leading to Noah and his son Shem, who remain faithful to God.

Shakespeare: (1564–1616) Of English birth, considered the world's greatest dramatist, authoring such masterpieces as *Hamlet*, *Macbeth*, and *King Lear*.

Shiva: In Hindu tradition is considered the Supreme God or a major deity along with Vishnu and Brahma. Known as the god of destruction and reproduction.

Sibyl: A prophetess of the ancient world, found in various holy sites in antiquity. There were nine Greek and one Roman sibyls, the most ancient of whom was the Delphic Sibyl, not to be confused with the Delphic Oracle.

Sichem: (Shechem) An ancient Canaanite city which was the first capital of the Northern Kingdom of Israel, led by Jeroboam, following the split with the Southern Kingdom of Judah (1 Kings 12:25).

Sidon: One of the most important and oldest of the Phoenician cities, inhabited perhaps as far back as 5000 B.C.E, considered sinful by Jesus but potentially repentant (Luke 10:13–14; Matthew 11:21–22).

Simon: Of the Biblical Simons, one was an Apostle of Jesus, originally named Peter, and another was Simon the Cyrenian, who helped Jesus carry the cross.

Socrates: A Greek philosopher, ca. 469–399 B.C.E, teacher of Plato, and practitioner of the Socratic method, by which one taught through interactive question-and-answer dialogue. Unlike Aristotle and Plato, Socrates left no writings.

Sodom: An Old Testament city on the Jordon River plain destroyed by God for the impenitent sins of its inhabitants (Deut. 29:23).

Solomon: King of Israel and son of King David, in the tenth century B.C.E. Builder of the First Temple in Jerusalem.

Sostratus of Cnidus: Born 3rd century B.C.E., a Greek architect and engineer. He designed the lighthouse of Alexandria, one of the Seven Wonders of the Ancient World (ca. 280 B.C.E.).

Spherus: A Greek philosopher and disciple of the Stoic philosopher Zeno of Citium, ca. 243 B.C.E.

spindle: Associated with the Sibyls during their prophesying because of its use by the three Fates—Clotho spun the thread of life onto her spindle, Lachesis measured its length, and Atropos cut it and chose the manner of death.

Spinoza: A great 17th century Dutch philosopher who thought reason was the path to knowledge. His work was censured by the Roman Catholic Church, and he, himself, was excommunicated by the Jewish community. He made a living grinding lenses, rejecting honors and professorships.

Spitzbergs: The Spitzbergen archipelago of Norway, near the Arctic Ocean, covered with pointed snow-capped mountains amidst glaciers.

Stellial: Scholars note that this may be the Latin word for "Star" (*Stella*) paired with a Hebrew ending.

Sterne: Novelist and satirist born in Ireland to an English soldier and his Irish wife. He spent most of his life in England, and became famous after writing *Tristram Shandy*. He influenced Diderot.

Strigoi: Immortal vampires in Roman mythology.

Swedenborg: A famous Swedish scientist (1688–1772) who at age 53 became a mystic, and around whose teachings a church was established.

Swift: Irish author and satirist, born in Dublin in 1667 C.E., who wrote *Gulliver's Travels*.

Syriac: The language of a Syrian people living in the Fertile Crescent in ancient times.

Talmud: A central religious text of Judaism.

Talos: A giant made of brass, created by Hephaestus (Vulcan), the god of Fire, to guard his original workshop on Crete.

Tarquin: Tarquinius Priscus, the fifth king of Rome, built the Circus Maximus in the 6th century B.C.E, to hold chariot races. It could seat an estimated 150,000 spectators.

Tauris: A peninsula in the northern Black Sea area (today's Crimea), part of Scythia, and the region where, according to legend, Iphigenia, the daughter of Agamemnon, was led by Artemis upon saving her life.

teals: Small ducks with brightly marked plumage.

Tell: William Tell was a Swiss hero who resisted the Hapsburgs when they claimed his homeland for themselves. This eventually led to the founding of the Swiss Republic.

Teutates: Celtic god identified with the Roman gods Mars and Mercury. An ancient verse of a canticle from Brittany reads: "On the red stone blood was spread / And in the Cranou, in the middle of the wood, / Under the oaks of Teutates, / People used to be slain without pity."

Thebaid: A region in Upper Egypt which was primarily desert, located beside the Nile, containing the city of Ombos, later becaming a place of retreat for Christian monks.

Thebes: Ancient city in Egypt, a city of great grandeur which was thought to be the oldest city in the world.

Theos: The Greek word for "deity" or "god."

Thersites: A coarse, rank and file soldier who spoke unwelcome truths about Agamemnon in the *Iliad*, reflecting those of Achilles, and thus becoming the archetypal social critic for all times, and especially thought of as such by 19th century philosophers.

Thessaly: A region on the Aegean Sea, near Thrace, on the eastern coast of what is now present-day Greece, and a military power in the 4th century B.C.E. incorporated into the Macedonian Empire by Philip II, the father of Alexander the Great.

Thomas: An Apostle who questioned the truth of Jesus' resurrection, known since as "Doubting Thomas" (John 20:24–29).

Thrace: A warrior people and a Trojan ally in the *Iliad*. Their lands were bordered by the Danube, the Aegean, the Black Sea and the Sea of Marmara. Orpheus is thought to have been Thracian.

Thryx: A name of unknown provenance, perhaps a variant of Thrax, son of Ares, the god of war, and the origin of the place-name Thrace. Or perhaps Thrym, King of the Frost Giants who stole Thor's hammer, and was subsequently killed by him.

Tiberius: Roman Emperor, 14–37 C.E., and a great general who expanded the empire. He was an introspective and serious man, who in 26 C.E., soon after losing his son, exiled himself from Rome, allowing others to run the government. He was not actively engaged during the last days of Jesus.

Tiburtine: A Roman sibyl, whose seat was the ancient Etruscan town of Tibur.

Timon: A long-lived Athenian Skeptic philosopher from ca. 279 B.C.E. who achieved great financial success as a Sophist, and authored three books of lampoons.

Timur: Turkic conqueror, 1336–1405, chiefly remembered for the barbarity of his conquests.

Titan: Titans were the gods who preceded the Olympians in Greek mythology. According to one legend, they were Giants who overthrew their father Uranus to rule the earth, only to be overthrown in turn by their offspring, Zeus and the Olympians.

Tivoli: An ancient town in central Italy known for its gardens.

Toldos: Refers to the *Sepher Toldos Jeshu* (*The Life of Jesus*), from the Kabbalah.

Torpedo: A bottom-dwelling fish called an "electric ray."

Torquemada: From 1483 until his death in 1498, the fanatical Grand Inquisitor of Spain.

Trajan: A column was built to celebrate the victory of the Roman Emperor Trajan over the Dacians in 106 C.E.

Tripod: A type of sacrificial alter used in ancient Greece. An example is the three-legged tripod used by the oracle at Delphi, on which she sat while delivering her prophecies.

Typhon: He was the most fearsome of all creatures in Greek mythology, a many-headed giant born to Gaia who tried to kill Zeus but was buried by him under Mt. Etna.

Tyr: The god of single combat, victory and heroic glory in Norse mythology, portrayed as a one-handed man, and equated with Mars.

Tyre: (Hebrew Zor, Latin Tyrus) An ancient Phoenician city in southern Lebanon, jutting out into the Mediterranean Sea, founded at the start of the third millennium B.C.E. Solomon received cedars from Tyre to build the Temple. Like the city of Sidon, it was considered sinful by Jesus, but potentially repentant (Luke 10:13–14).

Ursa: Latin feminine for "bear," and referring to the constellations Ursa Major and Ursa Minor. The Welsh, Vikings, and Germanic tribes associated the seven brightest stars of Ursa Major with a chariot of their gods or heroes, thus perhaps one source of Hugo's reference to horses within this context.

Venus: The Roman goddess of Love.

Vesper: The Roman equivalent of Hesperos, in Greek mythology. It is the Evening Star, the planet Venus in the evening.

Vesta: In Roman mythology she was a virgin goddess who represented home and family.

vibrios: Microorganisms that cause cholera.

Vignola: One of the great Italian architects of 16th century Mannerism.

Vishnu: One of the supreme gods in Hinduism.

Vitruvius: Marcus Vitruvius Pollio (ca. 80–15 B.C.E.) was a Roman writer, architect and engineer, who authored *De architectura*, the only surviving major book on architecture from classical antiquity.

voghi: Hugo's rendering of "yoghi," or "yogi," a male practitioner of yoga.

Voltaire: French writer of genius, born in 1694 C.E. A *philosophe*, he wrote in every field, including drama, poetry, science, and history.

volvox: A protozoan forming multi-cellular colonies. Often seen as algae in shallow water.

Zaim: Chief or leader in Islamic culture.

Zebulun: The Israelite Tribe of Zebulun, the sixth son of Jacob (Genesis 46:14).

Zend: The *Zend Avesta* is Zoroastrianism's holy book. Zend means "commentary." Associated particularly with the Parsis, the last of the followers of Zoroaster, in Persia, now present-day Iran.

Zerubbabel: Credited with laying the foundation of the Second Temple in Jerusalem upon return from the Jewish exile in Babylonia (Ezra 1–5). An important figure in

Freemasonry.

Zion: Thought by scholars to mean "to be dry," "to protect," "ridge of a mountain," or "fortification," it is a term referring to the Jewish people, land of Israel, a hill or mountain, or to Jerusalem itself. (2 Sam. 5:7; 1 Kings 8:1; 1 Chron. 11:5; Isaiah 40:9, 60:14; Jer. 31:12, Zech. 9:13, Psalms 2:6, 48:2)

Zoilus: A Greek Cynic philosopher and scholar ca. 400 B.C.E., known for his harsh critique of Homer.

Zoroaster: (Zarathustra) The ancient prophet, and founder of Zoroastrianism, at one time in antiquity one of the world's largest religions. It was the Persian state religion for centuries. Zoroaster was a great observer of the stars.

NOTES

1. Matthew Josephson, *Victor Hugo* (Garden City, New York: Doubleday, Doran & co., 1942), 88–90.

2. Hugo, in his mysterious work, reduced all prose, philosophy, oratory, and history to poetry, and, as he was poetry incarnate, he essentially seized for himself alone, amongst thinkers, orators and storytellers, the very right to self-expression itself. (Hugo, dans sa tâche mystérieuse, rabattit toute la prose, philosophie, éloquence, histoire au vers, et, comme il était le vers personnellement, il confisqua chez qui pense, discourt ou narre, presque le droit à s'énoncer.)

Stéphane Mallarmé, *Œuvres complètes,* t. II (Paris: Gallimard, 2003), 205.

3. Gaëtan Picon, *Surrealists & Surrealism*, trans. James Emmons (Geneva: Éditions d'Art Albert Skira S.A., 1995), 46.

4. André Breton, "On Magic Art," in *What is Surrealism—selected writings* Book Two, edited and translated by Franklin Rosemont (New York: Monad Press, 1978), 293.

5. Gaston Picard, "Ce que pensent de Victor Hugo quelques écrivains d'aujourd'hui," *Les Nouvelles littéraires, artistiques et scientifiques*, no. 236, avril 23 (1927): 5, (microfiche).

6. Victor Hugo, *Poésie*, t. I, ed. Bernard Leuilliot (Paris: Éditions du Seuil, 1972), 9.

7. Graham Robb, *Victor Hugo: a biography* (New York: W. W. Norton & Company, 1997), 317–18.

8. Victor Hugo, *The Letters of Victor Hugo: From Exile, and After the Fall of the Empire*, ed. Paul Meurice (Boston: Houghton, Mifflin & Co., 1898), 116.

9. [M]on père est satisfait d'avoir enfin son rêve réalisé: être dans une île et avoir

la mer à ses pieds. Adèle Hugo, *Le Journal d'Adèle Hugo*, t. I, ed. F.V. Guille (Paris: Lettres Modernes Minard, 1968), 246.

10. John Pringle Nichol, *Victor Hugo: a sketch of his life and work* (London: S. Sonnenschein, 1893), 71.

11. Ibid., 69–70.

12. Robb, *Victor Hugo: a biography*, 318.

13. Poëte, tu fais bien! Poëte au triste front,
  Tu rêves près des ondes,
Et tu tires des mers bien des choses qui sont
  Sous les vagues profondes!

Victor Hugo, Introductory epigraph from *Les Contemplations*, t. I (Paris: Hachette, 1868), 7.

14. Georges Édouard Lemaître, *From Cubism to Surrealism in French Literature,* rev. ed. (Cambridge: Harvard University Press, 1947), 26.

15. Gwendolyn Bays, *The Orphic Vision: seer poets from Novalis to Rimbaud* (Lincoln:University of Nebraska Press, 1964), passim 108–21. Henry Prais, in "The Lilith Myth in Victor Hugo's *La Fin de Satan* and Its Source," from *Myth and Legend in French Literature* (ed. Keith Aspley, David Bellos, and Peter Sharratt [London: The Modern Humanities Research Association, 1982] 155-172), demonstrates how the portions of the poem devoted to the character Lilith have been greatly influenced by Hugo's reading of a chapter on Jewish religious practices written by Venetian Rabbi Leon de Modena in the 1807 *Cérémonies et coutumes religieuses de tous les peoples du Monde,* a book found in Hugo's Guernsey library.

16. Une comparaison entre *la Fin de Satan* et *le Testament de la Liberté* paraît encore plus instructive. Comme chez Victor Hugo, nous assistons d'abord, chez l'abbé Constant, à la chute "de l'ange qui, en naissant, refusa d'être esclave", et qui entraîna dans la nuit "une pluie de soleils et d'étoiles par l'attraction de sa gloire": mais Lucifer, l'Intelligence proscrite, enfante deux sœurs, Poésie et Liberté, et "l'esprit d'amour empruntera leurs traits pour soumettre et sauver l'ange rebelle."

Auguste Viatte, *Victor Hugo et les illuminés de son temps* (Montreal: Les Éditions de L'Arbre, 1942), 171.

17. Mon père parle des révélations faites par les Tables, puis il arrive enfin à sa propre religion, qui se résume dans ce grand mot *Amour.* Ce poème se termine par des points suspensifs, c'est-à-dire qu'il ne se termine que devant l'infini. Il était deux heures et demie lorsque mon père a terminé son poème, ce poème à 1946 vers, ce dénombrement des religions qui ont cherché à trouver Dieu sans jamais y

arriver. Kesler, l'athée, commence pourtant à croire en Dieu, dont ce poème gigantesque est l'échelle de feu. Il s'en va en disant: C'est aussi beau que *L'Apocalypse*, et nous nous retirons tous, émus et éblouis....Mon père resté seul, grimpe dans sa chambre, et va rechercher au ciel le rayon de lune, ami qui s'était assis près de lui dans cette pauvre salle à manger de l'exil. Il regarde la lune.

Adèle Hugo, *Le Journal d'Adèle Hugo*, t. IV: 1855, ed. F.V. Guille and Jean-Marc Hovasse (Paris: Lettres Modernes Minard, 2002), 169.

Hugo wrote of this evening's reading in his MS (folio 3r) as well, adding: "J'ai regardé ensuite l'éclipse de lune, visible cette nuit-là à Jersey." (I then watched the lunar eclipse, visible this evening on Jersey), hence Adèle's reference to his gazing at the moon.

18. Hugo, *The Letters*, 128–9.

19. Ibid., 130.

20. Ibid., 137–8.

21. Alain Montandon, *Espaces domestiques et privés de l'hospitalité* (Clermont-Ferrand: Presses Universitaires Blaise Pascal, 2000), 194.

22. J'ai reçu votre noble lettre et votre beau livre. L'art est comme l'azur, c'est le champ infini: vous venez de le prouver. Vos *Fleurs du Mal* rayonnent et éblouissent comme des étoiles. Je crie bravo de toutes mes forces à votre vigoureux esprit.

Victor Hugo, *Correspondance II (*1849–1866*)* (Paris: Albin Michel-Librairie Ollendorff, Imprimerie nationale, 1950), 272.

23. Comte de Lautréamont, *Maldoror & The Complete Works of the Comte de Lautréamont*, trans. Alexis Lykiard (Cambridge: Exact Change, 1994), 256.

24. C'est une tentative vers l'idéal. Rien de plus....[L]orsque plusieurs autres parties de ce livre auront été publiées, on apercevra le lien qui, dans la conception de l'auteur, rattache *la Légende des Siècles* à deux autres poëmes, presque terminés à cette heure, et qui en sont, l'un le dénoûment, l'autre le couronnement: *la Fin de Satan,* et *Dieu.*

L'auteur...a esquissé dans la solitude une sorte de poëme d'une certaine étendue où se réverbère le problème unique, l'Être, sous sa triple face: l'Humanité, le Mal, l'Infini; le progressif, le relatif, l'absolu; en ce qu'on pourrait appeler trois chants, *la Légende des Siècles, la Fin de Satan, Dieu.*

Victor Hugo, *La Légende des siècles,* t. I. (Paris: Hachette, 1920), 17–18.

25. Hugo, *The Letters*, 140.

26. Hinduism is noticably absent from Hugo's catalogue of religions, but India's ancient sacred texts, introduced to him in his youth by German scholars Friedrich

Schregel and Baron Ferdinand Eckstein during the height of Europe's Oriental Renaissance, were of long-standing interest to him. Their influence reasserted itself during this period, particularly in his writing of *Dieu.*

27. …chaque religion progrès sur la précédente, et lui répliquant, la spiritualisation de plus en plus dégagée jusqu'à l'arrivée et à l'évanouissement dans l'esprit pur.

Victor Hugo, *Poésie,* t. 3, ed. Bernard Leuilliot (Paris: Éditions du Seuil, 1972), 377.

28. Dieu n'a qu'un front: Lumière! et n'a qu'un nom: Amour! Ibid., 348.

29. Ce sera une des grandeurs de ce grand dix-neuvième siècle d'avoir posé, dans une sorte d'immense débat public et libre, avec toute latitude laissée à la négation comme à l'affirmation, en dehors et au-dessus des religions, la question suprême: *Dieu.*

Nous sommes de ceux que sollicite et qu'étreint ce point d'interrogation formidable, sans cesse aperçu sur l'horizon, sombre le jour, lumineux la nuit.

De là ce poème, dont nous publions aujourd'hui la première partie, *Le Seuil du gouffre.*—La deuxième partie paraîtra plus tard et sera intitulée *L'océan d'en haut.*

La première partie aborde la question. La deuxième conclut.

Ibid., 377.

30. Étriens l'immensité, saisis l'éternité,
Retiens, arrache, prends toute cette ombre en fuite,
Divulgue le secret de l'abîme, ébruite
Dieu, malgré le mystère et malgré l'infini.

Ibid., 389.

31. Anthony Hartley, ed., *The Penguin book of French verse 3: The Nineteenth Century* (Baltimore: Penguin Books, 1967), xxiii–xxiv.

32. Personne ne peut contester la sincérité du grand poëte et qu'il fut vraiment et réellement un voyant, à la manière de l'Anglais Blake.

Paul Claudel, *Œuvres complètes,* t. 15 (Paris: Gallimard, 1959), 34–5.

33. Et je pense aussi que Victor Hugo ne fut pas la seule âme en peine de cette lande pleine de ruines et de fouilles qu'est la littérature du XIXe siècle. Dans ce cimetière bêché par les lémures titubent d'autres grands hallucinés, Blake, le Gœthe du *Second Faust,* Michelet, Carlyle, Ibsen, Wagner qui fut le premier éclairé d'un rayon rédempteur, Nietzsche enfin qui fut dévoré tout vivant par le monstre dont les autres n'étaient que poursuivis.

Ibid., 35.

34. Algernon Charles Swinburne, *Studies in prose and poetry* (London: Chatto & Windus, 1894), 242–47.

35. Ibid., 170–71.

36. Paroles de celui qui songe en écrivant ce livre.

Victor Hugo, *A bilingual edition of the major epics of Victor Hugo*, vol. II, trans. E. H. and A. M. Blackmore (Lewiston, New York: Edwin Mellen Press, 2002), 441; Victor Hugo, *Œuvres Complètes de Victor Hugo*, *Poésie XI, La Fin de Satan. Dieu.* (Paris: Imprimerie nationale, 1911), 274.

37. Mon père lit une pièce de vers de son poème de *Satan Pardonné.* Cette pièce de vers s'appelle *Nemrod.* Ce poème est fait contre ces trois fléaux du vieux monde: la Guerre, la Peine de Mort, la Prison. La Guerre sort du clou qu'ençonça Caïn, le premier criminel, dans la tête d'Abel son frère. Ce clou sert de glaive à Nemrod qui incarne la guerre. La Peine de Mort sera représentée par le gibet du Christ.... La Prison s'incarnera dans la Bastille. La Révolution détruira la Prison par la Prise de la Bastille. Adèle Hugo, *Le Journal d'Adèle Hugo*, t. III: 1854, ed. F.V.Guille (Paris: Lettres Modernes Minard, 1984), 460–61.

38. W. W. M., "From Our Paris Correspondent," in *The Southern Messenger*: devoted to every department of literature and the fine arts (Richmond: Jno. R. Thompson, 1851), 578, http://bit.ly/P8xOV3.

39. La mort de l'Homme-Dieu est, à l'avis de mon père, un admirable sujet de poème.

Adèle Hugo, *Le Journal d'Adèle Hugo*, t. III, 460–61.

40. Contrairement à tous les Satans classiques qui n'aiment pas Dieu et qui conséquemment, loin de souffrir de son absence, doivent être très heureux d'en être débarrassés, le Satan romantique du poème de mon père aime Dieu et sa souffrance consiste à en être éloigné.

Ibid., 462.

41. John Andrew Frey, *A Victor Hugo Encyclopedia* (Westport, Connecticut: Greenwood Press, 1999), 99.

42. Lucretia S. Gruber, "Alfred de Vigny's 'Eloa': A Modern Myth," *Modern Language Studies*, vol. 6, no. 1, Spring (1976): 74, http://www.jstor.org/stable/3194396.

43. The great bronze soul who laments in heaven above!

From "*À Louis B…*" (To Louis B…) in the collection *Les Chants du crépuscule.*

44. Mme. Agnes Mary Frances (Robinson) Duclaux, *Victor Hugo* (New York: Henry Holt and Company, 1921), 259–60.

45. Dans la *Corde d'Airain*, dans *Dieu*, dans la *Fin de Satan,* dans la pièce sur la mort de Gautier, l'artiste septuagénaire, qui a vu mourir tous ses émules, qui a pu voir naître de soi toute une génération de poëtes, et même profiter des enseigne-

ments inappréciables que le disciple donnerait au maître si le maître durait, le vieillard très illustre atteint le plus haut point de la puissance poétique et de la noble science du versificateur.

Paul Valéry, *Situation de Baudelaire* (Paris: Chez Madame Lesage, 1924), 27–8.

46. Picard, "Ce que pensent de Victor Hugo," 5.

47. Victor Hugo, *Poésie*, t. I, 9.

48. Florian Rodari, *Shadows of a Hand*: the drawings of Victor Hugo, trans. Judith Hayward and Mark Hutchinson (The Drawing Center New York in association with Merrell Holberton Publishers, London, 1998), 23.

49. J.R. Ireson, *Victor Hugo: A Companion to his Poetry* (Oxford: Clarendon Press, 1997), 5.

JERSEY AND GUERNSEY

50. Philip Stevens, *Victor Hugo in Jersey* (Shopwyke Hall, Chichester, Sussex: Phillimore, 1985), 27.

51. Ibid., 25.

52. Ibid., 26.

53. Id.

54. Id.

55. *A Guernesey*

Ces rocs de l'océan ont tout, terreur et grâce,
Cieux, mers, escarpement devant tout ce qui passe,
Bruit sombre qui parfois semble un hymne béni,
Patience à porter le poids de l'infini
Et, dans ces fiers déserts qu'un ordre effrayant règle,
On se sent croître une aile, et l'âme devient aigle.

Victor Hugo, *Œuvres inédites de Victor Hugo, Tout la lyre,* t. I (Paris: J. Hetzel et A. Quantin, 1888), 115.

A NOTE ON HUGO'S ART

56. Vincent van Gogh, *The Complete Letters of Vincent van Gogh*, vol. III (Greenwich, Connecticut: New York Graphic Society, 1958), 243.

57. ...des choses que j'appelle mes dessins à la plume....Cela m'amuse entre deux strophes. Léon Cellier, *Baudelaire et Hugo* (Paris: José Corti, 1970), 137.

58. ...ces traits de plume quelconques, jetés plus ou moins maladroitement sur le papier par un homme qui a autre chose à faire....

Victor Hugo, *Œuvres Complètes de Victor Hugo: Actes et Paroles: II. Pendant l'exil.* 1852–1870 (Paris: Édition Hetzel-Quantin, [n.d.]), 291.

59. Philippe Burty, *Maîtres et Petits Maîtres* (Paris: G. Charpentier, 1877), 328.

60. J'ai fini par y mêler du crayon, du fusain, de la sépia, du charbon, de la suie et toutes sortes de mixtures bizarres.... Cellier, *Baudelaire et Hugo*, 137.

61. Philippe Burty, "Sept dessins de gens de letters," *The Academy: a weekly review of literature, science, and art*, July–December, vol. VIII (London: Robert Scott Walker, 1875): 316, http://bit.ly/Voewyb.

62. Pierre Georgel, *Drawings by Victor Hugo*: catalogue (London: Victoria and Albert Museum, 1974), section III (1852–1860).

63. Burty, "Sept dessins de gens de lettres," *The Academy*, 316.

64. Id.

65. Pierre-Georges Jeanniot, "Victor Hugo's Home at Guernsey," *Scribner's Magazine*, vol. XXI, January–June (1897): 113–14, http://bit.ly/Thdzuc.

66. Rather than a drawing of the dawn, it appears to be no more than the word "AUBE" drawn on paper, which appealed to Breton's surrealist sense of irony and playfulness.

LOUIS MORÉRI

67. Abraham A. Avni, "Hugo's Alleged Fabrications of Names and Anachronisms," *Modern Language Notes*, vol. 79, no. 3, French Issue, May (1964): passim 264–269, http://www.jstor.org/stable/3042836.

68. Moréri est la mine où Victor Hugo descend tous les jours et plusieurs fois par journée. Moréri lui donne l'histoire, qu'il se charge de rendre pittoresque, surtout les noms propres bizarres, étranges, inquiétants, qui réveillent l'attention et la tirent à eux, comme une couleur éclatante tire à elle les yeux.

Albert Cim, *Récréations littéraires: curiosités et singularités, bévues et lapsus, etc.* (Paris: Hachette, 1920), 109.

69. Victor Hugo, *Dieu (Le Seuil du gouffre),* ed. René Journet and Guy Robert (Paris: A. G. Nazet, 1961).

On page 145 Journet and Robert speak of Hugo's library at Hauteville-House. Researchers discovered Hugo's 1683, 2 volume edition of the Moréri, probably purchased in Jersey. Other resource books found there were Dom Calmet's *Histoire universelle*,

Nicolas Gueudeville's *Grand Théâtre historique*, the Abbé Prévost's *Histoire générale des Voyages*, Ernest Feydeau's *Histoire des usages funèbres et des sépultures des peuples anciens*, Louis-Mayeul Chaudon's *Nouveau Dictionnaire historique*, as well as a French translation of *Lives of Eminent Philosophers* by Diogenes Laërtius. In n. 3 of a prefatory note by Jean Gaudon, page 415 in *Œuvres complètes: IX*. Édition chronologique, edited by Jean Massin, reference is made to other books discovered by P. Berret and J.-B. Barrére in Hugo's library: the works of the Abbé Banier, Chompré, and Bayle, as well as the *Dictionnaire* of Trévoux and the *Encyclopédie* of Renier. Also present was an 1807 edition of *Cérémonies et coutumes religieuses de tous les peuples du Monde,* edited by Richard Simon. A comprehensive list of the works in the Hauteville-House library can be found at http://bit.ly/14dS6bB.

A NOTE ON THE TRANSLATION

70. The JR had stated their policy of reproducing, in the body of their text, Hugo's primary line from the MS, if it was not crossed out. Their rationale had been that they did not know what variant Hugo would have chosen, he having shown no past pattern in his choice of variant. If we study the twenty instances in "L'Esprit humain" where at least one of the six important editions other than the JR—the 1891 HQ, the 1911 IN, the 1950 BP, the 1969 Club français du livre (CF), the 1972 Éditions du Seuil (hereafter the ES), and the 1986 Robert Laffont edition (RL)—chooses a variant not found in the primary line, we find that there is a consistency, of sorts. The editions seem to be divided into two camps, the three earliest editions and the later ES, versus the JR, CF, and RL. The CF and the RL are accounted for in that they reproduce the JR text to the letter, just as the IN, BP, and ES appear to defer to the HQ edition. Of the twenty instances of variants chosen, the HQ, IN, and BP all chose the same variant eighteen times, ten times from above the line, once from below the line, once from the left margin, and six times from Hugo's later version (see "Publication History of *Dieu*" in the Introduction, as well as the E.H. and A.M. Blackmore Foreword where is discussed Hugo's two versions of "L'Esprit humain") of this part of the poem, on folio 16r, versus the JR choice from the earlier version, on folio 17r, that transition point in the MS where the two versions are merged (with some slight overlap). The ES concurs seventeen of the eighteen times. The last two variant divergences are rare cases of the JR reproducing left-hand margin variants, while, in one instance all four others reproduce the right-hand column primary verses, and in the other instance the BP and the ES reproduce the right-hand primary verses, the IN concurs with the JR,

and the HQ reproduces verses not found in the MS.

In terms of stanzaic spacing and punctuation of the text, the JR, CF, and RL for the most part stayed faithful to the MSS. The ES, on the other hand, took liberties, as it saw fit, as did the HQ to an even greater extent. The BP, although at times tending to emulate the HQ, was fairly independent in its own use of stanzaic and punctuation changes, as was the IN. In general, the HQ, IN, BP, and ES were idiosyncratic in the liberties they took with the MS, while the JR, CF and RL stayed faithful to it.

71. August 12th, 1870, three days before returning to France, Hugo reiterated in a note written on the folder of the MS (found on folio 1r) that "Le Seuil du Gouffre" was to start the poem, but named the second part "Dieu," not "L'Océan en haut" as he had named it in 1869. As the entire poem is entitled *Dieu*, I have reverted to his 1869 preference to avoid confusion.

THE PUBLICATION HISTORY OF *DIEU*

72. Sheila Gaudon, ed., *Correspondance entre Victor Hugo et Pierre-Jules Hetzel: t. I* (1852–1853) (Paris: Klincksieck, 1979), 76.

73. Sheila Gaudon, ed., *Correspondance entre Victor Hugo et Pierre-Jules Hetzel: t. II* (*janvier* 1854–*avril* 1857) (Paris: Klincksieck, 1979), 336.

74. Mon père nous parle ce matin du projet qu'il a de publier le poème de *Dieu* tout de suite; [il] répond pleinement à ce que demande Mme Sand, suite et continuation des *Contemplations*; il faut battre le fer quand il est chaud.

René Journet and Guy Robert, "Pourquoi Victor Hugo n'a-t-il pas publié son poème 'Dieu' ?," *Cahiers de l'Association internationale des études françaises* 19, no. 19 (1967): 226, doi:10.3406/caief.1967.2345.

75. Colette V. Michael, "Light/Darkness and the Phenomenon of Creation in Victor Hugo," in *Analecta Husserliana: The Yearbook of Phenomenological Research*, vol. XXXVIII, ed. Anna-Teresa Tymieniecka (Dordrecht: Kluwer Academic Publishers, 1992), 146.

76. ...conseille de faire un contraste de variété, de publier de la prose.

René Journet and Guy Robert, "Pourquoi Victor Hugo," 227.

77. Ce que nous faisons? Lui termine *Dieu* et *La Fin de Satan*; dans ce moment il ne nous lit rien; mais il s'éveille à cinq heures du matin pour écrire. L'immense succès des *Contemplations* l'a mis en verve; tu sais probablement qu'Hetzel vient de lui en acheter encore 5 mille exemplaires. Ça se traduit en balcons et en jets d'eau dans la nouvelle maison.

Gaudon, *Correspondance entre Victor Hugo et Pierre-Jules Hetzel,* t. II, 18.

78. Vos volumes de *Dieu* et *Satan* trouveront embusqués tous les ennemis que *les Contemplations* avaient mis en déroute.

En me souvenant de ce que vous m'avez dit à Guernesey, j'imagine que vous avez en portefeuille de quoi consterner tous ceux qui vous attendent avec des articles tout faits à vos ouvrages annoncés *Dieu* et *Satan*, je veux parler des *Petites Épopées*. Si vous êtes prêt pour ces deux volumes ou pour l'un des deux auquel *le Revenant* est une merveilleuse réclame, je suis sûr d'un second triomphe.

Victor Hugo, *Œuvres Complètes de Victor Hugo: Poésie V. La Légende des siècles*, t. I. (Paris: Imprimerie nationale, 1906), 614.

79. Journet and Robert, "Pourquoi Victor Hugo," 229.

René Journet and Evelyn Blewer published an undated fragment, following two fragments dated 1870, on pp. 359–60 of *Chantiers* (Paris: Robert Laffont, 1990), which began: "M. Ch. Éd [= mon cher Éditeur]," in which Hugo is writing to an unnamed publisher stating that he plans to publish *Dieu*. Journet and Guy Robert published the same text in their earlier *Dieu (fragments)* (Paris: Flammarion, 1969, 34), describing it as a rough draft of a letter to the publisher Albert Lacroix, probably from spring of 1869. The same letter is printed as a rough draft attributed to the year 1864, with Lacroix as recipient, in *Correspondance II (*1849–1866*)* (Paris: Imprimerie nationale, 1950), 483.

80. ...[A]vant de partir pour la France, en août 1870, Hugo met le poème *Dieu* dans deux malles qu'il dépose le 13 dans une banque de Guernesey. Ces malles, il ne les rouvrira qu'en avril 1875, lors d'un bref séjour qu'il fait à Guernesey. Dans l'intervalle, il n'a pas pensé à la publication de *Dieu*, et dans la suite il n'y pensera plus guère. A peine discerne-t-on çà et là une marque d'intérêt témoignée à cette œuvre: en 1876, par exemple, le poème *À l'Homme* porte la rubrique: "Pour le poème *Dieu*"; mais cette mention a été biffée, et ce poème est entré en 1877 dans la Seconde Série de *La Légende*. Journet and Robert, "Pourquoi Victor Hugo," 229.

81. Jean Gaudon *et al.*, " 'Discussions': Communication de MM. Journet et Robert," *Cahiers de l'Association internationale des études françaises* 19, no. 19 (1967): 302, http://bit.ly/PzImNc.

82. Ibid., passim 301–02.

83. Après, il continuera à travailler à une des parties de son poème *Dieu,* mais de nombreux projets interviendront, et il est vrai de dire que son pouvoir créateur sera de moins en moins à la hauteur du grand poème *Dieu*.

Ibid., 302.

84. It is commonly accepted, and reflected in bibliographies and library catalogues, that there was no general volume numbering of this 48 volume edition, only particular volume numbering within the genres, and that the order of genres is: I. Poésie (16 vol.)–II. Philosophie (2 vol.)–III. Histoire (3 vol.)–IV. Voyages (2 vol.)–V. Drame (5 vol.)–VI. Roman (14 vol.)–VII. Actes et paroles (4 vol.)–VIII. Œuvres diverses (2 vol.).

Upon examination of the forty-eight volumes, one discovers that the publishers did in fact assign a general volume number, as well, to at least the first thirty-one volumes published, including the first volume of *La Légende des siècles*, in accordance with their preconceived numbering plan for the entire completed set. I have found thirteen such numbered volumes, numbers 1, 2, 3, 8 (twice), 9, 15, 17, 18, 19, 20, 21, and 31, all published 1880–1882 but for the volume of *La Légende des siècles* (one of the number 8's), which was published in 1883. They fall sequentially within three genres, Poésie, Drame, and Roman, and include number 1, *Odes et ballades*, the first volume in the Poetry genre, and number 31, *Quatrevingt-treize*, the last (14th) volume in the Novel (Roman) genre.

The general volume numbering indicates that the publishers' intended order of the first three genres was: Poésie, Drame, and Roman (not Poésie, Philosophie, Histoire), and it seems probable that the genres Philosophie, Histoire, Voyages, Actes et Paroles, and Œuvres diverses complete their intended order, based on their publication dates. Many of these numbered volumes were not published in that order, that is, chronologically, according to their final place in the preconceived plan. Had this volume numbering continued, following the last-minute addition of three more volumes of *La Légende des siècles* in 1883, and the addition of drama volume V, *Torquemada. Amy Robsart. Les Jumeaux*, published in 1889, further volume number duplications would have resulted. Thus was the system abandoned in 1883, following publication of *La Légende des siècles*, vol. I.

85. Victor Hugo, *Chantiers*, ed. René Journet (Paris: Robert Laffont, 1990), IX–X.

86. In a 1927 interview conducted by Frédéric Lefèvre, Simon said:

> This edition was 'invented' by Paul Meurice in 1903....There remain a large number of unpublished texts. All those which are connected to some book will be published in the appendix of that book. What will remain will be published, according to the wishes of Hugo, in a last volume, under the title: *Océan.*
>
> (Cette édition fut 'inventée' par Paul Meurice en 1903....Il reste un grand nombre d'inédits. Tous ceux qui se rattachent à un livre quelconque seront publiés en appendice de ce livre. Ce qui restera sera publié, selon le désir de Hugo, dans un dernier volume, sous le titre: *Océan.*) Frédéric Lefèvre, "Une Heure Avec M. Gus-

tave Simon—Exécuteur testamentaire de Victor Hugo," *Les Nouvelles littéraires, artistiques et scientifiques*, no. 236, avril 23 (1927): 4, (microfiche).

87. Victor Hugo, *Œuvres Complètes: Poésie IV,* eds. Jacques Seebacher and Guy Rosa (Paris: Robert Laffont, 1986), X.

88. Et il éprouvait une joie à lire, à relire ces manuscrits, qu'il allait puiser dans une armoire bretonne placée auprès de son lit. C'étaient de chers trésors inconnus du public et il avait une jouissance infinie en songeant aux surprises qu'il ménageait aux lecteurs.... Gustave Simon, "Paul Meurice—Souvenirs Intimes," *La Revue de Paris*, year 13, vol. 3, Mai-Juin (1906): 90, http://bit.ly/VojPhk.

89. —Je voudrais surtout faire les volumes les plus difficiles et ceux pour lesquels j'ai le plus de souvenirs personnels; mais je n'achèverai pas l'édition. Songez donc, quarante ou quarante et un volumes! *Le Rhin* va paraître; après, ce sera la *Fin de Satan* et *Dieu*....J'ai retrouvé des fragments inédits de *Dieu*, d'une grande beauté. Ibid., 89.

90. ...près de mille fragments de toute grandeur, les uns sur une page pleine, ce sont les plus rares, les autres au dos d'une enveloppe, d'une bande de journal, d'une convocation, d'une circulaire ou d'un prospectus; quand il tombait sous la main du poëte quelques lettres adressées à ses enfants ou à sa femme, la partie restée libre était utilisée; certains vers sont disposés sur un espace d'un centimètre de hauteur. Cet océan de vers portait pour titre: Dieu. Au lieu de publier tout ce dossier en Reliquat,...nous en avons extrait les passages s'adaptant au texte publié en 1891 et nous les avons intercalés au cours du volume....

Victor Hugo, *Œuvres complètes de Victor Hugo: Poésie XI. La Fin de Satan. Dieu.* (Paris: Imprimerie nationale, 1911), 627.

91. ...préférable, dans l'intérêt même de l'œuvre, de la présenter, autant que possible, comme une œuvre finie; on a dû, pour la concordance des rimes, supprimer des passages entiers; des lignes de points, au milieu d'une période intéressante, n'auraient-elles pas distrait et dérouté le lecteur de l'édition originale?

Dans cette édition-ci, qui a un caractère tout documentaire et définitif, et qui s'adresse aux travailleurs et aux chercheurs, nous croyons devoir rétablir dans leur intégralité tous les vers de Victor Hugo.

...[I]l se trouve aujourd'hui considérablement augmenté et en quelque sorte complète; il n'était pas encore relié quand nous l'avons eu entre les mains, nous y avons introduit des pages entières portant la mention: DIEU, ou le titre de l'une des divisions....

Id.

92. Guy Rosa, "Problèmes de l'édition critique des manuscrits: Hugo, Flaubert," *Revue d'histoire littéraire de la France*, 85, no. 2 (1985): 275.

93. Although usually listed in bibliographies as critical editions, Guy Rosa speaks of them as "establishing the text" ("Problèmes de l'édition critique," 276); Michael Riffaterre of the 1960 edition as "containing all the variants" ("La Poesie Metaphysique de Victor Hugo: style, symbols et thèmes de *Dieu*," *The romanic review*, 51, [1960]: 268); and Hugo scholars and translators E.H. and A.M. Blackmore of *Contribution aux études sur Victor Hugo: vol. 2. (Le texte de La fin de Satan)* as a "variorum edition" (Hugo, *A bilingual edition of the major epics of Victor Hugo*, vol. II, 421).

94. At Hugo's home on July 23rd, 1885, two months after his death, and lasting until February 25th, 1887, Hugo's notary, maître Gâtine, began the painstaking process of notarizing the as-yet-uncertified work, including the unpublished manuscripts and fragments. ["Fragments" (État de la question—L'état des manuscrits de Hugo à sa mort; la "cote Gâtine"), Groupe Hugo, Université Paris 7 Equipe 19° siècle, http://groupugo.div.jussieu.fr/Fragments/Pour_Presentation_et_aide.htm]

According to the report of this process found in the notary's main filing cabinet by Jacques Seebacher, the notarizing of the prologue to *Dieu*, "Le Seuil du gouffre," occurred March 27th, 1886. [Document SEEBACHER—Extraits concernant les papiers, relevés par Jacques SEEBACHER (saisie Jacques CASSIER), 6, http://groupugo.div.jussieu.fr/Groupugo/Textes_et_documents/CGASTINE.pdf]

When Gâtine or an assistant notarized Hugo's MSS, he used a rubber stamp specifically created for the purpose, atop which was the phrase "Inv[re] SS[on] V. Hugo," and at the bottom the phrase "Me GATINE, N[re]." Across the middle of the stamp were spaces for the *Cote* (portfolio number) and the *pièce* (piece or part) number. Below the impression of the stamp left on each MS folio, the agent signed his initials.

95. The red numbering system appears to be that of the IN, given that the amount and order of the 'Voice' texts in the MS are mirrored in the IN text, different as they are from those of the HQ. By increasing the contrast (in Photoshop) of highly magnified, high-resolution images of the manuscript's pagination, one can quite often also see faint pagination in two other hands, as well, one to the right of the red numbers and the second written over and partially obscuring the first. The obscured, less extensive pagination coincides with the text of the HQ's last six 'Voices.' The more extensive pagination on top of it, appears to be an early pagination of the IN, mirroring, as it does, the final sequence of 'Voices.' In fact it appears to be a further development of the

first pagination, simply adding more voices to its initial sequence, which is what the IN indeed did. The first pagination is perhaps that of Meurice or an assistant, when he was preparing the MS for the HQ edition, and can be seen in other MSS, such as that of *Notre-Dame de Paris*. The later IN pagination can be seen accompanying it. Further study might reveal pertinent information.

96. Hugo *Dieu (fragments)*, vol. 1, passim 7–13.

97. …un résidu imposant qu'ils organisèrent aussi méthodiquement que possible: d'où les quelque trente-cinq volumes manuscrits intitulés *Océan* ou *Tas de pierres*: des fragments de plus en plus petits classés par genres ou par sujets. Les derniers volumes de la série…sont véritablement des fourre-tout: bribes à peine lisibles, notes de tout genre, parfois pratiques, ou intimes….La matière était débordante…. Des publications ultérieures ont picoré dans ce qui restait, sans l'épuiser.

Hugo, *Chantiers*, X.

98. En examinant le contenu de certaines cotes dans les cahiers de concordance de Guy Robert ou dans l'Extrait de l'Inventaire fait par Jacques Seebacher, on a l'impression que d'une sorte de capharnaüm, le notaire, ou l'un de ses clercs, a extrait, parfois au hasard, une brassée de papiers….Fragments vers….Fragments de prose pour la plupart sans lien apparent….Manuscrits de toutes sortes sans lien apparent….

Ibid., XII.

99. Il faut donc se résigner à la conclusion inévitable: *Dieu* n'existe pas.

Victor Hugo, *Œuvres complètes: IX,* Édition chronologique, ed. Jean Massin (Paris: Club français du livre, 1968), 410.

100. The editors' task of piecing together the poem *Dieu* was a difficult one. I will give some brief examples of the varied readings of the MS by different editors. The verse numbers are those of this edition. The IN began line 71 with the words *Il poursuivit*, replacing the HQ's *Que sui-je encore*, words that are found neither in the other editions, nor in the MS as a variant phrase. On line 219, the HQ substituted the word *lever* for *lueur*, the latter apparently a misreading by the HQ. Lines 251-254 have been added by the IN and other editions, as have lines 308-324 and 327-34. They were marked for deletion by Hugo. Lines 357-368 and continuing through line 4 of the ES text's "Variante A," verses found at this juncture in the JR as well, have been placed by the HQ, the IN, and the BP after "Les Voix." The first line of this section of verses in the HQ, *Je ne me lassais pas! et je continuai* has been changed in the IN to *Et, sombre, j'attendis; puis je continuai*, which is the primary verse from the MS. The editors of the HQ seemed to have modified it. The only other edition using the

HQ version was published in 1929 by Charpentier et Fasquelle, Paris, an apparent reproduction of the HQ text. The only variant shown in the MS is the word *morne* written above the word *sombre.*

Lines 5-7 of the ES's Variant B read:

Dans le prodigieux silence du ciel noir.
Et je restai muet, regardant, sans pouvoir
Deviner d'où venait cette gaieté terrible.

These verses were published in the BP as well, and are found in the right-hand column of folio 22r. Those in the IN, CF, and RL read:

Dans ce prodigieux silence où le néant
Semblait vivre, insondable, immobile et béant.

with no third verse. Those two verses were published as Hugo's primary text in the JR, although they are written in the left-hand column of 22r, and are alternative verses added by Hugo. This is another rare example of the JR publishing a variant as primary verse, but by doing so, they retained complete, rhymed couplets. In place of these two verses the HQ published three different verses altogether:

De nuage en nuage, au fond du ciel grondant.
Et je restai muet, grave et me demandant
Ce que ma question avait de si risible.

A search for these three verses among the variants, fragments, and notes in the MS, other critical editions, chronological editions or variorum editions of this work revealed only the half-line *Et je restai muet*...from the BP and ES verses above. I did find them in a Brussels literary journal, *Revue générale*: Volume 54, 1891, quoting the line while reviewing that 1891 edition, as well as the single line *Ce que ma question avait de si risible* in what was originally a 1911 thesis on Hugo alexandrines, by Auguste Rochette, subsequently published by Hachette as *L'Alexandrin chez Victor Hugo*, p. 352. It was a quote from the Hetzel reissue of *Dieu*, used to illustrate a certain usage of the hemistich in Hugo's verse. The only other edition of that work containing those three lines is once again the Charpentier et Fasquelle 1929 edition.

Perhaps they were on a manuscript fragment subsequently lost. Perhaps the editors, themselves, created rhymed verses to match their next stanza which began: *Cependant par degrés l'ombre devint visible* (the other editions left that first line standing alone as an incomplete couplet).

The poem "Le Jour," added as epilogue to the HQ, IN, BP, and JR, was moved, in a rearranged form, to the main text of "L'Esprit humain" as "Conclusion A" and "Variante A" by the CF and ES, respectively. The RL excluded it altogether.

The MS of *Dieu* can be found at http://gallica.bnf.fr/ark:/12148/btv1b6000826p.r=victor+hugo.langEN and the MS of *La Fin de Satan* can be found at http://gallica.bnf.fr/ark:/12148/btv1b6000828h.r=victor+hugo.langEN.

TRANSLATOR'S NOTE: English passages cited from French editions identified in the text or notes are my own translations. Passages cited from published English translations identified in the notes are the work of those translators unless otherwise indicated.

BIBLIOGRAPHY

I. WORKS BY VICTOR HUGO

Hugo, Victor. *A Bilingual Edition of the Major Epics of Victor Hugo, vol. II.* Translated by E. H. and A. M. Blackmore. Lewiston, New York: Edwin Mellen Press, 2002.

———. *Boîte aux letters.* Edited by René Journet and Guy Robert. Paris: Flammarion, 1965.

———. *Chantiers.* Edited by René Journet. Paris: Robert Laffont, 1990.

———. *Dessins de Victor Hugo.* Edited by Theophile Gautier. Engraved by Paul Cheney. Paris: Castel, 1863.

———. *Dieu (fragments).* Edited by René Journet and Guy Robert. 3 vol. Paris: Flammarion, 1969.

———. *Dieu (Le Seuil du gouffre).* Edited by René Journet and Guy Robert. Paris: A. G. Nazet, 1961.

———. *Dieu (L'océan d'en haut).* Edited by René Journet and Guy Robert. Paris: A. G. Nazet, 1960.

———. *La Légende des siècles,* t. I. Paris: Hachette, 1920.

———. *La Légende des siècles. La Fin de Satan. Dieu.* Edited by Jacques Truchet. Paris: Gallimard, 1950, 1997.

———. *Les Contemplations*, 2 vol. Paris: Hachette, 1922.

———. *Les Contemplations*, 2 vol. Paris: Michel Lévy Frères–J. Hetzel–Pagnerre, 1856.

———. *Œuvres complètes: IX–XI.* Édition chronologique. Edited by Jean Massin. Paris: Club français du livre, 1968–69.

———. *Œuvres Complètes: Poésie IV.* Edited by Jacques Seebacher and Guy Rosa. Paris: Robert Laffont, 1986.

———. *Œuvres complètes de Victor Hugo. Édition définitive d'après les manuscrits originaux.* Paris: J. Hetzel et A. Quantin, 1880–1889. 48 vol.

———. *Œuvres complètes de Victor Hugo.* Paris: P. Ollendorff; Albin Michel; Imprimerie nationale, 1904–1952. 45 vol.

———. *Œuvres complètes de Victor Hugo, Poésie XI, La Fin de Satan. Dieu.* Paris: Imprimerie nationale, 1911.

———. *Œuvres inédites de Victor Hugo*: *Dieu*, Troisième Édition. Paris: J. Hetzel et A. Quantin, 1891.

———. *Œuvres inédites de Victor Hugo*: *La Fin de Satan.* Paris: J. Hetzel et A. Quantin, 1886.

———. *Poésie*, 3 vol. Edited by Bernard Leuilliot. Paris: Éditions du Seuil, 1972.

———. *Selected Poems of Victor Hugo: a bilingual edition.* Translated by E. H. and A.M. Blackmore. Chicago: University of Chicago Press, 2001.

———. *The Letters of Victor Hugo: From Exile, and After the Fall of the Empire.* Edited by Paul Meurice. Boston: Houghton, Mifflin & Co., 1898.

———. *Victor Hugo, l'homme océan.* Under the direction of Marie-Laure Prévost. Paris: Bibliothèque nationale de France; Paris: Seuil, 2002.

———. *Victor Hugo: Selected Poems.* Translated by Brooks Haxton. New York: Penguin Books, 2002.

———. *Victor Hugo: Selected Poetry.* Translated by Steven Monte. New York: Routledge, 2002.

———. *William Shakespeare,* Cinquième Édition. Paris: Librairie Internationale, 1869.

II. OTHER WORKS

Avni, Abraham A. "Hugo's Alleged Fabrications of Names and Anachronisms."

Modern Language Notes, vol. 79, no. 3, French Issue, May (1964): 264–269. http://www.jstor.org/stable/3042836.

Bays, Gwendolyn. *The Orphic Vision: seer poets from Novalis to Rimbaud.* Lincoln: University of Nebraska Press, 1964.

Biès, Jean. *Littérature Française et Pensée Hindoue des origines à 1950.* Paris: C. Klincksieck, 1974.

Blackmore, E. H. and A. M., eds. *Six French Poets of the Nineteenth Century.* Oxford: Oxford University Press, 2000.

Breton, André. *What is Surrealism—selected writings* Book Two. Edited and translated by Franklin Rosemont. New York: Monad Press, 1978.

Burty, Philippe. *Maîtres et Petits Maîtres.* Paris: G. Charpentier, 1877.

———. "Sept dessins de gens de lettres". *The Academy: a weekly review of literature, science, and art*, July–December, vol. VIII (London: Robert Scott Walker, 1875): 315–317. http://bit.ly/Voewyb.

Cellier, Léon. *Baudelaire et Hugo.* Paris: José Corti, 1970.

Cim, Albert. *Récréations littéraires: curiosités et singularités, bévues et lapsus, etc.* Paris: Hachette, 1920.

Claudel, Paul. *Œuvres complètes,* t. 15. Paris: Gallimard, 1959.

Duclaux, Agnes Mary Frances (Robinson). *Victor Hugo.* New York: Henry Holt and Company, 1921.

Fasquelle, Eugène, ed. *Correspondance entre Victor Hugo et Paul Meurice.* Paris: Bibliothèque-Charpentier, 1909.

Frey, John Andrew. *A Victor Hugo Encyclopedia.* Westport, Connecticut: Greenwood Press, 1999.

Gaudon, Jean, Pierre Albouy, Maurice Piron, and Guy Robert . " 'Discussions': Communication de MM. Journet et Robert." Cahiers de l'Association internationale des études françaises, 19, no. 19 (1967): 300–02. http://bit.ly/PzImNc.

Gaudon, Sheila, ed. *Correspondance entre Victor Hugo et Pierre-Jules Hetzel: t. I* (1852–1853). Paris: Klincksieck, 1979.

Gaudon, Sheila, ed. *Correspondance entre Victor Hugo et Pierre-Jules Hetzel: t. II* (janvier 1854–avril 1857). Paris: Klincksieck, 1979.

Georgel, Pierre. *Drawings by Victor Hugo: catalogue.* London: Victoria and Albert Museum, 1974.

Glachant, Paul and Victor. *Papiers D'Autrefois.* Paris: Librairie Hachette, 1899.

Gogh, Vincent van. *The Complete Letters of Vincent van Gogh*, vol. III. Greenwich, Connecticut: New York Graphic Society, 1958.

Gruber, Lucretia S. "Alfred de Vigny's 'Eloa': A Modern Myth." *Modern Language* Studies, vol. 6, no.1, Spring (1976): 74–82. http://www.jstor.org/stable/3194396.

Hartley, Anthony, ed. *The Penguin book of French verse 3: The Nineteenth Century.* Baltimore:Penguin Books, 1967.

Hugo, Adèle. *Le Journal d'Adèle Hugo*, tome I: 1852. Edited by F.V. Guille. Paris: Lettres Modernes Minard, 1968.

———. *Le Journal d'Adèle Hugo*, tome III: 1854. Edited by F.V. Guille. Paris: Lettres Modernes Minard, 1984.

———. *Le Journal d'Adèle Hugo*, tome IV: 1855. Edited by F.V. Guille and Jean-Marc Hovasse. Paris: Lettres Modernes Minard, 2002.

Ireson, J.R. *Victor Hugo: A Companion to his Poetry.* Oxford: Clarendon Press, 1997.

Jeanniot, Pierre-Georges. "Victor Hugo's Home at Guernsey." *Scribner's Magazine*, vol. XXI, January-June (1897): 108–119. http://bit.ly/Thdzuc.

Josephson, Matthew. *Victor Hugo.*Garden City, New York: Doubleday, Doran & co., 1942.

Journet, René and Guy Robert. *Contribution aux études sur Victor Hugo: Le texte de "La Fin de Satan"*. Paris: Belles Lettres, 1979.

———. "Pourquoi Victor Hugo n'a-t-il pas publié son poème 'Dieu'?." *Cahiers de L'Association internationale des études françaises*, 19, no.19 (1967): 225–231. doi:10.3406/caief.1967.2345

Lautréamont, comte de. *Maldoror & The Complete Works of the Comte de Lautréamont.* Translated by Alexis Lykiard. Cambridge: Exact Change, 1994.

Lefèvre, Frédéric. "Une Heure avec M. Gustave Simon—Exécuteur testamentaire de Victor Hugo." Les Nouvelles littéraires, artistiques et scientifiques, Sixième Année, no. 236, avril 23 (1927): 3–4. (microfiche).

Lemaître, Georges Édouard. *From Cubism to Surrealism in French Literature.* rev. ed. Cambridge: Harvard University Press, 1947.

Leuilliot, Bernard. "Éditer Victor Hugo." *Romantisme: revue du dix-neuvième siècle*, no. 6 (1973): 111–123. doi:10.3406/roman.1973.4959.

Mallarmé, Stéphane. *Œuvres complètes*, t. II. Paris: Gallimard, 2003.

Michael, Colette V. "Light/Darkness and the Phenomenon of Creation in Victor Hugo." In *Analecta Husserliana: The Yearbook of Phenomenological Research*, vol. XXXVIII. Edited by Anna-Teresa Tymieniecka. Dordrecht: Kluwer Academic Publishers, 1992.

Montandon, Alain. *Espaces domestiques et privés de l'hospitalité.* Clermont-Ferrand:

Presses Universitaires Blaise Pascal, 2000.

Neefs, Jacques and Claude Mouchard. "Dieu, *manuscrit.*" In *Hugo de l'Écrit au livre,* edited by Béatrice Didier and Jacques Neefs. Saint-Denis: Presses universitaires de Vincennes, 1988.

Nichol, John Pringle. *Victor Hugo: a sketch of his life and work.* London: S. Sonnenschein, 1893.

Page, Curtis Hidden. "Current French Poets and Novelists." *Poet Lore* 18, Spring (1907): 113–122.

Picard, Gaston. "Ce que pensent de Victor Hugo quelques écrivains d'aujourd'hui." *Les Nouvelles littéraires, artistiques et scientifiques,* Sixième Année, no. 236, avril 23 (1927): 5. (microfiche).

Picon, Gaëtan. *Surrealists & Surrealism.* Translated by James Emmons. Geneva: Editions d'Art Albert Skira S.A., 1995.

Rainey, Thomas. *Ocean Steam Navigation and the Ocean Post.* New York: D. Appleton & Co., 1858. http://bit.ly/SdEZ1t.

Riffaterre, Michael. "La Poésie Métaphysique de Victor Hugo: style, symboles et thèmes de Dieu." The romanic review, 51 (1960): 268–276.

Robb, Graham. *Victor Hugo: a biography.* New York: W. W. Norton & Company, 1997.

Rodari, Florian. *Shadows of a Hand: the drawings of Victor Hugo.* Translated by Judith Hayward, Mark Hutchinson. London: The Drawing Center New York in association with Merrell Holberton Publishers, 1998.

Rosa, Guy. "Problèmes de l'édition critique des manuscrits: Hugo, Flaubert." *Revue d'histoire littéraire de la France* 85, no. 2 (1985): 275–284.

Schwab, Raymond. *La Renaissance Orientale.* Paris: Payot, 1950.

Simon, Gustave. "Paul Meurice—souvenirs intimes." *La Revue de Paris* 3, Mai–Juin (1906): 61-96. http://bit.ly/VojPhk.

Stevens, Philip. *Victor Hugo in Jersey.* Shopwyke Hall, Chichester, Sussex: Phillimore, 1985.

Swinburne, Algernon Charles. *Studies in prose and poetry.* London: Chatto & Windus, 1894.

Valéry, Paul. *Situation de Baudelaire.* Paris: Chez Madame Lesage, 1924.

———. *The Art of Poetry.* Translated by Denise Folliot. New York: Pantheon Books, 1958.

Viatte, Auguste. *Victor Hugo et les illuminés de son temps.* Montreal: Les Éditions de l'Arbre, 1942.

SWAN ISLE PRESS is an independent, not-for-profit, literary publisher dedicated to publishing works of poetry, fiction and nonfiction that inspire and educate while advancing the knowledge and appreciation of literature, art, and culture. The Press's bilingual editions and single-language English translations make contemporary and classic texts more accessible to a variety of readers.

For more information on books of related interest or
for a catalog of new publications contact:

www.swanislepress.com

GOD AND THE END OF SATAN

DIEU ET LA FIN DE SATAN

Designed by Andrea Guinn
Typeset in Bulmer
Printed on 50# Glatfelter Natural

SWAN
ISLE
PRESS